a brit's guide

to

rlando

and

walt disney world

2006

 ★

simon & susan veness

foulsham

LONDON • NEW YORK • TORONTO • SYDNEY

foulsham

The Publishing House, Bennetts Close, Cippenham, Berkshire, SL1 5AP, England

Foulsham books can be found in all good bookshops or direct from
www.foulsham.com

While every effort has been made to ensure the accuracy of all the information
contained within this book, neither the author nor the publisher can be liable for any
errors. In particular, since prices, times and any holiday or hotel details change on a
regular basis, it is vital that each individual check relevant information for themselves.

ISBN 0-572-03157-2

Text copyright © 2006 Simon Veness

Series, format, logo and layout design copyright © 2006 W. Foulsham & Co. Ltd

A CIP record for this book is available from the British Library

Look out for the latest editions in this series:
A Brit's Guide to Las Vegas, Karen Marchbank
Choosing A Cruise, Simon Veness
A Brit's Guide to Disneyland Resort Paris, Simon Veness
A Brit's Guide to New York, Karen Marchbank with Amanda Statham

SPECIAL THANKS

First and foremost to Susan, who is now my partner in every sense, and makes
this job so much more worthwhile and enjoyable.

Special thanks for this edition go to: Travel City Direct, The Walt Disney
Company, Alamo Rent A Car, Virgin Holidays, Universal Orlando,
Orlando/Orange County Convention and Visitors Bureau, Kissimmee
Convention and Visitors Bureau, Synergy PR and Anheuser-Busch Parks,
The Renaissance Orlando Resort, Alexander Holiday Homes, The Reunion
Resort, The Bahama Bay Resort, Lorraine Ellis (Get Married In Florida),
Margie and Michelle at Boggy Creek Airboats.

My sincere thanks also go to all the hard-working people at Foulsham who
help to bring my work to life every year, plus editor Julia Thorley.

Printed in Malaysia

Contents

FOREWORD   PAGE 5

1. Introduction

(or, Welcome to the Holiday of a Lifetime). Getting to grips with Orlando,
what's in store, facts and figures, theme park tickets, climate, visas,
the attractions outlined, what's new and central Florida festivals.   PAGE 6

2. Planning and Practicalities

(or, How to *Almost* Do It All and Live to Tell the Tale). When to go, the
main tourist areas, the principal holiday companies, holiday strategy, how to
beat the crowds, clothing and health matters, travellers with disabilities,
Disney special occasions, learning American-speak, weddings, safety advice,
plus the new *Brit's Guide* Personalised Itinerary Planner.   PAGE 19

3. Driving and Car Hire

(or, The Secret of Getting Around on Interstate 4). Arriving in Orlando,
the main roads and tourist roads, car hire guide, learning to drive on
the wrong side of the road, Orlando for non-drivers.   PAGE 48

4. Accommodation

(or, Making Sense of American Hotels, Motels and Condos). Understanding
American-style accommodation, Walt Disney World Resort hotels,
Disney Hotel Plaza, Budget hotels, Standard hotels, Superior hotels,
Deluxe hotels, Universal Orlando, resorts and holiday homes, B&B;
buying a home.   PAGE 60

5. Disney's Fab Four

(or, Spending the Day with Mickey Mouse and Co). More ticket info,
ratings, tactics, plus full guides to the Magic Kingdom Park, Epcot,
Disney-MGM Studios and Disney's Animal Kingdom Theme Park.   PAGE 93

6. Five More of the Best

(or, Expanding Orlando's Universe). Full guide, ratings, tickets and tactics
to Universal Studios Florida, Islands of Adventure, SeaWorld Adventure
Park and Discovery Cove, and Busch Gardens.   PAGE 146

7. The Other Attractions

(or, One Giant Leap for Tourist Kind). The Kennedy Space Center,
Astronaut Hall of Fame, Cypress Gardens Adventure Park, Historic Bok
Sanctuary, Silver Springs, Gatorland, Fantasy of Flight. International Drive:
Ripley's Believe It Or Not, Titanic – The Exhibition, Skull Kingdom,
Fun Spot, Magical Midway, WonderWorks, SkyVenture. Downtown Orlando:
Orlando Science Center, Orange County History Center, The Holy Land
Experience. The water parks: Disney's Typhoon Lagoon Water Park,
Disney's Blizzard Beach Water Park, Wet 'n Wild, Water Mania.   PAGE 194

8. Off The Beaten Track

(or, When You're All Theme-Parked Out). A taste of the real Florida: Winter Park, Boggy Creek Airboat Rides, Balloon Flights, Excursions: Everglades, Bahamas and More, Warbird Adventures, Green Meadows Petting Farm, Osceola County Pioneer Museum, Reptile World Serpentarium, Disney and cruising, Seminole County, Florida Eco-Safaris, Disney's Wilderness Preserve. Beaches: St Pete's/Clearwater, Cocoa Beach and Daytona. Sports: golf, mini-golf, fishing, water sports, horse riding, spectator sports and Disney's Wide World of Sports™, fitness centres, rodeo, motor sport.

PAGE 222

9. Orlando by Night

(or, Burning the Candle at Both Ends). Downtown Disney, Cirque du Soleil, DisneyQuest, Disney's Boardwalk, Universal's CityWalk, The Pointe Orlando. Dinner shows: Disney shows, Arabian Nights, Pirate's Dinner Adventure, Medieval Times, Sleuth's Mystery Dinner Shows, WonderWorks: The Outta Control Magic Show, Dolly Parton's Dixie Stampede, Chamber of Magic, Fiascos. Nightclub scene: live music, The Social, clubs, bars.

PAGE 251

10. Dining Out

(or, Man, These Portions Are Huge!). Full guide to local-style eating and drinking, rundown of the fast-food outlets, best family restaurants, American diners and speciality restaurants.

PAGE 270

11. Shopping

(or, How to Send Your Credit Card into Meltdown). Your duty-free allowances, full guide to the main tourist shopping complexes, discount outlets, flea markets, malls, supermarkets and speciality shops.

PAGE 292

12. Going Home

(or, Where Did the Last Two Weeks Go?). Avoiding last-minute snags, returning the car, full guide to Orlando International and Orlando Sanford airports and their facilities for the journey home. Where next? (guide to Orlando's low-cost airlines).

PAGE 305

13. Your Holiday Planner

Example of how to plan for a 2-week holiday with a Disney 5-Day Premium Ticket and 4-Park Orlando FlexTicket. Theme Parks' Busy Day Guide

PAGE 312

INDEX PAGE 314

COPYRIGHT NOTICES PAGE 319

ACKNOWLEDGEMENTS PAGE 320

Foreword

Much has happened since I sat down to write the Foreword to the last edition – all of it positive. The launch of the Brit's Guide *website – www.askdaisy.net/orlando – has given us an extra dimension, while our Itinerary Planning Service has taken off to a degree we never imagined in our wildest dreams. It has become a major source of information and feedback for us, meaning we have an even better idea of what people want from their Orlando holiday – and how to cater for it in these pages. There has also been a change in our 'editorial' situation. Susan, my long-time principal research assistant, is now my full-time partner in every sense, and we are looking forward to continuing to develop the* Brit's Guide *together from our home base about five minutes away from Mickey and Co!*

For newcomers to the Brit's Guide, *we like to think of this as the definitive source of insider info on all that lies in store for you in this amazing Central Florida wonderland. This is where the fun really starts and you can begin preparing for a truly magical and memorable time. Orlando has developed in astonishing fashion since Walt Disney World opened in 1971, and it continues to grow and change on an annual basis. Nowhere else in the world is your choice of attractions so broad and detailed. Of course, that means it can be confusing and potentially expensive, not to mention exhausting, but you have definitely made the right start by choosing us to provide the full inside track.*

This 11th edition of Britain's best-selling guidebook to the US represents the most user-friendly and authoritative companion to all that lies in store, especially if used with our website. I believe we write and research with a tourist's eye for detail and value, including all the info you really need to know. We aim to give you a good idea of what to expect and how to plan and budget for it. Our online Personalised Itinerary Planner (see page 46) then goes a step further with the chance for us to tailor-make your holiday campaign.

As mentioned, the area remains vigorously engaged in making things newer, bigger and better almost by the week, and we have completely overhauled our Accommodation and Dining Out chapters to stay abreast of all the changes. It is quite a challenge keeping up with it all, but we can't pretend it isn't also great fun! The bottom line is there is so much to do and see, we are determined to help you get the most out of your visit. More significantly, you'll get the inside track on how to have the best holiday, at the best price and with the least fuss. Prepare to be amazed (and tired!) by what's in store, but don't say we didn't tell you so. Now, excuse us while we put our feet up for a while… have a nice day now.

Simon and Susan Veness
(visit us at www.askdaisy.net/orlando or email simonveness@yahoo.co.uk)

1 Introduction
(or, Welcome to the Holiday of a Lifetime)

Welcome to the most exciting holiday experience in the world, bar none, guaranteed. This area of central Florida we call 'Orlando' is a vast conglomeration of adventure rides, thrills, fun and fantasy the like of which exists nowhere else, and we are not talking just about the amazing *Walt Disney World Resort* here.

First off, you need to be aware of the bewilderingly extensive and complex nature of this tourist wonderland. Disney remains the leading attraction, but there is an extremely strong supporting cast, led by Universal Orlando and SeaWorld.

There is something to suit all tastes and ages – young or old, families, couples or singles – but it exacts a high physical toll. You'll walk a lot, queue a lot and probably eat a lot. You will have a fabulous time, but you'll end up exhausted as well. It is not so much a holiday as an exercise in military planning.

Eight theme parks

In simple terms, there are now eight major theme parks that are essential holiday fare here, and at least one of those will require 2 days to make you feel it has been well and truly done. Add on a day at one of the water parks, a trip to see some of the wildlife or other more 'natural'

attractions, and the lure of the nearby Kennedy Space Center, and you already have 12 full days of pure adventure-mania. Then mix in the night-time attractions of *Downtown Disney*, Universal's CityWalk and a host of dinner shows, plus the lure of world-class shopping, and you get an idea of the awesome scope of the place. Even with 2 weeks, something has to give – just make sure it isn't your patience/pocket/sanity!

So, how do you get full value from what is still, without doubt, a truly magical holiday? There is no guaranteed answer, but we have some pretty solid guidelines to steer you in the right direction and help avoid the more obvious pitfalls. Central to all of them is **planning**. At the back of this guide there is a useful 'calendar' to use as a ready reference guide. Don't be inflexible, but be aware of the time demands of the parks and allow a quiet day or two by the pool or at one of the smaller attractions to recover. With so much on offer, it simply isn't possible to 'Do it all', so try to ensure you get full value for what you do decide to do.

Also, you must be aware of the vast *scale* of everything here. It is well spread out and it takes time even to get from park to park. But do stop to admire the clever detail and imagination of what's on offer, especially in the Disney parks.

Orlando

Orlando itself is a relatively small but bright young city that has been taken over to the immediate southwest by *Walt Disney World Resort in Florida*, to give it its full title, which opened with the *Magic Kingdom Park* in 1971 and has led to a massive tourist expansion ever since. New attractions pop up all the time and it is easy to get carried away by the artificial (and highly commercial) fantasy of it all.

The tourist area we call Orlando actually consists of 3 counties. Orange County is the home of the city of Orlando, but part of *Walt Disney World* is in Osceola County, with Kissimmee its main town. Seminole County, home of Orlando Sanford airport, is north of Orange County.

The local population numbers slightly fewer than 2 million, of which almost 250,000 are actively employed in the tourist business. But, in 2005, some 52 million people were expected to make Orlando their holiday choice, spending in excess of $21 billion in the area.

Britain accounts for more than 40 per cent of all foreign visitors to Orlando, and in 2004 that was 1 million of us. Those figures represent a huge increase in recent years (even allowing for a dip after September 11), with the international airport seeing its traffic boom from 8 million passengers in 1983 to a record 31.1 million in 2004. In addition, the Metro Orlando area boasts some 113,000 hotel rooms and 4,000-plus places to eat. And shopaholics have the choice of an amazing 250 shopping centres, including 30 malls. But let's give you a quick taste of the main attractions.

Walt Disney World Resort in Florida

This is where the 'Magic' really starts – and the effect is vividly real. This vast resort actually consists of four distinct, separate theme parks, 20 speciality hotel resorts, a camping ground, 2 water parks, a sports complex, 5 18-hole golf courses, 4 mini-golf courses and a huge shopping and entertainment district *(Downtown Disney)*. It covers 47sq miles (122sq km). The likes of Alton Towers and Thorpe Park would comfortably fit into its car parks! Indeed, Alton Towers, Britain's biggest theme park, is 60 times smaller. On average, there are estimated to be 200,000 visitors within those 47sq miles at any one time. The Disney organisation does things with the most style, but the others have caught on fast and are rapidly creating new amenities.

Intriguingly, only half of Disney's massive site has been built on, leaving plenty of room for new developments, while even the existing parks have potential for an extra ride or two, and there are always new projects on the drawing board. Disney maintains an extremely high level of customer service and is always looking at ways to refresh existing attractions. Everyone who works for them is officially a Cast Member, not just staff, and they take that ethic to heart.

Here's a quick rundown of what's on offer:

Magic Kingdom Park: this is the essential Disney, including the fantasy of its wonderful animated films, the adventures of the Wild West and Africa, the excitement of thrill rides like Space Mountain (a huge indoor roller-coaster), the 3-D film fun of Mickey's PhilharMagic and the splendour of the daily parades and fireworks.

FLORIDA

How far from Orlando to . . .

Bradenton 130 miles/210km	Key West 375 miles/604km
Clearwater 110 miles/176km	Miami 220 miles/354km
Cocoa Beach 40 miles/64km	Naples 230 miles/370km
Cypress Gardens . . . 40 miles/64km	Sarasota 140 miles/225km
Daytona 60 miles/97km	Silver Springs 80 miles/129km
Fort Lauderdale . . 205 miles/330km	St Augustine 120 miles/193km
Fort Myers 190 miles/306km	St Petersburg 105 miles169km
Jacksonville 155 miles/250km	Tampa 75 miles/120km
Key Largo 294 miles/470km	Venice 160 miles/257km

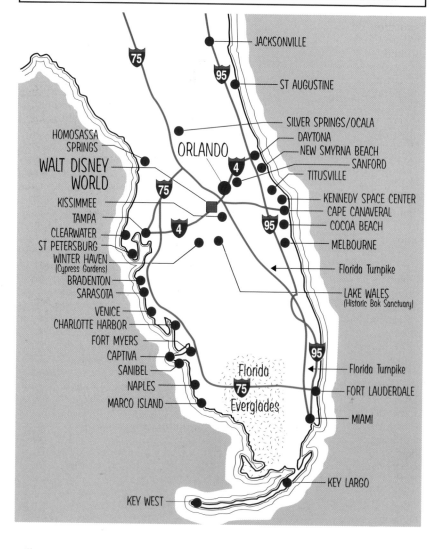

Having fun in the water parks

Epcot: Disney's look at the world of tomorrow through the gates of Future World, plus a potted journey around the globe in World Showcase. More educational than adventurous, it still possesses some memorable rides, including Test Track, Mission: SPACE and the superb new Soarin', along with superb dining options.

Disney-MGM Studios: here you can ride the movies in style, meeting up with Star Wars™, the Muppets and Indiana Jones; drop into the fearsome Tower of Terror or the high-speed Rock 'n' Roller Coaster; learn how films are really made; and enjoy the thrills and spills of the epic new Lights, Motors, Action!™ Extreme stunt Show.

Disney's Animal Kingdom: billed as 'a new species of theme park', this delivers another contrasting and entertaining scenario. With realistic animal habitats, including a 100-acre (40.5-ha) safari savannah, captivating shows and several terrific rides, it offers a pleasant change of pace from the other parks.

Disney's Typhoon Lagoon Water Park: bring your cozzie and spend a lazy day splashing down water-slides and learning to surf in the world's biggest man-made lagoon.

Disney's Blizzard Beach Water Park: the big brother of all the water parks, this has a massive spread of rides and slides in a 'snowy' environment.

Downtown Disney: this incorporates *Pleasure Island*, Marketplace and the West Side with themed restaurants, a cinema multiplex, the *DisneyQuest* arcade of interactive games, Virgin Megastore and world-famous Cirque du Soleil® company. New Year's Eve is the *Pleasure Island* theme, with seven nightclubs.

The picture-perfect **Wedding Pavilion**, which appears in many brochures and offers marriage ceremonies in fairytale style, is another Disney feature.

The other parks

If you think Orlando is all about Disney, you will be pleasantly surprised at the huge range of other attractions on offer.

Universal Orlando is the other big resort development, with 2 theme parks, water park, wonderful entertainment district and 3 speciality hotels: **Universal Studios:** here you Ride The Movies as you encounter Jaws, the Men In Black and Back to the Future, the Shrek 4-D show and Revenge of the Mummy ride, plus Woody Woodpecker's KidZone and the amazing Terminator 2: 3-D show. **Islands of Adventure**: new in 1999, Universal's second park is a superb blend of thrill rides, family attractions, shows and eye-catching design, with some of the most technologically advanced hardware in the world.

Wet 'n Wild: although on International Drive (I-Drive), this water park is Universal-owned and offers plenty of fun rides and slides.

Susan at Islands of Adventure

SeaWorld: don't be put off thinking it's just another dolphin show, this is the place for the creatures of the deep, with killer whales being the main attraction, a bright, refreshing atmosphere (check out the new Waterfront district and Blue Horizons show) and a pleasingly serious ecological approach, plus thrill rides Journey to Atlantis and Kraken. SeaWorld also has an exclusive neighbour, **Discovery Cove,** which offers the chance to swim with dolphins, among other things.

Busch Gardens: the sister park to SeaWorld, here it's creatures of the land, with a good mix of rides and shows. Highlights are the new SheiKra mega-coaster, the Rhino Rally ride, Myombe Reserve, a close-up look at the endangered central African highland gorillas, the Edge of Africa 'safari' experience, and the Haunted Lighthouse 3-D film show. A real family treat, plus a must for coaster fans.

BRIT TIP: Be very careful not to buy too much in the way of tickets. Travel agents often pressure people into buying more than they need, and you simply will not get full use out of, say, a 14-day Disney ticket and an Orlando FlexTicket in just a 2-week holiday.

More attractions include: **Kennedy Space Center:** the dramatically upgraded home of space exploration; **Silver Springs:** a close look at Florida's nature via jeep and boat safaris through real swampland, with a delightful, natural feel; **Fantasy of Flight:** an aviation museum experience with the world's largest private collection of vintage aircraft, plus fighter-plane

simulators; and **Cypress Gardens:** Florida's oldest 'theme park', reborn in 2004 with coasters and other rides, as well as their wonderful gardens.

Disney tickets

Most people buy one of the multi-day passes that allow you to move between the theme parks on the same day and grants unlimited access to the transport system (always get your hand stamped if you leave one park but intend to return). Make no mistake, you can't walk between the parks (except for a fairly long haul between Epcot and Disney-MGM Studios), and trying to do more than one in a day is hard work. The choice of tickets is bewildering, so make sure you buy ONLY what you need.

BRIT TIP: Buy Disney and Universal/SeaWorld tickets in advance, NOT at the park gates. You will save time AND money as there is a built-in advance purchase discount.

In 2004, Disney introduced a brand new ticket system called **Magic Your Way,** which is horribly complicated for the first-timer. Happily, they also brought in a simplified range of tickets for the UK, which makes life easier. All multi-day passes offer savings against buying **1-Day Tickets,** but, unlike the old system, unused days now expire after a certain time, unless you buy an upgrade at the parks. If you just turn up at the ticket booths, you must choose from the *Magic Your Way* menu: first, the number of days you require (from 1-10); then if you want *Park Hopping* (which allows you to visit more than one park on the same day for a flat rate $35); then you have the *Plus*

Choosing a ticket

Ticket Type	Park	Allowance
1-Day Ticket	Any Disney park, Universal Orlando parks, SeaWorld or Busch Gardens; not available in advance	Access to one park ONLY for one day
5-Day Premium Ticket	*Magic Kingdom Park, Epcot, Disney-MGM Studios, Disney's Animal Kingdom Theme Park*	Access for 5 days, with multiple parks on same day; plus 3 visits to water parks, Pleasure Island and/or DisneyQuest; valid for 14 days after first use (non-expiration option may be purchased)
7-Day Premium Ticket	*Magic Kingdom Park, Epcot, Disney-MGM Studios, Disney's Animal Kingdom Theme Park*	Access for 7 days, with multiple parks on same day; plus 3 visits to water parks, *Pleasure Island* and/or *DisneyQuest*; valid for 14 days after first use (non-expiration option may be purchased)
14-Day Ultimate Ticket	All Disney parks; available only in advance in the UK	Unlimited access to all the attractions, including water parks, *Pleasure Island*, *DisneyQuest* and *Disney's Wide World of Sports Complex*™ for 14 days after first use; no non-expiration option
21-Day Ultimate Ticket	All Disney parks; available only in advance in the UK	Unlimited access to all the attractions, including water parks, *Pleasure Island*, *DisneyQuest* and *Disney's Wide World of Sports Complex*™ for 21 days after first use; no non-expiration option
Annual Pass	*Magic Kingdom Park, Epcot, Disney-MGM Studios, Disney's Animal Kingdom Theme Park*; includes numerous discounts for shops, restaurants and tours	Unlimited admission and free parking for 365 days after purchase date. If ordered online, you get a voucher which must be activated at a park. The 365 days start on the day you first activate the pass
Premium Annual Pass	All Disney parks; includes numerous discounts for shops, restaurants and tours	Unlimited admission and free parking for 365 days after purchase date; plus discounts on sports and recreation
2-Day 2-Park Ticket	Universal Studios, Islands of Adventure, CityWalk	Access to both parks, including both on same day, plus clubs of CityWalk
3-Day 2-Park Ticket	Universal Studios, Islands of Adventure, CityWalk	Access to both parks, including both on same day, plus clubs of CityWalk
Universal Bonus Pass (5 days for the price of 2)	Universal Studios, Islands of Adventure, CityWalk; available online only	Access to both parks, including both on same day, plus clubs of CityWalk, for 5 consecutive days from first use
4-Park FlexTicket	Universal Studios, Islands of Adventure, SeaWorld and Wet 'n Wild, plus CityWalk	Access to all 4 parks, with multiple parks on same day, for 14 days from first use, plus clubs of CityWalk
5-Park FlexTicket	Universal Studios, Islands of Adventure, SeaWorld, Wet 'n Wild, Busch Gardens	Access to all 5 parks, with multiple parks on same day, for 14 days from first use, plus clubs of CityWalk
Value Ticket	SeaWorld and Busch Gardens	One day at each park

ORLANDO – MAIN ATTRACTIONS AND ROUTES

A   Magic Kingdom Park
B   Epcot
C   Disney-MGM Studios
D   Disney's Animal Kingdom Park
E   Universal Orlando
F   SeaWorld Adventure Park
G   Busch Gardens
H   Kennedy Space Center/
     US Astronaut Hall of Fame
I   Cypress Gardens
J   Historic Bok Sanctuary
K   Silver Springs

L   Gatorland
M   Disney's Typhoon Lagoon Water Park
N   Disney's Blizzard Beach Water Park
O   Fantasy of Flight
P   Water Mania
Q   Wet 'n Wild
R   Discovery Cove by SeaWorld
S   Holy Land Experience
T   Ripley's Believe It or Not
U   Titanic – The Exhibition
V   Orange County History Center
W   Downtown Disney area

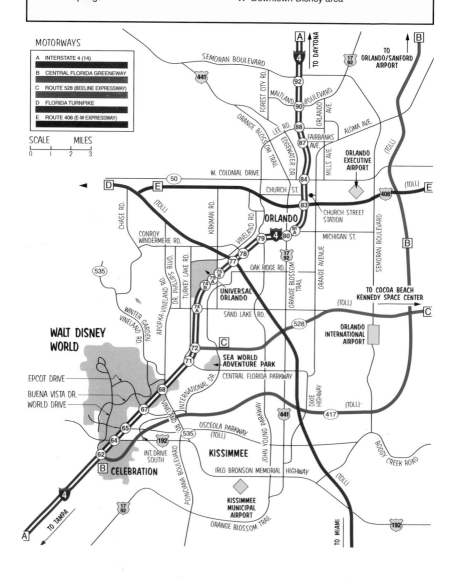

MOTORWAYS

A	INTERSTATE 4 (14)
B	CENTRAL FLORIDA GREENEWAY
C	ROUTE 528 (BEELINE EXPRESSWAY)
D	FLORIDA TURNPIKE
E	ROUTE 408 (E-W EXPRESSWAY)

SCALE   MILES
0   1   2   3

© Disney

Sleeping Beauty

Pack option (which gives you 2–5 extra visits to the water parks, Pleasure Island and DisneyQuest, for $45); finally you must choose whether or not to buy the *Non-expiration* option for your tickets (at $10–$55). The savings increase with the more days you buy (1 day ticket = $59.75, 10 days = $208).

The bonus of coming from the UK means there are really only 4 tickets to consider, all of which are sold in advance (2 exclusively in Britain), and all of which represent good value. They are the 5- and 7-Day Premium Ticket, and the 14- and 21-Day Ultimate Ticket (see Chart on page 11).

Other tickets

When it comes to Universal Orlando, SeaWorld and Busch Gardens, the choice is simpler. Again, you have **1-, 2-** and **3-Day Tickets** (in 2005, the **3-Day Ticket** was extended to give 14 successive days' admission with various UK ticket agencies). However, much better value are the **Orlando FlexTickets**, which are valid for 14 days from first use. There is also a Universal Bonus Pass online at www.universalorlando.com for 5 consecutive days for the price of a 2-day ticket. For CityWalk, there is a **CityWalk Party Pass** ($9.95 plus tax) or a **Party Pass with Movie** ($12), as the centre has a 20-screen

cinema. You can also get **Dinner with a Movie** for $19.95 (choice of one main meal at any of 7 CityWalk restaurants). A trip to the exclusive **Discovery Cove** includes a free **7-Day Pass** for either SeaWorld or Busch Gardens, too.

With price hikes every year, it is worth buying your tickets as soon as you book. However, **tour operators** can be above gate prices for the convenience of being able to book early and budget for your main costs, so we recommend shopping around at the following, who all offer competitive prices and the early-booking convenience, as well as providing the actual tickets (as opposed to vouchers that need to be exchanged at the ticket booths): **Keith Prowse Attraction Tickets** (0870 123 2425, www.keithprowse tickets.com), who also offer various Florida excursions (notably to the Kennedy Space Center, Naples & Everglades, Clearwater, Miami and Manatee Swims) plus an array of Orlando options like Shop Til You Drop and a 2-Day Gatorland ticket, plus tickets to all of the major American sports; **Attraction Tickets Direct** (0845 130 3876, www.attractionticketsdirect.com), Britain's biggest direct-sell Orlando ticket broker, who have a price guarantee, no credit card fees and promise free delivery in 7 days (plus dinners shows, a Manatee Swim, Orlando Magic basketball, Kennedy Space Center and Space Shuttle Launch tickets, as well as an online Florida Forum and info centre); and **Holiday Travel Essentials** (01444

Typhoon Lagoon's Crush 'n Gusher

© Disney

COCONUT

231486, www.attraction tickets4less.com). There are numerous others, but these 3 all guarantee the right product, with the right service and local knowledge (see also page 194).

Don't forget to plan your main theme park days with the benefit of our **Busy Day Guide** on page 313. You simply cannot do the parks in one big chunk and not expect to end up exhausted, especially if you hit, say, the Magic Kingdom, on one of its busier days.

The climate

The next question is when to go? Florida's weather does vary from bright but cool winter days in November, December and January, with the odd drizzly spell, to furiously hot and humid summers punctuated with tropical downpours.

BRIT TIP: The humidity levels – up to 100% – and fierce daily rainstorms in summer take a lot of visitors by surprise, so carry a lightweight, rainproof jacket or buy a cheap plastic poncho locally.

The most pleasant option is to go in between the two extremes, in spring or autumn. You will also avoid the worst of the crowds. However, as most families are governed by school holidays, July to September remain the most popular months for British visitors, and so this guide contains advice on how to get one jump ahead of the high-season crush. If you do need to visit during summer, opt for the second half of August, as many US schools have resumed by then.

And now to business: it's big, brash and fun, but above all it's American and that means everything is well organised, with a tendency towards the raucous rather than the reserved. It's clean, well maintained and anxious to please: Floridians generally are an affable bunch, but they take affability to new heights in the theme parks, where staff are almost painfully keen to make sure you 'have a nice day'.

Tipping

Close to every American's heart is the custom of tipping. With the exception of fast-food restaurant servers, just about everyone who serves in hotels, bars, restaurants, buses, taxis, airports and other public amenities will expect a tip. In bars, restaurants and taxis, 15 per cent of the bill is the usual rate while porters expect $1/bag and chambermaids $1/day per adult when they make up your room. As all service industry workers are taxed on the basis of receiving 15% in tips, whether they receive it or not, it's important not to forget those few extra dollars.

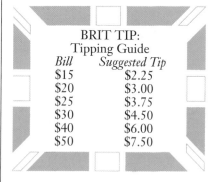

BRIT TIP:
Tipping Guide

Bill	Suggested Tip
$15	$2.25
$20	$3.00
$25	$3.75
$30	$4.50
$40	$6.00
$50	$7.50

Visa requirements

Here's where the media have provided some extremely misleading information of late. Holiday visitors to America do NOT need a visa providing they hold a valid machine-readable passport showing they are a

Orlando timeline

Here's the full list of how the area has grown since Disney first opened its doors in Florida.

1971: *MAGIC KINGDOM PARK* (MK)

1973: Pirates of the Caribbean and Tom Sawyer Island (MK); Church Street Station; SEAWORLD (SW)

1974: Star Jets (now Astro Orbiter) (MK)

1975: Space Mountain and WEDway People Mover (now Tomorrowland Transit Authority) (MK); Central Florida Zoo

1976: River Country; Mystery Fun House (closed 2001)

1977: WET 'N WILD (WW)

1980: Big Thunder Mountain Railroad (MK)

1982: *EPCOT* (E)

1983: Journey into Imagination pavilion (now Imagination) (E); Medieval Times Dinner Tournament

1984: Morocco pavilion (E)

1986: The Living Seas (E)

1987: Fort Liberty

1988: Wonders of Life and Norway pavilion (E); Mickey's Birthdayland (now Mickey's Toontown Fair) (MK); Flying Tigers Warbird Restoration Museum; Arabian Nights Dinner Show

1989: DISNEY-MGM STUDIOS (MGM); Body Wars and Cranium Command (E); Typhoon Lagoon, Pleasure Island, Green Meadows Petting Farm

1990: Star Tours and Honey I Shrunk the Kids Movie Set Adventure (MGM); Mickey's Starland (replaced Mickey's Birthdayland) (MK); UNIVERSAL STUDIOS (U)

1991: Jim Henson's Muppet*Vision 3-D (MGM); SpectroMagic parade (MK); Terror On Church Street (closed 1999)

1992: Splash Mountain (MK); The Voyage of the Little Mermaid (MGM); Ripley's Believe It or Not!

1993: New production of Hall of Presidents (MK); Kumba in Busch Gardens (BG); A World of Orchids; Splendid China (closed 2003)

1994: Legend of the Lion King (MK); Innoventions (E); Honey, I Shrunk the Audience (replaced Captain EO) (MGM); Food Rocks (replaced Kitchen Kabaret) (E); The Twilight Zone™ Tower of Terror (MGM); Planet Hollywood

1995: The Circle of Life (E); Extra TERRORestrial Alien Encounter (MK); Blizzard Beach; Disney's Wilderness Lodge; Fantasy of Flight; Disney's All Star Sports Resort

1996: Mickey's Toontown Fair (replaced Starland) (MK); Ellen's Energy Adventure (E); Disney's The Hunchback of Notre Dame (closed 2003)(MGM); Fantasia Gardens; Mini-Golf; Celebration; Boardwalk; Pirate's Dinner Adventure; Montu (BG); Disney's All Star Music Resort

1997: *Downtown Disney* West Side; *Disney's Wide World of Sports Complex*; Skull Kingdom; The Edge of Africa (BG); Disney's All Star Movies Resort

1998: DISNEY'S ANIMAL KINGDOM THEME PARK (AK); Buzz Lightyear's Space Ranger Spin and Enchanted Tiki Room – Under New Management (MK); Fantasmic! (MGM); Journey to Atlantis (SW); *DisneyQuest*; Disney Cruise Line; The Pointe*Orlando; WonderWorks; Lake Buena Vista Factory Stores

1999: Sounds Dangerous starring Drew Carey and Rock 'n' Roller Coaster starring Aerosmith (MGM); Kali River Rapids and Maharajah Jungle Trek (AK); Test Track (E); The Many Adventures of Winnie the Pooh (MK); Gwazi (BG); Cirque du Soleil®; ISLANDS OF ADVENTURE (IoA) and CityWalk; Titanic – The Exhibition

2000: Journey Into Your Imagination (now Journey Into Your Imagination with Figment) (E); Storm Force and Flying Unicorn (IoA); Kraken (SW); Discovery Cove; Guinness World Records Experience (then Hard Rock Vault); Orlando Premium Outlets

2001: Who Wants to Be A Millionaire – Play It! (MGM); The Magic Carpets of Aladdin (MK); Rhino Rally (BG); The Holy Land Experience; Disney's Animal Kingdom Lodge;

2002: Chester and Hester's DinoRama, TriceraTOP Spin and Primeval Whirl (AK); Men in Black – Alien Attack (U); The Scriptorium: Center for Biblical Antiquities (Holy Land Experience)

2003: Mission: SPACE (E); Mickey's PhilharMagic (replaced Legend of the Lion King) (MK); Jimmy Neutron's Nicktoon Blast and Shrek 4-D (U); Waterfront, Odyssea, Sharks Deep Dive (SW). R L Stine's Haunted Lighthouse (BG). Dolly Parton's Dixie Stampede; Festival Bay; Hard Rock Vault (now closed); Mall at Millennia; Disney's Pop Century Resort

2004: Wishes firework display and Stitch's Great Escape (MK); Revenge of The Mummy (U); Fusion and Mistify (SW); Cheetah Chase and KaTonga (BG); The Blast (WnW); Disney's Saratoga Springs Resort & Spa; Disney's Pop Century Resort

2005: Lights, Motors, Action!™ Extreme Stunt Show (MGM); Soarin' (E); Cinderellabration (MK); Crush 'n' Gusher (TL); Fear Factor Live (U); Blue Horizons (SW); SheiKra (BG); Disco H2O (WnW)

2006: Expedition Everest (AK); Ron Jon's Surf Park (Festival Bay)

British citizen (ALL members of the family must have their own passport that does not expire for 90 days from the time of entry). Instead, all you do is fill in a green visa waiver form (usually given out on your flight or when you check in) and hand it in with your passport to the US immigration official who checks you through after landing.

However, British subjects AND those who do not have a *machine-*

Lazy River at Omni Champions Gate Resort

> BRIT TIP: US immigration now requires that ALL visitors (ages 14–79) give fingerprint and photo ID on arrival. It slows things down a touch, but the process is pretty simple – first, left index finger then right index finger on their glass panel, then stand still for the camera.

readable passport DO need a visa (£60), and should apply at least 2 months in advance to the US Embassy. Also, as of October 2006, anyone applying for a *new* British citizen passport *will* have to apply for a visa if the new passport does not include biometric data. As it is unlikely the technology to include biometric data on British passports will be set up in time, this is potentially a major inconvenience, but this deadline has already been

Cadillac Diner in Kissimmee

postponed twice and it is possible it will be delayed again. Please check with the US Embassy website (see below) for up to date requirements.

Some travellers may NOT be eligible to enter under the visa waiver programme and will have to apply for a special restricted visa or they may be refused entry. This applies to those who have been arrested in the past (even if the arrest did not result in a conviction), have a criminal record (the Rehabilitation of Offenders Act does not apply to US visa law), or have a certain serious communicable illness (and the US counts AIDS sufferers in this category), or have previously been refused admission into, deported from, or have previously overstayed in the US on the visa waiver programme (minor traffic offences that did not result in an arrest and/or conviction do not count).

In England, Scotland and Wales write to the Visa Office, US Embassy, 5 Upper Grosvenor Street, London W1A 2JB (0891 200 290). In Northern Ireland, write to US Consulate General, 3 Queens House, 14 Queen Street, Belfast BT1 6EQ. You can call 09055 444 546 (£1.30/minute) for more detailed advice, or visit www.usembassy.org.uk.

Orlando skyline

What's new

In keeping with Orlando's tradition for providing an ever-changing profile of attractions, there is much that is new in this region of the Sunshine State.

Walt Disney World remains at the forefront with their 'Happiest Celebration on Earth' festivities throughout the parks until the end of 2006. This celebration, to mark the 50th anniversary of *Disneyland Resort in California*, featured new attractions in each of the parks in May 2005, with another blockbuster ride due to open in spring 2006. That is when *Disney's Animal Kingdom Park* will unveil **Expedition Everest** – a unique high-speed coaster , designed like a runaway train that careers both backwards and forwards around the glaciers, canyons and caverns of a 200-ft (60-metre) high 'Everest' in search of the mythical Yeti.

Around the other parks, Universal Orlando opened **Fear Factor Live** in summer 2005, an interactive version of the popular American reality TV show, while SeaWorld added a major new show, **Blue Horizons**, a mixture of theatre and animal interaction. SeaWorld has also announced plans for a new, adjacent water park, but this will not be ready before 2007 at the earliest. Busch Gardens has opened a stunning new coaster, the truly awesome **SheiKra** – the world's highest and fastest 'dive' coaster –

and the all-new **Cypress Gardens** continues to add new facets all the time, with a 6-acre water park in summer 2005.

Elsewhere, the spectacular **Reunion Resort** (which includes three golf courses) continues to develop new features and a major new hotel/condo development is springing up next to the Lake Buena Vista Factory Stores shopping complex. **The Lake Buena Vista Resort Village & Spa** is a huge project featuring 1,875 2-, 3- and 4-bedroom luxury apartments in a hotel-like setting. The upmarket **Shingle Creek Resort** should also be up and running in 2006, behind the Convention Center off Universal Boulevard. At the increasingly impressive **Belz Festival Bay** mall, June 2006 should see the opening of Ron Jon's Surf Park, a first-of-its kind complex offering some unique challenges and entertainment, while **The Pointe Orlando** continues a major rebuilding project to add new shops and restaurants. More new outlet stores can also be found at **The Loop** in Kissimmee and the **Prime Outlets** (formerly Belz Factory Outlet World), where another big facelift started in 2005.

Of course, for all the latest info, make sure you check our own website – www.askdaisy.net/orlando – to keep you fully up to date with everything to do with this holiday wonderland!

Revenge of the Mummy

Central Florida festivals

Here are some major – and unusual
– annual events that are worth
keeping an eye out for in 2006 (and
even planning your holiday around).
**Blue Spring Manatee Festival, Jan
29** (www.themanateefestival.com):
beautiful Blue Spring State Park is
home to the wonderful manatee, and
special celebrations are staged around
their seasonal migrations, with craft
shows, park tours and interpretive
programmes. In Orange City, it's
worth seeing at any time of year. (Off
Exit 118 on Interstate 4 or I-4.)
Florida State Fair, Feb 9–20
(www.floridastatefair.com): this 100-
year-old (in 2004) fair just outside
Tampa (right on I-4) draws almost
half a million people to its mix of
fairground rides, art, crafts, livestock
and live entertainment and offers a
huge variety of dance, contests and
competitions. A real Florida
showcase.
**Silver Spurs Rodeo, Feb 17-19
and Oct 20-22 (tbc)**
(www.silverspursrodeo.com): a
twice-yearly celebration of an
original American sport, this is held
at the new Osceola Heritage Park in
Kissimmee and features some top
quality events, plus associated crafts
and activities. (Just off the eastern
end of Highway 192.)
**Plant City Strawberry Festival,
Mar 2–12** (www.flstrawberry
festival.com): one of the most
unusual and fun events – a fully
grown country fair based on the
local produce, but with concerts,
shows, exhibitions and parades, plus
lots of activities for kids. One of
Florida's great social events. (Off
Exit 19 on I-4.)
**Daytona Beach Bike Week, Mar
3–12** (www.officialbikeweek.com): a
celebration of all things two-wheeled
and mechanical, with races at
Daytona Speedway, concerts,
parades and street festivals.
**Sidewalk Arts Festival, Mar
17–19** (www.wpsaf.org): Winter
Park is home to one of America's
most prestigious fine arts festivals,
with three days of art, food, music
and children's events, 9am–5pm.
Fun 'n Sun, Apr 4-10 (www.sun-
n-fun.org): the annual aviation
spectacular in Lakeland, with
museums, vintage planes, aerobatics
and much, much more. One of the
biggest in the USA. (Off Exit 27 on
I-4.)
**Zellwood Corn Festival, May
26–28 (tbc)** (www.zellwoodcorn
festival.com): another offbeat but
fun offering, with the festival
featuring corn-eating contests,
carnival rides, live entertainment,
games, arts and crafts. (25
miles/40km north-west of Orlando,
take Route 436 to Route 411.)
Independence Day, July 4: a
huge national holiday throughout
the country, but watch out for big
annual special events at Lake Eola
(downtown Orlando), Lakefront
Park (Kissimmee), Mount Dora,
Celebration and Winter Park, as
well as the main theme parks.
**Great Outdoor Festival, Nov
11-12 (tbc)** (www.floridakiss.com):
right at the end of Kissimmee's
annual 8-week Anglers' Challenge (a
huge local fishing festival that
attracts devotees from all over the
US) is this environmental
celebration of family fun, races, live
music and outdoor recreation
exhibits, at the Silver Spurs Arena at
Osceola Heritage Park.

Plan your visit

The next few chapters will help you
plan your days and tell you
everything you need to know to
make your holiday perfect. Draw up
a rough itinerary and then fine tune
it with our help here, our website
www.askdaisy.net/orlando, the UK
Discussion Boards on
www.wdwinfo.com and with your
Personalised Itinerary Planner (see
page 46).
    Now read on and enjoy…

Planning and Practicalities
(or, *How to* Almost *Do It All and Live to Tell the Tale*)

There is one simple rule once you have decided Orlando is the place for you. Sit down and PLAN what you want to do very carefully. This is not the type of holiday you can take in a freewheeling, carefree 'make it up as you go along' manner. Frustration and exhaustion lie in wait for all those who do not have at least a basic plan of campaign.

First of all work out WHEN you want to go, then decide WHERE in the vast resort is the best place for you. Then consider WHAT sort of holiday you are looking for, WHO you want to entrust your holiday with and finally HOW MUCH you want to try to do.

When to go

If you are looking to avoid the worst of the crowds, the best periods to choose are October to December (but not the week of Thanksgiving in November or between Christmas and New Year), early January up until 2 weeks before Easter (avoiding President's Day in February) and April (after Easter) to the end of May. Orlando gets down to some serious tourist business from Memorial Day (the last Monday in May, the official start of the summer season) to Labor Day (the first Monday in September and the last holiday of summer), peaking on July 4, a huge national holiday. The Easter holidays are similarly uncomfortable (although the weather is better), but easily the busiest is Christmas time, starting the week before December 25 and lasting until January 2. It is not unknown for some of the parks to close to new arrivals by mid-morning.

The best combinations of good weather and smaller crowds are in April (avoiding Easter) and October. However, few of the attractions are affected by rain (roller-coasters and water rides close only if lightning threatens) and you'll be one jump ahead if you have waterproofs as the crowds noticeably thin out if it rains. All the parks sell cheap, plastic ponchos (cheaper at Wal-Mart or other supermarkets). In the colder months, take a few warm layers for early morning queues then, when it heats up, leave them in the park lockers. When it gets too hot, take advantage of the air-conditioned attractions and restaurants (and drink LOTS of water).

BRIT TIP: Thanksgiving is always the fourth Thursday in November; George Washington's birthday, or President's Day, is the third Monday in February. Try to avoid those weeks!

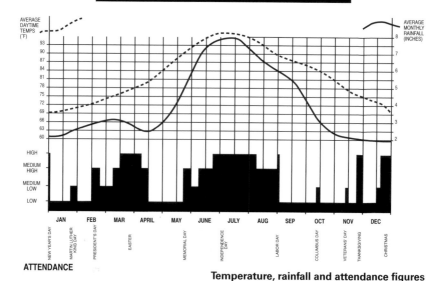

Temperature, rainfall and attendance figures

Where to stay

The choice of where to stay is equally important. Inevitably, there is a huge choice of location and price. As a guide, four main areas make up the greater Orlando tourist conglomeration:

Walt Disney World Resort in Florida: some of the most sophisticated, convenient and fun places to stay are to be found in Disney's great range of hotels. The same imagination that has gone into creating the theme parks has been at work on the likes of *Disney's Polynesian Resort* and *Disney's Animal Kingdom Lodge*. They all feature free, regular transport to the parks, your own resort ID card (so you can charge meals and souvenirs to your room, and have your purchases delivered to the hotel), free parking

and the BIG bonus of the **Extra Magic Hours**. This allows Disney resort guests entry to one theme park each day, either a full hour before the official opening time or three hours after closing, meaning you can do many of the main attractions with only a fraction of the crowds. Many resorts also have great kids' clubs and baby-sitting services. The drawbacks here are that, with the exception of *Disney's All-Star* and *Disney's Pop Century Resorts*, their hotels are among the most expensive, especially to eat in, and are a fair drive from Universal and other attractions. It makes a good 1-week holiday though.

> BRIT TIP: Having the use of a pool where you are staying is a major plus for relaxing at the end of a busy hot day.

Lake Buena Vista: a loosely defined area around the eastern fringes of *Walt Disney World Resort in Florida* and along Interstate 4 (I-4), this again features some upmarket

Disney's Grand Floridian Resort & Spa

© Disney

Mövenpick Dream Castle Hotel at Disneyland Resort Paris

hotels. It is also handy for all the Disney fun, with most hotels offering free transport to the parks, while there is also excellent dining and shopping. Still a bit pricey, but its proximity to I-4 makes it convenient for much of Orlando.

International Drive: this ribbon development, known as I-Drive, lies midway between Disney and downtown Orlando and is therefore an excellent central location. Running parallel to I-4, it is about 20 minutes' drive from Disney, closer to Universal and SeaWorld. It is also a well-developed tourist area in its own right, with great shops, restaurants and attractions like Wet 'n Wild, Ripley's Believe It Or Not, WonderWorks and Skull Kingdom. The downside is it gets congested with tourist traffic in peak periods, especially the evenings. But it does represent good value for money and is one of the few areas with extensive pavements, making it easy to explore on foot. A sub-district off I-Drive is the Universal area of Kirkman Road and Major Boulevard, where new hotels are regularly being added.

Kissimmee: budget holiday-makers can be found in their greatest numbers along the tourist sprawl of Highway 192 (the Irlo Bronson Memorial Highway), an almost unbroken 20-mile (32-km) strip of hotels, motels, restaurants and shops. It offers some of the best economy accommodation in the area

and is handy for all Disney's attractions, although it is furthest away from Universal Orlando and downtown Orlando. A car is most advisable here, although the ongoing BeautiVacation project (to enhance the heavily built-up stretch of 192 from Formosa Gardens east to Hoagland Boulevard with pavements, landscaping, bus shelters, benches and water fountains) has made it a much better location for getting around on foot or by bus.

> BRIT TIP: Phase II of the BeautiVacation of Highway 192 will continue until summer 2006, meaning serious roadworks from Route 535 to Hoagland Boulevard. Use (toll) Osceola Parkway to beat the traffic.

Split holidays

Florida has so much to offer that many people opt to split their holiday by having a week or two in Orlando as well as a week elsewhere, such as the Gulf Coast, Miami or Florida Keys. The Atlantic coast has some great beaches only an hour's drive to the east, the magnificent Florida Everglades are some 3–4 hours to the south, and there are more wonderful beaches and pleasant coast roads to the west. Great shopping is to be found almost everywhere, while Orlando

Toon Lagoon at Universal

has some stunning golf courses along with plenty of opportunities to play or watch tennis, baseball and basketball, or go fishing, boating or canoeing.

The main tour companies offer a huge variety of packages, with some popular cruise-and-stay options. If you can afford the time (and expense), the best option is to have 2 weeks in Orlando itself, then a week relaxing on one of Florida's many fabulous beaches. A 2-week, half-and-half split is a regular choice, but can make your time in Orlando rather hectic, unless your additional week is somewhere like Cocoa Beach (near the Kennedy Space Center) and gives you the chance to return to Orlando for the day. Several companies offer a worthwhile 10-day Orlando and 4-day coast split. Fly-drives offer the greatest flexibility, but there is a lot to tempt you in just 2 weeks and you may find it better to book a 1-centre package that includes a car and accommodation so you can still travel around but avoid too much packing and unpacking.

Travel companies

There is serious competition for your hard-earned holiday money and the travel companies have been working hard to keep the cost of an Orlando holiday down, whether you fly-drive, book your own flights or take a package. Shop around to get the best value for your holiday £, but make sure you book with an ABTA agent for security should anything go wrong. At the last count, there were some 65 tour operators offering holidays to Florida. Here is a rundown of the biggest and best:

Travel City Direct: the UK's largest independent direct-sell Florida specialist, with more than 150,000 customers a year, it offers a wide range of holidays at ultra-competitive prices (because you book direct), including fly-drives, 1- and 2-centre holidays, private pool villas and Caribbean cruises. New features include a dedicated (and well-written) Disney brochure and their own tie-up with Carnival Cruise Line for a range of tempting Caribbean cruise add-ons. A sharp reservations team (and improved online booking) has excellent local knowledge and can advise on where to stay, what to do and keep you up to date with what's new. In 2005 it introduced its exclusive Freetime Check-In service at its Welcome Lounge at Lake Buena Vista Factory Stores. This allows guests to make the most of their last day by checking in luggage early on the morning of departure – and reducing the amount of time needed at the airport. Simply pre-book this new service for only $5 per person at the Welcome Lounge. Freetime Check-In is also free to Sunshine First and Premium clients.

Most flights year-round are now with its in-house branded airline (Gatwick and Manchester, eight flights a week in summer), using Air Atlanta Europe Boeing 747s and with one of the most generous seat pitches (32in/82cm of leg room) for a charter, plus free drinks, meals and headsets in all classes (unlike many). There is an economy cabin (the Sunshine Cabin), the Sunshine Upper Deck (no under-9s allowed, still economy-size seats but better service and meals, 30kg luggage allowance and priority check-in and disembarkation, from an extra £99) and Sunshine First (22 seats with a 50in/127cm pitch that recline almost flat, upgraded menus and individual video screens, 40kg luggage allowance, priority boarding and late check-in, all from £249 extra).

You can also pre-book seats on most flights (for £20 return or £69 for a family of four). They have a double baggage allowance offer (£15/person, or £99 for a family of four if buying pre-bookable seats too) allowing you to increase your limit from 20kg to 40kg (useful if you are shopping in Orlando). Other flights depart from six regional airports, including Belfast and Cardiff.

Travel City Direct has three dedicated arrivals centres and its own check-in for selected flights at Orlando Sanford airport, as well as the smart Welcome Lounge at Lake Buena Vista Factory Shops, open 7 days a week (plus one on I-Drive in peak season). Travel City Direct can be found on Teletext page 298 on ITV, for direct bookings call 0870 950 5128 or visit www.travelcity direct.com.

Airlines: Travel City Direct, plus Air Atlanta Europe, BA, Virgin, US Airways, Continental Airlines and charters.

Airport: Orlando Sanford (Travel City Direct, Air Atlanta Europe and charters), Orlando International (BA, US Airways, Virgin and Continental).

Virgin Holidays: the UK's biggest scheduled tour operator to Florida, Virgin offers the most extensive programme to the Sunshine State, with a vast variety of combinations – more than 180 properties to choose from, including Miami, the Keys, New York, Boston, the Caribbean and some tempting Disney cruises, as well as the Florida coasts. A strong selling point is Virgin's non-stop scheduled service to Orlando (from Manchester and up to 17 times a week from Gatwick) with award-winning in-flight entertainment, free drinks, kids' packs, meals and games. It has a wide choice of accommodation (including most Disney resorts) and is popular for fly-drives, flying into Orlando and out of Miami, and vice versa. New in 2006 is a Value Collection of hotels to help the budget-conscious, plus flights into Fort Myers.

There are flight upgrades to its Premium Economy (highly recommended; extra leg room and bigger seats from £195 one way) and the superb Upper Class service (from £555 one way; with seats that recline fully, plus personal attention and service and free use of the Virgin Atlantic Clubhouse in UK airports).

You can pre-book seats free of charge (on 0871 231 0231) no more than 180 days before departure and even check in the evening before your flight at Gatwick. You can now pre-book the Virgin Clubhouse at Gatwick at £35/person. Virgin also has a valuable *Downtown Disney* Check-In service for return flights, allowing guests to check in the morning of departure, freeing up the rest of the day to enjoy at leisure (exclusively free for Virgin Holidays customers).

Orlando is also popular as a wedding venue, and Virgin can provide wedding co-ordinators for ceremonies throughout Florida. Other bonuses include single-parent discounts, a top-class service for passengers with disabilities, 'kids eat free' deals at selected hotels (and a free meal at the Hard Rock Café for all Orlando guests), next-day pick-up for hire cars and some excellent non-driver packages, plus a chartered bus from Orlando to Miami or Fort Lauderdale. Uniquely, it now has a prestige car hire option that includes the all-American Hummer. Call 0871 222 1232 or visit www.virgin.com/holidays.

Airline: Virgin Atlantic.
Airports: Orlando International, Miami, Fort Myers.

Thomson: another of the largest, mass-market operators, Thomson has an excellent reputation in Orlando, having a large team of reps and Service Centres on I-Drive, and offers 7 departure airports (including Birmingham, Cardiff, Newcastle, Glasgow and Belfast).

You can pre-book your seats (£17 adult, £7 child), while good in-flight entertainment and kids' packs are provided (with its Thomsonfly charter airline).

Thomson price packages well for the family market, with hundreds of free child places (for early bookers), special children's fares (from £49 first child) and 'kids eat free' and 'extra value' hotels, while offering a decent selection of cruises, coastal resorts for 2- or even 3-centre holidays (including Miami and Key West) plus pre-bookable golf packages. An increased range of private villas (sleeping up to 10) is available, as are wedding packages (from £665-£725) at Magnolia Acres, the Wyndham Palace or Wyndham Orlando hotels.

Flight upgrades cost £60 (for extra leg room) and £150 (£169 in summer 2006) for Premium service (with free drinks, wider seats, choice of meals, entertainment and priority boarding). Call 0870 550 2567 or book online at www.thomson.co.uk.
Airline: Thomsonfly and other charters.
Airport: Orlando Sanford.
Airtours: also in the leading group who take around 100,000 visitors to Orlando each year, Airtours flies from 7 UK airports with good in-flight entertainment, and seat-back TVs (on selected flights). It offers an excellent Premiair Gold upgrade (extra leg room and baggage allowance, free bar, pre-selected menu, late UK check-in) and have some novel 10- and 11-night packages (from Manchester and Gatwick only) for a more flexible choice, plus a wide range of car hire options and upgrades. There is an Airtours service desk at the huge McDonald's on I-Drive and Sand Lake Road and Welcome Meetings are imaginatively held in Universal's CityWalk (with free parking), so you can hit the fun straight away. There are some good 2-centre combos, including a week at a Disney resort and a week on I-Drive. Airtours also have a range of 'Drive and Stay' holidays, including new packages that combine a fly-drive with the first 3 or 4 nights at a Disney or Universal hotel. Early bookers get the pick of Airtours' special offers, including guaranteed free child places, free pre-bookable seating, and free in-flight meals. Premiair Gold upgrades are available (£179), as are extra-leg-room seating (£70), 25kg luggage allowance (per person) and low deposit. Call 0870 900 8639 or visit www.airtours.co.uk.
Airline: MyTravel.
Airport: Orlando Sanford.
First Choice: a comprehensive programme to Florida from 4 UK airports (Gatwick, Manchester, Nottingham East Midlands, and Glasgow) using First Choice Airways. Its revamped (and highly popular) long-haul flight service features personal seat-back entertainment, more leg room, wider seats and all meals included – plus premium cabin upgrades giving even more room, complimentary drinks, entertainment on demand and personal widescreen TV. Star Class is the standard service, with a generous 33-inch seat pitch and 7-in seatback TVs, while Star Class Premier features a 36-inch pitch with leather seats, a 9-in TV screen, 30 channels to choose from and a choice of meals (for £149 extra for adults, £99 for children). There is also a special Disney preview channel and activity packs for children. Outstanding value in the charter flight world. Holidays

Kids have fun on Virgin flights

are available throughout Orlando and the Gulf Coast plus a dedicated programme to *Walt Disney World Resort in Florida* featuring all on-site resorts. First Choice has a family-friendly touch offering hotels (mainly the 3- and 4-star variety) with themed Kidsuites and 'kids eat free' deals, plus villas and apartments. There is a meet-and-greet service at Orlando Sanford airport, plus a new service desk at the Holiday Inn Resort on I-Drive. Visit the website www.firstchoice.co.uk or request a brochure on 0870 750 0001.

Airline: First Choice Airways.
Airport: Orlando Sanford.

Other First Choice brands selling Florida are: **First Choice Disney** for all Disney hotels and extensive information on how to enjoy *Walt Disney World*; **First Choice Villas** for a solely villa-based holiday; **First Choice Premier** for a selection of 5-star hotels (0870 750 0001 or www.firstchoice.co.uk for all three); **Eclipse Direct**, a direct-sell operator with a standard range of accommodation around Orlando (0870 501 0203, www.eclipse direct.co.uk); and **Sunstart**, the budget operator, featuring mainly 2- and 3-star hotels (0870 243 0636, www.firstchoice.co.uk).

British Airways Holidays: another company to benefit from its own direct, scheduled air service, BA Holidays offers great flexibility with almost any duration and combination possible. Beach add-ons, 2 centres – both coasts and the Florida Keys – and an extensive selection of quality but great-value private homes and condominiums are all on offer. BAH also flies to Miami and Tampa, opening up plenty of fly-drive and multi-centre possibilities. However, you won't find them in most travel agents as they only do direct-sell, but their packages are all well tried and trusted. BA flights also come with the option to upgrade to the luxurious Club World (with wonderfully fully flat beds) or World Traveller Plus (larger seats with more leg room), plus special kids' meals and seat-back TVs. BA Holidays were also the only UK operator to offer *Disney's Magical Express* from the beginning, the innovatory transfer service that whisks you straight to your Disney resort, with your luggage being delivered for you without you having to touch it again after the flight check-in. Call 0870 243 3406 or browse online at www.baholidays.com.

Airline: British Airways.
Airport: Orlando International.

Thomas Cook: two choices are available under the famous Cook banner: the main Thomas Cook brochure and a specialist Thomas Cook Signature programme, (see right). The regular Thomas Cook brand has 46 properties on offer (from budget to luxury, and villas that sleep up to 10), mainly using their Thomas Cook charter airline (from 6 UK airports – Birmingham, Cardiff, Gatwick, Glasgow, Manchester, Newcastle), which has replaced the old jmc brand. Their Premium cabin upgrade is available at £139/person, while extra legroom seats (for £30 each way), pre-bookable seating and VIP lounge facilities (at selected UK airports) are all on offer, along with children's packs and extras such as champagne and chocolates (for a charge). In-

Kids always have great fun at Disney!

© Disney

flight meals are an optional £10 each. Book one of the Select properties and you qualify for free in-flight drinks, headphones and an enhanced 30kg luggage allowance. Thomas Cook also has one of the best punctuality records of all the charter airlines and its in-flight service is one of the best, from my observations. Many hotels come with the 'kids eat free' bonus, and its car hire has a free upgrade if you book Alamo Gold or fully inclusive insurance. There is even a 'next day' car collection service, meaning you don't have to drive straight away on arrival but can pick up your car the following day from one of 5 Orlando locations (or a transfer option – at £35/person – if you are not driving). You can either book through their own High Street agencies, by phone (0870 750 5711), online at www.thomascook.com or via Thomas Cook TV (Sky Guide channel 648, ntl:home channel 857). It offers some good wedding packages (from £1,399 per couple at a Disney location, to just £439 in Winter Park), and some tempting 2-centre options (including the Bahamas, Jamaica, Miami, a week's Orlando stay with a week's fly-drive, and a week in 2 different Gulf Coast resorts) and cruises.
Airline: Thomas Cook and Monarch.
Airport: Orlando Sanford.
Thomas Cook Signature: now here's an operation to compete with the Virgins of this world – a more quality-conscious and selective offering using ONLY scheduled air services (although their prices are still pretty competitive). It tends to suit repeat visitors especially, and bonuses include early booking discounts, free night offers (stay 6 and get another free), 'kids eat free' and free room upgrades at many hotels. Its ticketing info and material is first class and there is a strong tailor-made element to the range of choice. Its selection of holiday homes is particularly good (with some of the most upmarket properties in the area), and the twin-centre options include both coasts, Miami, the Keys, as well as the rest of the USA and the Caribbean. New for 2006 is a stand-alone Disney brochure for all its US resorts, plus good cruise deals. Call 0870 443 4453 or visit www.tcsignature.com.
Airlines: Virgin Atlantic, British Airways, American Airlines, Continental Airlines, United.
Airports: Orlando International, plus Miami and Tampa.
Funway Holidays: the sister company of America's largest tour operator and a leading specialist in holidays to the US, Funway offers a tailor-made service to match Orlando with any option, providing total flexibility of choice from no less than 17 UK airports. Its Orlando private homes are a big feature of its Florida programme but it also serves up an array of hotels throughout the Sunshine State, including all the Disney resorts, and its low children's prices (for early bookers) make it consistently among the best-priced for a family of 4. It also uses only scheduled airlines (with an option to upgrade to Virgin's Premium Economy from £140 each way). Its 2-centre choices include the Gulf Coast, Miami, the Florida Keys and the Caribbean, which gets a dedicated brochure in 2006. Added bonuses include 'kids eat free' hotels, free kids' clubs, free hotel nights and free transport to the theme parks at selected hotels. Look at www.funwayholidays.co.uk or call 0870 444 0770 for a brochure.
Airlines: various scheduled, including Virgin Atlantic, British Airways and Continental.
Airport: Orlando International.
Style Holidays: one of the UK's top Florida specialists (and a Thomas Cook-owned company), Style offers a huge selection of villas

with private pools (from 2-6 bedrooms), self-catering apartments and a wide range of hotels, as well as fly- drive options. All properties are in named, well-described locations and can be booked either as a package with hire car or on an accommodation-only basis. Its comprehensive brochure has an excellent range of Gulf Coast villas (some right on the beach), apartments and luxury resorts, all of which can be twinned with Orlando. Style also feature excellent in-resort service. For a brochure, call 0870 444 4474 or visit www.style-holidays.co.uk.

Airlines: Various charters.
Airport: Orlando Sanford.

Jetsave: Florida specialist Jetsave puts the accent on flexibility, with a wide range of choice, including a new tie-up with flights on Thomsonfly from Manchester to Orlando Sanford. For accommodation, you have the full selection of hotels (especially the kid-friendly variety and all Disney's resorts), apartments and holiday homes (or villas as we would call them), and simple, accurate star ratings are given for each property. They also work closely with Disney and Universal to offer good prices on the various theme park tickets. Jetsave use Virgin Atlantic as their primary airline from Gatwick and Manchester so customers can fly any day and stay for any duration. Flight upgrades with Virgin are available, including Club Orlando, their unique Premium Economy Plus service from Manchester. Jetsave can also tailor-make a holiday in Florida with any combination of flights, accommodation and resorts, including self-drive itineraries and offer a wedding service for those wanting to get married in the Sunshine State. Visit www.jetsave.co.uk or call 0870 161 3402.

Airlines: Virgin Atlantic, British Airways, Thomsonfly.

Airport: Orlando International and Orlando Sanford (Thomsonfly).

Cosmos: another familiar holiday company name, Cosmos has a long history in Florida and focuses on the key resort areas in Orlando and the Gulf Coast (Clearwater, St Pete's Beach and Naples). With a full range of hotels (including Disney and Universal), suites and villas, it offers 7-, 14- and 21-night holidays on a package, fly-drive and flight-only basis, and is particularly well-priced for car hire. Coach transfers are also available to all Orlando hotels (at £32/person). With flights (on Monarch) from Gatwick, Manchester and (in high season) Glasgow, it also offers the Monarch Premium cabin upgrade (for £159/person), which provides wider seats with extra legroom, personal entertainment systems, complimentary headsets, amenity packs, free bar choice, enhanced in-flight meals, extra baggage allowance (30kg), dedicated check-in and priority boarding and baggage reclaim. Extra legroom seats are also available at £60/person. Call 0870 99 06 880 or visit www.cosmos-holidays.co.uk.

Airlines: Monarch.
Airport: Orlando Sanford.

A number of other companies worth checking include: the high-quality style of **Kuoni** (call 01306 747 734 or visit www.kuoni.co.uk); **Trailfinders** (the UK's largest independent travel firm, 0845 058 5858 or download its online brochures at www.trailfinders.com); **USAirtours** (tailor-made US itineraries, many with villas in Orlando; 08712 100 500, www.usairtours.co.uk); **Travelbag** (0800 052 5000, www.travelbag.co.uk); **Transolar Holidays** (another US specialist, also great for attraction ticket offers on 0151 630 3737 or www.transolarholidays.com); **Premier Holidays** (more tailor-made choice, 0870 889

0850, www.premierholidays.co.uk); and **Ebookers** (the travel agent arm of Flightbookers, 0800 082 3000, www.ebookers.com).

For flight-only offers, try **Flight Centre** (0870 499 0040 or www.flightcentre.co.uk), **Airline Network** (0870 700 0543, www.airline-network.co.uk), **Dial A Flight** (0870 333 4488, www.dialaflight.com; also for villas, hotels and car hire) and the excellent **Cheap Flights** (an internet-only service, www.cheapflights.co.uk). A look at **Teletext** page 222 or www.teletextholidays.co.uk) often reveals special deals, as do www.expedia.co.uk, www.lastminute.com and www.opodo.co.uk. A new internet company, **Vacation Florida**, website www.vacation-florida.co.uk, and partner website www.cheapestflights.co.uk, 0800 015 8030), offer the full range of flights, packages and car hire. You might also consider the well-designed Disney specialists **The Holiday People** (0870 240 2510, www.theholidaypeople.com) for more than just tickets, while **Holiday Travel Essentials** (0870 036 0063, www.worldwide-attractions.co.uk) also offers accommodation and car hire, in addition to tickets.

Apart from the charter airlines, there are only a handful of choices for direct flights to Orlando, notably Virgin Atlantic, British Airways and Aer Lingus (from Dublin), but you can often save money on indirect flights with the likes of Delta (via Atlanta or Cincinnati), American Airlines (via Dallas, New York or Raleigh Durham), Continental (via Houston or Washington), Northwest (via Detroit) , United (via Dallas or New York) and even Icelandair (via Reykjavik). The obvious drawback is the extra length of journey time, and you can often arrive in Orlando late in the evening after the connecting flight. However, it does give you the chance to break the journey up, and places like Detroit and Atlanta can often process international passengers much quicker than Orlando, meaning less hassle when you arrive in Florida.

Two new operations with a scheduled flight element worth keeping an eye on are Gatwick-based Excel Airways (and sister company Freedom Flights, who sell through travel agents – www.freedomflights.com) and Manchester's Air Scandic. In 2005, **Excel** operated direct flights to Orlando Sanford airport once a week, with modern in-flight service on its Boeing 767s. Look up more on www.xl.co.uk. **Air Scandic** operates in summer, from Manchester (Mon and Thur), Glasgow (Sun and Mon), Newcastle and Belfast (both Wednesday) to Orlando Sanford, and at Christmas/New Year from Manchester and Gatwick (Wednesday only), operated by Pure Flights. Some flights (using a Boeing 757) have a refuelling stop at Gander in Canada, making for a 10-hour-plus flight. Call 0870 777 0747 or look at www.pureflights.com.

Finally, for those looking to book things themselves but wanting help with Disney accommodation, meal reservations, etc, the excellent **Dreams Unlimited Travel** service is the answer. Visit www.dreamsunlimitedtravel.com for the essential information on this no-cost service that can save time, money and hassle. Other Orlando hotels (with some serious discounts) feature on its DreamsRes online booking service plus a discount ticket agency, TicketRes.

Clearwater Beach

What to see when

Once you arrive, the temptation is to head for the nearest theme park, then the next, and so on. Hold on! If there is such a thing as theme park indigestion, that's the best recipe for it. Some days at the parks are busier than others, while it is highly inadvisable to attempt 2 of the main parks on successive days at peak times. So here's what you can do.

With the aid of the Holiday Planner on pages 312–13 (or the *Brit's Guide* Personalised Planner – see page 46), make a note of all the attractions you want to see over the length of your stay. The most sensible strategy is to plan around the eight 'must-see' parks – *Magic Kingdom Park, Epcot, Disney-MGM Studios, Disney's Animal Kingdom Theme Park*, Universal Studios, Islands of Adventure, SeaWorld and Busch Gardens. If you have only a week, drop Busch Gardens (it's furthest away from Orlando) and concentrate on Disney, Universal Studios and SeaWorld. Space travel fans will be hard-pressed not to include the Kennedy Space Center, but it would probably bore young children.

As a basic rule, the *Magic Kingdom Park* is the biggest hit with children, and families often find it requires 2 days. The same can be said of *Epcot*, but there are fewer rides to amuse the younger ones. Only the most fleet of foot, given the benefit of relatively low crowds, will be able to negotiate *Epcot* in a day. *Disney's Animal Kingdom Theme Park* is also a little short on attractions for the youngest visitors (unless they really love their animals), but it still requires nearly a whole day. *Disney-MGM Studios* is usually possible to do in a day (not forgetting the early evening Fantasmic! show), while SeaWorld occasionally needs rather longer and Universal Studios can be a 2-day park at its busiest. Islands of Adventure will almost certainly keep everyone, except possibly under-5s, busy all day, too. Busch Gardens, extremely popular with British families, is another full-day affair, especially as it is a 75–90-minute drive away in Tampa to the south-west. However, an early start to the Kennedy Space Center (an hour's drive away to the east) will mean you can be back in your swimming pool by teatime.

All the attractions are described in detail in Chapters 5–8, so it's best to try to get an idea of the time requirements of them all before you pick up your pencil.

Smaller attractions

Of the other, smaller-scale attractions, the nature park of Silver Springs is a full day out as it also involves a near 2-hour drive to get there, and the revamped Cypress Gardens will certainly keep you occupied all day, but everything else can be fitted around your Big Eight Itinerary. The water parks provide a good place to spend a relaxing afternoon, while Historic Bok Sanctuary is another quieter spot to while away half a day or so. There are also a number of smaller-scale attractions in Orlando that will probably keep the children amused for several hours (often after the major theme parks have closed).

Gatorland is a unique look at some of Florida's oldest inhabitants and is a good combination with Boggy Creek Airboats. Ripley's

Feeding the jungle crocs at Gatorland

Believe It Or Not museum and WonderWorks interactive house of fun are both good family centres for several hours. Add in the terrific haunted house attraction Skull Kingdom and the more old-fashioned lure of go-karts and other fairground-type rides at Fun Spot or Magical Midway (all on the I-Drive corridor), and you have a full day of alternative fun and frolics. Aviation fans must not miss a trip to Fantasy of Flight (further down I-4) for a novel experience.

DisneyQuest, another part of the *Downtown Disney* area, is a hugely imaginative interactive 'arcade' that guarantees several hours' fun (especially for older children). Each main area is also well served with creatively designed mini-golf courses that will absorb any excess energy for an hour or two.

Evenings

The evening entertainment harbours a similarly wide choice of extravagant fun-seeking. By far the best, and worth at least one evening each, are *Downtown Disney's Pleasure Island*, Universal's CityWalk and The Pointe Orlando area. All will keep you busy until the early hours. Dinner shows provide a lot of fun – 2-hour cabarets based on themes like medieval knights, pirates, Arabian Nights and murder mysteries that all include a hearty meal. Rounding it up is the huge variety of nightclubs and bars, many offering live music.

What to do when

There are several general guidelines for avoiding the worst of the tourist hordes, even in high season. The vast majority of fun-seekers in town are American, who tend to arrive at weekends and head for the main theme parks first. That means Monday is generally a bad time to

visit the *Magic Kingdom Park*, as is Saturday, and Wednesday is usually humming at *Epcot*. Disney's *Extra Magic Hours* programme, which allows its hotel guests entry to one park a day either an hour early or three hours after regular closing time, also creates a greater build-up of crowds, so, if you are NOT staying at a Disney hotel, avoid the following parks day by day: Sunday, *Disney-MGM Studios*; Monday, *Epcot*; Tuesday, *Disney's Animal Kingdom* and *Disney-MGM Studios*; Wednesday, *Magic Kingdom*; Thursday, *Epcot*; Friday, *Magic Kingdom*; Saturday, *Disney's Animal Kingdom*. The *Animal Kingdom* is also the hardest to get round when it's crowded. *Disney's Blizzard Beach* and *Typhoon Lagoon* water parks hit high tide at the weekend, and Thursday and Friday in summer.

At Universal Orlando, the picture is different as there are no early entry days, and the busiest days are usually the weekends as the locals tend to visit then. This often means Monday is quietest at both Universal and Islands of Adventure, getting busier through the week, with the former being slightly more crowded.

If *Walt Disney World* is humming in the early part of the week, that makes it a good time to visit SeaWorld, Busch Gardens, Silver Springs or the Kennedy Space Center. Avoid Wet 'n Wild and Water Mania at the weekends when the locals come out to play. The Busy Day Guide on page 313 shows you at a glance the busiest and quietest days at each park.

BRIT TIP: In the first edition of the *Brit's Guide* for 1995, a typical burger-and-chips park meal cost around $5.65. Now it is more likely to be $8–10.

2

BRIT TIP: If your hotel is not far away, take a break from the park for a couple of hours and return for a siesta or a swim. Have your hand stamped for re-entry when you leave (your car park ticket will be valid all day) and then return to enjoy the spectacular evening entertainment, often the best part of the day.

Ensuring you get the most out of your days at the main parks is another art form, and there are several practical policies to pursue. The official opening times seldom vary from 9am but arriving early is highly advisable. Apart from the advantage of being near the head of the queues (and you will encounter some SERIOUS queues, or lines as the Americans call them), the parks sometimes open earlier than scheduled if the crowds build up before the official hour. So, you can be a step ahead of the masses by arriving at least 30 minutes before opening time, or an hour early during the main holiday periods. Apart from anything else, you will be better placed to park in the wide open spaces of the public car parks and catch the tram to the main gates (anything up to half a mile away). Once you've put yourself in pole position, don't waste time on the shops, scenery and other frippery that will lure the unprepared first-timer. Instead, head straight for

BRIT TIP: The water IS safe to drink in the US but it may not taste great, as they tend to put a lot of fluoride in it.

some of the main rides and get a few big-time thrills under your belt before the main hordes arrive. You will quickly work out where the most popular attractions are as the majority of early birds will flock to them. Use Chapters 5 and 6 to help plan your park strategies.

You can also benefit from doing the opposite of what the masses do after the initial rush has subsided. Try not to have all your meals in the parks, too. While they still represent great value for money, eating out has become expensive here, and it can be $10/person for even a basic counter-service meal. Instead, having a good buffet breakfast at somewhere like the Ponderosa or Golden Corral means you won't need lunch and can save $$$s!

Pace yourself

Another word of warning: Disney's parks, notably the *Magic Kingdom*, stay open late for the main holidays, occasionally until midnight, and that can be a long day for children. Therefore, it is important to pace yourself, especially if you have been among the first through the gates.

There are plenty of options to take time off for a drink or a sit-down somewhere air-conditioned, and you can benefit from the American propensity to take mealtimes seriously by avoiding lunchtime (12 noon–2pm) and dinnertime (5.30–7pm). So, after you've had a couple of hours of park going, it pays to take an early lunch (i.e. before midday), plunge back into it all for another 3 hours or so, have another snack mid-afternoon and then return to the main rides, as the parks quieten down a little in late afternoon.

Finally, a word about shopping in Orlando – it's world class. Your battle plan should include at least a day to visit one of the spectacular malls, as well as the discount outlets and speciality centres like Old Town in Kissimmee, the excellent Orlando Premium Outlets, and the likes of The Pointe Orlando and Festival Bay on International Drive.

Clothing and comfort

The most important part of your holiday wardrobe is your footwear – you will spend a lot of time on your feet, even at off-peak periods. The smallest of the parks covers 'only' 100 acres (40ha), but that is irrelevant to the amount of time you will spend queuing. This is not the time to break in new sandals or trainers! Comfortable, well-worn shoes or trainers are essential. Otherwise, you need dress only as the climate dictates. T-shirts and shorts are quite appropriate in all the

> BRIT TIP: Don't be tempted to pack a lot of smart or formal clothing – you really won't need it in hot, informal Florida.

parks (swimwear is not acceptable away from pool areas) and nearly all restaurants will happily accept informal dress.

If, after a long day, you feel the need for a change of clothes or a sweater for the evening, take advantage of the handy lockers (unlimited use all day, even if you change parks). All the parks are also well equipped with pushchairs (or strollers) for hire, and baby services

Festival Bay

The Gaylord Palms Wedding Pavilion

are located at regular intervals. It is *vital* to use high-factor sun creams at all times, even during the winter months when the sun may not feel strong but can still burn. Nothing is guaranteed to ruin your holiday like severe sunburn. Orlando has a sub-tropical climate and requires higher factor sun creams than the Mediterranean. Use sun block on sensitive areas like your nose and ears, and splash on the after-sun lotion liberally at the end of the day. You will also need waterproof sun cream for swimming. Skincare products are widely available and usually inexpensive (especially at Wal-Mart, Kmart or Target).

> BRIT TIP: One of the best ways to keep cool in the Florida sun is to visit a supermarket and buy a simple mist spray fan (about $7.99) which you carry with you and just refill with water.

Wear a hat if you are out in the hottest part of the day, and try to avoid alcohol, coffee and fizzy drinks until the evening as they are dehydrating and make you susceptible to heatstroke. You will need to increase your fluid intake significantly during the summer months in Orlando, but stick to still

2

CityWalk

soft drinks such as Gatorade, a squash-like energy drink, or water.

> BRIT TIP: If you fear the onset of blisters, buy some moleskin footpads from the nearest supermarket.

Want to see more?

If, like me, you want to make the most of every holiday opportunity, you could also travel a little further afield in America with the help of their highly efficient low-cost airline system. Orlando represents an excellent base from which to explore the delights of New York, Washington, St Louis, Chicago, Atlantic City, plus the Bahamas, Puerto Rico, Cancun and Aruba in the Caribbean, all of which are only 2 hours' flight away, or go even further to glittering Las Vegas or Los Angeles. With the benefit of cheap hotel deals (check out www.hotels.com), you can seriously spread your wings (ahem) by using the likes of **Spirit Airlines** (from Orlando International and Tampa airports) and **TransMeridian Airlines** (from Orlando Sanford airport). Skip ahead to pages 310 and 311 for more details on how to

extend your holiday. Repeat visitors may like to consider this, and it represents only a small additional investment after going all the way to Florida.

Medical aid

Should you require medical treatment, whether for sunburn or other first aid, consult your tour company's information about local hospitals and surgeries. In the event of a medical, or other, **emergency**, dial 911 as you would 999 in Britain.

It cannot be over-stressed you should have comprehensive travel and health insurance (see page 35) for any trip to America as there is NO National Health Service and ANY form of medical treatment will need to be paid for – and is expensive. Keep all the receipts and reclaim on your return home.

Emergency out-patients departments can be found with **Centra Care** at Florida Hospital Medical Center in 13 Orlando locations and can provide hotel in-room services (407 238 2000) and free transport (407 239 6463). Open from 8am-5, 6, 7, 8 or 9pm, Centra Care centres can be found at 12500 S Apopka-Vineland Road near the Crossroads shopping centre and Downtown Disney at Lake Buena Vista (until midnight on weekdays – 407 934 2273); 7848 West Irlo Bronson Memorial Highway (192), in Formosa Gardens Village (407 397 7032); 6001 Vineland Road, near Universal Studios (407 351 6682); and 4320 West Vine Street, near Medieval Times (407 390 1888). Sand Lake Hospital on 9400

Jurassic Park Splashdown!

Top 10 things to do for free

While Orlando has a magnificent array of paid-for attractions, there are still many things you can do that don't cost a cent.

1) Peabody Duck March: turn up at 11am or 5pm at the Peabody Hotel to see the resident mallards get the Red Carpet Treatment as they either arrive or leave their lobby fountain 'home'.

2) Lakeridge Winery and Vineyards: join a free wine-tasting tour and you'll know why Lakeridge (in nearby Clermont) has won more than 300 awards. Be sure to designate a driver as sample sizes are generous! 10am–5pm Mon–Sat, 11am–5 pm Sun (www.lakeridgewinery.com).

3) Disney's Boardwalk Resort: free nightly entertainment includes jugglers, comedy skits and live music. Time your visit to coincide with the 9pm IllumiNations fireworks extravaganza at nearby *Epcot.*

4) Morse Museum: this superb little museum in tranquil Winter Park, dedicated to American paintings, ceramics and representative arts from the 19th and 20th Centuries, is free from 4-8pm every Friday Sept-May (see also www.morsemuseum.org and page 222).

5) Pianoman Bob Jackson: Disney's Port Orleans Riverside Resort hosts some excellent free entertainment with Pianoman Bob on Wed-Sun evenings, doing the Chicken Dance and singing along with old favourites in a family-friendly atmosphere.

6) Lake Eola Park: take a walk on the mild side in the heart of downtown Orlando. The kids can play or feed the swans, and there is live musical entertainment in summer at the Disney Amphitheater (see Parks & Recreation at www.cityoforlando.net).

7) Fort Christmas Historical Park: 20 miles (32km) east of Orlando in the town of Christmas is this replica of an 1837 US Army fort from the Seminole Indian Wars, with exhibits, video presentations and restored homes, and special events at some weekends; 10am–5pm Tue–Sat, 1pm–5pm Sun (www.nbbd.com/godo/FortChristmas).

8) Leu Gardens: just north of downtown Orlando, this sanctuary of peace and quiet, with wildlife, nature trails and the 1880s' Leu House Museum is free every Monday from 9am–noon (www.leugardens.org).

9) Sanford Museum: some quaint history is well presented through the personal collections of city founder Henry S Sanford (11am–4pm Tue–Fri). Combine a visit with a walking tour, including the new Riverwalk (www.ci.sanford.fl.us/cf03.html).

10) Old Town, Kissimmee: the biggest vintage car parade in the US every Saturday, with cars on display from 1pm and the parade at 8.30pm, a Friday Night Cruise (classic cars from 1978–85) at 8.30pm and Motorcycle Mania Thursdays at 6pm, plus live music (www.old-town.com).

2

BRIT TIP: The summer is
mosquito time. Buy a
spray-on insect repellent.
Alternatively, try any of
Avon's Skin So Soft
skincare products, which
can work wonders at
keeping bugs at bay.

Turkey Lake Road has an
emergency out-patients dept (407
851 6478). The **East Coast Medical
Network** (407 648 5252) also make
hotel 'house calls' 24 hours a day.
House Med Inc operates
MediClinic, a walk-in facility on
2901 Parkway Boulevard, Kissimmee
(open daily 9am–9pm), and Orlando
Regional Healthcare System
(operator of Sand Lake Hospital) has
Walk-In Medical Care centres on
I-Drive (407 351 3035 and 407 239
6679) open 8am–8pm. A 24-hour
tourist-orientated **dentist** is
J Antonellis on W Colonial Drive
(407 292 8767). The two largest
chemists (drug stores in the US) are
CVS (formerly Eckerd Drugs) and
Walgreens, and their branches at
908 Lee Road and 6201 I-Drive
(among others) are open 24 hours a
day. If you take regular prescription
drugs, check with your doctor or
pharmacist to see if they have a
different name in the US. Many do
(adrenaline is known as epinephrine)
and it is worth finding out and
carrying the drug with both names
in case of an emergency. (Many
thanks to Valerie Mulcare-Tivey for
this advice.) Another reader points
out the American term for
paracetamol is acetaminophen.

Travel insurance

Having said you should not travel
without insurance, you shouldn't pay
too much for it. Travel agents can be

expensive or may imply you need to
buy their policy when you don't. In
all cases make sure you are covered
in the USA for: **medical cover** of at
least £2m; **personal liability** up to
£2m (though this won't cover
driving abroad; you would still need
Supplementary Liability Insurance
with your car-hire firm);
cancellation or **curtailment** cover
up to £3,000; personal property
cover up to £1,500 (but check on
expensive items, as most policies
limit single articles to £250); **cash
and document** cover, including
your passport and tickets; and finally
that the policy gives you a 24-hour
emergency helpline. If you want to
go horse riding, check your policy
includes **dangerous sports cover**.

Shop around at reputable dealers
like **American Express** (0800 700
737), AA (0870 606 0483), **Bradford
& Bingley** (0800 435642), **Club
Direct** (0800 074 4558), **Columbus**
(0845 330 8518), **Direct Travel**
(01903 812 345), **Norwich Union**
(0800 121007), **Options** (0870 876
7878), **Premier Direct** (0990 133
218), **Thomas Cook** (0845 600
5454), **Worldcover Direct** (0800
365 121) and **Worldwide Travel
Insurance** (01892 833 338).

Florida with children

We are often asked what we think is
the right age to take children to
Orlando, and there is no set answer.
Some toddlers take to it instantly,
while some 6- or even 7-year-olds
are overwhelmed. Quite often, the
best attractions for young children
are the hotel swimming pool or the
tram ride to a park's front gates!
Some love the Disney characters
instantly, while others find them
frightening. There is simply no
predicting how they will react, but I
do know my oldest boy at 4½ loved
just about every second of his first
experience (apart from the fireworks
– see page 37) and still talks about it.

Orlando theme park attendances 2004

(As estimated by *Amusement Business* magazine)
1 *Magic Kingdom*, 15.2 million (up 8% on 2003)
2 *Epcot*, 9.4 million (up 9%)
3 *Disney-MGM Studios*, 8.3 million (up 5%)
4 *Disney's Animal Kingdom*, 7.8 million (up 7%)
5 Universal Studios, 6.7 million (down 3%)
6 Islands of Adventure, 6.3 million (up 3%)
7 SeaWorld, 5.6 million (up 7%)
8 Busch Gardens, 4.1 million (down 5%)

© Disney

Cinderella-style wedding

Yes, a 3-year-old may not remember much, but they WILL have fun and provide you with some great memories, photos and video.

Here are some top tips for travelling with youngsters – with thanks to the folks at www.wdwinfo.com for chipping in (additional tips are given in the theme parks chapters).

The flight: try to look calm (even if you don't feel it) and relaxed. Small children soon pick up on any anxieties and make them worse. Pack a bag with plenty of little bits for them (comics, sweets, colouring books, small surprise toys, etc) and keep vital 'extras' like Calpol (in sachets, if possible), change of clothes, small first-aid kit (plasters, antiseptic cream, baby wipes), sunglasses, hat and sunscreen in your hand luggage.

Once you're there: take things slowly and let your children dictate the pace, to a large extent. In hot, humid summer, only the most placid children (and few under 5s, in my experience) will happily queue for an hour or more at a ride, so use Disney's FastPass system (see page 94) and Universal's equivalent (see page 149). The heat, in particular, can result in grizzly kids in no time, so take breaks for drinks and splash zones or head for attractions with air-conditioning. Remember to carry your small first-aid kit. Things like baby wipes always come in handy, and it is a good idea to take spare clothes, which you can leave in the lockers at all the main parks. Going back to the hotel for an afternoon snooze is a good idea – you will dodge the worst of the heat and crowds.

In the sun: carry sun cream and sun block at all times and use it frequently, in queues, on buses, etc. A children's after-sun lotion is also advisable. And make sure they drink a lot of water or non-fizzy drinks. Tiredness and irritability are often the result of mild dehydration.

Dining out: look for 'kids eat free' deals in many places, as they can apply to children up to 12, and take advantage of the many buffet options (see Chapter 10, Dining Out) to fill the family up or for picky eaters. 'Many restaurants do Meals To Go if you want a quiet meal in

Travel City Direct jumbo

travelcitydirect.com

2

Feeding the giraffes at Busch Gardens

Hurricane alert?

Florida was hit by an unprecedented four hurricanes in 2004, three of which affected Orlando, with a lot of resultant publicity and worry. But the simple fact is this was the worst weather for more than a century and the big storms are incredibly rare in central Florida. The hurricane 'season' runs from June–November, with August and September the most storm-prone months. However, even the extremes of 2004 caused no significant damage to the theme parks and the biggest inconvenience for tourists was losing electricity for a few days. In the unlikely event of a major storm, switch your TV to the Weather Channel and follow their advice to stay safe.

your own accommodation without the worry of the kids playing up!' says LisaG on www.wdwinfo.com. Try to let your children get used to the characters and the size of them before you go to one of the many fab Disney character meals.

Having fun: let your children do some of the decision-making and be prepared to go with the flow if they find something unexpected they like (the many squirt fountains and splash zones in the main parks are an example – bring swimsuits and/or a change of clothes!). The Orlando rule of 'You Can't Do It All' applies especially with children. And beware the evening fireworks, as they are loud and youngsters can get distressed (my eldest – then 4 – had to be taken out of *Epcot* in a hurry!). The resort hotels around the *Magic Kingdom* offer safer ways to view the fireworks – at a distance!

BRIT TIP: Avoid making phone calls from your hotel room – it's hugely expensive. It's cheaper to buy a local phonecard and use a normal payphone. British tri-band mobiles are also costly to use in the US. To call home from the US, dial 011 44, then drop the first 0 from the UK area code.

All the parks have **Baby Centers** for nursing mothers and can provide baby food and nappies on request (check the park map for the locations). The centres can even provide spare children's underpants for those little 'accidents'! All of Disney's hotel gift shops stock baby food and nappies. Expectant mothers are strongly advised not to ride some of the more dynamic attractions and coasters, and there will be clear warnings on park maps and at the rides themselves. Basically, the rides to avoid are: *Magic Kingdom:* Space Mountain, Splash Mountain; *Epcot:* Test Track, Body Wars, Maelstrom, Mission: SPACE; *Disney-MGM Studios:* Tower of Terror, Rock 'n' Roller Coaster starring Aerosmith, Star

Lost river voyage at Silver Springs

American-speak

Many words and phrases have a different meaning across the Atlantic. For instance, when Americans say the first floor, they mean the ground floor, the second floor is really the first, and so on. (NB: NEVER ask for a packet of fags. Fag is a crude, slang term for homosexual.) Here are a few everyday words to help you:

American	English		American	English
Check or tab	Bill		Diaper	Nappy
Restroom	Public toilet		Stroller	Pushchair
Bathroom	Private toilet		Faucet	Tap
Eggs 'over easy'	Eggs fried both sides but soft		Collect call	Reverse charge phone call
Eggs 'sunny side up'	Eggs fried on just one side (soft)		Gas	Petrol
			Trunk	Car boot
Biscuit	Savoury scone		Hood	Car bonnet
Seltzer	Soda water		Fender	Car bumper
Soda	Fizzy drink		Freeway	Motorway
Broiled	Grilled		Divided highway	Dual carriageway
Shrimp	King prawn		Denver boot	Wheel clamp
Eggplant	Aubergine		Turn-out	Lay-by
Zucchini	Courgette		No standing	No parking OR stopping
Chips	Crisps		Ramp	Slip road
Entree	Main course		Intersection	Junction
Graham cracker	Digestive biscuit		Yield	Give way
Crib	Cot		Purse	Handbag
Cot or rollaway	Fold-up bed		Quarter	25 cents
			Dime	10 cents
			Nickel	5 cents

Tours; *Disney's Animal Kingdom:* Dinosaur!, Primeval Whirl, Kali River Rapids, Kilimanjaro Safaris; *Universal Studios Florida:* Back To The Future – The Ride, Men In Black – Alien Attack, Revenge of the Mummy, Earthquake, Jimmy Neutron ride (unless you use the static seats); *Islands of Adventure:* Incredible Hulk Coaster, Dr Doom's Fearfall, Popeye and Bluto's Bilge-Rat Barges, Dudley Do-Right's Ripsaw Falls, Jurassic Park River Adventure, Dueling Dragons; *SeaWorld:* Wild Arctic (avoid simulator ride), Journey to Atlantis, Kraken. *Busch Gardens:* SheiKra, Gwazi, Kumba, Montu, The Python, The Scorpion, Congo River Rapids, Stanley Falls Log Flume, Tanganyika Tidal Wave, The Phoenix, Sandstorm, Crazy Camel.

Travellers with disabilities

The parks pay close attention to the needs of holiday-makers with disabilities. There are few rides that cannot cater for them, while wheelchair availability and access is almost always good. For hearing-impaired guests, there are assistive listening devices and reflective captioning at attractions where a commentary is part of the show, and guidebooks in Braille are available, plus rest areas for guide dogs. All Disney hotels have disabled-accessible rooms – call 407 939 7807 or visit www.disneyworld.com – and Disney publishes a *Guidebook for Disabled Guests* (as does Universal), available in all 4 main parks (and online). Life-jackets are always on hand at the water parks, and there are special tape cassettes for blind guests. If you require help while queuing or have children with special needs, call in at any Disney guest relations office to ask about what provisions are available.

Disabled drivers should take their orange car badge with them as this is honoured in the US and there are

BRIT TIP: Pushchairs are essential, even if your children are a year or two out of them. The walking involved wears kids out quickly and a pushchair can save a lot of discomfort (for dads especially!). You can take your own, hire them at the parks or, better still, buy one at a local supermarket for around £12.

designated parking areas at all theme parks. For local assistance, **Walker Medical & Mobility Products** (407 518 6000) specialises in 3-wheeled electric scooters and wheelchair rentals, with free delivery and pick-up even from holiday villas. **Rainbow Wheels** (407 977 3799, www.rainbowwheels.com) hires out full-size or mini vans equipped for wheelchair users. The discussion forums on www.wdwinfo.com also include a board geared to visitors with disabilities.

Reader Les Willans confirms: 'Orlando is superb when it comes to accessibility for wheelchair users like myself, but Americans often use quite offensive language, such as the term "handicapped", when referring to the disabled.'

Orlando for grown-ups

It may sound daft to include information specifically for adults, but it is an often overlooked aspect that you don't need to have kids in tow to enjoy Orlando. In fact, I've often felt the place is actually too good for kids! There is so much clever detail and imagination, it is usually the grown-ups who get the most out of the experience. In fact, as many couples and singles visit the parks as families.

Certainly, when you look at some of the entertainment on offer at *Pleasure Island* and CityWalk, the downtown district and The Pointe Orlando, the great range of bars and fine restaurants, with a good number of romantic offerings, it is easy to see the attraction for those 21 and over. As well as Florida being a key honeymoon destination, its friendly, social atmosphere provides an ideal place for singles, while couples without children can also take advantage of the late opening hours at the parks and clubs like Jellyrolls at *Disney's Boardwalk Resort*.

Orlando for seniors

The more mature traveller can also benefit from a healthy dose of the Sunshine State. And, if my parents (both into their senior years) are any guide, they will have just as much fun, within slightly different parameters. For the older person, staying in a Disney hotel is highly recommended as it removes the stress of driving. The extra cost is offset, my parents felt, by the beauty and convenience of their surroundings. In the parks, they found there was still plenty for them to do, even if they weren't keen on most of the thrill rides (although just watching can be entertainment enough!). *Epcot* and *Disney's Animal Kingdom* both have much to engage the older visitor, while the shows of *Disney-MGM Studios* make that a popular choice, too, and the *Magic Kingdom Park*, while 'probably the noisiest of all the parks', still represents an essential experience.

The *Downtown Disney* area can feel a bit frenetic for the senior crowd, but *Disney's Boardwalk Resort* is popular and the whole of the *Epcot* resort area offers much in the way of fine dining and relaxation. In fact, this is often a prime area for seniors, notably the quieter *Disney's Yacht and Beach Club Resorts*, and the superb

Top 10 Romantic Restaurants

1 Tchoup Chop, Universal's Royal Pacific Resort
2 California Grill, *Disney's Contemporary Resort*
3 Todd English's bluezoo, *Walt Disney World Dolphin Resort*
4 Zen, Omni Orlando Resort at Champion's Gate
5 Jiko, *Disney's Animal Kingdom Lodge*
6 The Boheme, Grand Bohemian Hotel
7 Manuel's on the 28th, Bank of America building, downtown Orlando
8 Old Hickory Steakhouse, Gaylord Palms Resort
9 Atlantis, Renaissance Orlando Resort
10 Le Jardins du Castillon, Park Avenue, Winter Park

Swan-Dolphin complex.

For my parents in particular, the attractions they highlight for their age group are: Jim Henson's Muppet Vision 3-D and Fantasmic! at *Disney-MGM Studios*; Kilimanjaro Safaris, the Maharajah Jungle Trek and Festival of the Lion King at *Disney's Animal Kingdom Theme Park*; Spaceship Earth, Soarin', Universe of Energy, Test Track and IllumiNations at *Epcot* (plus the wonderful gardens and architecture); The Haunted Mansion, Jungle Cruise, Pirates Of The Caribbean and the monorail ride to the *Magic Kingdom*; watching the children at the many parades and character greetings; dinner at the California Grill in *Disney's Contemporary Resort*;

shopping at Orlando Premium Outlets; most of Universal Studios, but less of Islands of Adventure (although they were wowed – as most are – by the Amazing Adventures of Spider-Man).

Weather-wise, March was just about ideal for them, but they wouldn't be keen to visit in the summer. Seniors can also take advantage of many discounts and special deals for their age group at the attractions as well as at many restaurants and hotels. The Official Visitor Center on I-Drive (see page 47) publishes a brochure of all the deals (www.orlandoinfo.com).

Repeat visitors

Repeat visitors create a large part of the Orlando market and are always on the lookout for something new after they have done all the main parks. To that end, our Off the Beaten Track chapter (see pages 222–50) is largely designed with them in mind. Listed here are 10 things worth doing once you have Been There and Done That:

1 Behind the scenes tours at the Disney parks
2 Pony rides at *Disney's Fort Wilderness Resort* and carriage rides at both Fort Wilderness and Disney's Port Orleans Resort

> **BRIT TIP:** If you have a fridge in your hotel, put drink cartons in the freezer overnight and they will be cool for much of the next day in your back-pack. Better still, buy a cheap cool bag, freeze it with some water bottles in, and leave it in the car – great after a day in the parks.

A romantic outing in Old Town, Kissimmee

3 A weekend visit to *Disney's Wilderness Preserve* in Poinciana, Kissimmee
4 The scenic boat ride and Morse Museum in Winter Park
5 Historic Bok Sanctuary in Lake Wales
6 Lunch or dinner (and a visit to the soup cannery!) at the eclectic Chalet Suzanne – also Lake Wales
7 Boggy Creek Airboats and Swamp Buggy Ride
8 The amazing SkyVenture on International Drive
9 Jazz evenings in Bosendorfer Lounge at The Grand Bohemian Hotel downtown
10 Friday night rodeo at Kissimmee Sports Arena

Measurements

American clothes sizes are smaller than ours, hence a US size 12 dress is a UK size 14, or an American jacket sized 42 is really a 44. Shoes are the opposite: a US 10 should fit a British size 9 foot. Their measuring system is also still imperial and NOT metric.

Wedding bells (with getmarriedinflorida.com)

Florida is a place increasingly sought after by couples looking to tie the knot (some 20,000 couples a year at the last count). Its almost guaranteed sunshine, lush landscape and natural beauty make it a big hit as a wedding backdrop. Orlando also offers some terrific services, from wedding co-ordinators, photographers, videographers, florists, transportation companies and cake makers to a wonderfully scenic range of venues such as Cypress Grove Park, Magnolia Acres, Southport Park, Winter Park, Harry P Leu Gardens, the many resort hotels and even golf courses. More unusual

ones include getting married in a hot-air balloon, helicopter, on the beach or a luxury yacht or in the pit-lane of the Richard Petty Driving Experience at *Walt Disney World Resort in Florida* or even at 145mph (233kph) around the speedway itself!

Walt Disney World's Wedding Pavilion offers true fairytale romance, with the backdrop of Cinderella Castle. You can opt for traditional elegance in this Victorian setting with up to 260 guests or the full Disney experience, arriving in Cinderella's coach with Mickey and Minnie as guests. Disney's wedding planners can tailor-make the occasion (407 828 3400).

All the main tour operators feature wedding options and co-ordinated services, and offer a variety of ceremonies. Prices vary from around £439 per couple to £1,980 (Disney's Premium Intimate Wedding package – Virgin). To obtain a marriage licence you can visit one of the local courthouses, which include the Osceola County Courthouse, Courthouse Square, Suite 2000, Kissimmee (just off Bryan Street in downtown Kissimmee) 8am-4pm Mon-Fri (407 343 3500); the Orange County Courthouse, 425 North Orange

SkyVenture sky diving

Avenue (Downtown Orlando) 7.30am-4pm Mon- Fri (407 836 2067); Clermont Courthouse, 1206 Bowman Street, Clermont (in Sunnyside Plaza) 8.30am-4.30pm (closed for lunch 12-1pm; 352 394 2018). All courthouses are closed on US Bank Holidays. Both parties must be present to apply for the marriage licence, which costs $93.50 (in cash, travellers cheques or by credit card) and is valid for 60 days, whilst a ceremony (equivalent to a British register office) can be performed at the same time by the clerk for an extra $20 (times vary according to courthouse visited). Passports and birth certificates are requested, and, if you have been married before, you should bring your decree absolute. After acquiring a licence, a couple can get married anywhere in Florida. Neither witnesses nor blood tests are necessary. You also do not have to be resident for a certain amount of time in Florida before you can get married. It is also now possible to obtain your licence prior to arriving in Florida. Just look up www.florida marriagelicencebypost.com for more details.

Of even greater significance is an internet business dedicated to organising weddings for couples from the UK. Run by Briton Lorraine Ellis, who has specialised in Orlando marriages for many years, www.getmarriedinflorida.com (407 384 0848) is the complete service and can provide all the necessary organisation and elements for the perfect wedding. (Susan and I can vouch for that ourselves!) Caterers, DJs, photographers, notaries and more are all at her fingertips. We can also add our recommendation for caterers Levan's (www.levans.com), the amazing www.andreacheesecake.com and excellent DJ Jeff Farley (407 877 4452). If you would prefer to get married in a church or other place of worship, contact the **Center of Light Church & Spiritual Center** on East Robinson Street (407 228 0101), the **First Baptist Church** on John Young Parkway (407 425 2555), **St Nicholas Catholic Church** on Sand Lake Road (407 351 0133) or **Trinity Lutheran Church** on East Livingston Street downtown (407 422 5704, www.trinitydowntown.org).

Disney special occasions

Birthday badges: free badges can be found at City Hall in the *Magic Kingdom Park* and Guest Services at *Epcot, Disney-MGM Studios* and *Disney's Animal Kingdom Theme Park*. Cast Members like to make a fuss over children (and adults!) wearing a birthday badge.

Birthday cakes: contact room service at your resort, or Guest Services at one of the parks. All Disney restaurants can offer cakes (starting at $7.99). Be sure to tell the Cast Member at check-in (or when you make your hotel reservation) as well as hostesses and/or servers in restaurants, if someone in your party has a birthday. While it is not guaranteed, Disney staff often go out of their way to make the day special. If characters know it's a birthday when they sign a child's autograph book, they may add a special birthday wish.

Birthday cruise: the IllumiNations cruises (to *Epcot*), the motorboat *Breathless* (from *Disney's Yacht and Beach Club Resorts*) and the pontoon boats from *Disney's Grand Floridian Resort* (to view the Wishes fireworks show) all host birthday events, with snacks and refreshments, and boats can be decorated (by Disney). Wishes cruises range from $188 to $258, while Illuminations Cruises cost $179–$258.

Birthday parties: *Disney's Yacht and Beach Club Resorts* arrange

2

BRIT TIP: If you shop at any Wal-Mart store in America, you can return faulty or wrong-size goods to your local Asda for a refund, provided you keep your receipts.

birthday parties for ages 4 and up. A 3-hour party for up to 12 guests is $300. Decorations, birthday cake, use of the games at the Sandcastle Club, arcade games (free), video games, Disney movies on TV and access to Stormalong Bay are included. Parties can be booked at either 11am or 12 noon. Menu is pizza, hot dogs, burgers, chips and soda. Call 407 934 3750.

The *Winter-Summerland Miniature Golf* hosts 2-hour birthday parties for 10 or more, including pizza, sodas, cake, party favours and a round of mini golf. Cost is $16.95 a head, plus tax. Call 407 WDW-PLAY, and you need to book at least one week ahead.

DisneyQuest has Birthday Tickets at $33 for adults, $27 per child (3–9), which includes admission, one meal coupon, one $5 Prize Play card and 20 per cent off merchandise at the Emporium (good only for the day of the event).

Safety first

While crime is not a serious issue in central Florida, this is still big-city America and, as with all big cities, you need to keep your wits about you. You don't leave your common sense at home.

The area has its own Tourist Oriented Policing Service (or TOPS), centred on I-Drive, with more than 70 officers patrolling purely the main tourist areas, arranging crime prevention seminars with local hotels and generally

ensuring Orlando takes good care of its visitors. You will often see the local police in these areas out on mountain bikes, and they are a polite, helpful bunch should you need their assistance or to ask them directions. Tourism is such a vital part of the local economy the authorities cannot afford to be seen not taking an active role against crime, hence the area has a highly safety-conscious attitude. However, it would be foolish not to stick to the usual safety guidelines when travelling abroad.

Emergencies

General: for police, fire department or ambulance, dial 911 (9-911 from your hotel room). It is a good idea to make sure your children are aware of this number, while for smaller-scale crises (mislaid tickets or passports, rescheduled flights, etc) your holiday company should have an emergency contact number in the hotel reception. If you are travelling independently and run into passport or other problems that require the assistance of the **British Consulate** in Orlando, its office is located in Sun Bank Towers, 200 South Orange Avenue, with walk-in visitors' hours 9.30am–noon and 2–4pm, or phone 9.30am–4pm on 407 426 7855.

Phonecards, which you need to make a call from a local payphone – and are much cheaper than using your hotel room – are available from most 7-Eleven stores or from your tour rep.

Hotel security

While in your hotel, you should always use door peepholes and security chains whenever someone knocks at the door. DON'T open the door to strangers without asking for identification, and check with the

Two-way radio rentals

Two-way radios are useful gadgets at the best of times, but they take on a popular new role in Orlando, in terms of both safety and convenience. Many families now buy these 'walkie-talkies' to keep in touch around the parks and it is common to see them in use. You can pick them up locally for as little as $20–$35 in stores like Wal-Mart, Best Buy, Circuit City, Radio Shack, Office Depot and Staples. However, they cannot be used in the UK as they use the same frequency as the emergency services.

hotel desk if you are still not sure. It is stating the obvious, but keep doors and windows locked at all times and always use deadlocks and security chains. It is still surprising how many people forget basic precautions on holiday (the local police never cease to be amazed at people leaving their common sense at home!). Always take your cash, credit cards, valuables and car keys when you go out (or put them in the safe), and don't leave the door open at any time, even if you just pop down the corridor to the ice machine.

Check hotels' safety precautions when you make a reservation: do rooms have electronic card-locks (which can't be duplicated) and do

Lake Buena Vista Factory Stores

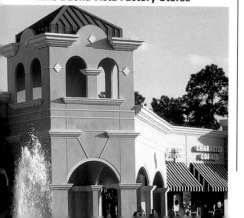

BRIT TIP: For your journey to the US, use a business address rather than your home address on all your luggage. It is less conspicuous and safer should any item be stolen or misplaced.

they have security staff? Most hotels can offer deposit boxes, and many rooms now have mini-safes to safeguard non-essential valuables. Don't be afraid to ask reception staff for safety advice for the surrounding areas or if you are travelling somewhere you are not sure about. Safety is a major issue for the Central Florida Hotel/Motel Association and hotel staff are usually well briefed to be helpful. Using a bumbag (the Americans call them fanny packs!) is a better bet than a shoulder bag or handbag.

Nothing is guaranteed to get the local police shaking their heads in disbelief than the tourist who goes round looking like an obvious tourist. The map over the steering wheel is a giveaway, but other no-nos are wearing large amounts of jewellery, carrying lots of camera equipment or flashing wads of cash around. The biggest giveaway is leaving a camera or camcorder on view in the car (also inadvisable as the heat build-up in summer can ruin some equipment).

BRIT TIP: If your room has already been cleaned before you go out for the day, hang the 'Do Not Disturb' sign on the door. Always keep your valuables out of sight, whether in the hotel or the car.

Arabian Nights chariot race

Finally, and this is VERY strong police advice, in the unlikely event of being confronted by an assailant, DO NOT resist or 'have a go', as it can often result in making the situation more serious.

Money matters

It is useful to know dollar travellers' cheques can be used as cash and can be readily replaced if lost or stolen, so it is not necessary (as well as not being advisable) to carry large amounts of cash around. However, sterling travellers' cheques can only be cashed in major banks – most outlets will not accept them. You will need to carry ID with you in many cases, though – the new UK driver's licence card is very useful for this.

Having a credit card is almost essential as they are accepted everywhere and provide extra buying security. In some cases, notably car hire, you can't operate without your flexible friend. Visa, Mastercard and American Express are all widely accepted. It is worth separating the larger notes from the smaller ones in your wallet to avoid flashing all your money in view. Losing £200 of travellers' cheques shouldn't ruin your holiday – but losing $300 in cash might. The Sun Banks in Disney's Magic Kingdom and Epcot are open 7 days a week if you need financial help. Some UK banks

(notably the Nationwide) have no currency conversion charges for using their credit card in the US, and you can then use American cash machines, or ATMs, as well. (Chase Bank has no transaction charge either.)

Take note: all Orlando prices, both in this book and on every price tag you see, do not include the 6–7 per cent Florida Sales Tax. There is also a 4–5 per cent Resort Tax on hotel rooms.

Car safety

Car crime has led to some lurid headlines in the past, especially in the Miami area in the mid-1990s. Once again, it pays to make basic safety checks before you set off. The first thing is to familiarise yourself with the car's controls BEFORE driving off for the first time – which button for the air-conditioning, which control operates the indicators and where are the windscreen wipers, etc.

Also, try to memorise your route in advance, even if it is only a case of knowing the road numbers. Most hire firms now give good directions to all the hotels, so check them before you set off – trying to drive with the map over the steering wheel is just asking for trouble.

Check the petrol tank is well filled and never let it get near empty.

Disney Cruise Lines

© Disney

Let us plan your holiday ...

... with our Personalised Itinerary Planner

In conjunction with the *Brit's Guide* website – www.askdaisy.net/orlando – our Personalised Itinerary Planner will help you get the very most out of your time in central Florida. We will design an itinerary tailored to your individual plans for the parks and attractions of Orlando. In your Planner (which usually runs to 30-plus pages on either a Word document or PDF file for a 2-week Orlando itinerary), we will indicate the best days to visit the parks to avoid the crowds, all the main show and parade times for the days you are there, a detailed touring plan for each park, any rides that may be closed for refurbishment, a shopping guide, updates on new rides, etc, and up-to-the-minute advice right from the source of the fun, plus a host of additional Brit Tips and Brit Picks (our special favourites) that we can't fit into the book.

All you have to do is visit the *Brit's Guide* website and click on the Itinerary Planner link. Fill out the online form with your travel dates, hotel and family details and what you would like to fit in to your visit. Submit the form, along with your payment, and you will receive an immediate acknowledgement of your requirements. A few days before you go, you will receive by e-mail your Personalised Itinerary Planner, which will consist of:

1   An official *Brit's Guide* welcome from Simon and Susan Veness.
2   A full day-by-day plan for the length of your holiday.
3   A touring strategy for ALL 8 main parks, the water parks and shopping centres, avoiding the crowds and taking advantage of the latest developments.
4   An alternative plan in case of bad weather.
5   All the main parade and fireworks times for the days you are there.
6   A note of any rides/shows that are closed during your visit.
7   A special selection of Brit Tips and local advice specifically for you.
8   Our Brit Picks – a guide to a range of personal favourites from restaurants to shops – that we feel may appeal to you most.
9   The ultimate insider knowledge, as both Simon and Susan are based in the heart of the Orlando magic and are fully up-to-date on all developments.

All in all, it adds up to the most comprehensive package of specialised holiday info anywhere, and it represents the secret to the most fun, in the most hassle-free way in the most exciting place on earth. What more could you ask for? Just check us out on www.askdaisy.net/orlando and we'll do the rest for you.

Please note: There is a minimum order period, so do check the website and make sure you apply for your planner in good time before your holiday. We are not a travel agency or ticket service and you MUST know your ticket requirements in advance.

Running out of 'gas' in an unfamiliar area holds obvious hazards. If you stray off your pre-determined route, stick to well-lit areas and ask directions only from official businesses like hotels and petrol stations or better still, a police patrol. Always try to park close to your destination where there are plenty of lights and DO NOT get out if there are suspicious characters lurking around. Always keep windows closed (you have air-conditioning, remember?), and don't hesitate to lock the doors from the inside if you feel threatened (larger cars have doors that lock automatically as you drive off). And don't forget to lock up when you leave the car. Not all rental cars have central locking, so it's wise to double check.

BRIT TIP: All American banknotes are the SAME green colour and size. It is only the picture of the president and denomination in each corner that change.

It is comforting to know a unique aspect of driving in Orlando is that none of the main tourist areas has any no-go areas. The nearest is the portion of the Orange Blossom Trail south of downtown Orlando. This houses a selection of strip clubs and 'adult bars' that can be downright seedy at night.

For more information on safety, contact the Community Affairs office of Orange County Police (407 836 3720) or the TOPS office (407 351 9368).

Know before you go

You can contact these organisations for advance tourist information. Florida Tourism (and their info-packed website www.visit florida.com) have an info line (0900 160 0555) (60p/minute) that lists all Florida destinations and gives other consumer lines in the UK, while they have a free information pack if you call 01737 644 882. The Orlando Tourism Bureau in London has a 24-hour information line (0800 018 6760), on which you can request their free *Destination Imagination* info pack or visit www.orlandoinfo. com/uk/. You can also visit the Kissimmee Convention & Visitors Bureau at www.floridakiss.com.

When you arrive in the area, it is also worth checking Orlando's ONLY official **Visitor Center** at 8723 International Drive (407 363 5872) for discounted attraction tickets, free brochures and accommodation advice and free

information pamphlets and maps. The Kissimmee CVB is at the eastern end of the Highway 192 tourist drag (407 847 5000 or 1-800 327 9159 in the States) and they have a toll-free accommodation line in the US (1-800 333 KISS).

You'll find information on all things Orlando and Disney on the fun and info-packed www.wdwinfo. com, to which I also contribute. The creation and maintenance of this independent site is a mind-boggling feat. It provides up-to-the-minute advice and assistance, including the complete range of theme park info (right down to park hours and ride height requirements), restaurant info, news, weather, facts, figures and tips, plus discounts throughout Orlando, excellent discussion boards and a chat forum.

The official sites aren't bad, although Disney's can be hard work: www.disneyworld.co.uk (for opening hours, rides, parades, etc, and bookings). Then see www.universalorlando.com, www.seaworld.com and www.buschgardens.com. The local newspaper's online service (www.orlandosentinel.com) is packed with info (especially for nightlife on associate website www.orlandocitybeat.com), while the free *Orlando Weekly* is also worth checking (www.orlandoweekly.com).

Among the many unofficial websites (not approved by Disney) are www.wdwmagic.com (great for Disney trivia and rumours), the well-designed www.wdisneyw.co.uk (with more pages for UK visitors), www.thedibb.co.uk ('Disney with a British accent') and www.orlando rocks.com (for all theme park addicts).

BRIT TIP: Don't forget our own website, www.asakdaisy.net/orlando for all the latest updates.

3

Driving and Car Hire
(or, The Secret of Getting Around on Interstate 4)

For the majority, introduction to Orlando proper comes immediately after clearing the airport via the potentially bewildering road system in a newly acquired, left-hand-drive hire car. Yet driving here is a lot easier and more enjoyable than driving in the UK. Anyone familiar with the M25 should find Orlando's roads FAR less stressful.

Before you get to your hire car, though, you need to be aware of your arrival details at Orlando International and Orlando Sanford airports (see also Chapter 12).

Arrival

Orlando International is one of the most modern and enjoyable airports in the world, but it does have a bewildering double baggage collection system for international arrivals. You disembark at a satellite terminal and collect your luggage straight after going through Immigration, and pass through the Customs check before putting your main baggage (NOT hand luggage) on another carousel that takes it to the main terminal while you ride the automated tram. There is then a secondary security screening upstairs, which can also cause a bit of a queue.

Once in the main terminal, you will be on Level 3 and need to descend to Level 2 (split into the A and B sides) for baggage reclaim (British Airways and Virgin are always on side B). Porters can help you to Level 1 for hire car pick-up (remember $1/bag tip), while trolleys need $3 in change – or a credit card – to operate (they are NOT free like UK airports). Taxis, buses and hotel shuttles are also on Level 1, while kerbside pick-up is on Level 2. If you have a driver meeting you, they will be waiting on Level 2, either at the bottom of the escalators or by your baggage reclaim belt. Several tour operators have help desks here, too. The public bus system, Lynx (see page 50), operates ONLY from the B side of Level 1, in spaces B12-14. Buses 11, 41 and 51 depart every half-hour (less frequently on Sundays and bank holidays) for Orlando city centre (about 45 minutes away) while Bus 42 serves International Drive (about a 60-minute journey).

If you are arriving late, consider staying at the **Hyatt Regency** hotel (see page 75) inside the airport rather

The Orlando airport train system

BRIT TIP: visit the website – www.orlandoairports.net – for a photo preview of the arrival process at the airport.

International Drive by night

than driving off tired. You will feel far more ready to drive the next day.

The hire companies with check-in desks at the airport are Dollar, National, L & M, Budget, Avis, and of course *Brit's Guide* partners **Alamo**, and all offer a full service (Alamo used to work out of a depot but is now on-airport, boosting its efficiency). A phone desk on Level 1 connects to another 15 companies at off-airport depots, including Hertz, Thrifty, Payless and Enterprise.

Off-airport rental firms have a free shuttle on Level 1 to take you to their depots, which gives you a preview of the roads before you take to them. Hertz and Avis are the biggest US companies, but Dollar and Alamo are tops for tourist business. Dollar is included in typical packages by Thomson, Airtours, Virgin, Style Holidays, Travel City and First Choice, while Alamo is the main client for Unijet, Funway, Jetlife, Jetsave, Kuoni, British Airways Holidays and Thomas Cook.

BRIT TIP: If you are hiring a car from one of the on-airport companies, save time by going to their desk to complete the paperwork BEFORE collecting your luggage on Level 2.

After completing your paperwork with Alamo or whoever, you walk out of Level 1, across the road to the multi-storey car park and collect your car. It's that simple. When you drive out of the airport, DON'T look for signs to 'Orlando.' The main tourist areas are south and west of the city proper, so follow the respective signs for your accommodation. For International Drive (or I-Drive), take the North Exit and the Beeline Expressway (Route 528) west until it crosses I-Drive just north of SeaWorld. The main hotel area of I-Drive is to the north, so keep right at the exit.

BRIT TIP: The Beeline Expressway (528) and Greeneway (417) are both toll roads, so keep some change in the car. Toll booths hate to change notes above $20 while some auto-tolls take ONLY coins.

For Kissimmee, Disney resorts and holiday villas in Clermont/Davenport, take the South Exit for 3 miles and pick up Central Florida Greeneway (Highway 417) west. For most Disney resorts, take Exit 6 and follow the signs; for *Animal Kingdom* resorts, use Exit 3 and take Osceola Parkway west. For eastern Kissimmee, come off Highway 417 at Exit 11, the Orange Blossom Trail (Highway 17/92), and go south. For west Kissimmee and Clermont/

Highway 192 in Kissimmee

Davenport (Highway 27), take Exit 2, turn right on to Celebration Avenue and left on to Highway 192, which runs west all the way to Highway 27.

Orlando Sanford Airport

Arriving at Sanford couldn't be easier. Once through Immigration (where queuing is simplified by having just two lines in its enlarged hall that feed through to the kiosks – like at the post office!), you collect your baggage, pass through Customs check and walk straight out to car hire, shuttle and taxi pick-up. The tour operator welcome desks and Dollar car hire offices are immediately in front of you, while **Alamo** has a large, new welcome centre that you reach via a covered walkway and boardwalk behind this, and its British-dedicated operation is usually pretty smooth. National, Avis, Enterprise, Thrifty and Hertz are also on-airport (turn sharp right out of Customs then take the first door on the right).

It may be further to the north and involve more driving (and taxis and shuttles are more expensive – a town car service would be $70 one-way to I-Drive and a taxi almost $60), but you usually save time overall by your quicker exit. There is just one main road out, on to East Lake Mary Boulevard, and you then pick up the Central Florida Greeneway

BRIT TIP: Don't want to drive? Consider a multi-centre stay within Orlando itself, staying first at, say, International Drive or Universal Orlando and then a Disney resort, to get the best out of the free or cheap transport options.

(Highway 417) South. The slip road on to this toll motorway is just under the fly-over on your LEFT, and you will need about $4.50 to reach Kissimmee or Disney or $3.75 to reach I-Drive (via the Beeline Expressway, Route 528). You can avoid the tolls by staying on Lake Mary Boulevard for 6 miles (10km) until you hit I-4, but you may encounter the 4-6pm snarl-up through the city centre. The Greeneway is an excellent, easy-driving introduction to Orlando roads, even if it does cost an extra few dollars.

For radio traffic news and reports, tune in to 1680AM. If you have a tri-band mobile phone, dial 511 for traffic info on I-4.

ORLANDO WITHOUT A CAR

Although being mobile is advisable, it is possible to survive without a car. However, few attractions are within walking distance of hotels, and taxis can be expensive. You also need to plan your campaign with greater precision to allow for extra travelling time (and, with children, taking buses can be tiring). If you decide not to drive, your best base is either *Walt Disney World Resort in Florida* (free transport throughout, but harder to get to the rest of Orlando) or International Drive (I-Drive) for its location, good pavements and the great I-Ride Trolley. Many hotels have free shuttles to some of the parks or a cheap regular mini-bus service. There are 4 main options: public transport, shuttle services, town car/limousine services and taxis.

Public transport

The reliable, cheap, but slightly plodding **Lynx bus system** (407 841 8240, www.golynx.com) covers much of Orlando. Its online System Map shows all its routes (or 'Links') and the main attractions. Worth noting are **Link 42** from Orlando International Airport to I-Drive; **Links 56** and **304**, from Kissimmee and the I-Drive area to Disney; **Link 18** from Kissimmee to downtown Orlando; **Link 55**, which covers Kissimmee's Highway 192 from Osceola Square Mall west to Secret Lake Drive; **Link 38**, I-Drive to downtown Orlando; and **Links 50** and **300**, from Disney to downtown.

Lynx fares are $1.50 a ride (transfers are free) or $12 for a weekly pass (children 6 and under go free with a full-fare passenger). The service is every 30 minutes in the main areas, every 15 minutes from 6-9am and 3.30-6.30pm, but remember to have the right change. Lynx bus stops are marked by pink paw-print signs and all buses are wheelchair accessible. There can be long queues for the buses out of Disney at closing time, and it may be more worthwhile getting Disney transport to Downtown Disney, spending some time there, then getting a cab back to your hotel (about $20-$25 to I-Drive).

The I-Drive area also has the great-value **I-Ride trolley**, which operates 2 routes along a 14-mile (23km) stretch of this tourist corridor. The *Main Line* runs from Universal Orlando resort area (Windhover Drive and Major Boulevard) in the north, via Prime Outlets shopping centre at the top of I-Drive, to SeaWorld via Westwood Boulevard and Sea Harbor Drive, and south to Orlando Premium Outlets. The *Green Line* basically covers Universal Boulevard, from the Orange County Convention Center up to the junction of I-Drive and Kirkman Road (407 354 5656, www.iridetrolley.com). Running every day, 7am-10.30pm at roughly 15-minute intervals (30 minutes on the Green Line), it costs 75c per trip (25c for seniors) – please have the

right change – or you can buy Unlimited Ride passes for 1, 3, 5, 7 or 14 days at $3, $5, $7, $9, $16. You can buy a 14-day pass at the official Visitor Center on I-Drive (see page 47) by Austrian Court and save $2. If you need to transfer between routes, ask for a transfer coupon when you board (transfers are free with Unlimited Ride passes). Kids 12 and under go free with an adult, and all trolleys have hydraulic lifts for wheelchairs. Passes are sold at 75 locations in the I-Drive area, including most hotel service desks.

Another regular service worth noting is from SeaWorld to Busch Gardens in Tampa, with 6 departure points daily from 8.15-9.30am. Called the **Busch Shuttle Express**, it costs $10 a person but is free if you have bought Busch tickets in advance (included in the 5-Park Orlando FlexTicket). For more details, see page 146.

Shuttle services

An alternative to public transport is the raft of well-organised firms that offer set-fee shuttles to the attractions and pick up at hotels. There are more than a dozen companies, offering everything from Hummer limos to buses. **Mears** (407 423 5566, www.mears transportation.com) has the most comprehensive service, from limousines to coaches, and typical round-trip shuttle fares would be: Airport-*Walt Disney World*, round-trip $29 adults, $21 under 12s, under 4 free ($17 and $13 one-way); Airport-I-Drive, $25 and $18 ($15 and $11 one way); Airport-Highway 192 in Kissimmee $41 and $32 ($23 and $19 one way); *Walt Disney World*-Universal Orlando, $14 round trip; I-Drive-*Walt Disney World*, $14; I-Drive or *Walt Disney World*-Kennedy Space Center, $21. Mears also offers a SuperPass service of 3,

BRIT TIP: A Town Car is an American term for a deluxe saloon, like a Cadillac or Lincoln.

4, 5, 6 or 7 days of unlimited service to and from the main area attractions (including airport transfers) from I-Drive or *Walt Disney World* for $63, $72, $85, $96, $107 ($56, $67, $78, $89, $100 per child 4–11). Additional days $15 each. You can book a Mears shuttle on arrival at one of their desks in the luggage halls, but it can be a long journey to your hotel if they have a full van.

Town Cars and Limousines

When it comes to limousine and Town Car services, look no further than *Brit's Guide* partner **Skyy Limousines**. Not only is it a dynamic, British-run company, all our readers qualify for a special 12½% discount by using the special coupon with sister company International Divers (see inside back cover) – call them on 407 352 4644 and ask for the *Brit's Guide* Discount). Skyy has some of the latest and smartest cars (including the amazing Hummer limo), personable staff and offers transportation throughout central Florida. It covers airport and cruise

Skyy limousine

transfers, special occasions, a night on the town and all-day services, and can also provide tailor-made services. Skyy offers several meal and limo combinations, great for the entire family, with dinner with the Disney characters followed by a drive around town and a visit to the Downtown Disney area. A real holiday highlight.

Skyy's Town Car service also specialises in airport transfers, trips to the beach, concerts and your own personalised excursions, and their rates are always competitive.

Quick Transportation (1888 784 2522; www.quicktransportation.com) also comes well recommended for airport transfers and tailor-made transport packages. Town cars cope with a family of 4, while its luxury vans cater for larger parties and it offers a 30-minute grocery stop, if required, for an extra $18.50. Luxury van rates (for up to 7) one way from the airport range from $47.50 to the I-Drive area up to $76 for the farthest parts of *Walt Disney World*. Up to 11 can use a van for a small additional fee per person. Larger parties may need a luggage trailer for $18.50 extra each way. Town car rates are $78.50 one way from the airport to anywhere in Greater Orlando and $150 round trip, while stretch limos are $120 and $240. It also serves all the theme parks and attractions while every Tuesday it organises a shuttle to Kennedy Space Center for $28 round trip.

Excursion services are also offered by *Brit's Guide* partners **International Divers** (407 352 5151, www.floridadolphintours.com) and **Real Florida Excursions** (see page 227).

Several shopping malls also have their own shuttle service. **Lake Buena Vista Factory Stores** collects guests free on a daily basis from more than 40 hotels in the Orlando and Kissimmee areas (check your hotel for details, or call 407 363

The I-Ride trolley

1093). **Orlando Premium Outlets** (407 390 0000) provides a hotel shuttle with Maingate Transportation at $6 round trip from the Lake Buena Vista area and $9 from Kissimmee hotels. **The Florida Mall** has a free shuttle twice daily from hotels in I-Drive and Lake Buena Vista (check with your hotel concierge, call 407 851 6255 or visit www.florida-mall-fl.com).

Taxis

For groups of 4 or 5, **taxis** can be a more cost-effective option than the shuttles. Orlando International to I-Drive would cost around $31 (plus tip), making it about $6 each for 5, $10 from I-Drive to Universal Orlando and $20 from I-Drive to *Downtown Disney*. You will find plenty of taxis waiting in ranks at the parks, hotels and shopping centres, but they don't cruise around looking for fares, so it is usually best to book one in advance. You also need to ensure you choose a reliable, fully insured company (Orlando has what are known as 'gypsy' cab drivers, who appear to be with reputable firms but often do not have full passenger insurance). Check that the name and phone number of the cab company is clearly displayed on the side, that the driver's ID and insurance are visible and their rates are shown on the window or inside the car. 'Gypsy' drivers look for fares

in the airport baggage hall, which is strictly illegal – all legitimate taxis should be in the rank on Level 1.

The **Mears** group (407 699 9999) has 3 firms who work (via computer system) through it – Checker Cabs, Yellow Cabs and City Cabs – all of which are reliable. Most taxis are metered but it is also acceptable to ask what the fare is in advance. Other reputable firms include **Central Florida Taxis** (407 851 7523 or freephone 1-800 441 3276 in Florida), **Star Taxis** (407 857 9999) and **Diamond Cab Co** (407 523 3333). Several hotels have Town Cars at their ranks, and these will not have meters, so you can either ask the fare or call one of the companies listed above yourself.

THE CAR

Ultimately, having a car is the key to being in charge of your holiday and, on a weekly basis, it tends to work out quite reasonable too. Weekly rental rates can be as low as $100 for the smallest car, an **Economy** (or sub-compact), usually a Corsa-sized hatchback; next up is the **Compact**, a small family saloon like a Vauxhall Astra; the **Midsize** (or Intermediate) is a more spacious 4-door, 5-seater like a Vectra; and the **Fullsize** would be a large-style executive car like an Omega, and you can go up the scale still, with **Premium**, **Luxury** and **Convertible**, plus the Minivan, a Renault Espace or VW Sharan type.

But beware these low starting rates. There are a number of essential insurances, taxes and

> BRIT TIP: Your first call for car hire should be to *Brit's Guide* partners **Alamo**. See inside the front cover for our special readers' offer.

> BRIT TIP: The boot size
> of American cars tends to
> be smaller than the British
> equivalent. And you will
> not get seven adults PLUS
> all their luggage in a 7-seat
> people carrier (van)!

surcharges, and these can take the
weekly rate up to $300 or more.
However, all the big rental
companies now offer all-inclusive
rates, which can work out
significantly cheaper if booked in
advance in the UK. Rates can be as
low as £150 a week, and you also
benefit from easier processing at the
Orlando end, making the whole
business quicker.

For other car rental companies,
you can try **Dollar** on 0800 252897,
Avis (0990 900 500), **Budget** (0880
181181), **Thrifty** (0990 168 238),
Hertz (0990 906090), **National**
(0345 222525), or **Suncars** (0990
005566).

The scale of the car-hire
operation is huge, with as many as
1,000 visitors arriving at a time. Most
British holiday companies offer 'free
car hire', but that does not mean it
won't cost you anything. It is only
the rental cost that is free and you
must still pay the insurance, taxes
and other extras BEFORE you drive
away (which makes the all-inclusive
packages even more attractive).

Having a credit card is essential,
and there are two main kinds of
insurance, the most important being
the Loss or Collision Damage

> BRIT TIP: Be firm with
> the car hire company
> check-in clerk; some can
> push you into having extras,
> like car upgrades, that you
> don't need.

Waiver (LDW or CDW). This costs
around $20 a day and covers you for
any damage to your hire car. You can
do without it, but the hire company
will insist on a deposit in the order
of $1,500 on your credit card (and
you are liable for ANY damage). You
will also be offered Supplemental
Liability Insurance (SLI) or
Extended Protection at around $13 a
day. This covers you against being
sued by any court-happy American
you may happen to bump into (not
essential, but good for your peace of
mind).

> BRIT TIP: Double-check
> that you have your driving
> licence BEFORE you leave
> home (both parts of it with
> the new photo-card type).
> Without it you will simply
> NOT be given a hire car.

Relatively new and again optional
is the Underinsured Motorists
Protection (in case somebody with
only minimal cover runs into you) at
around $6 a day. Drivers under 25
have to pay an extra $20 a day, while
all drivers must be at least 21. Other
rental costs include local and Florida
state taxes, which add $8 a day to
your final bill, and Airport Handling
Tax and Access Fee at $6-7 a day.
Then there's petrol, although this is
still much cheaper than in the UK.
Ask to return the tank full yourself,
as this will save a few dollars on their
fill-up option.

For those on a tight budget, you
can cut costs by arranging travel
insurance through specialists like
Extrasure (01242 518300), whose
Americasure policy offers both
LDW and SLI at around £5 a day.
You may still need to leave a credit
card imprint with the hire firm, but
they should accept these policies
(but do still check in advance).

You may also feel a little jet-lagged for the first day or two, but this can be reduced by avoiding alcohol and coffee on the plane and drinking plenty of water.

Most people soon find driving in America is a pleasure rather than a pain, mainly because nearly all hire cars are automatics and rarely more than a year old. And, because speed limits are lower (and rigidly enforced), you won't often be rushed into taking the wrong turn. Keep your foot on the brake when you are stationary as automatics tend to creep forward, and always put the automatic gear lever in 'P' (for Park) after switching off.

Controls

All cars have air-conditioning, which is essential for most of the year. Turn on the fan with the A/C button or it will not work! Don't worry if a small pool of liquid forms under the car – it's condensation off the A/C unit. Power steering is also universal and larger cars have cruise control, which lets you set the desired speed and take your foot off the accelerator. There will be two buttons on the steering wheel, one to switch the cruise control on, the other to set the desired speed. To take the car off cruise control either press the first button again or simply touch the brake.

> BRIT TIP: With an automatic, you probably won't be able to take the keys out of the ignition unless you put the car in 'Park' first.

The handbrake may also be different. Some cars have an extra foot pedal to the left of the brake, and you need to push this to engage the handbrake. To release it, you pull the tab just above it, if there is one, or give a second push on the pedal. The car probably won't start unless the gear lever is in 'P'. To put the car in 'D' for Drive, you also have to depress the main brake pedal. D1 and D2 are extra gears for steep hills (none in Florida!). Not all cars have central locking, so make sure you lock ALL the doors before leaving it.

Getting around

Your car-hire company should provide you with a basic map of Orlando, plus directions to your hotel. Insist they give you these, as all the hire companies make a big point of this in their literature. Try to familiarise yourself with the main roads in advance and learn to navigate by the road numbers (as those are mainly given on the signposts) and the exit numbers of the main roads.

Signs and road names

The system of signposting and road-naming can be confusing. For instance, you cannot fail to find the main attractions, but retracing your steps back to the hotel can be tricky because they often take you out of the parks a different way. (Disney is notoriously poor at sign-posting to help find your way out. A good tip is to get a copy of its Transportation Guide/Map from Guest Services at any park to help navigation.)

> BRIT TIP: On the Greeneway (417) heading south, just after Exit 34, it appears to split into two where it meets Highway 408. Stay in the RIGHT lane to stay southbound.

BRIT TIP: Be organised – get your directions in advance off the internet at excellent map sites like www.mapquest.com.

It is vital to learn the main road numbers (and directions, either east-west or north-south) around the attractions so you know where you are heading, and whether you want I-4 east or west or 192 as you exit *Epcot* or *Disney-MGM Studios*.

Exits off I-4 and other main roads can be on EITHER side of the carriageway, not just on the right. This potential worry is offset by the fact you can overtake in ANY lane on multi-lane highways, not just the outside ones. Therefore, you can sit in the middle lane until you see your exit. However, you don't get much advance notice of turn-offs.

Orlando has yet to come up with a comprehensive tourist map of its streets and the maps supplied by the car-rental companies tend to be simplified. It helps that none of the main attractions is off the beaten track, but the support of a front-seat navigator can be useful. Around town, road names are displayed at every junction, hung underneath the traffic lights suspended ABOVE the road. This road name is NOT the road you are on, but the one you are CROSSING. Once again there is no advance notice of each junction and the road names can be difficult to read as you approach them,

especially at night, so keep your speed down if you think you are close to your turn-off, to get in the correct lane. If you do miss a turning, most roads are on a grid system, so it is usually easy to work your way back.

BRIT TIP: The Osceola Parkway toll road that runs parallel to Highway 192 is a much easier route into *Walt Disney World Resort in Florida* from much of Kissimmee and costs only $1.50. Use Sherberth Road for Disney access from west 192.

Occasionally, you will meet a crossroads where no right of way is obvious. This is a **4-way stop**, and the priority goes in order of arrival. So, when it's your turn you just indicate and pull out slowly (America doesn't have many roundabouts, so this is the closest you will get to one).

Tolls and traffic lights

For the toll roads, have some change handy in amounts from 25c to $2. They all give change (in the GREEN lanes), but you will get through much quicker if you have the correct money (in the BLUE lanes). On minor exits of Osceola

Disney's Boardwalk Resort

© Disney

Getting around on two wheels is popular at some Disney resorts

Parkway and the Greeneway, there are auto-toll machines only, so keep some loose change in the car.

As well as the obvious difference of driving on the 'wrong' side of the road, there are several differences in procedure. The most frequent British errors occur at traffic lights (which are hung above the road, not on posts). At a red light it is still possible to turn RIGHT, providing there is no traffic coming from the left and no pedestrians crossing, unless otherwise specified (signs will occasionally indicate 'No turn on red'). Turning left at the lights, you have the right of way with a green ARROW, but you have to give way to traffic from the other direction on a SOLID green.

The majority of accidents involving overseas visitors take place on left turns, so take extra care here. There is also no amber light from red to green, but there IS an amber light from green to red. A flashing amber light at a junction means proceed but watch for traffic joining the carriageway, while a flashing red light indicates it is okay to turn if the carriageway is clear.

Restrictions

Speed limits are always well marked with black numbering on white signs and the police are pretty hot on speeding, with steep on-the-spot fines. Limits vary from 55-70mph (88-113kph) on the Interstates and can change frequently – where there is also a 40mph (64kph) minimum speed – to just 15 or 20mph (24 or 32kph) in built-up areas.

Flashing orange lights over the road indicate a school zone and school buses must not be overtaken in either direction when they are unloading and have their hazard lights on. U-turns are forbidden in built-up areas and where there is a solid line down the middle of the road. It is illegal to park within 10ft (3m) of a fire hydrant or a lowered kerb, and never park in front of a yellow-painted kerb – they are stopping points for emergency vehicles and you will be towed away. Never park ON a kerb, either.

Seat belts are compulsory for all front-seat passengers, while child seats must be used for under 4s and can be hired from the car companies at around $8 a day (better still, bring

International Drive

your own). Children aged 4 or 5 must either use a seat belt, whether sitting in the front or back, or have a child seat fitted.

You must put your lights on in the rain, and park bonnet first. Reverse parking is frowned upon because number plates are often found only on the rear of cars and police then can't see them. If you park parallel to the kerb you must face the direction of the traffic. You must pull to the side of the road to allow emergency vehicles to pass when they have lights and/or sirens going. **Disabled drivers** should note their UK orange disabled badge IS recognised in Florida for parking in the well-provided disabled spaces.

Finally, DON'T drink and drive. Florida has strict laws, with penalties of up to 6 months in prison for first-time offenders. The legal blood-alcohol limit is lower than in Britain, so it is safer not to drink at all if you are driving. It is also illegal to carry open containers of alcohol in the car.

Bonus for AA members: your membership is recognised by the equivalent AAA in the US and you also benefit from a number of special offers. Take your AA card with you and, where you see the AAA 'Show & Save' signs in hotels, shops and restaurants, just produce it to enjoy the same money-saving benefits as the locals (notably a coupon book at the Orlando Premium Outlets). Visit www.aaasouth.com then click on the Savings link for the full low-down.

Accidents

In the unlikely event of having an accident, no matter how minor, you must contact the police before the cars can be moved (except on the busy I-4). Car-hire firms will insist on a full police report for the insurance. If you break down, there should be an emergency number for the hire company in their literature

or, if you are on a major highway, raise the bonnet and wait for one of the frequent police patrol cars to stop (or dial *FHP on your mobile). Always carry your driving licence and hire agreement forms in case you are stopped by the police.

Key routes

The main route through Orlando is Interstate 4 (or I-4), a 4-, 6- or 8-lane motorway linking the two coasts. Interstates are always indicated on blue shield-shaped signs. For most of its length, I-4 travels east-west but, around Orlando, it swings north-south, although directions are still given east (for north) or west (for south). All main motorways are prefixed I, the even numbers generally going east-west and odd numbers north-south. Federal Highways are the next grade down, numbered with black numerals on white shields, while state roads are known as Routeways and prefixed SR (black numbers on white circular or oblong signs). All the attractions of Walt Disney World, plus those of SeaWorld and Universal Orlando are well sign-posted from I-4. Historic Bok Sanctuary is a 45-minute drive from central Orlando (south) west on I-4 and Highway 27, while Busch Gardens is 75-90 minutes down I-4 to Tampa.

International Drive (or I-Drive) is the second key local roadway, linking a 14½-mile (24-km) ribbon of hotels, shops, restaurants and

BRIT TIP: All Interstate exits have been renumbered recently, so repeat visitors must be aware that I-4 exit numbers may be different from the last time they were there.

BRIT TIP: There are long-standing roadworks on I-4 south of Kissimmee and these can cause much longer journeys to and from Tampa.

attractions like Wet 'n Wild, The Mercado centre and Belz Festival Bay. (I-Drive South, from Highway 192 north to Route 535, is NOT the main stretch, although they will eventually link up.)

From I-4, take Exits 71, 72, 74A or 75A going (north) east, or 75B, 74A or 72 going (south) west. To the north, I-Drive runs into Oakridge Road and the South Orange Blossom Trail, which leads to downtown Orlando (Junctions 82C–84 off I-4). I-Drive is also bisected by Sand Lake Road and runs into World Center Drive (536), to the south, also convenient for Disney's attractions.

I-Drive is a major tourist centre and makes an excellent base, especially to the south of Sand Lake Road, near The Mercado, as it is fully pedestrian-friendly. It's a 20-minute drive to Disney and 10 minutes from Universal. However, it can be congested at peak times, especially around Sand Lake Road in the evening, so try to use Universal Boulevard instead.

The other main tourist area is the city of **Kissimmee**, south of Orlando and south-east of Disney. Its features are grouped along a 19-mile (31km) stretch of the Irlo Bronson Memorial Highway (192), which intersects I-4 at Junction 64B, and is only 10 minutes from *Walt Disney World*, 20 from SeaWorld and 25 from Universal. The downtown area of Kissimmee is off Main Street, Broadway and Emmett Street and is ideal for walking. A handy visual

along **Highway 192** is the Marker Series from Formosa Gardens (Number 4) to just past Medieval Times (Number 15). These highly visible signs are good locators for hotels, restaurants and attractions.

Fuel

Nearly all American petrol, or 'gas', stations are self-service and most require you pay before filling up. However, the pumps usually allow you to pay by credit card without having to go into the cashier's office. Always use unleaded fuel and, to activate the petrol pump, you may need to first lift the lever underneath the pump nozzle. **RaceTrac** and **Hess** petrol stations are often the cheapest. The two Hess stations in *Walt Disney World* are, surprisingly, among the cheapest in the area. Petrol stations in Lake Buena Vista just outside Disney are outrageously expensive!

Local maps

The best and most up-to-date free maps are the bright orange Welcome Guide-Map (also full of discount coupons), available in the main tourist areas, and the pull-out map inside the Kissimmee-St Cloud Visitors' Guide (from the official Visitor Center on East Highway 192, call 407 847 5000). AA members are well catered for (see page 58), but the best paid-for maps are the Trakker series, with four products covering Orlando: the Pocket Map ($4.95) is almost as detailed as the AAA ones, while the City Slicker (a laminated fold-out of the main areas, $5.95) is useful in the car. Trakker also does a full Orlando Street Atlas ($16.95) (407 447 6485 in Orlando, www.trakkermaps.com). Now, let's go on to the next vital step, your holiday accommodation…

4 Accommodation
(or, Making Sense of American Hotels, Motels and Condos)

To list all the accommodation in this area would fill a book. Metro Orlando has the second highest concentration of hotels in the world and more are being built all the time – with in excess of 113,000 rooms and still counting. Therefore what follows is a general guide to the bigger, better and budget types.

HOTELS

American hotels, particularly in the tourist areas, tend towards the motel type. The facilities and service are fine, but you won't necessarily be located in one main building. Your room may be in one of several blocks arranged around the pool, restaurant or other facilities. Room size rarely alters, even from 2- to 4-star accommodation; extra amenities and services give a hotel extra star rating. A standard room usually has 2 double beds and will comfortably accommodate a family of 4 (couples should ask for a king room, with an extra-size bed). All hotels should offer non-smoking rooms.

The other feature of motel-type accommodation is the lack of a restaurant in some cases. This is because American hotels operate almost exclusively on a room-only basis – meals are usually extra – so you may have to drive to the nearest restaurant (of which there are many – see Chapter 10) just for breakfast. So check the dining facilities before you book.

Most hotels are big, clean, efficient and great value. You'll find

Suite things

Suites hotels are virtually unknown in the UK but provide a combination of hotel and apartment, with extra value for large families or groups. Typically, a suites room gives you a living room and kitchenette, including microwave, coffee-maker, fridge, cutlery and crockery, while many offer a complimentary continental breakfast (or better). All have pools and grocery stores or snack bars. They vary only in the number of bedrooms (although a couple do have restaurants) and can usually sleep 6-10 people.

plenty of soft-drink and ice machines, with ice buckets in all the rooms (although it's much cheaper to buy drinks from the nearest supermarket). All accommodation will be air-conditioned and, when it is really hot, you have to live with the drone of the A/C unit at night. Don't turn it off when you go out, even if it is cool in the morning, or the room will be like an oven by your return. If you need a more spacious room, look for one of the many Suites hotels here, which provide sitting rooms and mini-kitchens as well as 1, 2 or even 3 bedrooms.

Note that the most expensive place from which to make a phone call is your hotel room. Most hotels add a 45–70 per cent surcharge (Disney resorts add a $15 'connection fee') to every call (you can also be charged for a call if no one answers, if it rings 5 or more times). Buy a phonecard instead (see page 43). Remember, too, hotel prices (in this book and in Orlando) are always per *room*. They will be cheaper out of the main holiday periods but can vary from month to month, with special deals at times. Always ask for rates if you book yourself and check if any special rates apply during your visit (don't be afraid to ask for their 'best rate' at off-peak times, which can be lower than published rates). There may be an additional charge ($5–15 per person) for more than 2 adults sharing the same room, plus there is a per night state tax and a resort fee that can add $10-$20 to the rate.

If you've just arrived and still need accommodation, head for 1 of the 2 official Visitor Centers: International Drive just south of The Mercado (on the corner of Austrian Court, open daily 8am–7pm); or on eastern Highway 192 in Kissimmee (open 8am–5pm), where they keep brochures and all the latest hotel deals. If you're happy with auction websites like www.priceline.com, you may pick up a bargain. Other agencies worth trying are **Know Before You Go** (407 425 5387 or 1800 230 5938, www.knowbefore ugo.com), who deal in discounted accommodation as well as attraction tickets, **Hotel Anywhere** (01444 410 555, www.hotelanywhere.co.uk) and, in the US, **Hotels.com** (1-800 246 8357, www.hotels.com).

As there is no widely accepted star rating, we group hotels into 1 of 4 ranges: Budget, Standard, Superior and Deluxe, where the rough price groups will be:

Budget	=	up to $50 per night
Standard	=	$51–99
Superior	=	$100–160
Deluxe	=	$161-plus

Our price guide is only a rough reckoner as rates can vary from month to month. The main factor to bear in mind is the extra facilities involved. Hence, a Deluxe grading

> **BRIT TIP:** Buy soft drinks at the supermarket, and a polystyrene cooler for about $4 that you can fill with ice from your hotel ice machine to keep drinks cold.

will include the highest level of facilities and service, while a Budget grade will be a more basic motel-type. A key factor in price, though, is your location – the closer to Disney and the other parks, the higher the price, so you can save money if you don't mind a longer drive to your accommodation.

Disney hotels

Our review of Orlando's hotels starts with *Walt Disney World Resort*. Conveniently sited on the doorstep of the main attractions – and linked by an excellent free transport system of monorail, buses and boats – Disney's hotels, holiday homes and campsites are all magnificently appointed and maintained. They range from the *Deluxe Grand Floridian Resort & Spa* to the Standard but still fun style of the new *Pop Century Resort* – and their imagination and attention to detail are as good as the theme parks. There are some 28,000 rooms, while *Fort Wilderness Resort & Campground* has 1,190 sites.

Grand accommodation comes at a price, though. A regular room at the

Disney's Beach Club Resort

© Disney

Grand Floridian can cost $500 a night in high season (suites can top $2,000) and even the Superior *Caribbean Beach Resort* can top $150 a night. Dining at resort hotels is not cheap either, and you'll find few fast-food outlets on site. Disney also have an additional category of **Home Away From Home** resorts – *Wilderness Lodge Villas, Old Key West, Boardwalk Villas,* the new *Saratoga Springs Resort & Spa* and *Fort Wilderness* cabins.

Staying with the Mouse is one of the great thrills, for the style, service and extras. The 21 resorts offer a superb array of facilities, and children especially love being a part of Disney full-time. The benefits are: **Resort ID card:** every guest receives a card with which to charge almost all your food, gifts and services while on site to your room account. **Package delivery:** in conjunction with your ID card, you can have park purchases sent back to your hotel gift shop. **Free parking:** with your ID card, there is no charge for your car at any of the parks. **Free transport:** forget the car and use the monorail-bus-boat network. **Refillable mugs:** all Disney resorts sell collectible drinking mugs, which are well worth buying (about $11.99 each) as you can then help yourself to refills at their self-service cafés. **Dining priority:** many Disney restaurants hold tables for resort guests and you can book up to 90 days in advance (2 years for dinner shows). Call 407 939 3463 or dial *55 on any resort phone. **Priority golf:** the best tee times are reserved for resort guests and can be booked 90 days in advance on 407 939 4653. **Children's services:** all resorts have in-room or group baby-sitting (subject to availability, so book in advance on 407 827 5444) and eight of the nine Deluxe resorts have supervised activity centres and dinner clubs (around $10/child per

hour), usually open until midnight. **Mickey on call:** what better way to wake up than with an alarm call from the Mouse himself? **Extra Magic Hours:** this is the BIG bonus, the chance to get into one of the parks either an hour early each day or for 3 hours after regular park closing, (see page 30) and do many rides with much-reduced crowds.

Standard resorts

Disney's All-Star Resorts were Disney's first foray into the more modestly priced market in 1994. Here you can stay in one of the 5 **Sports**-themed blocks (Surfing, Basketball, Tennis, Baseball and American Football) centred around a massive food court, two swimming pools, a games arcade and shops; the **Music**-themed version (Jazz, Rock, Broadway, Calypso and Country); or the **Movies** complex (Mighty Ducks, 101 Dalmatians, Fantasia, Love Bug and Toy Story). The latter is possibly the most imaginative, with its Fantasia pool and kids' play areas, and the most popular blocks are Toy Story and 101 Dalmatians (both non-smoking). All 3 centres, which total 5,760 rooms, have pool bars, shops, laundry facilities, video games rooms and a pizza delivery service. Bright and compact (if a little tight for families of 4 with older children), they are well designed for families who want to enjoy all the Disney conveniences but without the full price tag. Close to *Disney's Animal Kingdom*, there is also a large **McDonald's** nearby if the resort's food courts don't appeal. Transport to all the parks (and Downtown Disney) is provided by a highly efficient bus service.

Disney's Pop Century Resort is in a similar vein, themed round the decades of the 20th century. There are 10 blocks with giant icons – such as yo-yos, Rubik's cubes and jukeboxes – and a riot of period sayings and visual gags. The first half of the resort (the **Classic Years**, 1950s–'90s) opened in December 2003 and features a huge 10-pin bowling lane incorporating one of the 3 pools (the others are shaped like a computer and a flower), a huge table football set-up and open-air Twister mats. Blocks are grouped around a main building housing a spacious check-in area (with large-screen TV showing Disney films, of course), a large food court, a lounge (with quick-breakfast bar), a Disney store and games arcade.

> BRIT TIP: To make a reservation at any *Walt Disney World* resort, call 407 934 7639. For information, visit www.disneyworld.co.uk.

The 177-acre (72-ha) complex also features a central lake, while the **Legendary Years**, the 1900s–40s, will have identical facilities when completed in the near future. It all adds significantly to Disney's budget-orientated offerings and has a well-organised bus service to the parks. The drawbacks? Long queues to check in for much of the afternoon and it has a rather hectic feel even late into the evening. You also need to request a hair-dryer from reception and rooms are, again, rather on the small side.

Superior resorts

Going up a level, **Disney's Caribbean Beach Resort** opened in 1988 (with a major refurb in 2003) and has 2,112 rooms spread over 5 Caribbean 'islands' (with inter-island bus service). Rooms are still relatively plain but comfortably sleep four, and the food court, main

restaurant, **Shutters**, and outdoor activities (with a lakeside recreation area with themed waterfalls, slides and games arcade) are a big hit with children. The 6 counter-service outlets in the food court at **Old Port Royale Town Center** (hub of this pretty resort) can get busy in the morning, and the Trinidad South and Barbados 'islands' are a fair walk from the centre. But it is an action-packed resort with some imaginative touches, like Parrot Cay Island Playground with its tropical birds and play area. Transport to the parks is purely by bus.

Disney's Port Orleans Resort opened in 1991 and is a 2-part complex (formerly Port Orleans and Dixie Landings) split into the 2,048-room **Riverside** – with a steamboat reception area, a great cotton mill-style food court, a full-service Cajun-themed restaurant and an old-fashioned general store (gift shop) – and the 1,008-room **French Quarter**, which has the **Sassagoula Floatworks and Food Factory** court, two bars, a games room and shopping arcade. The Riverside includes **Ol' Man Island**, a magnificent 3½-acre (1.5-ha) playground with swimming pool, kids' area and a fishing hole, while the French Quarter has Doubloon Lagoon, with Mardi Gras dragon slide, alligator fountains and play area. The eye-catching landscaping and design vary from rustic Bayou backwoods to turn-of-the-century New Orleans. Transport for both sections is by bus to the parks and bus or boat to *Downtown Disney*.

Disney's Coronado Springs Resort is possibly the best value of this trio as it is newer (built in 1997) and has slightly more facilities for its 1,921 rooms spread over 125 acres (50ha): 4 pools, including the massive Lost City of Cibola, 2 games arcades, a boating marina, bike rentals, restaurant, food court and convenience store, lounge bar, gift shop, beauty salon and health club, business centre and two guest launderettes. Constructed in a scenic Mexican/Spanish theme in three 'villages' (Casitas, Ranchos and Cabanas), Coronado is an often-overlooked treasure. Check out the **Maya Grill** and its New Latino cuisine. Coronado is also only 5 minutes from *Disney's Animal Kingdom* and is well served by the bus network.

Deluxe resorts

More than anything, Disney specialises in high-quality hotels with all manner of special design features, amenities and splendid restaurants. All 9 Deluxe resorts offer a Concierge level, which adds an exclusive, personalised service, and a private lounge with meals and snacks. The first 2 (refurbished several times since) opened with the *Magic Kingdom Park* in 1971. Situated on the monorail, right next to the park, the 15-storey **Disney's Contemporary Resort** has 1,030 rooms (in the process of being extensively refurbished in a chic, modern style), a cavernous foyer, shops, restaurants, lounges, a real sandy beach, a marina, 2 pools (1 with water-slide), 6 tennis courts, a video games centre and health club – and fabulous views, especially from the superb, hotel-top **California Grill** (one of the most romantic settings in Orlando; try to get a

Disney's Contemporary Resort

© Disney

> **BRIT TIP:** Disney resort restaurants CAN (and should) be visited even if you are not staying there. You can book in advance at any of the parks, from any Disney phone (dial *55) or on 407-WDW-DINE.

reservation to coincide with the park's fireworks).

Don't miss **Chef Mickey's** here for a breakfast or dinner buffet with your favourite characters, while the monorail runs right *through* the hotel – fascinating for kids. Rooms are large and well furnished. Within walking distance of the *Magic Kingdom Park*, transport to the other parks is by bus.

Disney's Polynesian Resort, the other 1971 original, is a South Seas tropical fantasy with modern sophistication and comfort. Beautiful beaches, lush vegetation and architecture are home to 853 rooms built in wooden long-house style, all with balconies and superb views. Also on the monorail line opposite the *Magic Kingdom*, it boasts a stunning 3-storey atrium, with 75 varieties of tropical plants, parrots and a waterfall.

The resort offers excellent eating: **'Ohana** is an entertaining and stylish dinner venue that also offers lively character breakfasts, while the **Kona Café** is slightly less formal but still with an extensive menu, and **Captain Cook's Snack Company** offers more basic counter-service fare. Then there are canoe rentals, a beautiful pool area with water-slide, a games room, shops and children's playground. **The Neverland Club** caters for 4-12s (4pm-midnight). Catch the monorail or a boat to the *Magic Kingdom*, and buses to the other parks. The Poly is also home to the nightly *Spirit of Aloha* dinner show (see page 260), which is open to non-resort guests and makes a great evening among the torch-lit paths and gardens. The Resort's beach area also makes a great location from which to view the nightly *Magic Kingdom* fireworks.

> **BRIT TIP:** Dine in superb South Seas style at 'Ohana's but don't ask for the salt – unless you want to spark an amazing reaction…

Next to open, in 1988, was **Disney's Grand Floridian Resort & Spa**, a true five-star hotel built like a hugely elaborate Victorian mansion, with 867 rooms, an impressive domed foyer and staff in period dress. Again on the monorail, one stop from the *Magic Kingdom*, the rooms and facilities are truly luxurious, hence mega prices, so it is worth a look even if you are not staying. It has 6 restaurants, including the top-of-the-range **Victoria and Albert's** (where the set, 6-course dinner with wine will cost $110+ each), the chic seafood-based **Narcoossee's** (one of our favourites), with its excellent view over Seven Seas Lagoon (for the nightly Electrical Water Pageant), and Mediterranean-styled **Citricos**. You will also find 4 bars and impressive sporting and relaxation facilities, notably the fabulous Spa and Salon. There's a wonderful second pool area, complete with zero-depth entry and water-slide. **The Mouseketeer Club** caters for 4-12s (4.30pm-midnight) and the **1900 Park Fare** restaurant is hugely popular for character breakfasts and dinners.

For young princesses, the Garden View Lounge hosts **My Disney Girl's Perfectly Princess Tea Party** (10.30am–noon; daily except Tue and Wed), featuring Princess

> **BRIT TIP:** Watch out for the free nightly **Electrical Water Pageant** on Bay Lake and Seven Seas Lagoon (see page 253), which you can see from all the *Magic Kingdom* resorts.

Aurora from *Sleeping Beauty* and with storytelling, sing-alongs and a princess parade, plus a princess doll and gifts for each child (3–11). The cost for 1 adult and child is a whopping $200, however (but reservations still advisable on 407 WDW DINE). The Garden View Lounge also serves a variety of traditional **Afternoon Teas** from 2–4.30pm daily from $8.50-$24.50 a head. Transport to the *Magic Kingdom* is by boat and monorail; by bus to the other parks.

The refined, almost intimate, **Disney's Yacht and Beach Club Resorts** added more quality when they opened in 1990 with 630 and 583 nautical-themed rooms respectively. Set around Crescent Lake next to the Epcot park, they help to form one massive resort area that is a delight to walk around at any time but especially at night. For dinner, the **Yachtsman Steakhouse** offers friendly, polished and elegant dining at the Yacht Club while the

Victoria and Albert's at Disney's Grand Floridian Resort & Spa

© Disney

sister hotel features **Cape May Café** for lovely character breakfasts and a nightly New England-style clambake buffet. **Beaches & Cream** can also be found here, a classic 1950s-style diner with some of the best burgers anywhere, plus delicious shakes and sundaes. Both resorts are set along a white-sand beach like a tropical island paradise and share water fun at **Stormalong Bay**, a superb 2½-acre (1-ha) recreation area with water-slides and a sandy lagoon. You can go boating or catch a water-shuttle to Epcot; other park transport is by bus. The **Sand Castle Club** here caters for 4-12s (4.30pm-midnight).

The unmistakable **Walt Disney World Swan** and **Dolphin** hotels also went up on Crescent Lake in 1990 and, while not actually owned by Disney, they conform to the same high standards. They have some of the most extensive facilities of all the resorts, a wonderful location, fabulous restaurants and a night-time view second to none, while they are usually slightly cheaper than the main Disney Deluxe resorts. They are within walking distance of *Epcot* and *Disney-MGM Studios*, *Disney's Boardwalk Resort* and the *Fantasia Gardens* Miniature Golf Courses, but also have boat service to both parks (and bus to the others). The 'entertainment architecture' style is extensive and fun, with The Swan featuring a 45ft (14m) statue on top, as well as 758 large rooms (including 55 suites), while the Dolphin (1,509 rooms, with 136 suites) is crowned by 2 even bigger statues. Both were extensively refurbished in 2003–4 with a luxury look by the original architect, Michael Graves. They now feature the popular Westin Heavenly Bed and unlimited access to high-speed in-room internet. This mega-resort boasts 17 restaurants, 4 tennis courts, 5 pools (1 an amazing grotto pool with hidden alcoves and water-slide), a

kids' pool and white-sand beach, 2 health clubs, bike and paddle boat rentals, a great range of shops, video arcade and the **Camp Dolphin** centre for 4-12s (5.30-midnight, $10/hour).

Even for non-guests, the Italian **Palio** (Swan), **Shula's Steak House** and, new to the resort, celebrity chef Todd English's **bluezoo** (both Dolphin) are worth seeking out (with seafood-themed bluezoo one our top-recommended restaurants, see page 290). **Fresh**, the Dolphin's Mediterranean-style market, serves breakfast and lunch, featuring all made-to-order menu items and both à la carte and tableside dining. At the Swan, the **Garden Grove Café** is set indoors in a tropical gazebo, with à la carte or buffet breakfasts – including character breakfasts on Saturday and Sunday. The restaurant is transformed in the evening into **Gulliver's Grill**, featuring à la carte menus, themed buffets and Disney characters every weeknight. **Tubbi's** in the Dolphin is open 24 hours. With its ideal location within walking distance of the 2 parks and the Boardwalk district, this is very nearly the perfect resort. Visit www.swandolphin.com or call 407 934 3000.

Disney's Wilderness Lodge opened in 1994 and is one of the most picturesque resorts, as well as being a great romantic destination. It is a detailed re-creation of a National Park lodge, from the stream running through the massive wooden balcony-lined atrium into the gardens, past the swimming pool (with hot and cold spas) to a geyser that erupts each hour. Offering authentic backwoods charm with true luxury, the resort is connected to the *Magic Kingdom* Park by boat and bus only (and buses to the other parks). Rooms are all spacious and with some lovely furniture, while the Courtyard View rooms are the best of the regular rooms (although at a slight premium). Deluxe rooms sleep up to 6 and the suites (at up to $815 a night) are truly sumptuous. It also has 2 restaurants: the brilliant **Artist's Point** (lunch and dinner) and the **Whispering Canyon Café** (lively breakfast and huge all-you-can-eat buffets) – plus a snack bar and pool bar. **The Cubs Den** is for 4-12s (4.30pm-midnight).

The **Villas at Wilderness Lodge** are a recent development of 136 studios and 1- and 2-bedroom villas. Facilities include living areas, fully equipped kitchens, private balconies and whirlpool baths. There is a quiet pool area, spa and health club.

Completing the Crescent Lake resorts next to *Epcot* in 1996 was the 45-acre (18-ha) **Disney's BoardWalk Inn and Villas Resort**, one of the most extravagant on-site hotels and a key ingredient in this entertainment 'district.' It features a 372-room hotel, 520 villas, 4 themed restaurants, a TV sports club and 2 nightclubs, plus an array of shops, sports facilities and a huge, free-form swimming pool with a 200ft (60m) water-slide, all on a semi-circular boardwalk around the lake. The effect is stunning, and the in-room attention to detail excellent. Highlights are the summer cottage-style villas, tapas-style restaurant **Spoodles** (breakfast and dinner) and the **Big River Grille Brewing Company** (lunch and dinner) for a great range of beers. Top of the lot is the expensive but superb seafood of the **Flying Fish Café** (dinner only). You can try the **Boardwalk Bakery** for a snack, while Spoodles has a quick-service window for takeaways. It is a delightful place to visit for a

BRIT TIP: If you visit no other Disney resort, you should definitely try The Boardwalk at some stage, preferably in the evening.

meal, the nightlife (especially **Jellyrolls** piano bar and the **ESPN Club**, the latter of which serves lunch and dinner) or just to wander the boardwalk. The **Harbor Club** caters for 4–12s (4pm– midnight). There is boat transport to *Epcot* and *Disney-MGM Studios* and bus service to the other parks.

Disney's Animal Kingdom Lodge opened in 2001, a stunning private game lodge on the edge of a 33-acre (13-ha) animal-filled savannah, which many rooms overlook. The pervasive African theme is almost overwhelming, and the effect of opening your curtains to a vista of giraffes and zebras is immense. This wonderful creativity comes before you consider the amenities of this 1,293-room resort: 2 restaurants, café, bar, elaborately themed 'watering-hole' main pool (with water-slide) and kids' pool, massage and fitness centre, large gift shop, children's play area and an awesome 4-storey atrium. The main restaurant, **Jiko**, is spectacular, but there is also the buffet-style **Boma**, a 'marketplace' restaurant featuring African dishes from a wood-burning grill and rotisserie for breakfast and dinner.

BRIT TIP: Jiko at *Disney's Animal Kingdom Lodge* offers an imaginative, New World cuisine menu, attentive service and authentic ambience.

The lavishness and detail are superb, right down to the guides who can tell guests about the 200 animals and their habitats, the African folklore stories around the outdoor firepit and the chance for children to become junior safari researchers while Mum and Dad do some wine-tasting (the hotel boasts the largest US collection of South

African wines). Rooms range from standard doubles to 1- and 2-bedroom suites, some of which have bunk beds. **Simba's Cubhouse** is for children aged 4-12 (4.30pm-midnight), and all Disney transport is by bus (with the *Animal Kingdom* barely 5 minutes away).

Home Away From Home resorts

Possibly the best value of all the Disney properties can be found at **Disney's Fort Wilderness Resort and Campground**, which opened with all the initial development in 1971. Situated on Bay Lake, almost opposite the *Magic Kingdom*, it offers impressive camping facilities and chalet-style homes that can house up to 6 in a 750-acre (304-ha) spread of Florida countryside. Two 'trading posts' supply fresh groceries and there are 2 bars and cafés plus a range of on-site activities, including two swimming pools, the thrice-nightly *Hoop-Dee-Doo Musical Revue*, Mickey's Backyard Barbecue (a character buffet dinner), campfire programme, films, sports, games and a prime position from which to view the nightly Electrical Water Pageant. You can rent bikes or take horse rides around the country trails, or go boating, while the Tri-Circle D ranch offers a small petting zoo. The **Trails End** restaurant (sit-down and takeaway) offers excellent value for its buffet breakfast, lunch and dinner, while **Crockett's Tavern** serves pizza and appetisers (dinner only). Buses and boats link

Fort Wilderness cabin

© Disney

the resort with other areas (and the short boat ride to the *Magic Kingdom* is a great start to any day).

Disney's Old Key West Resort (originally Disney's Vacation Club resort when it opened in 1992) is primarily a 5-star holiday ownership scheme (one of five Disney timeshare, or Vacation Club, properties), but the 1-, 2- or 3-bed studios in a Key West setting can also be rented nightly when not in use by members. Facilities include 4 pools, tennis courts, games room, shops and fitness centre plus **Olivia's** restaurant (for superb Key Lime Pie!). Transport to all parks is by Disney's bus service.

> **BRIT TIP:** No regular Disney hotel room will accommodate more than 4. For larger groups, consider Old Key West, Saratoga Springs, the Boardwalk Villas, Wilderness Lodge Villas, Fort Wilderness cabins or one of the Deluxe resorts.

Disney's Saratoga Springs Resort & Spa is the newest member of the line-up, a 65-acre (26-ha) apartment complex opposite *Downtown Disney* with some wonderful views over the lake and right next to the beautiful Lake Buena Vista Golf Course. When the third phase is completed in 2007, it will boast 828 units, from standard 2-bed hotel-style studio rooms to huge 2-storey, 3-bedroom apartments sleeping 12. The first phase of 184 rooms opened in May 2004, another 368 in 2005 and another 176 are due in 2006. The theme is the 1880s' New York resort of the same name, with a peaceful, gracious look and a great array of facilities, from the free-form, zero-depth entry main pool (with water-slide and squirt-fountain play area), a smaller quiet pool, the health-conscious dining room (the **Artist's Palette**, offering breakfast, lunch and dinner, plus groceries), a large video arcade, tennis courts and a wonderful full-service spa and gym. This is spacious, elegant accommodation for large groups. The standard 1-bedroom apartment can sleep 4; the 2-bed version sleeps 8 and there's a 3-bed, 3-bath villa. All but the hotel-style studios have a kitchen (with dishwasher and microwave), washer, dryer, whirlpool bath and DVD player with TVs in the living room and each bedroom. The resort includes a guest services desk, room service, baby-sitting and child-minding services and a water launch to the shops and entertainment of Downtown Disney. Rates for the 3-bed villas top $1,000 a night, but the 1-bed units are more modestly priced and, although it is a Disney Vacation Club property, some rooms are available to the general public. Transport to all the parks is by Disney's bus service.

Disney Hotel Plaza

In addition to the official hotels, there are another seven 'guest' hotels on Disney property at the **Disney Hotel Plaza** on the doorstep of *Downtown Disney*. There's a free bus service to the attractions and guaranteed admission to the parks, and you can make reservations for shows and restaurants before the public, but they tend to be more expensive than similar hotels outside Disney property (although the convenience of being able to walk to *Downtown Disney* and the Crossroads shopping plaza is worth a lot).

The well-priced **Holiday Inn in the Walt Disney World Resort** (formerly the Courtyard by Marriott) has 323 extra-large rooms

in a 14-storey tower and 6-storey annex with glass-walled lifts, three heated swimming pools – including one for kids – small gym, games room, **Courtyard Café & Grill**, snack bar and lounge/bar, plus lovely gardens (407 828 8888; Standard). Similarly, the tropically themed **Best Western Lake Buena Vista** has 325 rooms with views over the Marketplace, in-room coffee-makers and hair-dryers, while the huge top-floor suites are magnificent. Garden-themed **Traders** is pleasant for breakfast or dinner, plus there is a quick-service deli, **Parakeets**, a lounge bar, and **Toppers** nightclub on the 18th floor, plus a large pool, video arcade and small gym (407 828 2424; Standard).

Going more upmarket, the **Grosvenor Resort** has 626 rooms, great service and colonial decor, plus 2 pools, a large hot tub and a children's pool and playground. There is a Disney character breakfast 3 days a week at **Baskerville's**, a sports bar, poolside bar and grill and a 24-hour café, **Crumpets**. You will also find the fun **MurderWatch** dinner theatre here on Saturdays. Extra facilities include tennis courts, basketball, volleyball and a state-of-the-art fitness centre (407 828 4444; Superior). The lovely **Hotel Royal Plaza** has a pleasant aspect, boasting 372 spacious and well-equipped rooms and 22 suites, with a full-service diner-restaurant (the **Giraffe Diner**, featuring an excellent breakfast buffet), lounge bar, deli-style café, landscaped pool area and pool bar, 4 tennis courts, a health club and fitness centre and

Disney's Yacht Club Resort

© Disney

Disney gift shop. Standard rooms include a sitting area and balcony (407 828 2828; Superior). For extra space with your accommodation, the contemporary **Doubletree Guest Suites** offers 229 family suites with every convenience, from in-room safe to cookies(!), wet bar, fridge and microwave. There are also excellent kids' facilities, with their own check-in area, pool, games room, cinema and video arcade. There is a casual restaurant, lounge and market, **Streamers**, while the large main pool also has its own bar, Other facilities include an exercise room, jogging trails and tennis courts (407 934 1000; Superior).

Arguably the standout property here is the **Wyndham Palace Resort & Spa**, an elegant, 27-storey cluster offering 1,014 rooms, many with a view of *Epcot*'s Spaceship Earth, a European-style spa, 3 heated pools, tennis courts, a marina with boat rentals and the superb **Arthur's 27** restaurant, with stunning views and a magnificent menu (opt for the set 4-course version at $68) for one of the most memorable dining experiences. Also try the **Top of the Palace Lounge** for a drink with a view! The chic **Watercress Café** is a great venue for breakfast and lunch, or a Sunday brunch with Disney characters (reservations not needed). The **Laughing Kookaburra Lounge** is a smart nightclub open to non-residents, and the themed **Outback Steakhouse** is a stylish one-off of this great chain restaurant (407 827 2727; Superior).

Top of the list (for service, mod cons and price) is the 10-storey, 814-room **Hilton**. With 2 excellent pools, 6 restaurants and lounges and a superb Health Club, it fully deserves its high rating. It is also the only 'outside' hotel to enjoy Disney's Extra Magic Hours feature, while there is a baby-sitting service and a character breakfast on Sundays. The

outstanding **Benihana** restaurant offers sushi, sashimi, chicken and great steaks, while **Finn's Grill** specialises in seafood (407 827 4000; Deluxe).

For more info on hotels in this area, go to www.downtowndisney hotels.com.

Beyond Disney

Once you move outside the confines of the *Walt Disney World Resort in Florida*, your hotel choice becomes much more diverse and complicated. The Budget and Standard types are the most common, and the area you stay in also has an effect on the price: the further you go from Disney on Kissimmee's Highway 192, the cheaper the hotel/motel, while parts of International Drive are more expensive than others (generally, north of Sand Lake Road is cheaper). Facilities vary little and what you see is usually what you get. All the big hotel chains can be found here, with rates as low as $30/room off-peak (but remember the tax and resort fee). Some also feature rooms with a kitchenette (what they call an 'efficiency') for a few extra dollars. Be prepared to shop around for a good rate, especially along Highway 192, where many hotels advertise rates on neon signs. Feel free to ask to see a room before you book (some of the motels can be pretty ordinary). So, looking at things from the price perspective, here is a guide to the main selections.

Budget hotels

Chain hotels can be found at their most numerous in this category and you will find few frills from what is an identikit bunch. All will have pools but only a handful have restaurants and none will have bars or lounges (although quite a few provide a free continental breakfast in their lobby). Conversely, many offer fridges and even microwaves that help to add real value. At the bargain basement end are **Motel 6** (1800 466 8356; www.motel6.com) and **Red Roof Inn** (1800 733 7663; www.redroof.com). The **Super 8 Motel** chain varies quite a lot, with its newer properties (notably on American Way, near Universal Orlando) being good value, but others looking old and tired (1800 800 8000; www.super8.com). Among the most consistent are **EconoLodge**, with a feature free continental breakfast (1877 424 6423; www.econolodge.com). At the upper end of the category are **Microtel Inn & Suites**, which tend to have much newer properties (1800 771 7171; www.microtel inn.com) as do **Travelodge** (also on American Way; 1800 578 7878; www.travelodge.com).

The **Days Inn** chain varies widely, from older properties to smart relatively recent ones, and with free continental breakfast (1800 329 7466; www.daysinn.com), while sister brand the **Days Suites** are smarter still, with some real mod cons. The **Rodeway Inn** chain has slipped from Standard into more Budget territory in recent years (1877 424 6423; www.choice hotels.com). **Knights Inn** (recently merged with **Villager Inns**; 1800 843 5644; www.knightsinn.com) is a smart choice in this area, and **Masters Inn** is another to offer free coffee and continental breakfast to boost their value (1800 633 3434; www.mastersinn.com).

BRIT TIP: Hotels designated Maingate East or Maingate West should be close to Disney's main entrance on Highway 192, although it is wise to check.

There are also dozens of smaller, independent outfits that offer special rates from time to time (especially a battery of cheap and cheerful motels along Highway 192 in Kissimmee). But a couple to look out for are the **Magic Castle Inn** and **Suites Maingate** in Kissimmee, which take some beating with their range of amenities (free continental breakfast, free Disney transport, in-room fridge, microwave, safe, kids' playground, guest laundry and picnic area (1800 446 5669; www.magic orlando.com) and the **Red Horse Inn** (formerly the Universal Inn) on International Drive (near Wet 'n Wild). This latter is a fun choice, with a striking Southwestern design theme and large, comfy rooms, all refurbished recently. There is a Cantina lobby bar (with free continental breakfast featuring Starbucks coffee) and a neat oasis-themed pool area. There is no restaurant but the neighbouring Sheraton Studio City is only a short walk away and a 24-hour Denny's is next door (407 351 4100, www.redhorseorlando.com).

Standard hotels

At first glance there may not seem too much difference here, as some of these are still firmly in motel-style territory. There should be generally smarter facilities but not all will have their own restaurant. The **Howard Johnson** chain tends to have older properties here, many with 'kids eat free' option and they usually have more spacious rooms (1800 446 4656; www.hojo.com). **Ramada** hotels represent good value at this level as some have complimentary breakfast (1800 272 6232; www.ramada.com) and **Quality Inns** are also a sound, popular choice, with a great reputation for value, while some of their hotels also boast an exercise room (1877 424 6423; www.choicehotels.com).

> **BRIT TIP:** Not all hotels provide hair-dryers, though they can often be ordered from the desk. For your own, you will need a US plug adaptor (with two flat pins). Their voltage is 110–120 AC (ours is 220) so appliances will be sluggish.

The **Comfort Inn** chain is equally identikit (perhaps not surprisingly as part of the big Choice Hotels worldwide group), but also offer a valuable free breakfast, and sister brand **Comfort Suites** often boast some smart, newer properties. The **Clarion Inn** (and Suites) is another notable Choice brand, and tends to include restaurants, although properties vary in age quite considerably. Its **Sleep Inn** brand is aimed more at business travellers but tends to have newer properties, and with a free breakfast (1877 424 6423; www.choicehotels.com). For pure no frills, clean and consistent chains with more space than many in this category (and kitchens in most hotels), look for **Extended Stay America**, while they also have Extended Stay Deluxe properties (formerly the Sierra Suites group), which are smarter (if more expensive). Sister brand **StudioPLUS** offer extra facilities (1800 804 3724; www.extendedstay america.com).

Fairfield Inns are the budget version of the impressive Marriott chain and usually have smart, new hotels, many with gymnasiums and most offering free breakfast (1800

228 2800; www.marriott.com). **Hampton Inns** (and Suites) are also above average in this category, with a free breakfast bar (and free tea/coffee in the lobby 24 hours a day; 1800 426 7866; www.hamptoninn.com) while **AmeriSuites** (the Hyatt chain's budget brand) is another good name, with large, well-fitted rooms and free hot breakfast (1877 833 1516; www.amerisuites.com).

Moving to the upper end of this category you find the **Best Western** group, all with good facilities, family-orientated but large (1800 780 7234; www.bestwestern.com), the smart **La Quinta Inn** (and Suites), which has some notable new hotels in Orlando (1866 725 1661; www.lq.com) and the **Holiday Inn** chain, who vary quite a lot but provide some great value (and well-equipped) hotels in the Standard/Superior range. Kids eat free (with their parents) at all properties and many include some sophisticated pools and extra facilities, like games rooms (1888 465 4329; www.holiday inn.com). Possibly the best overall value here, though, is provided by the **Radisson** group, which has some excellently priced hotels in the area, all above average for amenities and services and most well situated for the parks (1888 201 1718; www.radisson.com).

There are also a handful of notable individual properties in this category. A firm personal choice is the **Seralago Inn Hotel** and **Suites Maingate East** (formerly a Holiday Inn), which also boasts deluxe suites, 2-room suites and Kidsuites, plus great kids' facilities (including free films in their own cinema), making it an outstanding family resort. Attention to detail (hair-dryers, coffee-makers, microwaves and fridges even in standard rooms), free Disney transport and its proximity to Old Town make for great flexibility and value. There's a children's check-in area, games

Monorail at Disney's Polynesian Resort

© Disney

BRIT TIP: It is usual in American hotels to tip the chamber maid by leaving $1 per adult each day before your room is made up.

arcade and pool, while under-13s eat breakfast and dinner free (1800 366 5437; www.seralagohotel.com).

The **Tropical Palms Fun Resort**, on Holiday Trail next to Old Town in Kissimmee, has well-equipped studio and 2-bedroom cottages with some great facilities (1800 647 2567; www.tropicalpalms.com), while the plush 2-bed, 2-bath studios of **Enclave Suites** (on Carrier Drive, just off I-Drive) are excellent value as kids eat free with parents, there's free breakfast and a superb array of resort-style facilities (1800 457 0077; www.enclavesuites.com). The **Dorsan Suites** is a new value-conscious condo hotel in east Kissimmee that offers studio and 1-bed suites, with extra facilities such as a pool bar, tennis, volleyball and a children's playground (1877 436 7726; www.dorsansuites.com).

Superior hotels

This is a category where you will find far fewer of each brand, and so we highlight a few worthy individuals as well as the chain details. All these properties will provide a good pool (often with extra facilities like a water-slide, kids pool and/or playground), at least one restaurant, bar and café, and extra in-room amenities, such as tea/coffee makers.

The **Doubletree chain** offer smart, modern properties with fewer frills than most but more spacious rooms (1800 222 8733; www.doubletree.com), while **Homewood Suites** (both part of the Hilton chain) provide extra room for larger

families in 1- and 2-bed suites with fully equipped kitchens, a free hot breakfast daily and a more upmarket feel with mid-range pricing (1800 3255 4663; www.hawthornsuites.com). Of particular note here is the recently refurbished and fun-styled **Doubletree Club Hotel** on Apopka-Vineland Road in Lake Buena Vista, which includes kids' club suites. The location at the entrance to *Downtown Disney*, pleasant bar and café, large pool deck and spacious, airy rooms mark this out as a real bargain (407 239 4646; www.doubletreeclublbv.com). The **Doubletree Hotel Universal Orlando** is a twin-tower complex with a smart resort feel, with spacious, tropical-themed rooms, a large pool, kids' playground, pool bar, arcade, hair salon, gym and sauna, plus a sports bar, full-service restaurant and food court. It also offers a free shuttle to Universal (across the road), SeaWorld and Wet 'n Wild (407 351 1000; www.doubletreeorlando.com).

For other good, spacious properties at below-average prices, look for the **Springhill Suites** and **Residence Inn** chains, which are both part of the Marriott group (along with the more upmarket **Courtyard** hotels). Residence Inn tend to be newer and feature free breakfast and exercise rooms but both Residence Inn and Springhill brands include microwave, fridge and tea/coffee-making facilities (1888 236 2427 in the US, 0800 221 222 in the UK; www.marriott.com). The **Marriott Village** complex, just off I-4 at Exit 68 in Lake Buena Vista, features a Fairfield Inn, Courtyard and Springhill Suites

Balcony at the Omni Hotel – Champions Gate

(www.marriottvillage.com), with 24-hour gated security, free *Walt Disney World* transport and great facilities.

A relative newcomer but highly worthwhile is the **Baymont Inn & Suites** group, which boasts several properties in the area (1866 999 1111; www.baymontinns.com), while the **Country Inn & Suites** are almost identical, newer hotels with spacious rooms and a pleasant country-house style lobby, which serves an extensive free breakfast (1888 201 1746; www.countryinns.com). The property on Universal Boulevard is possibly the best, with 170 standard rooms with in-room safe, coffee-maker, hair-dryer and iron/ironing board, while the 48 king suites include microwave and fridge. It is 1 mile (1.6km) from Universal Orlando and half that from Wet 'n Wild, yet much quieter than many I-Drive hotels (407 313 4200).

If you want a slightly more upmarket touch, the **Staybridge Suites** (1888 697 5292; www.stay bridge.com) and the **Hawthorn Suites** (1800 527 1133; www.hawthorn.com) feature wonderfully spacious 1- and 2-bed suites that will comfortably sleep up to 6 and fully fitted kitchens, plus a hearty free breakfast and free local phone calls. However, to our mind the best suites examples here are the **Embassy Suites** properties. The **Embassy Suites Hotel International Drive South** (407 352 1400, www.embassysuites orlando.com) is the most prominent and consistently gets good reader feedback. It is exceedingly smart, with excellent service, and spacious rooms (either standard 2-room suites sleeping 4 or double-doubles, sleeping 6) providing 2 TVs, coffee-maker, fridge and microwave. There's a neat outdoor pool deck, kids' splash pool and indoor pool, plus a sauna, steam room and gym. The Sedona Café and Hurricane's Lounge give it a real edge in dining

options, and it also offers a free Disney shuttle service and transport to the other parks from $4-8/person.

Sheraton hotels are well represented in Orlando and boast a smart, revamped look in recent years (as part of the Starwood group). Several are themed and feature extra facilities and good dining options (1800 325 3535; www.sheraton.com). A novel choice is the African-themed **Sheraton Safari Hotel** in Lake Buena Vista, which sports a water-slide, heated pool and kids' pool, free transport to Disney parks and 'kids eat free' with parents. Rooms are well equipped, with hair-dryers, coffee-makers and ironing boards, and with a good selection of shops and restaurants nearby, including *Downtown Disney*. It has 489 safari-themed rooms, including 96 huge suites (407 239 0444; www.sheraton safari.com).

The 21-storey **Sheraton Studio City Hotel** is an I-Drive icon near Universal Orlando and features a neat 1950s' film theme throughout. Facilities include a heated outdoor pool and paddling pool, games room, mini-golf, fitness room, an excellent restaurant and free shuttle to Universal, Wet 'n Wild and SeaWorld. All rooms have coffee-makers and Nintendo games (407 351 2100; www.sheratonstudio city.com). A third worthy example is the recently remodelled **Sheraton World Resort**, just off the main I-Drive. Set in 28 acres (11ha) and with 1,102 rooms and extra-large suites, the resort offers 3 pools, 2 kiddie pools, a playground and mini-golf and well-furnished rooms. Dining options are fairly standard, but the tropical grounds give it a more upmarket feel (407 352 1100, www.sheratonworld.com).

Marriott is another well-represented group in central Florida, with some of the smartest hotels in this category. They often provide extra facilities and more landscaped grounds, with a choice of restaurants and some of the largest standard rooms, as well as suites. The **Orlando World Center Marriott** is a *Brit's Guide* favourite and an impressive landmark on Disney's outskirts, set in 200 landscaped acres (810ha) and surrounded by a golf course. An elaborate lobby and its range of facilities (7 restaurants, 4 pools, tennis courts and a health club) make it expensive, but it is conveniently situated and has one of the most picturesque pool areas, plus the whizziest glass-fronted lifts. It does get busy with convention business, though. 'Try their Christmas Day Buffet,' says reader Roy Carlisle. 'Pricey but brilliant.' (407 239 4200; www.marriottworldcenter.com).

The **Hilton** chain is notable here mainly for its **Grand Vacation Club** holiday ownership resorts, which are also available on an individual rental basis at times. They feature some superb facilities and wonderfully spacious accommodations (studios, and 1-, 2- and 3-bed villas). Its 2 properties on I-Drive, by SeaWorld and Orlando Premium Outlets, are especially eye-catching (1800 230 7068; www.hiltongrandvacations.com). The **Hyatt** group is also rare in tourist territory, but one prime example is the **Hyatt Regency** at Orlando International Airport, especially if you arrive late and could benefit from a first-night rest. It has 2 excellent restaurants and a smart pool deck, plus a fitness room, lounge and business centre. The 446 rooms are superbly spacious, especially the corner rooms, and many feature internal balconies overlooking the 6-storey airport atrium. Surprisingly, there is no noticeable aircraft noise and none of the bustle you would expect of an airport hotel. Staying there gives the distinct advantage of collecting your hire car in the morning rather than straight after a long flight (407 825 1234, http://orlandoairport.hyatt.com).

Wyndham Hotels & Resorts are also anything but mass market material, but it has 2 contrasting properties in the area (in addition to its smart *Downtown Disney* hotel). The **Wyndham Orlando Resort** in the heart of I-Drive boasts a formidable line-up of facilities (3 swimming pools, a full-service restaurant and bar, a deli and an ice cream shop, 2 pool bars, a pool restaurant, tennis courts, a kids' club and game arcade, and a health club) in its beautifully landscaped grounds but without the high price tag you would expect. The resort covers 42 acres (17ha), which takes some getting around, but it is one of the best all-round hotels for the money. The **Wyndham Palms Resort & Country Club**, tucked away in a quiet corner of Kissimmee, is primarily a holiday ownership property but it also offers hotel rentals, often at terrific rates. And it is a truly luxurious resort with just about every facility you can think of, plus an impressive array of beautiful 1-, 2- and 3-bed villas that sleep up to 12 (1877 747 4747; www.wyndham.com).

Crowne Plaza Hotels have made a mark for themselves in recent years with some fabulous new properties in this category. They feature excellent pool areas, whirlpools, good quality restaurants, fitness centres and ultra-comfortable rooms. The **Crowne Plaza Orlando Universal** is a fine example of this Superior elegance, with 304 rooms and 94 suites in 2 distinct, stylish blocks and a spectacular circular atrium. Two restaurants, a cocktail lounge, guest laundry and baby-sitting facilities, plus its huge heated pool, add up to excellent quality and value in an ideal location on Universal Boulevard's junction with Sand Lake Road (407 781 2107, www.crowneplazauniversal.com).

WALT DISNEY WORLD AND LAKE BUENA VISTA ACCOMMODATION

1 Disney's Contemporary Resort
2 Disney's Polynesian Resort
3 Disney's Wilderness Lodge
4 Disney's Grand Floridian Resort & Spa
5 Walt Disney World Swan
6 Walt Disney World Dolphin
7 Disney's Caribbean Beach Resort
8 Disney's Yacht Club Resort
9 Disney's Beach Club Resort
10 Disney's Boardwalk Resort
11 Disney's All-Star Resorts
12 Disney's Port Orleans Resort (French Quarter)
13 Disney's Port Orleans Resort (Riverside)
14 Disney's Coronado Springs Resort
15 Disney's Saratoga Springs Resort & Spa
16 Disney's Old Key West Resort
17 Disney's Fort Wilderness Resort & Campground
18 Disney's Animal Kingdom Lodge
19 Disney's Pop Century Resort
20 Hilton at Walt Disney World
21 Grosvenor Resort
22 Wyndham Palace Resort & Spa
23 Doubletree Guest Suites Resort
24 Best Western at Walt Disney World
25 Hotel Royal Plaza
26 Holiday Inn in the Walt Disney World Resort
27 Hyatt Regency Grand Cypress
28 Orlando World Center Marriott
29 Embassy Suites Resort Lake Buena Vista
30 Extended Stay America Deluxe
31 Radisson Inn Lake Buena Vista
32 Staybridge Suites by Holiday Inn
33 Sheraton Vistana Resort
34 Sheraton Safari Resort
35 Holiday Inn Sunspree Resort
36 Marriott Village
37 Doubletree Club Hotel
38 Nickelodeon Family Suites
39 Lake Buena Vista Resort Village & Spa

One last group is the **Rosen Hotels & Resorts** of Florida. Four of its hotels are purely Budget-minded properties of the Choice Hotels company on I-Drive (including the Brit-popular Quality Inn Plaza and Quality Inn International), but its other two are worthy of individual note. The **Rosen Plaza Hotel** is a distinctive 800-room block with excellent resort facilities – including 2 restaurants, a pizza shop, deli, fitness centre and nightclub – and spacious, recently redecorated rooms (with 32 suites; 1800 627 8258; www.rosenplaza.com). And the spectacular 24-storey **Rosen Center Hotel** is currently their star property, opposite The Pointe Orlando, the third largest hotel in Orlando. It caters mainly for the convention trade (it is next door to the massive Convention Center), but also offers excellent facilities with its 1,334 rooms and 80 suites. It has a huge swimming grotto, tennis courts, exercise centre, 2 top-quality restaurants (including the excellent, seafood-based **Everglades**), a deli and 2 bars (1800 800 9840; www.rosencenter.com).

However, in autumn 2006 Rosen Hotels will open the grand **Shingle Creek Resort** in the middle of the Shingle Creek Golf Club, just to the east of I-Drive behind the new Convention Center. With 1,500 rooms and suites, a full-service spa and state of the art fitness centre, it promises to be a stunning and genuinely Deluxe development.

When it comes to other notable individuals in the Superior category, there are only a few non-chain properties hereabouts.

The **Nickelodeon Family Suites by Holiday Inn** (almost opposite Orlando World Center Marriott, on I-Drive South) opened in May 2005 after a major transformation from the Holiday Inn Family Suites, making for a wonderfully striking and kid-friendly holiday choice.

Characters from the Nickelodeon TV station adorn strategic points and there is plenty of live character interaction (notably at breakfast). Suites come complete with bunk or twin beds, a TV and video-console system. The existing water features were enhanced to form 2 sprawling pools with water-slides, flumes, poolside game areas and a games room. The suites feature 1, 2 and 3 bedrooms, a living room and bathroom, microwave and fridge (and full kitchen with some). The Nicktoons Café features buffet dining (plus à la carte in the evening), with 'kids eat free' at all times. There is also a food court, pool bar and grill, and the Nick@Nite Lounge. It all makes for a striking and fun (if rather raucous) holiday base in an excellent location close to Disney (1866 462 6425; www.nickhotel.com).

Other one-off suites properties worthy of note include the well-appointed **Buena Vista Suites** (1800 537 7737; www.bvsuites.com) and the eye-catching **Caribe Royale Resort** (1800 823 8300, www.caribe royale.com), both on World Center Drive just off the lower end of I-Drive. The former is the more basic type, with spacious 2-room suites, a full free breakfast, heated pool, whirlpool, tennis courts, gift shop, mini-market and the Citrus Bar and Grill. The Caribe Royale is the 5-star version, with a choice of 1-bed suites and 2-bed villas, a super pool area with water-slide, tennis courts, 2 fitness rooms and one of the best free breakfast buffets in town. Its Venetian Room is a real treat for lovers of fine continental cuisine, and there are 4 other cafés and lounges.

Nickelodeon Family Suites

Deluxe hotels

When it comes to the finest hotels, it is very much a question of individuals. All the best hotel groups are here – Hyatt Regency, Westin, Renaissance, Peabody, Ritz-Carlton and Loews – and you can be sure of a magnificent range of facilities, outstanding service and, usually, at least one 5-star restaurant. Many are also off the beaten track – away from the usual tourist frenzy but within striking distance of the parks.

A prime example of this is the **Celebration Hotel** in the Disney-inspired town of Celebration. Just off Highway 192, the Central Florida Greeneway and I-4, this unique hotel offers a refreshing small-town America style. It has an elegant lounge and two reception desks, and you are a long way from the usual tourist hurly-burly. With 115 rooms in its 1920s wood-frame design, the Celebration has a classy ambience and a wealth of high-quality touches, notably in the ultra-comfy rooms. These come in a choice of an attic-like Retreat, Traditional (with either 1 king or 2 queen-size beds), Studio or a 2-room Suite and are all beautifully furnished. Lovely artwork, courteous staff and a good array of facilities – pool, Jacuzzi and fitness centre, plus the superb Plantation Room Restaurant (excellent buffet breakfasts and a range of 'new Florida' dishes) – mark this out as a real gem. It is within a short stroll of the town's shops, restaurants and lakeside walks, and there's an inexpensive shuttle service to the parks. This member of The Kessler Collection Hotels Group (Sheraton Safari, Doubletree Castle, Sheraton Studio City, Red Horse Inn and Westin Grand Bohemian) is also ideal for a quieter or romantic stay (407 566 6000, www.celebration hotel.com).

Another Kessler Collection hotel, the **Westin Grand Bohemian**, has added a touch of class to the downtown scene. It features an early 20th-century Austrian theme, with the accent on fine art, fine dining and good service. Its 14 storeys make it a major landmark, and it boasts the wonderful **Boheme** restaurant, and one of the most stylish bars I have been to – the **Bösendorfer Lounge** – with great live entertainment nightly, plus a 14th-floor concierge suite, heated pool, spa, fitness centre, art gallery and an in-hotel Starbucks coffee lounge. The rooms are superbly appointed, with high-speed internet access, mini-bars, radio/CD players and huge interactive TVs, plus there are 36 sumptuous suites. All rooms feature the ultra-comfy Westin Heavenly Bed (407 313 9000, www.grandbohemianhotel.com).

One of the newest – and most dramatic – properties is the 1,406-room **Gaylord Palms Resort** on the junction of I-Drive South and Osceola Parkway (ideal for Disney). A cross between a convention centre and a vast turn-of-the-century Florida mansion, it features $4\frac{1}{2}$ acres (2ha) of indoor gardens, fountains and landscaped waters under a glass dome. Three intricately themed indoor areas bear witness to a great level of creativity, and the resort offers every creature comfort, with an array of restaurants and bars, an adults-only pool, family activity pool and beach (with octopus water-slide), full-service spa, children's daycare centre and a range of shops. Standard rooms are some of the smartest and most spacious in the area, while the suites are enormous, and there is even a hotel-within-a-hotel, as the central Emerald Tower offers an even more upmarket room choice and concierge facilities. One area is landscaped like the Everglades, with native plants, trees and animals; another copies the old-world charm of St Augustine – with replica Spanish fort – while the third

BRIT TIP: The Gaylord Palms features Christmas celebration, ICE!, a winter wonderland of ice sculptures, snow scenery and even an ice slide. This is a ticketed event (early Nov to Jan 2) at $18.95 for adults, $14.95 for over 55s and $8.95 for 4-12s but is well worth seeing.

BRIT TIP: For a novel attraction, don't miss Peabody's twice-daily, red-carpet Duck March, when their trademark ducks take up residence 11am–5pm in the lobby fountain.

reproduces the offbeat style of Key West, with a mock-up marina and sailboat (and a fun-themed daily **Sunset Celebration** with live entertainment) and the rooms are themed after each area. To walk into the resort's marbled lobby and cavernous interior at night is like entering a future world.

The elaborate settings add to the resort's signature fine dining, with the choice of **Old Hickory Steakhouse** (naturally aged Black Angus beef a speciality), **Sunset Sam's** (for fine seafood) and the Spanish buffet-style **Villa de Flora** (with 6 show kitchens). The Canyon Ranch Spa Club is one of the region's largest with a state-of-the-art spa, fitness facilities and beauty salon. There are 13 shops, plus the **Planet Java** coffee shop, **Auggie's Jammin' Piano Bar**, **Gaylord Yacht Bar** and the **St Augustine Piazza** (407 586 0000, www.gaylord palms.com).

Top of the range for quality on International Drive is the **Peabody Orlando**, a luxurious, 891-room tower block, with an Olympic-size pool, health club, 4 tennis courts and some superb restaurants, notably the gourmet **Dux** (jacket advisable), classy Italian **Capriccio**, and the amazing **B-Line Diner** (see page 273). Service is superb and the style is a cut above normal tourist fare –

just check out the Royal Duck Palace! Larger-than-average rooms and some huge suites add to the quality, but rates are impressive and convention business can make it hectic (407 352 4000, www.peabody orlando.com).

Universal Orlando

When Universal decided to build its own hotels, it partnered with the Loews hotel group. Consequently, it ended up with 3 of the best. They also come with a rare privilege – **Universal Express**, front-of-line access to the main attractions of both parks.

The 53-acre (21-ha), 1,000-room **Royal Pacific Resort** has an exotic South Seas feel, transporting you back to a 1930s' luxury hotel in the tropics, and you really feel as if you have stepped into another world as you cross the bamboo bridge into the elegant lobby, faced by the splendid Orchid Garden courtyard. The extensive use of rich, dark woods, cool stone floors and masses of greenery (58,000 plants and 2,500 trees) give the place an opulent, colonial feel, while the rooms and facilities are equally impressive. Standard rooms feature hand-carved Balinese furniture, among many refined touches, and there is also a Club level of accommodation, with separate lounge and extended facilities, and some superlative suites. Islands Dining Room offers breakfast, lunch and dinner in a setting of oriental simplicity

All Universal resort guests have a number of exclusive privileges: **resort ID** card (for buying food, merchandise and other items throughout Universal Orlando); **free water taxi** transport; **priority seating** at most restaurants (show your room key card); **package delivery** to your room; the chance to buy a special **Length of Stay pass** (for unlimited parks access while you are at the resort); and, most importantly, **Universal Express** no-wait access to all the rides all day just by showing your room key card. For all Universal hotels, call 407 224 7117 or go to www.universalorlando.com.

(children have their own buffet area with TV screen), while fine dining is taken to a new dimension by a magnificent restaurant run by top American chef Emeril Lagasse called **Tchoup Chop** (possibly the best in Orlando, see page 291). There is a pool snack bar and luau garden area (with the Wantilan Luau buffet on Saturdays, featuring a Polynesian feast and dinner show). The huge free-form pool is ideal for kids, with zero-depth entry at one end and a boat-shaped interactive play area of squirting fountains. Add a health club (with Jacuzzi, sauna and gym), kids' club (with computer games, TVs and organised activities), video games room and 2 shops.

The **Hard Rock Hotel** is possibly the coolest hotel in Orlando. This icon of rock chic is themed as a former rock star's home, with 650 rooms and suites in California mission style. High ceilings, wooden beams, marble floors and eclectic

The Hard Rock Hotel

artwork give an eye-catching style, with a rock-star theme to most public areas, music memorabilia, black-suited foyer staff and fairly constant music. The 14-acre (6-ha) site includes 3 bars (including the ultra-cool Velvet Bar), 2 restaurants (the full-service **The Kitchen** and the 5-star, dinner-only **Palm Restaurant**), plus a take-away café, a fitness centre, gift shop, kids' club (for the 4-14s) and games room. The lido area that is the hotel's focus is terrific, with a large, free-form pool and 240ft (73m) water-slide, two Jacuzzis, a beach and volleyball court, shuffleboard, and life-size chess and draughts. The pool even has an underwater sound system! The rooms (including 14 Kidsuites) are big, modish, beautifully furnished in the hotel's chic style and wonderfully comfortable.

The **Portofino Bay Hotel** is the jewel in Universal's crown, a splendid re-creation of the famous Italian port and a stunning resort with every facility. The elaborate porticos, genuine *trompe l'oeil*

> BRIT TIP: For some wonderful gift shopping, check out Portofino Bay's Galleria Portofino for some magnificent art and jewellery.

painting, harbourside piazza and faithful ornamentation of the waterfront make it one of the most memorable settings in Florida, and the 750 rooms are impeccably appointed, with lashings of Italian style. Standard rooms are true luxury, with huge beds, spacious bathrooms, mini-bar and coffee facilities, ironing board and hair-dryer, while the exclusive Villa rooms feature butler service and private pool. There are 18 fun Kidsuites with separate themed

KISSIMMEE ACCOMMODATION

1 Country Inn & Suites at Calypso Cay
2 Buena Vista Suites
3 Caribe Royale Resort
4 Radisson WorldGate Resort
5 Renaissance World Gate Hotel
6 Summer Bay Resort
7 Omni Orlando Resort at Champions Gate
8 Magic Castle Inn & Suites Maingate
9 Seralgo Inn Hotel & Suites Maingate East
10 Holiday Inn Maingate West
11 Holiday Inn Nikki Bird Resort
12 La Quinta Inn Lakeside
13 Celebration Hotel
14 Gaylord Palms Resort
15 Comfort Suites Maingate
16 Tropical Palms Fun Resort
17 Nickelodeon Family Suites by Holiday Inn
18 Orange Lake Resort
19 Villages at Mango Key
20 Liki Tiki Village
21 Wonderland Inn
22 Comfort Suites Resort Maingate East
23 Hampton Inn Maingate West
24 Reunion Resort
25 Hampton Inn at Maingate East
26 La Quinta Inn & Suites Orlando Maingate
27 Quality Suites Maingate East
28 Dorsan Suites
29 Wyndham Palms Resort & Country Club
30 Windsor Palms Resort

LAKE TOHOPEKALIGA

rooms that include TV, CD player, Sony Playstation and play area.

The resort facilities are equally breathtaking – a Roman aqueduct-style pool with water-slide, a completely enclosed kids' play area and wading pool, a separate quiet pool, Jacuzzis, a full (if expensive) health spa, business centre, gift shops and video games room. There is also the Campo Portofino activity centre for kids 4–14, daily 5pm–11.30pm ($10/hour for the first child, $8/hour for each additional child). The Portofino also boasts 8 restaurants and lounges, including the 5-star (and very romantic) **Bice Ristorante**, the boisterous **Trattoria del Porto**, **Mama Della's**, an authentic Italian family dining experience (watch out for Mama herself!), an aromatic deli, a pizzeria and gelateria. It is only a short boat ride from Universal, but it feels light years away in terms of its tranquil ambience.

Stepping back outside Universal, the superb **Renaissance Orlando Resort** (788 rooms on Sea Harbor Drive) is a real *Brit's Guide* favourite for its style, service and genuine hospitality. It boasts a massive 10-storey atrium lobby and some equally enormous rooms and suites, an extensive (recently remodelled) pool area with bar and grill, tennis courts, fitness centre with sauna and steam room, and kids' play areas and activities. There is even a full service spa, with the option for in-room couple's massage. It is home to one of the most romantic restaurants in town, the seafood-themed **Atlantis** (see page 288), plus a regular breakfast, lunch and dinner offering, Tradewinds, a coffee shop and a locally renowned Sunday buffet. There is a choice of bars and shops, and all rooms have recently been renovated to a high standard. The hotel offers some great packages in conjunction with SeaWorld, which is a 2-minute walk across the car park,

and their rates are often the best in the Deluxe category (1800 327 6677; www.marriott.com).

Another high-quality offering is the new golfing paradise of the **Omni Orlando Resort at Champions Gate**. With 730 rooms and suites, and overlooking a superb golf set-up with 2 Greg Norman-designed courses, this is an imposing hotel with an impressive array of facilities, including a David Leadbetter golf academy, main swimming pool and activity pool (including a 'lazy river' feature, fountains and water-slide), four restaurants (notably the superb Asian cuisine of **Zen** and the chic **David's Club** bar-restaurant), coffee bar, deli, 3 lounge bars, state-of-the-art health club and full service Spa. Just 10 minutes south of Disney and right off I-4, this is well situated yet slightly off the beaten track for those looking for something different (especially golfers). Set in 1,200 landscaped acres (486ha) and with a magnificent vista as you walk in the front doors, it suits both the business traveller and leisure-seeker alike (407 390 6662, www.omnihotels.com and www.championsgategolf.com).

The area's first genuine Deluxe resort is also still one of the very best. The **Hyatt Regency Grand Cypress** (which opened in 1984) is a mature 1,500-acre (608-ha) resort with a unique mix of facilities, including the only 9-hole pitch-and-putt golf course in town, 27 holes of regular golf (designed by Jack Nicklaus), a golf academy, boating lake and even an equestrian centre. The elegant, welcoming lobby is just the start of a wonderfully luxurious adventure, on the doorstep of Disney and yet blissfully self contained (on Winter Garden-Vineland Road, just around the corner from the Crossroads plaza at Lake Buena Vista). The 750 rooms and generous-sized suites are all beautifully furnished, but it is the amenities once you step outside the room that are so memorable. The huge free-form swimming pool, complete with Jacuzzis, waterfalls and slide, the white sand beach, health club and the magnificent array of restaurants all make for a sumptuous stay. **Cascades** is the ideal venue for a casually elegant lunch, **Hemingways** is their Key West-styled dinner venue and **La Coquina** is the specialist gourmet restaurant, with a novel Chef's Table inside the kitchen four evenings a week. There is then a sports bar and grill, three lounge bars, pool bar, a deli-style café and a general store (407 239 1234; http://grand cypress.hyatt.com).

Finally, the luxury element is taken to the full at the 500-acre (200-ha) **Grande Lakes Orlando**, a combination of a 584-room, 5-star Ritz-Carlton Hotel, a 1,000-room JW Marriott Hotel, a 40,000sq ft (3,700sq m) health spa, an 18-hole Greg Norman-designed golf course, tennis centre and a range of shops and 11 restaurants, including the outstanding **Norman's**, featuring the 'new world' cuisine of celebrity chef Norman Van Aken. Located on the edge of a forestry preserve, it feels secluded and remote – quite a feat in this area. It is slightly off the beaten tourist track – at the junction of John Young and Central Florida Parkway – yet only 2 miles (3km) from SeaWorld, 7 miles (11km) from Universal Orlando and 10 miles (16km) from Disney and Orlando International Airport.

The **Ritz-Carlton** is the first of the company's properties in central Florida, and the scale and detail are wonderful: lush gardens, abundant lakes and streams, Venetian-inspired architecture and a wealth of genuine antiques. It has a large, sloped-entry pool, kids' pool, 3 floodlit tennis courts, a signature shop and 5 restaurants, plus a separate children's check-in and the excellent Ritz Kids

Club (for 5-12s; $10/hour, $55 full day, including lunch), while all the restaurants offer child menus. The rooms are gorgeous – beautifully furnished, with high-quality products in the marbled bathrooms – and feature plasma-screen TVs, radio/CD, mini-bar, hair-dryer, slippers and robe, and all have balconies.

> BRIT TIP: Head for the Ritz-Carlton's lobby lounge for afternoon tea or drinks in style with a magnificent view, especially at sunset.

There are 66 spacious suites and 92 Club rooms on the top 2 floors, with concierge and butler service, food and drink presentations in the Club Lounge, and Bvlgari amenities. Two Kidsuites feature a separate bedroom and bathroom, with toys, games, TV and video games for great child appeal (and safety – the balcony is closed off). Other Ritz-Carlton features are their **horse-drawn carriage rides** around the vast property on Friday and Saturday ($40 for a family of 6, including hot chocolate, souvenir photo and children's gift; $60 for a couple's starlight ride, with champagne, rose and photo; and $600 for the grand romantic experience, with a private dinner under the gazebo) and outdoor concerts, with a kids' playground and a firework finale.

The **JW Marriott** is the new flagship hotel for the Marriott group, with Spanish-Moorish design, a formal Italian restaurant, French brasserie, Starbucks coffee lounge and a pool bar and grill. It also has a unique 'lazy river' mini water park (providing the largest pool deck in Florida), plus a children's zero-depth-entry pool, splash fountain and a separate kids'

INTERNATIONAL DRIVE ACCOMMODATION

1 Peabody Orlando
2 Wyndham Orlando Resort
3 Renaissance Orlando Resort
4 Sheraton Studio City
5 Red Horse Inn
6 Days Inn Lakeside
7 Holiday Inn Express
8 Quality Inn International
9 Quality Inn Plaza
10 Embassy Suites Jamaica Court
11 Howard Johnson Plaza
12 Howard Johnson Inn
13 Rosen Plaza Hotel
14 Crowne Plaza Orlando Universal
15 Enclave Suites
16 Quality Suites at Parc Corniche
17 Villager Premier
18 Staybridge Suites by Holiday Inn
19 Comfort Suites

20 The Doubletree Castle
21 Rosen Center Hotel
22 Hawthorn Suites
23 Holiday Inn & Suites at Universal
24 Best Western Plaza
25 Embassy Suites I-Drive South
26 Doubletree Hotel at Universal Orlando
27 Portofino Bay Hotel
28 Hard Rock Hotel
29 Amerisuites Convention Center
30 Sheraton World Resort
31 Extended Stay America Deluxe
32 Homewood Suites
33 Country Inn & Suites
34 Royal Pacific Resort
35 Grande Lakes Orlando
36 Holiday Inn Convention Center
37 Shingle Creek Resort & Golf Club
38 Hilton Grand Vacations Club at SeaWorld

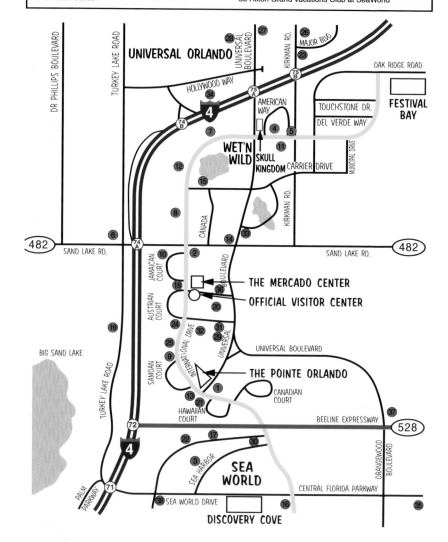

check-in. And, while the Marriott is more convention orientated, it is still well geared for families with all the facilities, a variety of shops and the option to use the Ritz Kids programme and dining options next door. Rooms are plush and ultra-comfortable, 70 per cent have balconies and there are 64 suites.

The golf course is immaculate, and every foursome is assigned a free caddie (virtually unknown for a public course in Florida). The beautiful citrus-tinged Health Spa is the best in the region, with a huge fitness centre and aerobics studio, lap pool (all free to guests at both hotels), lovely spa-cuisine restaurant and a huge array of massages and therapies. The pricing is suitably upscale, but it is a rare holiday treat (407 206 2400/2300, www.grandelakes.com).

RESORTS AND HOLIDAY HOMES

A fast-growing accommodation area in Orlando, purpose-built resorts and holiday homes, provide a valuable way for large families and groups to stay together and cut costs by self-catering. The homes, whether individual houses, collections of houses, resorts or condominiums (apartment blocks), usually have access to excellent facilities, such as pools and recreation, and are equipped with microwaves, TVs and washer-dryers. For these, a hire car is essential, but the savings are quite significant. They also defy the conventional hotel categorisation, hence they have their own section here.

Holiday resorts

This accommodation type combines the best of hotels, suites and villas, although some of the resort-style, purpose-built complexes double as timeshare resorts (or 'vacation

ownership'). A cross between condominiums and motels, they have the advantage of great in-resort facilities. They include the extensive **Orange Lake Resort** (4½ miles/7km west of Maingate on Highway 192; 1800 877 6522; www.orange lake.com) with a mixture of 2-bed, 2-bath villas and suites, golf, water sports and cinema, and the **Villages at Mango Key** (on Lindfields Boulevard, 4 miles west of Maingate; 407 397 2211; www.mangokey.com), smart, new 2- and 3-bed townhouses, with pool, Jacuzzi, tennis and volleyball.

Liki Tiki Village on the western fringe of Highway 192 is a timeshare set-up that often has good-value apartments to rent on a weekly basis. Its newest blocks offer huge 2-bed flats, with well-equipped kitchens (with coffee- and ice-makers), while the 64-acre (26-ha) complex boasts 2 pools, a mini water park, tennis courts, paddle boats, bikes, poolside bar and grill and free continental breakfast Mon–Fri when timeshare presentations are held – but you don't have to attend the timeshare hard-sell (407 239 5000, www.island one.com).

Another extensive operation is the **Sheraton Vistana Resort**, just off the lower end of I-Drive in Lake Buena Vista, where facilities include fitness centres with steam and sauna rooms, 7 pools and 13 tennis courts, basketball, volleyball and shuffleboard, games rooms, bike rental and mini-golf to back up their luxurious 1- and 2-bed villas sleeping 4 to 8 (407 238 5000, www.starwoodvo.com). The **Windsor Palms Resort** (just off West Highway 192 in Kissimmee) is

Liki Tiki Village

also popular, offering private owner-operated 3-, 4-, 5- and 6-bed pool homes and 2- and 3-bed condos with a clubhouse with gym, tennis courts, an Olympic-sized pool, a kiddie pool and spa, basketball, billiard room, playground and a 50-seat cinema showing recent films (1800 503 1127; www.windsorpalms resort.com).

The wonderful **Bahama Bay Resort**, on Lake Davenport in Kissimmee (at the west end of Highway 192, by Highway 27), opened in 2003 and is spread over 70 acres (28ha), with 498 condos (of 2 and 3 bedrooms, all with balconies) in 38 buildings, 2 and 3 storeys high. The resort-style community is woven with tropical landscaping that includes water features, a recreation centre and clubhouse, restaurant and snack bar, internet café, fitness centre, sauna and spa (the fabulous **Eleuthera Spa & Salon**), tennis, basketball and volleyball, 4 heated pools and kiddie pools. You can fish in the lake, which has a sandy beach, plus there is a video arcade and small cinema. There's a regular shuttle to the theme parks for a small charge. The 4 types of condo offer 2-bed, 2-bath (sleeping 6, with a sofa-bed in the lounge) and 3-bed, 2-bath (sleeping 8, again with sofa-bed), with fitted kitchen, laundry room/washer-dryer, living room and dining area. The Grand Bahama 3-bed condo boasts 1,739sq ft (162sq m) of space and is one of the most elegant (call 001 44 0870 160 9632 in the UK, or visit www.bahamabay.com).

The **Summer Bay Resort** (also on West Highway 192) is a mixture of Budget motel (The Inn at Summer Bay), Standard hotel (an award-winning Holiday Inn Express), some 3-bed vacation homes and new 1-, 2- and 3-bed villas and condos. The 700 rooms, spread over 64 acres (26ha) are smart enough, plus the facilities include outdoor, heated pools and kiddie pools, an elaborate children's water-play area, mini-golf, clubhouse with volleyball, tennis, basketball, shuffleboard and fitness room, video arcade, gift shop and snack bar. The lake provides jet-skis, paddle boats, water-skiing and more, plus daily kids' activities and organised sports. Even those in The Inn and Holiday Inn (which has its own pool deck and breakfast area) benefit from the clubhouse facilities, while there is a Denny's diner and Publix supermarket next door. It represents amazing value at the budget end, and wonderful accommodation in the condos, and is still only 15 minutes from Disney (1800 654 6102, www.summerbayresort.com).

The **Lake Buena Vista Resort Village & Spa** opens in 2006 with the first of what will be 14 blocks of stylish 2-, 3- and 4-bed condos, right next to Lake Buena Vista Factory Stores on Highway 535. A sneak preview in summer 2005 revealed a hugely impressive set-up of resort accommodations – all with full kitchens, Jacuzzi tubs, digital TVs and internet available. The completed Village will feature 4 pools, whirlpools, children's play areas, tennis courts, club-house, fitness centre and full-service spa, plus restaurants, pubs and shops. It should be a luxurious proposition when open, but check www.lbvresort village.com in the meantime.

The final option is arguably the grandest, the **Reunion Resort and Club**, of keen interest to golfers and all who appreciate the 5-star touch. On Highway 532 in Kissimmee, just off Exit 58 of I-4 south of Disney (the exit for Champions Gate), this fledgling 'community' will boast 8,000 units when complete, with hotels, condos and luxury homes set around 3 superb golf courses (designed by Arnold Palmer, Tom Watson and Jack Nicklaus). There will be an area of restaurants and shops, a water park, riding stables, swimming pools and other recreation, while every unit will have room service, personal concierge (for dining, tee times, stocking the fridge, etc) and airport escort. The homes range from modest 3-beds to grand 8-beds (costing more than $750,000), but all are available for rent (and some for sale). The condos vary from 1- to 3-bed, 2-bath apartments, all immaculately furnished and with stunning views over the golf courses. Much is still to be finished in the next 2 years, but the golf courses are working, plus an array of condos and homes. Only those who stay here can play on the courses, but the scale and imagination of the resort make it quite awesome (1877 738 6466, www.reunionresort.com).

Holiday homes

Vacation homes to rent are big business in central Florida and now account for a huge slice of the British market as they are ideal for repeat visitors, large groups and those who like their own privacy and facilities. They tend to be grouped in newly built estates and several are 'gated' communities for added security. Nearly all offer a private pool and the largest can sleep up to 16. Some are classed as executive homes, and this usually means more facilities (DVD, games consoles, barbecues, etc) rather than any increase in size. If you're booking independently, there are several key questions to ask before you book:

Do you need to go to an office some way away to pick up the keys or do they have a combination-lock box at the house? Is there a local contact if anything goes wrong (some owners do not live in Florida) or is the property maintained by an on-the-spot company? Do they offer a security bonding for your cash

booking, and are they members of a reputable organisation like the Better Business Bureau of Central Florida? If it's winter, is the pool heated, and how much do they charge for heating? Finally, are they as close to Disney as they say – some homes can be down in Polk County, 30–40 minutes' drive away. One final warning – once you have sampled pool-at-home life, you may never go back to a hotel!

The bottom line is you need to do your homework and shop around as you would for any significant purchase, and check with organisations like the Central Florida Property Managers' Association (www.cfpma.com). The following all pass the *Brit's Guide* credibility test.

Welcome Homes USA has condos, villas and private homes to rent in the Kissimmee area, with some smart properties at a broad range of prices. Its houses (3- to 5-beds) come with communal or private pools. Homes are only 10-15 minutes' drive from Disney in residential areas and feature everything from dishwashers to spoons (1800 818 4552, www.welcomehomesusa.com).

For similar great value and excellent properties, family-owned (since 1981) **Alexander Holiday Homes**, also in Kissimmee, manages 260 properties, from standard condo villas to luxury executive homes sleeping up to 10, all with pools and immaculately furnished, within 15 minutes of Disney. This company was the first of its kind in Orlando, and still offers a highly personable, efficient service. It was only the third management company in Florida to earn a lofty AAA rating (the American Automobile Association) and definitely gets a *Brit's Guide* recommendation. It also shows prices in UK and US currency and even offers an airport meet-and-greet service to ensure you get to your home OK. Its website is full of useful area info, as well as providing photo tours of all its homes (1800 621 7888 in the US, 0871 711 5371 in the UK; www.floridasun shine.com).

Premier Vacation Homes offers a good range of spacious properties with 2-6 beds, sleeping up to 14, in secure residential communities within a 15-minute drive of Disney. The homes are privately owned and have been purchased and furnished as vacation homes, with screened pools, 2 TVs, fully equipped kitchens (including dishwasher, washer-dryer, microwave and coffee-maker), at least 1 king or queen bed, and free local phone calls. Maid service can be added for a fee. The **Luxury** homes (2-4 beds) are the standard accommodation, while **Executive** homes (3-6 beds) are bigger, with an extra TV, VCR and a gas barbecue (407 396 2401, or 0500 892 634 in the UK, www.premier-vacation-homes.com).

Another company we know well and can highly recommend is British-owned **Florida Leisure**, which pays great attention to detail. With almost 100 homes (2-7 beds) in the Kissimmee area (most just 2-3 years old) for rent, it prides itself on a personal touch and offers some of the biggest and newest properties. Many are in the Executive range, with the fullest range of amenities in

BRIT TIP: You'll find Marmite, Ribena, McVitie's, etc, at the Publix supermarkets on Highway 192, or the 24-hour Goodings stores at Crossroads and on I-Drive.

addition to their private, screened pools, and often in a secure, gated community. You can see them all online (in photo and video) plus lots of local info, especially for restaurants and golf. Its handy office is in Lake Buena Vista Factory Stores (407 870 1600; www.florida leisure.com).

An alternative, UK-based company is **Sun Villas Florida Direct**, launched in September 2001 by a former managing director of Lunn Poly to provide a bespoke holiday offering villa accommodation, flights, attraction tickets and car hire. It has a variety of properties from Orlando down to Sarasota and Naples, and maintains consistently high standards (01926 336 611; www.SVFDirect.com).

ResortQuest is a relatively new name here, but not a new company. The former Advantage Vacation Homes is now part of a nationwide umbrella providing a growing list of properties throughout Florida. None of its 2-6 bed homes (the majority on West Highway 192 and Highway 27 in Clermont and Davenport) is more than 5 years old, while many are 2–3 years at most. It also manages an increasing portfolio of condos (in the Bahama Bay and SunLake Resorts), with a big new development under way next to its offices on West Highway 192. It offers 24-hour management, with a courteous and efficient staff (plus an attraction ticket service), open 9am–10pm daily. Its holiday homes are rated Bronze, Silver, Gold or

The Bahama Bay Resort

RENTAL ACCOMMODATION

1 Cumbrian Lakes
2 Eagle Pointe
3 Indian Pointe
4 Country Creek
5 Bass Lake Estates
6 Lake Berkley Reserve
7 Four Winds Estates
8 Montego Bay
9 Chatham Park
10 Hamilton's Reserve
11 Indian Wells
12 Buena Ventura Lake
13 Hunters Creek
14 Oak Island
15 Formosa Gardens
16 Indian Creek
17 Rolling Hills
18 Windsor Palms
19 Indian Ridge
20 Lindfields
21 Sunset Lakes
22 Emerald Isle
23 Polo Park
24 Fairways Lake
25 Davenport Lakes
26 Bass Lake
27 Lake Davenport Estates
28 Magnolia Glen
29 Bahama Bay Resort
30 Wellington Reserve
31 Highlands Reserve
32 Westridge
33 Hampton Estates
34 Florida Pines
35 Calabay Parc
36 Village at Tuscan Ridge
37 Santa Cruz
38 Loma Del Sol
39 Loma Vista
40 West Haven
41 Happy Trails
42 Omni Orlando Resort at
   Champions Gate
43 Gibson Park
44 Bentley Oaks
45 Bridgewater Crossing
46 Sunridge Woods
47 Reunion Resort
48 Pinewood Country Estates
49 Thousand Oaks

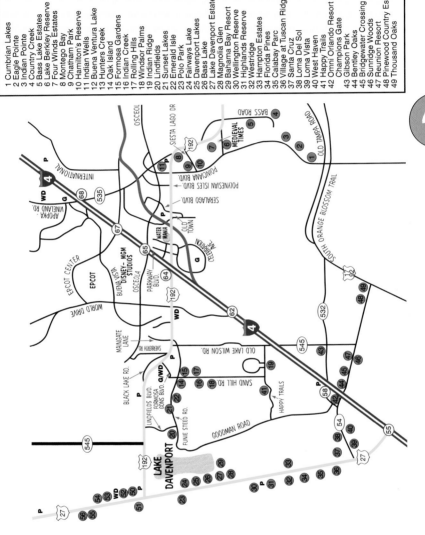

Platinum, with the difference in quality measured in the extras rather than size or facilities (larger-screen or plasma TVs, tiled floors rather than carpeting and perhaps a Jacuzzi). All include private, screened pools, fully equipped kitchens, hair-dryer, iron/ironing board, washer-dryers and the usual supply of linens and kitchen equipment. A typical 3-bed home would comfortably cater for 6-8, while the largest house sleeps 12 in style.

Its newest properties on Highway 27 usually have communal playgrounds and tennis courts. Extra options include gift baskets, daily or mid-stay cleaning, welcome food pack and airport meet-and-greet (1800 527 2262, www.resort quest.com). Finally, **Florida Choice Vacation Homes** provides townhouses (3-4 beds with communal pools and recreation facilities), standard and executive homes (3-7 bed private properties), some with heated pools and with free local phone calls. There is optional maid service and cot and highchair rentals (407 847 0284, www.floridachoice.com).

Bed and breakfast

Bed and breakfast in Orlando is offered in a more upscale, almost boutique style. Principle among them is the **Wonderland Inn** in Kissimmee, an 11-room, restored Historic Registry property off the beaten track but only 10 minutes from the Highway 192 area. Each room has a delightful, individual touch, and several are designed for singles as well as doubles, plus one honeymoon suite. The staff are wonderfully attentive and even the lovely gardens have an old-fashioned charm light-years from the hectic tourist whirl. It also offers a 4-course Romantic Candlelight Dinner

served in the gazebo (weather permitting) and a Romantic Getaway Package that includes a 3-hour limo service, dinner, breakfast in bed, a massage or two, champagne and chocolates (1877 847 2477, www.wonderlandinn.com).

The pretty Lake Eola district downtown has two fine B&Bs. **The Veranda** has 12 intimate, cottage-style rooms, ranging from Queen Studio and King Suites to a lovely honeymoon suite in landscaped gardens with a private courtyard, pool and spa area. Breakfast consists of fresh pastries, seasonal fruits, juices, tea and coffee, and it's a quiet spot, although it's an easy walk to some good restaurants and shops (1800 420 6822; www.theveranda bandb.com). The nearby **Eo Inn** is a genuine boutique hotel and spa (with a huge range of treatments), featuring 17 deluxe rooms. The lush grounds, rooftop terrace and lake vistas provide a refreshing alternative to the hotel experience (407 481 8485, www.eoinn.com).

BUYING A HOLIDAY HOME

The quality of life, the favourable exchange rate and fabulous weather are all compelling reasons to consider acquiring your own vacation home, for holidays, investment, a winter retreat or as a retirement home. But, apart from the fact it is easy to be starry-eyed on holiday, there are companies willing to exploit naive tourists. Therefore, you need to do your homework, especially to understand the terminology of US property buying.

If you have looked in the window of a realtor (a US estate agent), you will have seen the tempting price differential compared with the UK. In the third quarter of 2004, the average price of a single family home in Florida rose by more than 8 per cent (to top $150,000) on the same period in 2003, making the idea even more alluring. New homes are all the rage (in fact, they can't build them fast enough) but this also means the quality varies, so you need to find a proven builder. **Greater Homes of Orlando** (407 869 0300, www.greaterhomes.com) has an unimpeachable reputation and gets full *Brit's Guide* approval. It is a family-run company that has been building here since 1965 and has sold almost 3,000 homes to British owners. It is a reliable and quality-conscious firm and its website carries essential info for anyone considering buying here (including mortgage terminologies). Its latest development, **Eagle Creek**, is a golf-community collaboration with British builder Jones Homes about 10 minutes from Orlando International airport with prices from $310,000. The highest recommendation we can offer is we bought a Greater Home in 2004 and could not be more satisfied with our purchase, the ease with which it was conducted and the after-sales care.

You will also find useful info on the **Alexander Holiday Homes** site (www.floridasunshine.com) and the Real Estate links on **Florida Leisure** (www.floridaleisure.com), a registered realtor that publishes a free Home Buying Guide, available from its website.

Other builders worth considering are **Beazer Homes** and **KB Homes**, both rated well above average for build quality. Owning a piece of the

BRIT TIP: Florida Leisure has a cruise booking agency, Cruise Planners, so if you fancy a week in Orlando and a week at sea (highly recommended), visit www.gocruiseplanner.com.

magic is tempting, but you must get all the facts first, then look for a company that specialises in selling to British buyers. A dozen or so firms primarily offer vacation-style properties, and several deal mainly with British buyers. Consider investigating one of the firms that allows you to fund your mortgage in sterling, through a UK bank, rather than the dollar equivalent. If you live in the UK and are paid in sterling, a US dollar mortgage can be costly and inconvenient. For instance, US mortgage companies often 'sell' new mortgages to another lender after closing a loan, making it hard to track. Repayment of a dollar mortgage with sterling is also subject to changing exchange rates. Two publications to note are *International Homes* and *Homes Overseas*, which both have Florida sections.

In this instance, one company we have come to know well through our contacts with the British-American Chamber of Commerce, and whom we have been happy to recommend for several years now, is the **British Homes Group Florida**. When we first met its team a few years back, it had just completed a market test in Orlando of a new British currency mortgage designed specifically for UK residents buying investment properties in Florida. The test was a great success and British currency mortgages are now available to UK buyers *anywhere* in the Sunshine State, from Orlando to Miami, Kissimmee to Naples.

This innovative mortgage programme, called *British Mortgages Abroad*, was developed in collaboration with Abbey National and is now offered by the British subsidiary of GE though the British Homes Group. It allows Brits to purchase buy-to-let villas and second homes using the Florida property (rather than the buyer's UK home) as security for a pound denominated mortgage, thus avoiding monthly payment currency exchange risk. Recognising the seasonality of rental income in Orlando, these UK mortgages also allow UK borrowers up to 6 payment 'holidays' in any one year (usually plenty of time to sell a villa if necessary), which takes much of the risk out of buying income properties in Florida.

British Home Loans Florida, the Group's fully licensed Florida mortgage brokerage company, also offers a broad selection of US dollar mortgages for UK buyers preferring to keep all their Florida transactions in US currency. The British Homes staff of British and American real estate and mortgage experts can also determine which is the best loan for you (with no obligation). British Home Sales Florida, the Group's estate agency (realtor), can search and find the ideal property for you anywhere in the state, with access to more than 20,000 properties in Central Florida alone. Try it for yourself for free by visiting www.BritishHomesGroup.com).

Mention the *Brits Guide* and you may even be offered one of its 'specials,' such as a free home valuation if you purchase a villa or arrange a UK or US currency mortgage through them. Call (in Florida) 407 396 9914, or (in the UK) 0800 096 5989 (24 hours), visit its website or its offices in Orlando at 2960 Vineland Road, Kissimmee (above the Edwin Watts golf shop at the T-junction of Routes 535/192).

But, whoever you go with, ensure they can refer you to experts in UK and US taxation, immigration, hazard insurance, structural warranties and other areas essential to hassle-free home-ownership in Florida. Property in Orlando has increased in value by 10-12 per cent over the last 10 years, but there is never any guarantee, and rates can fluctuate.

Bob's Buying Tips

Bob Mandell (Chairman of Greater Homes) offers these essential tips for anyone looking to buy a holiday home – from his company or anyone else:
1 Get references from UK owners and check management company references.
2 Look up the Better Business Bureau for Central Florida.
3 Ensure the product has a warranty.
4 Walk through the community and talk to people there.
5 Ensure the documentation allows you to let it on a short-term basis.
6 Make sure you have all the proper US fees, registrations and taxes.

A typical holiday pool-home

5

The Theme Parks – Disney's Fab Four

(or, Spending the Day with Mickey Mouse and Co.)

By now you should be prepared to deal with the main business of any visit to Orlando: *Walt Disney World Resort in Florida* and the other main theme parks of Universal Orlando, SeaWorld and Busch Gardens.

If you have only a week, this is where you should concentrate your attention but even then you may decide Busch Gardens is a bridge too far. If you have less than a week, you should focus on seeing as much of *Walt Disney World Resort* as possible. There is SO much packed into every park and the main tourist areas, even 2 weeks is scarcely enough to give first-timers more than an outline of central Florida.

> BRIT TIP: Offers of 'Free' Disney tickets usually means timeshare firms, who also have several 'official' visitor centres. I-Drive has the *only* genuinely Official Visitor Center.

Buying your tickets in advance is highly advisable, but work out your requirements first – you wouldn't get full use out of, say, a 7-Day Premium ticket AND a 5-Park Orlando FlexTicket in just a 2-week holiday. There are so many ticket outlets these days, you need to check what measure of security they offer (ABTA bonding, etc) and what they do in case of lost or stolen tickets

during shipping. Try to use your credit card for all purchases – there is built-in additional security (for our list of recommended ticket outlets, see page 13). You will also find **discount coupons** in tourist publications distributed in Orlando for many of the smaller attractions (or from the Guest Services desk at your hotel – it's worth asking), while the **tour operators'** welcome meetings usually have special offers and tickets for the latest excursions.

The **Official Visitor Center** at 8723 International Drive (in the Gala Center on the corner of Austrian Row; 407 363 5871, www.orlandoinfo.com; see map on page 81) is also worth checking out for discounts. Equally, the Universal Attractions booths at several shopping malls (notably Orlando Premium Outlets) have great deals (3 days for the price of 2, 2-for-1 drinks, etc) on many attractions. It IS possible to bag free tickets by attending timeshare presentations,

The Jungle Cruise

© Disney

but they can easily take half a day of your precious holiday. Other sites worth visiting for discounts, etc, are the *Orlando Sentinel*'s info-based www.go2orlando.com, www.orlando savings.com and www.orlando. floridacouponsavings.com for free coupons.

Ratings

We judge all the rides and shows on a unique rating system that splits them into **thrill rides** and **scenic rides**. Thrill rides earn T ratings out of five (hence a TTTTT is as exciting as they get) and scenic rides get A ratings out of five (an AA ride is likely to be over-cute and missable). Obviously, it is a matter of opinion to a certain extent, but you can be sure a T or A ride is not worth your time, a TT or AA is worth seeing only if there is no queue, a TTT or AAA should be seen if you have time, but you won't miss much if you don't, a TTTT or AAAA ride is a big-time attraction that should be high on your list of things to do, and finally a TTTTT or AAAAA attraction should not be missed! The latter will have the longest queues, so you should plan your visit around them. Some rides have height restrictions and are not advisable for people with back, neck or heart problems, or expectant mothers. Where this is the case we say 'Restrictions: 3ft 6in/106cm', and so on. Height restrictions

BRIT TIP: If you DO want to check out timeshare options, look first at Disney Vacation Club for the guaranteed way to secure memorable holidays. Call 407 566 3300 or visit http://dvc.disney.go.com/dvc.

(strictly enforced) are based on the average 5-year-old being 3ft 6in/106cm tall, 6s being 3ft 9in/114cm and 9s being 4ft 4in/132cm.

Disney's FASTPASS Service

Another essential aid to queuing is **Disney's FASTPASS Service**. Most of the parks' main attractions have this wonderful service that allows you to roam while you wait for an allotted time to ride. How it works: insert your main park entrance ticket into the FASTPASS (FP) turnstile (to the side of the attraction's entrance) and you get another ticket giving you a period of time in which to return for your ride with only a minimal wait (NB: you need one FP ticket for every person who wants to ride, not just one per group). You can hold only one FP ticket per 2-hour period, although once you've used it you can get another. If you start by going to one of the FP rides, collecting your ticket and returning later, you can by-pass a lot of standing in line. You can also get another FP as soon as your 'window' opens: if your time slot for Space Mountain in Magic Kingdom Park is 10–11am, you could get another FP for, say, Buzz Lightyear's Space Ranger Spin at 10.05am and then go and ride Space Mountain! Many people still miss this, but it is FREE (FASTPASS rides are indicated by FP in attraction descriptions).

With Young Ones

All Disney's parks offer pushchair rental, and you can save 10 per cent by purchasing a multi-day rental at your first park. Then, show your ticket each time at the rental counter and avoid the queue. Return your receipt at the end of the holiday for a $1 refund. Children of ALL ages seem to get a big thrill from

BRIT TIP: Purchase a lanyard for your park tickets if you plan to use FastPass often. This keeps your tickets together and easily accessible.

collecting autographs from the various Disney characters, and most shops sell handy **autograph books** for this purpose.

Pal Mickey

If you want the ultimate theme park friend, to help you queue, offer tips, play games and help find the characters, just ask Mickey – Pal Mickey, that is. This is a high-tech 10½-in (27cm) tall cuddly toy that talks to you (using wireless communication around the parks) as a kind of tour guide, with hints (e.g. in *Disney-MGM Studios:* 'Fantasmic! will be starting in about an hour'), insider info (on Main Street USA: 'See the names written on those second-storey windows? Those folks helped Walt build his *Magic Kingdom!*') and interactive games while you queue (and that still work when you get back home). Sounds fun? Wait for the price – Pal Mickey costs a whopping $65.

Cast Members

Disney Cast Members (or CMs) are renowned for their helpful and cheerful style and are always willing to assist, offer advice or just stop and chat. Interaction with CMs often provides some of the best memories of a visit. So, if you've had exceptional service or a CM has gone out of their way to help you, let Disney know as they value such feedback (and CMs get credit for it, too). Call in at Guest Relations on your way out (or City Hall at the *Magic Kingdom* Park) and record your vote of thanks.

Child swap

Where families have small children, but Mum and Dad both want to try a ride, you DON'T have to queue twice. When you get to the front of the queue, tell the operator you want to do a 'child swap'. This means Mum can ride while Dad looks after junior and, on her return, Dad can have his go.

Happiest Celebration On Earth

May 2005 saw the launch of the 50th anniversary of *Disneyland Resort in California* in Anaheim, Los Angeles, Walt's original theme park, and to celebrate, every Disney park around the world joined *The Happiest Celebration on Earth*. The Florida parks are no exception, with an **18-month festival**, lasting until October 2006, and a host of new elements throughout. In the *Magic Kingdom* Park, look out for **Cinderellabration**, a lively stage show from *Disneyland Tokyo*; *Epcot* has the amazing **Soarin'** ride from *Disneyland California*; *Disney-MGM Studios* now has **Lights, Motors, Action!™ Extreme Stunt Show**, the sensational stunt show from *Disneyland Paris*; and *Disney's Animal Kingdom* will boast **Expedition Everest™** as arguably THE great new ride (from April 2006).

5

BRIT TIP: Smoking is not permitted in the parks, apart from a handful of designated areas. Check park maps for exact locations. All restaurants are strictly non-smoking.

Character dining

Having a meal with Mickey and Co. (or Winnie the Pooh, or Cinderella or Mary Poppins) is one of the great Disney experiences – even if you don't have children! It is also often the best way to meet your favourite characters without long, hot waits. All reservations can be arranged up to 90 days in advance by phoning 407 WDW DINE (939 3463), calling at any Guest Services desk, or by touching *55 on a Disney resort phone.

Some meals are difficult to get. **Cinderella's Royal Table** at the *Magic Kingdom* sells out 90 days in advance, within the first few minutes. **Chef Mickey's** and the **Princess Storybook** meals also go quickly. If you cannot book in advance, try calling the day you'd like to dine or, as a last resort, show up to see if there have been any cancellations. You must check in at the podium 5 minutes prior to your time and you will be given the next available table. Some characters don't enter the restaurant so, if they are in the lobby, you'll want to meet them before you are seated. Dining is all-you-can-eat, served buffet, pre-plated or family-style.

Inside the restaurant, characters circulate among the tables giving attention to each group (particularly when children are holding the camera!). Character interaction is top-notch, especially if you dine off-hours when the restaurant is slower. Be sure to bring your autograph book, a fat pen or marker (easier for the characters to hold) and plenty of film or an extra digital card for your camera. Some characters are huge, and children may be put off by them. If you aren't sure how they'll react, see how they are with the characters in the park before booking a character meal. **Price range:** breakfast $16.99–19.99 for adults, $8.99–9.99 for children; lunch $17.99–19.99 and $9.29–9.99; dinner $21.99–25.00 and $9.99–10.99.

The meals

Magic Kingdom: **Crystal Palace** (breakfast, lunch or dinner with Winnie the Pooh Tigger, Eeyore and Piglet – especially good for smaller children); **Cinderella's Royal Table** (for the Once Upon a Time Breakfast, with Cinderella, Fairy Godmother, Belle, Jasmine and Snow White, and Fairytale Lunch. Credit card needed to book, $10/$5 charged for no-shows); **Liberty Tree Tavern** (dinner with Chip 'n' Dale, Meeko, Minnie and Pluto).

Epcot: **Garden Grill** (lunch or dinner with Farmer Mickey, Pluto, Chip 'n' Dale); **Princess Storybook Dining** (breakfast, lunch and dinner; an alternative to Cinderella's, with some of Belle, Jasmine, Snow White, Pocahontas, Mulan, Sleeping Beauty and Mary Poppins but NOT Cinderella. Credit card needed to book, $10/$5 charged for no-shows).

Disney's Animal Kingdom: **Donald's Restaurantosaurus** (breakfast with Donald, Goofy, Pluto and sometimes Mickey).

Disney Resorts: **Chef Mickey's** (Contemporary Resort; breakfast or dinner with Mickey, Minnie, Goofy, Pluto, Chip 'n' Dale – peak times book up quickly); **1900 Park Fare** (Grand Floridian Resort and Spa; breakfast with Alice and her Wonderland Friends, dinner with Cinderella, Perla, Suzy, Fairy Godmother and, sometimes, Prince Charming – again, book early); **Wonderland Tea Party** (Grand Floridian Resort and Spa; 1.30–2.30pm Mon–Fri, 3–10s only, $28.17, lunch, activities and storytelling with Alice and friends); **'Ohana** (Polynesian Resort; breakfast with Mickey, Minnie, and Chip 'n' Dale); **Cape May Café** (Beach Club Resort; breakfast with Goofy, Chip 'n' Dale and Pluto); **Mickey's Backyard Barbecue** (Fort Wilderness; $39 and $25, games, storytelling, live entertainment, music and dancing with Mickey and Co; unlimited beer, wine, iced tea and lemonade – seasonal); **Walt Disney World Swan** (Garden Grove Café; Sat breakfast with Goofy and Pluto. Gulliver's Grill; 6pm dinner with Timon and Rafiki Mon–Fri, Goofy and Pluto Sat and Sun).

Magic Kingdom Park

The starting point for any visit has to be the *Magic Kingdom*, the park that best embodies the genuine enchantment Disney bestows on its visitors. It's the original development that sparked the tourist boom in Orlando back in 1971. In comparative terms, the *Magic Kingdom Park* is similar to the *Disneyland Park* at *Disneyland Resort Paris* and *Disneyland California*. Outside those, it has no equal as a captivating day out for all the family. However, although superficially some rides are the same as those in Paris or Los Angeles, there are key

> BRIT TIP: For the smoothest entry by road from West Highway 192, take Seralago Boulevard opposite the Holiday Inn Hotel & Suites next to Old Town, turn left on to a non-toll stretch of Osceola Parkway and follow the signs to your chosen park. On East 192, turn off on Sherberth Road, go north to the first traffic lights and turn right, then pick up the Disney signs.

differences, notably on Pirates of the Caribbean, Big Thunder Mountain Railroad and the Haunted Mansion. And Space Mountain is a completely different ride from Paris.

We will now attempt to steer you through a typical day at the park, with a guide to the main rides, shows and places to eat, how to park, how to avoid the worst of the crowds and

how much you should expect to pay.

The *Magic Kingdom* takes up just 107 acres (43ha) of Disney's near 31,000 acres (12,555ha) but attracts almost as many visitors as the rest put together. It has 7 separate 'lands', like slices of a large cake, centred on Florida's most famous landmark, Cinderella Castle. More than 40 attractions are packed into the park, not to mention numerous shops and restaurants (although the eating opportunities are less impressive than in *Epcot* and *Disney-MGM Studios*).

It's easy to get overwhelmed by it all, especially as it gets so busy (even the fast-food restaurants have big queues in high season), so study the notes and plan your visit around what most takes your fancy.

Location

The *Magic Kingdom Park* is situated at the innermost end of the vacation kingdom, with its entrance Toll Plaza three-quarters of the way along World Drive, the main entrance road off Highway 192. World Drive runs north–south through *Walt Disney World*, while the Interstate 4 (I-4) entrance, Epcot Drive, runs east–west. Unless you are staying at a Disney resort, you have to pay the $8 parking fee at the Toll Plaza and that brings you to the massive car park.

Cinderella's Golden Carousel

© Disney

5

The Magic Kingdom Park at a glance

Location	Off World Drive, Walt Disney World
Size	107 acres (43ha) in 7 'lands'
Hours	9am–7pm off peak; 9am–10pm Washington's birthday (see page 19), spring school holidays; 9am–11pm high season (Easter, summer holidays, Thanksgiving and Christmas)
Admission	Under 3 free; 3–9 $48 (1-day base ticket), $155 (5-Day Premium), $196 (7-Day Premium); adult (10+) $59.73, $193, $233. Prices do not include tax.
Parking	$8
Lockers	Yes; under Main Street Railroad Station; $7 ($2 refund)
Pushchairs	$10 and $18 (Stroller Shop to right of main entrance); $8 and $16/day for Length of Stay
Wheelchairs	$10 ($1 deposit refunded) or $35 ($10 deposit refunded) (Main Ticket Centre or Stroller Shop)
Top Attractions	Splash Mountain, Space Mountain, Mickey's PhilharMagic, Big Thunder Mountain Railroad, Pirates of the Caribbean, most rides in Fantasyland
Don't Miss	Share A Dream Come True Parade, SpectroMagic Parade (certain nights) and Wishes fireworks (certain nights)
Hidden Costs	**Meals** — Burger, chips and coke $7.78 / 3-course dinner $35 (Cinderella's Table) / Kids' meal $3.99
	T-shirts — $19–28
	Souvenirs — $1–350
	Sundries — Spray fan (handy when it's hot) $15.96, or Silhouettes: $7; with oval frame $13.95

The majority arrive between 9.30 and 11.30am, so the car parks are busiest then, which is another good reason to get here EARLY. If you can't make it by 9am during peak periods, you might want to wait until after 1pm, or even later when the park is open as late as 11pm. Remember to note on your parking ticket exactly what area you parked in and the row number, e.g. Mickey, Row 30. You will struggle to remember otherwise, and all hire cars look the same!

A motorised tram takes you from the car park to the Transportation and Ticket Center at the heart of the operation. Unless you already have your ticket (which will save you valuable time), you have to queue up at the ticket booths. From here, the monorail or a ferryboat will bring you to the doorstep of the *Magic Kingdom* itself. The monorail (straight ahead) is quicker, if there isn't a queue, otherwise bear left and take a slower ferryboat. If you are staying at a Disney hotel, the resort buses deliver you almost to the park's front door (or the monorail or boat will if you are staying at one of the *Magic Kingdom* resorts).

Finally, the *Magic Kingdom* is the only 'dry' park, i.e. there is no alcohol on sale. You may also find one or two attractions closed for refurbishment, but you will never be short of things to do!

Main Street USA

Right, we've finally reached the park itself… but not quite. Hopefully you've arrived early and are among the leading hordes aiming to swarm through the main entrance. The published opening time may say 9am, but the gates *can* open up to 45 minutes earlier.

You will find yourself in **Main Street USA**, the first of the seven 'lands'. At opening time, there is an informal Welcome Parade, with costumed singers and dancers, and the Character Train then arrives at Main Street Station to bring a variety of characters for a friendly meet-and-greet in Town Square (get those autograph books ready!). A family is then chosen at random to sprinkle some 'pixie dust' to open the park officially for the day. Immediately on your right is

BRIT TIP: Reader Roy Williams says: 'We bought a bright, 3-in plastic ball that we fixed to our car aerial in the car park, enabling us to find it easily on our return.' You could also leave a familiar, non-valuable item in the window for extra help. Visit www.aerialbuddies.co.uk for a selection of fun aerial accessories!

Exposition Hall, a photographic centre featuring archive film material, interactive games, a mini cinema showing Disney classics and some cartoon photo opportunities. On your left is **City Hall**, where you can pick up a park map and daily schedule (if you haven't been given them at the Toll Plaza) and make bookings for the restaurants (highly advisable at peak periods). You can also find out where the characters will appear and when. Ahead of you is **Town Square**, where you can take a one-way ride on a horse-drawn bus or fire engine and visit the **Car Barn** mini museum. The Street itself houses the park's best shopping (check out the massive Emporium), plus the **Walt Disney World Railroad** (AAA), a Western-themed steam train that circles the park and is one of the better attractions when the queues are long elsewhere (although Town Square station is also the busiest).

BRIT TIP: Save paying up to three times more for your drinks by bringing your own bottled water in a backpack to all the parks and use the many drinking fountains for refills.

For dining, the Italian-style **Tony's Town Square Restaurant** serves lunch and dinner, **The Plaza Restaurant** offers salads and sandwiches (lunch and dinner), and **The Crystal Palace** (breakfast, lunch and dinner) is buffet-style food with Winnie the Pooh, Tigger and Co. Quick bites can be bought from **Casey's Corner** (hot dogs, chips and soft drinks), **Main Street Bakery** (coffee and pastries), **Main Street Cinema** and **Main Street Confectionary** (chocolate and sweets) and the **Plaza Ice Cream Parlor**. Disney characters also appear

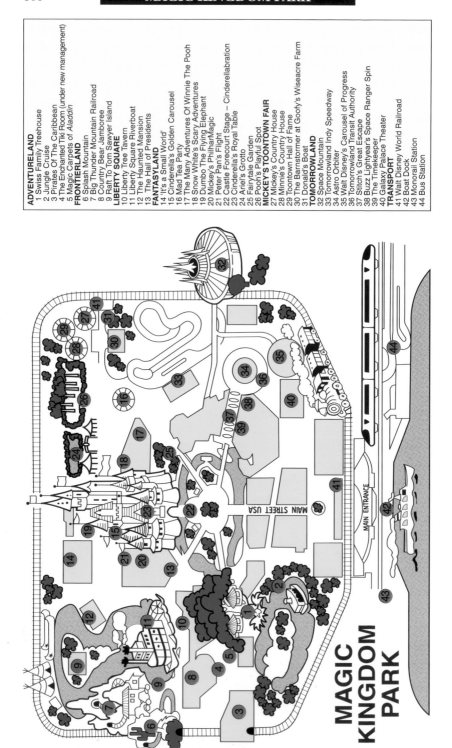

ADVENTURELAND
1 Swiss Family Treehouse
2 Jungle Cruise
3 Pirates Of The Caribbean
4 The Enchanted Tiki Room (under new management)
5 Magic Carpets of *Aladdin*

FRONTIERLAND
6 Splash Mountain
7 Big Thunder Mountain Railroad
8 Country Bear Jamboree
9 Raft To Tom Sawyer Island

LIBERTY SQUARE
10 Liberty Tree Tavern
11 Liberty Square Riverboat
12 The Haunted Mansion
13 The Hall of Presidents

FANTASYLAND
14 'It's a Small World'
15 Cinderella's Golden Carousel
16 Mad Tea Party
17 The Many Adventures Of Winnie The Pooh
18 Snow White's Scary Adventures
19 Dumbo The Flying Elephant
20 Mickey's PhilharMagic
21 Peter Pan's Flight
22 Castle Forecourt Stage – Cinderellabration
23 Cinderella's Royal Table
24 Ariel's Grotto
25 Fairytale Garden
26 Pooh's Playful Spot

MICKEY'S TOONTOWN FAIR
27 Mickey's Country House
28 Minnie's Country House
29 Toontown Hall of Fame
30 The Barnstormer at Goofy's Wiseacre Farm
31 Donald's Boat

TOMORROWLAND
32 Space Mountain
33 Tomorrowland Indy Speedway
34 Astro Orbiter
35 Walt Disney's Carousel of Progress
36 Tomorrowland Transit Authority
37 Stitch's Great Escape
38 Buzz Lightyear's Space Ranger Spin
39 The Timekeeper
40 Galaxy Palace Theater

TRANSPORT
41 Walt Disney World Railroad
42 Boat Dock
43 Monorail Station
44 Bus Station

MAGIC
KINGDOM
PARK

Main Street, USA

periodically outside Exposition Hall.

Look out for the **Guest Information Board** at the top of Main Street (on the left) that gives wait times for all the attractions. The **Baby Center** (for nursing mothers) can also be found at the top of Main Street, to the left next to the Crystal Palace, along with the park's First Aid station.

Unless you are a late arrival, give Main Street no more than a passing glance and head for the end of the street to the real entrance to the park. This is where you await the official opening hour for the famous 'Rope drop', and you should adopt one of three tactics here, each aimed at doing some of the most popular rides before the queues become substantial (wait times of an hour-plus for Splash Mountain are not unknown).

One: if you fancy the 5-star, log-flume ride Splash Mountain, keep

Find the characters

Can't find Mickey and Co? This is often one of the main laments of those who come in unprepared. Check in at **City Hall** and they will be able to tell you where they can be found. In fact, City Hall is your best friend for a variety of queries, from the location of baby facilities to meal bookings (but there are NO baby facilities at City Hall). Character meet-and-greets are also shown on all park maps with a Mickey's glove icon.

left in front of the Crystal Palace with the majority of the crowd, who will head for the same place.

Two: if you have young children who can't wait to have a ride on Cinderella's Golden Carrousel or the other Fantasyland rides, stay in the middle and pass around the Castle.

Three: if the thrills of the indoor roller-coaster Space Mountain appeal first, move to the right by The Plaza Restaurant and you'll get straight into Tomorrowland.

Now you'll be in pole position for the initial rush (and it will be a rush, believe me; take care if you're here with small children).

5

Adventureland

If you head to the left (effectively going clockwise around the park – always a good idea), you will enter Adventureland. If you're going to Splash Mountain first, you pass the Swiss Family Treehouse on your left and bear right through an archway (with toilets on your right) into Frontierland, where you turn left and Splash Mountain is straight in front of you. Stopping in Adventureland, however, these are the attractions:

Swiss Family Treehouse: this imitation Banyan tree is a clever replica of the treehouse from Disney's 1960 film *Swiss Family Robinson*. It's a walk-through attraction where the queues (rarely long) move steadily if not quickly, providing a fascinating glimpse of

Cinderella Castle

the ultimate treehouse, complete with kitchen, rope bridges and running water! AA.

Jungle Cruise: it's not so much the scenic, geographically suspect boat ride (where the Nile suddenly becomes the Amazon) that is so amusing here as the patter of your boat's captain, who spins a non-stop yarn about your adventure that features wild animals, tropical plants, hidden temples and sudden waterfalls. Great detail but long

> **BRIT TIP:** When you are faced by more than one queue for an attraction, head for the left-hand one. Almost invariably this moves slightly quicker.

queues, so visit either early morning (opens at 10am) or late afternoon (evening queues are shortest, but you'll miss some of the detail in the dark). AAAA (FP).

Pirates of the Caribbean: one of Disney's most impressive attractions that involves their pioneering work in audio-animatronics, life-size figures that move, talk and, in this instance, lay siege to a Caribbean island! Your underground boat ride takes you through a typical pirate adventure and the wizardry of the special effects is truly amazing. It's worth having several rides here, although it may be a bit spooky for very young children. Queues are rarely long and almost non-existent late in the day. AAAAA.

The Enchanted Tiki Room (under new management): a bird-laden, audio-animatronics show features Iago (from *Aladdin*) and Zazu (from *The Lion King*) leading a colourful 16-minute revue that will appeal especially to younger children. Queues are rare (and it is air-conditioned if you need to cool down!). AAA.

Magic Carpets of Aladdin: here, in an Agrabah-themed area styled after the animated film, this ride spins you up, down and around as you try to dodge the spitting camel! Your 'flying carpet' tilts as well as levitates, but it is basically simple stuff geared for younger children (and virtually identical to the Magic Carpets of Agrabah in the *Walt Disney Studios in Disneyland® Resort Paris*). TT (TTTT under 5s).

Shrunken Ned's Junior Jungle Boats: this costs an extra 50c for kids to try their hand at steering rather tame toy boats. T.

Disney **characters** also turn up outside the Pirates of the Caribbean and Magic Carpets rides, while the best of the shopping is in the Pirates Bazaar here. For food, you have **Aloha Isle** (yoghurt and ice cream), **Sunshine Tree Terrace** (fruit, snacks, yoghurt, tea and coffee), and the more substantial tacos, nachos and taco salads of **El Pirata y el Perico Restaurante**.

Frontierland

Passing through Adventureland brings you to the target for many of the early birds. This Western-themed area is one of the busiest and is best avoided from late morning to late afternoon.

Splash Mountain: based on the 1946 classic Disney cartoon *Song of the South*, this is a watery journey into the world of Brer Rabbit, Brer Fox and Brer Bear. The first part is all jolly cartoon scenery and fun with the main characters and a couple of minor swoops in your 8-passenger log boat. The conclusion, a 5-storey plummet at 45 degrees into a mist-shrouded pool, will seem like you are falling off the edge of the world! A huge adrenalin rush, but busy almost all day (try it first thing or during one of the parades to avoid the longest queues). You'll also get

VERY wet! Restrictions: 3ft 4in/
101cm. TTTTT (FP).

Big Thunder Mountain Railroad:
when Disney does a roller-coaster
you can be sure it will be one of the
classiest, and here it is, a runaway
mine train that swoops, tilts and
plunges through a mock abandoned
mine filled with clever scenery. You
should ride at least twice to
appreciate all the detail, but again
queues are heavy, so go first thing
(after Splash Mountain) or late in
the day. Restrictions: 3ft 4in/101cm.
TTTT (FP).

Country Bear Jamboree: now
here's a novelty, a 16-minute musical
revue presented by audio-
animatronic bears! It's great family
fun with plenty of novel touches
(watch for the talking moose-head).
Again, you'll need to beat the crowds
by going early morning (open at
10am) or early evening. AAA.

Frontierland Shootin' Arcade:
this is the only other attraction in
the park to cost extra (50c), as you
shoot the animated targets. TT.

Tom Sawyer Island: take a raft
over to an overgrown playground of
mysterious caves, grottos and mazes,
rope bridges and Fort Sam Clemens,
where you can fire air guns at
passing boats (open at 10am). A
good get-away in the early afternoon
when the crowds are at their biggest,
while **Aunt Polly's Dockside Inn** is
a refuge within a refuge for snacks
and soft drinks. TT.

Frontierland shops sell cowboy
hats, guns and badges as well as
Native American and Mexican
handicrafts. For food, try **Pecos Bill
Café** (salads, sandwiches and
burgers), **Frontierland Fries**
(McDonald's fries and drinks) or the
Turkey Leg Cart (massive, smoke-
grilled turkey legs). For shopping,
try the nicely themed **Briar Patch**
and the **Prairie Outpost** for some
interesting gifts.

Liberty Square

Continuing the clockwise tour
brings you next to a homage to post-
Independence America. A lot of the
historical content will go over the
heads of British visitors, but it still
has some great attractions.

Liberty Square Riverboat: cruise
America's 'rivers' on an authentic
paddle steamer, be menaced by
Native Americans and thrill to the
stories of How the West Was Won
(open at 10am). This is also a good
ride to take at the busiest times of
the day, especially early afternoon.
AAA.

The Haunted Mansion: a clever
delve into the world of ghost train
rides that is neither too scary for
kids nor too twee for adults. Not so
much a thrill ride as a scenic
adventure. Watch out for the neat
touch at the end when your car picks
up an extra 'passenger'. Longish
queues during much of the day,
however (so a good one for a
FastPass). AAAA or TTTT for
under 6s (FP).

The Hall of Presidents: this is
the attraction that is likely to mean
least to us, a 2-part show that is first
a film about the history of the
Constitution and then an audio-
animatronic parade of all 43
American presidents (open at 10am).
Technically it's impressive, but dull
for youngsters, although it is another
air-conditioned haven. AAA.

Shopping here includes **Ye Olde
Christmas Shoppe** and **The
Yankee Trader**, while eating
opportunities consist of the full-
service **Liberty Tree Tavern**
(hearty soups, steaks and traditional
dishes like meatloaf and pot roast,
plus dinner with Mickey and Co.),
Columbia Harbour House
(counter-service fried chicken or
shrimp, fish and salads) and **Sleepy
Hollow** (a picnic area serving
snacks, fresh fruit and drinks).

5

Fantasyland

Leaving Liberty Square, you walk past Cinderella Castle and come into the park's spiritual heart, the area with which young children are most enchanted. The attractions are designed with kids in mind, but some of the shops are quite sophisticated.

'It's a Small World': this recently revamped attraction could almost be Disney's theme ride, a family boat trip through the different continents, each represented by hundreds of dancing, singing audio-animatronic dolls in delightful set-piece pageants. It sounds twee but it actually creates a surprisingly striking effect, accompanied by an annoyingly catchy theme song that young children adore. Crowds peak in early afternoon. AAAA.

Dumbo the Flying Elephant: parents hate it but kids love it and all want to do this 2-minute ride on the back of a flying elephant that swoops in best Dumbo style (even if the ears do not flap). Ride early here or expect a long queue. TT (TTTT under 5s).

Mad Tea Party: again, the kids will insist you take them in these spinning, oversized tea cups that have their own 'steering wheel' to add to the whirling effect. Actually,

The Mad Tea Party

they're just a heavily disguised fairground ride. Again, go early or expect crowds. Characters from *Alice In Wonderland* also visit from time to time. TT (TTTT under 5s).

The Many Adventures of Winnie the Pooh: building on the timeless popularity of Pooh, Piglet and Co., this family ride offers a musical jaunt through Hundred Acre Wood with some clever special effects (get ready to 'bounce' with Tigger!) and another original soundtrack. AAA (AAAAA under 5s) (FP). In front of the ride is **Pooh's Playful Spot**, a new themed Hundred Acre Wood play area with slides, climbs and the ever-popular pop-jet fountains (guaranteed to get youngsters good and wet!).

Snow White's Scary Adventures: this lively indoor ride tells the cartoon story of Snow White with a

'It's a Small World'

Wishes Fireworks Show

few ghost train effects that may scare small children. Good fun, though, for parents and kids. Again, you need to go early or late (or during the main parade) to beat the queues. TTT (TTTTT under 5s).

Cinderella's Golden Carrousel: the centrepiece of Fantasyland shouldn't need any more explanation other than it is a vintage carousel ride that kids adore. Long queues during the main part of the day, though. T (TTT under 5s).

Mickey's PhilharMagic: this dramatic and utterly fun 3-D 10-minute film show has a host of in-theatre special effects as Donald tries to conduct the Enchanted Orchestra – to comic effect. Set in the PhilharMagic Concert Hall, it features a 150ft (46m) wide screen to immerse guests in the richly animated 3-D world of *Beauty & The Beast, The Little Mermaid, The Lion King, Peter Pan* and *Aladdin*, with the hapless Donald surviving a string of adventures before Mickey brings him back to earth. The lavishness of the theatre, the artistry of the new animation, the interweaving of the special effects (you can even 'smell' the food on-screen!) and the all-round family entertainment add up to one of Disney's most enjoyable attractions. There is no scare factor at work here (although the sudden plunge into darkness at one point and the noise of the 'orchestra' can sometimes spook young children),

while you'll be enchanted when Tinkerbell seems to fly right out of the screen to hover in front of you. AAAAA (FP).

Peter Pan's Flight: don't be fooled by the long queues, this is a rather tame ride, although it is still a big hit with kids. Its novel effect of flying up with Peter Pan quickly wears off, but there is still a lot of clever detail as your 'sailing ship' journeys over London to Neverland. AA (AAAAA under 6s) (FP).

Cinderellabration: as part of the *Happiest Celebration On Earth*, this elaborately staged spectacular picks up where the classic animated film ends. Mickey and Minnie join in to help Cinderella in becoming a princess, with the Fairy Godmother sprinkling her 'magic' around the Castle Forecourt with some beautiful lighting and other special effects. Young children will enjoy the pageant of princesses but it will not interest older children. AA (AAAA under 9s).

Ariel's Grotto, behind Dumbo, offers the chance to meet The Little Mermaid (which draws a queue at peak periods), while periodically in the **Fairytale Garden**, on the corner of the Castle facing Tomorrowland,

Big Thunder Mountain

you can listen to *Storytime with Belle*. *The Sword In The Stone* show is also re-enacted several times a day near Cinderella's Golden Carrousel.

Eating opportunities are at **The Pinocchio Village Haus** (pizza and Italian), the **Enchanted Grove** (ice drinks and juices), **Scuttle's Landing** and **Mrs Potts' Cupboard** (for ice creams and sundaes). **Cinderella's Royal Table** is a fine setting for the hugely popular character breakfast and lunch (dinner is also served, but without Cinderella and Co.). The majestic hall, waitresses in costume and well-presented food – salads, seafood, roast beef, prime rib and chicken – provide a memorable experience. It's a touch pricey for dinner, though. Shop at **Tinkerbell's Treasures**, the excellent **Sir Mickey's, Fantasy Faire** and **Pooh's Thotful Shop**.

Mickey's Toontown Fair

In the top corner of Fantasyland (just past the Mad Tea Party) is the shrub-lined entrance to **Mickey's Toontown Fair** (open at 10am). It is easy to miss, but it does have a station on the railroad. Its primary appeal is to young children as they can meet their favourite characters. Exceptionally kid-friendly and well landscaped, it features a huge merchandising area, the **County Bounty** – wallets beware! There is also the **Toon Park** playground to give youngsters the chance to let off some steam. **Mickey's Country House:** here is a walk-through opportunity to see Mickey at home and have your picture taken with him in the Judge's Tent. AAA (plus TTTTT for the photo opportunity!). **Minnie's Country House:** this is a chance to view Minnie's home and 'unique memorabilia', all designed in a Country and Western style. AAA. **Mickey's Toontown Fair Hall of**

Fame: three opportunities to meet a host of other Disney favourites in the Villains Room, Mickey's Pals and Famous Faces. TTTTT (for kids!).

The Barnstormer at Goofy's Wiseacre Farm: a mini roller-coaster just for the young uns, its masterful design features a swoop right through the barn itself (although it is a pretty short ride after the slow-moving queue). TTT (TTTTT for 4–8s). Restrictions: 3ft/91cm.

Donald's Boat: parents beware, youngsters get seriously wet here! If you've seen the pavement fountains at Epcot (see page 116), prepare for more watery delights as this boat-themed playground spouts off in all sorts of wonderful ways. Ideally, bring a change of clothes or swimsuit for the kids. It's also a great place to revitalise tired or irritable children. AAAA (under 10s).

Check out the **Toontown Farmers Market** for fruit, snacks and drinks.

Tomorrowland

The last of the 7 'lands,' this has a cartoon-like space-age appearance, guaranteed to appeal to youngsters, while it also boasts some of the more original shops.

Space Mountain: this is one of the 3 most popular attractions, and its reputation is deserved. It is a fast, tight-turning roller-coaster completely in the dark save for occasional flashes as you whiz through 'the galaxy'. Don't do this after eating! The only way to beat the crowds is to go either first thing, late in the day or during one of the parades (or, of course, get a FastPass). Restrictions: 3ft 8in/111cm. TTTTT (FP). Children will also gravitate to the **Tomorrowland Arcade** as you exit the ride.

Tomorrowland Indy Speedway: despite the long queues, this is a rather tame ride on supposed race tracks that just putt-putts along on rails with little real steering required (children must be 4ft 4in/132cm to drive alone). T (TTTT under 6s).

Astro Orbiter: a jazzed-up version of Dumbo in Fantasyland, this ride is a bit faster, higher and features 'rockets'. Large, slow-moving queues are another reason to give this a miss unless you have children. TT (TTTT under 10s).

Walt Disney's Carousel of Progress: this will surprise, entertain and amuse. It is a 100-year journey through 20th-century technology with audio-animatronics and a revolving theatre that reveals different stages in that development. Its 22-minute duration is rarely threatened by crowds (open only at peak periods). AAA

Tomorrowland Transit Authority: a neat 'future transport system', this offers an elevated view of the area, including a glimpse inside Space Mountain, in electro-magnetic cars. Queues are usually short. AAA (TTT for under 8s).

Stitch's Great Escape!: this 15-minute experience has replaced the Alien Encounter and is good family fun (although not perhaps for children frightened by the dark or loud noises). It is a unique audio-animatronic 'prequel' to Disney's *Lilo & Stitch*, with visitors being 'recruited' into the madcap Galactic Federation prison service. However, things go hilariously wrong as a new prisoner (Stitch) arrives and proceeds to cause havoc. There are 2 pre-show areas and then 'recruits' are ushered into a sit-down chamber (with shoulder restraints) where Stitch is let loose to bounce, dribble and even

BRIT TIP: Get more value for your money at the parks by ordering sodas 'without ice' to get a full cup.

belch over the unsuspecting audience. Good fun for kids if rather baffling for adults. Restrictions: 3ft 2in/101cm. AAA (FP).

Buzz Lightyear's Space Ranger Spin: kids will not want to miss this chance to join the great *Toy Story* character in his battle against the evil Emperor Zurg. Ride into action against the robot army – and shoot them with laser cannons! A sure-fire family winner, especially as you get to keep score. TTT (TTTTT for under 8s; FP).

The Timekeeper: a combination of high-tech audio-animatronics and 360-degree film wizardry gives you an amusing plunge into time travel in the company of the zany robot Timekeeper (voiced by Robin Williams) and his camera-equipped assistant Nine-eye (open only at peak periods). AAAA.

The Galaxy Palace Theater hosts live musical productions, featuring Disney characters and talent shows, at various times of the day. For food, **Cosmic Ray's Starlight Café** has burgers, chicken, pasta, soups and salads, **The Plaza Pavilion** does pizza, subs and salads, **Auntie Gravity's** (ouch!) **Galactic Goodies** serves ice cream and juices, the **Lunching Pad** (double ouch!) offers smoked turkey legs, snacks and drinks. Recent addition the **Tomorrowland Terrace Noodle Station** offers a more healthy line-up of Asian stir-fry, soup and vegetarian dishes. Shopping highlights include **Mickey's Star Traders** and **Merchant of Venus**.

Having come full circle, you are now back at Main Street USA and it's best to return here in early afternoon to avoid the crowds and have a closer look at the impressive array of shops.

The afternoon highlight, however, is the **Share A Dream Come True** parade. This 6-part extravaganza is designed as a flurry of classic Disney moments frozen inside giant snow

5

BRIT TIP: To watch a parade, sit on the left side of Main Street USA (facing the Castle) to stay in the shade if it's hot. People start staking out the best spots an HOUR in advance.

globes full of special effects. All the favourite characters feature, along with a typically Disney new musical score. Watch out for the chance to join in as the parade stops to allow characters to select people to dance and play act with. The globes themselves feature some outstanding effects, with *Aladdin* taking to the air on his flying carpet, the Wicked Queen turning into the evil old hag, and snow in the leading globes. It is a dazzler for all ages, but is especially popular with children. AAAAA. At Easter and Christmas, the daily parade takes on extra seasonal charm with appearances by the Easter Bunny and Father Christmas.

There's more

If you think the park looks good during the day, prepare to be amazed at how wonderful it appears at night – some of the lighting effects are astounding. When the park is open into the evenings (during the main holiday periods and weekends), you can see the **SpectroMagic parade** (when there are two a night, the second is less crowded), which is a mind-boggling light and sound festival full of glitter and

razzamatazz, with the Disney characters at the centre of a multitude of sparkling lights and fibre-optic effects. It is difficult to do it justice in words, so just make sure that you see it. AAAA.

Firework finale

Most nights at the *Magic Kingdom Park* conclude with the stunning **Wishes** firework show, behind the Castle and with a broad vista to the rear of the park. With a clever soundtrack narrated by Jiminy Cricket and featuring memorable moments from an array of Disney classics, it is magnificently choreographed and culminates in a sequence of pyrotechnic explosions (many of them designed especially for this show), which truly dazzle the eyes and mind. Starting with an appearance by Tinkerbell (from the Castle's top turret), it continues for 12 minutes of typical Disney emotional heart-tugging and is the perfect pixie-dust farewell to a day at this park. AAAAA.

The monorail IS quicker than the ferry when you leave the park, but you will need to be patient at peak times – it can take up to an hour to get back to your car. Also, if the crowds get too heavy during the day, you CAN escape by leaving in early afternoon (get a hand-stamp for re-admission and keep your car park ticket, which is valid all day) and returning to your hotel for a few hours' rest or a dip in the pool. Alternatively, catch the boat

BRIT TIP: Main Street USA closes half an hour after the rest of the park, so you can avoid the mad rush for the car parks by lingering here and enjoying an ice cream or coffee.

SpectroMagic Parade

© Disney

BRIT TIP: After the fireworks crowd exits, you are often allowed to take the Resort Only monorail back to the Transportation & Ticket Center, rather than stand in the queues for the main monorail.

transport to one of the Disney resorts for an hour or two – *Disney's Fort Wilderness* is especially fun for young children and boasts the great value **Trails End Buffet** for lunch or dinner.

Halloween and Christmas

Two additional annual events in the *Magic Kingdom Park* are **Mickey's Not So Scary Halloween Party** (on selected dates in October) and **Mickey's Very Merry Christmas Party** (late November and December), which provide a separate, party-style ticketed event from 7pm to midnight, with most of the rides open and extra themed fun

and games. The Halloween event sees many visitors dress up for the typical American trick-or-treat fun, and there are plenty of treats and sweets for youngsters on the way. With special music, story-telling, parades and fireworks (and some wonderful lighting effects), plus a free family photo, tickets go on sale about six months in advance and sell out quickly. The Christmas party sees 'snow' on Main Street and an array of magnificent festive decorations and theming. There is free hot chocolate and cookies, plus a family photo, as well as a parade and more fireworks. The whole atmosphere is truly enchanting, although the evening is occasionally liable to some unfriendly Florida weather. Halloween party tickets cost $42.55 for adults and $35.10 per child on the day (or $37.23 and $29.77 in advance), while the Christmas party is $46.81 and $37.23 (or $41.49 and $31.90 in advance). Book in advance on 407 934 7639.

Finally, one of the park's little-known 'secrets' is the **Keys to the Kingdom**, a 4–5-hour guided tour

5

Magic Carpets of Aladdin

© Disney

of many backstage areas, including the service tunnel under the park, and entertainment production buildings. It costs an extra $58 (including lunch; not available for under 16s). Call 407 939 8687 for more information. **Disney's Family Magic Tour** is a 2-hour guided adventure that takes you on a search for clues throughout the park at $25/person or you can experience **Disney's The Magic Behind Our Steam Trains** tour ($40/person; no under 10s) as you join the crew who prepare the park's trains each day.

MAGIC KINGDOM PARK with children

Here is a rough guide to the rides which appeal to different age groups. Obviously, children vary in their likes and dislikes but, as a general rule, you can be fairly sure the following will have most appeal to the ages concerned (height restrictions have been taken into account):

Under 5s
Walt Disney World Railroad, Main Street Vehicles, Jungle Cruise, The Enchanted Tiki Room (under new management), Country Bear Jamboree, Liberty Square Riverboat, 'It's a Small World', Peter Pan's Flight, Mickey's PhilharMagic, Cinderellabration, Cinderella's Golden Carrousel, Dumbo The Flying Elephant, Many Adventures of Winnie The Pooh, Mickey's Country House, Donald's Boat, Tomorrowland Indy Speedway (with a parent), Buzz Lightyear's Space Ranger Spin, Tomorrowland Transit Authority.

5–8s
Walt Disney World Railroad, Pirates of the Caribbean, Jungle Cruise, Swiss Family Treehouse, The Timekeeper, Magic Carpets of *Aladdin*, The Enchanted Tiki Room (under new management), Country Bear Jamboree, Cinderellabration, Liberty Square Riverboat, Tom Sawyer Island, Big Thunder Mountain Railroad, Splash Mountain, Haunted Mansion, Mickey's PhilharMagic, Snow White's Scary Adventures, Mad Tea Party, Many Adventures of Winnie The Pooh, Mickey's Country House, Donald's Boat, The Barnstormer at Goofy's Wiseacre Farm, Tomorrowland Indy Speedway (with parent), Tomorrowland Transit Authority, Buzz Lightyear's Space Ranger Spin, Walt Disney's Carousel of Progress, Astro Orbiter, Stitch's Great Escape! and Space Mountain (with parental discretion).

9–12s
Pirates of the Caribbean, Big Thunder Mountain Railroad, Splash Mountain, Country Bear Jamboree, The Haunted Mansion, Mad Tea Party, Mickey's PhilharMagic, The Barnstormer at Goofy's Wiseacre Farm, Tomorrowland Indy Speedway (without parent), Buzz Lightyear's Space Ranger Spin, Stitch's Great Escape!, The Timekeeper, Astro Orbiter, Space Mountain.

Over 12s
Pirates of the Caribbean, Big Thunder Mountain Railroad, Splash Mountain, Mickey's PhilharMagic, Haunted Mansion, Buzz Lightyear's Space Ranger Spin (Disney/Pixar), The Timekeeper, Stitch's Great Escape!, Mad Tea Party, Astro Orbiter, Space Mountain.

Epcot

Epcot actually stands for 'Experimental Prototype Community Of Tomorrow' but it might be more accurate to say Every Person Comes Out Tired. For this is a BIG park, with a lot to see and do, and much leg-work required for its 300-acre (122-ha) extent. Actually, it is not so much a vision of the future as a look at the world of today, with a strong educational and environmental message. At almost 3 times the size of the *Magic Kingdom Park*, it is more likely to require a 2-day visit (although under 5s might find it less entertaining) and your feet in particular will notice the difference!

Epcot at a glance

Location	Off Epcot Drive, *Walt Disney World*
Size	300 acres (122ha) in Future World and World Showcase
Hours	9am–6pm Future World (except Test Track, Innoventions, Spaceship Earth, Honey I Shrunk the Audience, 9am–9pm), 11am–9pm (World Showcase)
Admission	Under 3 free; 3–9 $48 (1-day base ticket), $155 (5-Day Premium), $196 (7-Day Premium); adult (10+) $59.73, $193, $233. Prices do not include tax
Parking	$8
Lockers	Yes; to left underneath Spaceship Earth and International Gateway; $7 ($2 refund)
Pushchairs	$10 and $18 ($1 deposit refunded); to the right underneath Spaceship Earth and International Gateway
Wheelchairs	$10 ($1 deposit refunded) or $35 ($10 deposit refunded), same location as pushchairs
Top Attractions	Mission: SPACE, Test Track, Spaceship Earth, Soarin'™, 'Honey, I Shrunk the Audience', Maelstrom, Universe of Energy, American Adventure
Don't Miss	IllumiNations: Reflections of Earth, Disney character bus (around World Showcase), live entertainment (including Off Kilter in Canada, JAMMitors in Innoventions plaza and Miyuki in Japan), and dinner at any of the World Showcase pavilions
Hidden Costs	**Meals** — Burger, chips and coke $7.78; 3-course dinner $33.97 (Le Cellier, Canada); Kids' meal $3.99–5.95
	T-shirts — $17–28
	Souvenirs — $1–995
	Sundries — *Epcot* 'Passport' $9.95

5

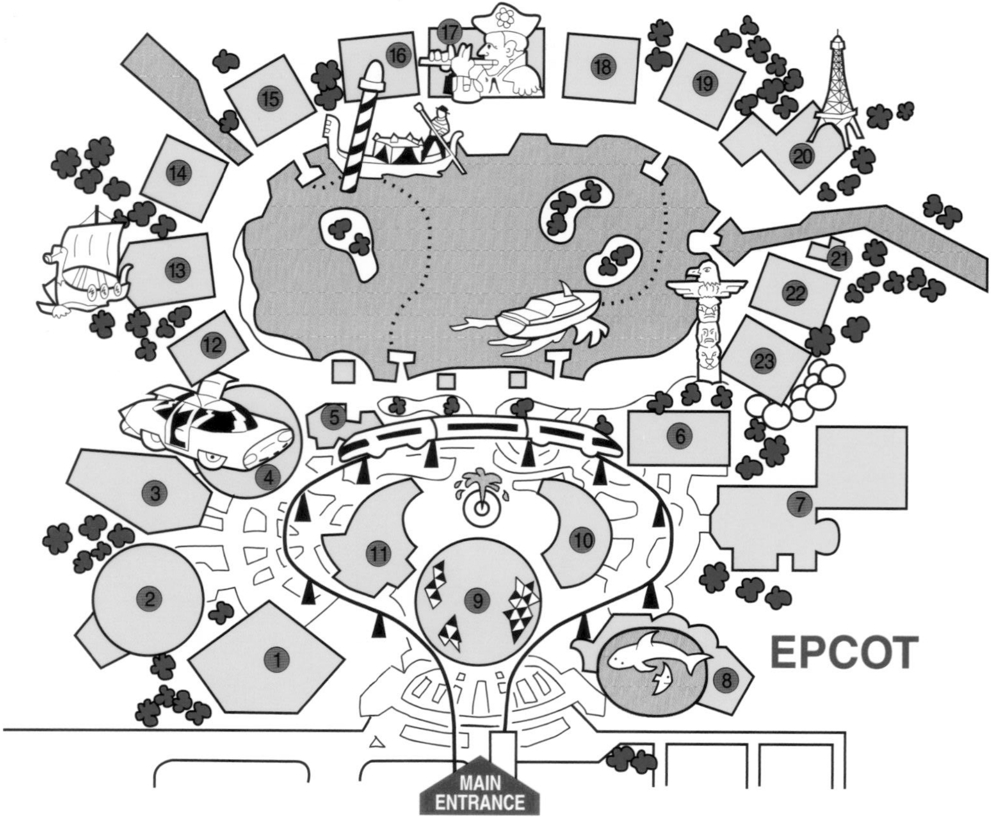

FUTURE WORLD

1 Universe Of Energy
2 Wonders Of Life
3 Mission: SPACE
4 Test Track
5 Odyssey Center
6 Imagination! (Including Honey, I Shrunk The Audience)
7 The Land (including Soarin')
8 The Living Seas
9 Spaceship Earth
10 Innoventions West
11 Innoventions East

WORLD SHOWCASE

12 Mexico
13 Norway
14 China
15 Germany
16 Italy
17 The American Adventure
18 Japan
19 Morocco
20 France
21 International Gateway (To Epcot Resort Hotels)
22 United Kingdom
23 Canada

EPCOT

MAIN ENTRANCE

Soarin'

Location

Epcot is located off Epcot Drive and the parking fee is again $8 as you drive into its main entrance (there is a separate entrance for guests at the *Epcot* resort hotels, called International Gateway). It opened in October 1982 and its giant car park is big enough for 9,000 vehicles, so a tram takes you from your car to the main entrance (although if you are staying at a Disney hotel you can catch the monorail, boat or bus service to its gates). And don't forget to note where you are parked (e.g. Create, row 78). Once you have your ticket, you pass through the turnstiles and wait in the immediate entrance plaza for Rope Drop, which is signalled by Mickey and Co. arriving on the Character Bus.

Epcot is divided into 2 distinct parts arranged in a figure of 8 and there are 2 tactics to help you avoid the worst of the crowds. The first or lower half of the '8' consists of **Future World**, with 7 different pavilions arranged around Spaceship Earth, which dominates the *Epcot* skyline) and Innoventions. The second part, or top of the '8', is **World Showcase**, a potted journey around the world via 11 internationally presented pavilions that feature a taste of each country's culture, history, shopping, entertainment and cuisine.

Once through the entrance plaza, you should aim to get the 3 big-time rides – Test Track, Mission: Space and Soarin' – under your belt first, then continue into World Showcase at its 11am opening time. Continue around World Showcase until 4 or 5pm, then return to Future World to catch up on the other attractions there, as the majority of the crowds will have moved on (apart from at the three main rides). As a general tactic, head first for the magnificent new **Soarin'**, then go across to the other side of Future World and grab a FastPass for **Test Track**. While you wait for your ride time, you can queue up for **Mission: Space** and perhaps even take in **Universe of Energy**.

Alternatively, if the rides don't appeal quite so much as a visit to such diverse cultures as Japan and Morocco, spend your first couple of hours in the Innoventions centres (busy from mid-morning), then head into World Showcase and you'll be ahead of the crowds for several hours. The other thing you should do early on is book lunch or dinner at one of the many fine restaurants around World Showcase (Mexico, Canada and Japan are all highly recommended). The best reservations go fast, but check in at Guest Relations (on the left of the Innoventions plaza) and they can give advice and make bookings.

5

Spaceship Earth

Future World

Here is what you will find in the first part of your *Epcot* adventure:

Universe of Energy: there is just the one attraction here but it is a stunner. **Ellen's Energy Adventure** is a 45-minute show-and-ride with comedienne Ellen DeGeneres and Bill Nye the Science Guy exploring the creation of fuels from the age of dinosaurs to their modern-day usages. The film elements convince you that you are in a conventional theatre, but then your seats rearrange themselves into 96-person solar-powered cars and you are off on a journey through the prehistoric era, with some realistic dinosaurs! Queues are steady but not overwhelming from mid-morning. AAAAA.

Mission: SPACE: this is the new cutting edge of Disney's attraction technology, a journey 30 years into the future to join the International Space Training Center. The space-age building alone prepares you for a major adventure as you enter through Planetary Plaza, with its giant replica planets (check out the model showing the Moon landings). At the main entrance you have a choice of four queues – FastPass Collection, Stand-by (the main queue), Single riders and FastPass return, and the clever organisation keeps lines to a minimum. As you enter the 'training facility', there are some superb models and graphics

BRIT TIP: If the thrills of Mission: SPACE and Test Track appeal to you most, head here FIRST when you arrive, grab a FastPass for Test Track, then ride the other. Mission: SPACE draws only half the queues of Test Track.

(like the giant revolving Gravity Wheel) to look at while you queue to reach Team Despatch. Here, the four 'ready rooms' form you into teams of four for the ride itself, and you will be either the Navigator, Engineer, Pilot or Commander, each with different functions to perform.

Once briefed (by actor Gary Sinise), you enter the Preparation Room to learn your mission – a flight to Mars. And then it is quickly into the ride vehicle – capsules that close down tightly with outer doors, shoulder restraints and screens that move forward to just 18in (46cm) from your face (this is NOT the ride for you if you suffer from claustrophobia). The sense of realism, with the control consoles, individual speakers and the countdown is magnificent, and the blast off feels VERY real as you experience some of the genuine forces of a rocket launch (it is part ride and part simulator).

Each member of the team has to perform their duties on cue (Sinise will 'prompt' you if you forget) and you experience a cleverly simulated sling-shot flight around the Moon and on to Mars, where the landing is an adventure in itself. It is a truly original, ultra-dynamic ride, but you should heed the advice to keep your head still and look straight into the screen or you WILL feel sick. It is way too intense for younger children, and there is no backing out once you blast off (parents could try it first to see if their children would enjoy it), while it is definitely not a ride for expectant mothers. Restrictions, 3ft 8in/112cm. TTTTT+ (FP).

As you exit the ride, there is an elaborate post-show with even more activities. **Space Base** is an excellent play area for children who can't ride (and those who just like to explore, climb, slide and crawl – enter through the gift shop if you just want to play here); **Space Race** is a neat game for two teams of 60 players, working in pairs, to propel their rocket to Mars with a series of on-screen challenges; **Expedition Mars** is a computer game to rescue stranded astronauts; and **Postcards from Space** can send a video e-mail of yourself in one of eight space 'scenes.' There is then the inevitable (and well-stocked) gift shop to negotiate on the way out. All in all, it is a mind-boggling experience, and a real taste of space 'exploration' without leaving the building!

Test Track: this is another big production, a 5½-minute whirl along Disney's longest and fastest track. It starts with an elaborate queue line that demonstrates General Motors' safety techniques and quality control, and prepares riders for a taste of the vehicle testing to come. The way the cars whiz around the outside of the building (at up to 60mph/97kph) provides a glimpse of what's in store. The reality is pretty good, too, as you are taken on a tour of a GM proving ground, including a hill climb test, suspension test (hold on to those fillings!), brake test, environment chamber, barrier test (beware the crash test dummies!) and the steeply banked, high-speed finale.

Once you regain your breath, there is a post-show area with a multimedia film, an animated presentation featuring future GM products and technological innovations, with a hint of virtual-reality driving, and the chance to view the latest GM models. Along with a smart gift store and ride photo opportunity, it makes for an extremely involved exhibit. A new **Kidcot** stop also adds some creative fun for youngsters. The downside is the HUGE queues it attracts, topping 2 hours at times, while the available FP service often runs out. Head straight here after opening or return in the evening to keep your queuing to bearable levels. If you are

on your own, save time by using the Singles Queue. Restrictions: 3ft 4in/101cm. TTTT (TTT for teens) (FP).

The Odyssey Center next door offers baby-care and first-aid facilities, telephones and restrooms.

Wonders of Life: this pavilion is the poor relation of the Future World line-up these days, to such an extent it is usually closed at off-peak times. When open, it offers **Body Wars**, a hectic simulator ride through the human body (quite a violent adventure, too, not recommended for people who suffer from motion sickness, anyone with neck or back injuries, or pregnant women. Restrictions: 3ft 4in/101cm). TTTT; **Cranium Command**, a hilarious theatre show set in the brain of a 12-year-old boy, showing how he negotiates a typical day. It is both audio-animatronic and film-based (see how many famous TV and film stars you can name in the 'cast'). AAAA; and **The Making of Me**, a sensitive film on the creation of human life, which therefore requires parental discretion for children as it has its explicit moments, although not without humour. AAA.

BRIT TIP: The Wonders of Life pavilion is a good place in which to spend time if you need to cool down, or if it's raining.

Imagination!: The 2-part attraction here starts with **Journey Into Imagination with Figment**, a recently revamped ride into experiments with imagination, in the company of Eric Idle (as Dr Nigel Channing of the Imagination Institute) and the cartoon dragon, Figment. The sight laboratory sees Figment having fun with a vision chart, the sound lab is a symphony of imaginative melodies and Figment's house is a truly topsy-turvy world (and watch out for the skunk in the smell lab!). It is gentle fun and rarely draws a crowd. AAA. (For fans of the original Dreamfinder ride here, Figment is prominent once again, while the ride's theme song, 'One Little Spark', makes a return.)

You exit into **Image Works – The Kodak 'What If' Labs**, an interactive playground of unusual sights and sounds, which will probably amuse children more than adults (although you may be tempted to part with more money on various cartoon images and select-your-own CDs).

Come out of the building and turn right for the fabulous 3-D experience of **'Honey, I Shrunk The Audience'**, as Rick Moranis reprises his hapless inventor character Wayne Szalinski. A neat 8-minute pre-show is the perfect prelude to the fun and games in store. If you have seen Jim Henson's Muppet*Vision 3-D at *Disney-MGM Studios* you'll have an idea of what to expect. Special effects and moving seats add to the feeling you have shrunk in size. And beware the sneezing dog! AAAAA (FP).

Germany Pavilion

© Disney

Outside, kids are always fascinated by the **Jellyfish** and **Serpentine Fountains** that send water squirting from pond to pond, and there is always one who tries to stand in the way and 'catch' one of the streams of water. Have your cameras and camcorders ready!

The Land: this pavilion features three elements that combine to make a highly entertaining but educational experience on food production and nutrition – plus the spectacular new Soarin'™ ride, which is a pure thrill and a huge draw.

Living with the Land: is an informative 14-minute boat ride that is worth the usually long queue. A journey through various types of food production may sound dull, but it is informative and enjoyable, with plenty to make children of all ages sit up and take notice through the three ecological communities, especially the greenhouse finale. AAAA (FP). Having ridden the ride, you can also take the **Behind The Seeds** guided tour through the greenhouse complex and learn even more about Disney's horticultural projects. It takes an hour ($6 for adults, $4 for 3–9s), but you have to book in person at the desk near the Green Thumb Emporium.

The Circle of Life is a 15-minute live-action/animated story, featuring characters from the film *The Lion King*, that explains environmental concerns and is easily digestible for kids. Queues are not a problem here. AAA.

Soarin'™ is *Epcot*'s latest and greatest, a hugely imaginative 'flight simulator' that offers an exhilarating ride for all ages, young and old equally. A copy of the Soarin' Over California simulator ride in *Disney's California Adventure* in Los Angeles, it features a breathtaking swoop over the notable landmarks of California, complete with aroma-vision (smell those orange groves!). An elaborate queuing area is arranged like an airport departure lounge, with the 'passengers' embarking on rows of seats that are then hoisted up into the air over a giant screen. The feeling is somewhat akin to taking a hang-glider ride as the special film, sounds and scents become all-encompassing. Feet dangling, you soar over the Golden Gate Bridge, sweep through a redwood forest and glide above Napa Valley with the wind in your hair. The finale includes a close encounter with a certain Disney theme park in LA! The ride's realism, magnificent music and superb technology ensure a 5-star experience – but also some serious queues. The lines move slowly and there is not much to keep your attention, so visit early or make use of a FastPass here. Restrictions, 3ft 4in/102cm. AAAAA (FP).

The **Sunshine Season Food Fair** offers the chance to eat some of Disney's home-grown produce, and there are healthy alternatives to the usual fast-food fare, while the **Garden Grill** restaurant is a slowly revolving platform that offers more traditional food, including roast meats, pasta, seafood and a vegetarian selection, all in the company of Mickey, Goofy, Pluto, Chip 'n' Dale.

The Living Seas: this pavilion does for the sea what The Land Pavilion does for terra firma (albeit without the clever rides, but with the addition of some character fun from

the film *Finding Nemo*). A 7-minute pre-show film leads on to a short journey to Sea Base Alpha by 'Hydrolator' (imagine an undersea lift simulator) and an elaborate marine research facility centred around a 5.7 million-gallon (25.9 million-litre) aquarium, with sharks, stingrays and other impressive denizens of the deep. This 2-level development takes you through 6 modules that present stories of undersea exploration and marine life, including a research centre that provides a close-up encounter with the endangered manatee. Plenty of interactive elements and educational touch-screens are on offer, plus additional fish tanks displaying Caribbean reef fish, jellyfish and the curious cuttlefish, while there is also an excellent demonstration of a diving chamber. Crowds are steady throughout the day, but queues rarely get too long – with one exception. **Turtle Talk With Crush** is a splendidly interactive – not to mention original – on-screen meet and greet with the cartoon surfer dude turtle from *Finding Nemo*. Crush is literally the star of the show as he swims up and engages children in the audience with some genuinely fun banter (with help from sidekick Dory). Next door, Bruce's Shark World is an elaborate photo opportunity with some more of the *Finding Nemo* characters. AAA.

The pavilion also includes the

5

Norway Pavilion

highly recommended **Coral Reef Restaurant** that serves magnificent seafood, as well as providing diners with a grandstand view of the massive aquarium. Dinner for 2 will cost around $70, which isn't cheap, but the food is first class.

Spaceship Earth: spiralling up 18 storeys, this attraction tells the story of communication from early cave drawings to modern satellite technology. It is one of the most popular rides, largely because of its visibility and location, hence you need to do it either first thing or late afternoon when the crowds have moved on from Future World into World Showcase. The highlight is the depiction of Michelangelo's painting of the Sistine Chapel, which will be lost on small kids, but it's an entertaining 15-minute journey all along. AAAA.

Innoventions West and East: these two centres of hands-on exhibits and computer games – subtitled **The Road to Tomorrow** –include a glimpse of Disney's latest investigations into virtual reality entertainment and other demonstrations of current and future technologies, especially the internet and computers, by the likes of IBM, Xerox, Compaq, Motorola and General Motors. Both sides are routed like a journey into the future and will reward enquiring minds in areas like **People At Play** and **Mouse House Jr.** In Innoventions West, the kids will gravitate to the free **Video Games of Tomorrow** selection presented by Disney Interactive and may take a bit of moving! Also worth waiting for are the 20-minute **Ultimate Home Theater Experience**, presented by Lutron, and the **Thinkplace** presented by IBM, featuring a demonstration of IBM's voice recognition technology. More interactive stuff is presented by the new **Where's the Fire?** exhibit, which takes a neat look at home fire safety.

In Innoventions East, you can send a video e-mail to friends in the **Internet Zone**, check out **The Underwriters Lab**, which offers an interactive area with various testing stations and Video D-Mail, and take the 15-minute walk through the **House of Innoventions**, full of smart gadgets and new technologies. You must also take a look at the latest form of transport here – the wonderful 2-wheeled Segway Human Transporter (which you can also pay to ride – see page 122) and try the new **Fantastic Plastics** (create your own robot to take home!).

Live entertainment is provided periodically in the Innoventions plaza, where innovative acts include the unique **JAMMitors** percussion group and the unusual **Kristos** dance troupe. The majestic fountains are also choreographed to an hourly music performance. Food outlets include the self-service **Electric Umbrella Restaurant** for lunch and dinner (sandwiches, pizza, burgers and salads) and the **Fountain View Espresso and Bakery** for tea, coffee and pastries. Look out also the new **Club Cool** (opening in December 2005) presented by Coca-Cola™, where you can check out the latest Coke-inspired products. You'll also find the huge gift shop **Mouse Gear** in Innoventions East, featuring stacks of quality *Epcot* and Disney souvenirs (and some wacky ceiling architecture!).

World Showcase

If you found Future World a huge experience, prepare to be amazed also by the equally imaginative pavilions around the World Showcase Lagoon. Each features a glimpse of a different country in dramatic settings. Several have either rides or films to show off their main tourist features, while in nearly every case the restaurants offer some of the best international fare in Orlando.

Mexico: starting at the bottom left of the circular tour of the lagoon and moving clockwise, your first encounter is the spectacular pyramid that houses Mexico. Here you will find the amusing boat ride **El Rio del Tiempo**, the River of Time, which gives you a potted 9-minute journey through the people and history of the country. Queues here tend to be surprisingly long from mid-morning to mid-afternoon. AAA. The rest of the pavilion is given over to a range of shops in the **Plaza de los Amigos**, which vary from pretty tacky to sophisticated, and the **San Angel Inn**, a dimly lit and romantic full-service diner offering traditional and tempting Mexican fare. Outside, on the lagoon, is the **Cantina de San Angel**, a fast-food counter for tacos, chilli and burgers. As in all the World Showcase pavilions, there is live entertainment and music.

> BRIT TIP: The Cantina de San Angel is a great spot from which to watch the nightly IllumiNations pyrotechnics show, but you need to arrive at least an hour early.

Norway: next up is Norway, which has the best ride in World Showcase, the Viking-themed **Maelstrom**. This 10-minute longboat journey through the country's history and scenery features a short waterfall drop and a North Sea storm. It attracts longish queues during the afternoon, so the best tactic is to go soon after World Showcase's 11am opening. TTT (FP). There are periodical Norwegian-themed exhibits in the reconstructed **Stave Church** and twice-daily guided tours (sign up at the Tourism desk), while kids can play on the **Viking boat**. The pavilion also contains a clever reproduction of Oslo's Akershus Fortress. The **Akershus Royal Banquet Hall** offers the Princess Storybook dining for breakfast, lunch and dinner, complete with a host of Disney princesses, and the **Kringla Bakeri Og Kafé** serves sandwiches, pastries and drinks.

China: the spectacular landscapes of China are well served by the pavilion's main attraction, the stunning **Reflections of China**, a 360-degree film in the circular Temple of Heaven. Here you are surrounded by the sights and sounds of one of the world's most mysterious countries in a special cinematic production, the technology of which alone will leave you breathless. Queues build up to half an hour during the main part of the day (but the waiting area is fully air-conditioned). AAAA. Two restaurants, the **Nine Dragons** (table service, decent if unremarkable food) and the **Lotus Blossom Café** (self-service, fairly predictable spring rolls and stir-fries), offer tastes of the Orient, while the **Yong Feng Shangdian Department Store** is a virtual warehouse of Chinese gifts and artefacts. Don't miss the periodic shows of Oriental music and acrobatics (including the stunning **Dragon Legend Acrobats**) on the plaza in front of the temple.

The **Outpost** between China and Germany features hut-style shops

> BRIT TIP: The lunch and dinner menus at the Nine Dragons restaurant are similar, so choose the lunch version – it's cheaper!

5

and snacks, with entertainment from Africa and the Caribbean.

Germany: this provides more in the way of shopping and eating than entertainment, although you still find strolling players and a magnificent re-creation of a Bavarian **Biergarten**, with lively Oktoberfest shows featuring the resident brass band at regular intervals. It also offers hearty portions of German sausage, sauerkraut and rotisserie chicken. The **Sommerfest** is fast food German-style (bratwurst and strudel). This pavilion has more shops than any of the others in *Epcot* and includes chocolates, wines, porcelain, crystal, toys and cuckoo clocks. An elaborate outdoor model railway is popular with children.

Italy: similarly, Italy has pretty, authentic architecture (including a superb reproduction of St Mark's Square in Venice), lively music and amusing Italian folk stories, 3 tempting gift shops (including wine, Perugina chocolates, Armani collectables, fine crystal, porcelain and Venetian masks), and a 5-star restaurant, **L'Originale Alfredo di Roma Ristorante**. It's a touch expensive, but the bustling atmosphere and decor add extra zest

China Pavilion

© Disney

to the meals, which include fettuccine, chicken, veal and seafood. Expect a 3-course meal to cost about $38. Watch out, too, here for **Sergio**, a madcap juggler who loves to involve his audience.

America: at the top of the lagoon and dominating World Showcase is **The American Adventure**, not so much a pavilion as a celebration of the country's history and Constitution. A colonial fife and drum band and wonderful a cappella group (Voices Of Liberty) add authentic sounds to the 18th-century setting, overlooked by a faithful reproduction of Philadelphia's Liberty Hall. Inside you have the spectacular American Adventure show, a magnificent film and audio-animatronic production lasting half an hour, which details the country's struggles and triumphs, its presidents, statesmen and heroes. It's a glossy, patriotic performance, featuring some outstanding audio-animatronic effects and, while some of it will leave foreign visitors fairly cold, it is difficult not to be impressed. Avoid at midday because of the queues. AAAA. If you have time pre-show, check out the **American Heritage Gallery** and its first full-time exhibition, Echoes of Africa, which explores the influence of African art on contemporary African–American artists.

Outside, handcarts provide touches of nostalgia and antiques, along with the **Heritage Manor Gifts** store, while **Liberty Inn** offers fast-food lunch and dinner. The **America Gardens Theater**, facing the lagoon, presents Disney fun and concerts from worldwide artists periodically.

Japan: next up on the clockwise tour, you will be introduced to typical Japanese gardens and architecture, including the breathtaking Chi Nien Tien, a round half-scale reproduction of a temple, some magnificent art exhibits (notably the Bijutsu-kan Gallery), musical shows and dazzling live entertainment (especially child-friendly **Miyuki**, a lovely lady who spins amazing candy creations out of toffee sugar). For one of the most entertaining meals in *Epcot*, the **Teppanyaki Dining Rooms** (as much an experience as a meal) and **Tempura Kiku** both offer a full, table-service introduction to Japanese cuisine while **Yakitori House** is the fast-food equivalent and the **Matsu No Ma Lounge** features sushi and cocktails. The restaurants are run by Mitsukoshi, as is the superb department store. Periodic live music features the **Matsuriza** traditional drummers.

Morocco: as you would expect, this is a real shopping experience, with bazaars, alleyways and stalls selling a well-priced array of carpets, leather goods, clothing, brass ornaments, pottery and antiques (seek out that Magic Lamp!). All of the building materials were faithfully imported for the pavilion, which was hand-built to give Morocco a great degree of authenticity, even by World Showcase's high standards. You'll be unable to keep your eyes off the clever detail around the winding alleyways and gardens, which can be enjoyed on daily (free) 45-minute walking tours.

The **Gallery of Arts and History** offers more historical and cultural insight into the country, while the Fez House depicts the style of a typical Moroccan home.

BRIT TIP: The Tangierine Café in Morocco is a peaceful haven in which to enjoy a quiet, healthy lunch, especially if you are vegetarian, while there is also a tempting coffee and pastry counter.

BRIT TIP: Kids: to get the best autographs from your Disney favourites, use a thick pen or pencil, as some characters have trouble writing otherwise!

Restaurant Marrakesh provides a full Moroccan dining experience, complete with traditional musicians and a belly dancer. It's rather pricey ($60 for the Moroccan feast for 2) but the atmosphere is lively and entertaining. However, better value can be had at **Tangierine Café**, with a healthy array of Mediterranean-style foods (hummus, tabbouleh, couscous, roast lamb, lentil salad and Moroccan breads) at more down-to-earth prices, and with several vegetarian options ($6.95–11.95). Watch out, too, for characters from Disney's film *Aladdin* and a new live musical show, MoRockin' with a variety of Arabic rhythms served up in fun style.

France: France is predictably overlooked by a replica Eiffel Tower, but the smart streets, buildings and the sheer cleanliness is a long way from modern-day Paris! This is pre-World War I France, with official buskers and comedy street theatre acts adding to the rather dreamy atmosphere (look out for **Le Serveur Amusant** for some eye-catching antics). Don't miss **Impressions de France**, another big-film production that serves up all the grandest sights of the country, accompanied by the music of Offenbach, Debussy, Saint-Saëns and Satie. Crowds get quite heavy from late morning. AAAA.

This is also the pavilion for a gastronomic experience with 3 restaurants, of which **Chefs de France** and **Bistro de Paris** are major discoveries. The former is an award-winning, full-service, and therefore expensive, establishment featuring top quality cuisine created by French chefs on a daily basis, while the latter, upstairs, offers more intimate bistro dining, still with an individual touch (and, if anything, slightly more expensive) and plenty of style (starters from $9–17, main courses $29–35). The Bistro books only 30 days in advance.

Alternatively, the **Boulangerie Patisserie** is a sidewalk café offering more modest fare (and some wonderful pastries, as you'd expect) at a more modest price. Shopping is also suitably chic, with a Guerlain perfumery, wine shop and patisserie.

United Kingdom: the least inspiring of all the pavilions, and certainly with little to entertain those who have visited a pub or shopped for Royal Doulton or Burberry goods. It is partly offset by some good street entertainers and the excellent Beatles tribute band, the **British Invasion**, but that really is the sum total here. **The Rose and Crown Pub** is antiseptically authentic, but you can get better elsewhere at these prices (ploughman's $12.99, cottage pie $14.99, fish and chips $15.99, and a

> BRIT TIP: The Rose and Crown dining room in the UK pavilion is a great place from which to see the nightly IllumiNations fireworks spectacular.

pint of Bass, Harp Lager or Guinness for a whopping $7). There is also a take-away **Harry Ramsden's** fish and chippie. Other shops are the Tea Caddy, the Magic of Wales, the Queen's Table, Crown And Crest (perfumes, heraldry) and the Toy Soldier (traditional games and Disney toys).

Canada: completing the World Showcase circle, the main features

here are **Victoria Gardens**, based on the world-famous Butchart Gardens on Vancouver Island, some spectacular Rocky Mountain scenery, a replica French gothic mansion, the Hôtel de Canada, and another stunning 360-degree film, **O Canada!** As with China and France, this showcases the country's sights and scenery in a terrific, 17-minute advert for the Canadian Tourist Board. It gets busiest from late morning to late afternoon. AAA. Resident band **Off Kilter** are also one of the most entertaining acts I've seen anywhere. Want to hear rock 'n' roll bagpipes? This is the group for you! **Le Cellier Steakhouse** is a modestly priced dining room offering great steaks, prime rib, seafood, chicken and several vegetarian dishes for lunch and dinner.

Around World Showcase are 11 **Kidcot Fun Stop** activity centres, at which children can play games and collect a special *Epcot* Passport to get stamped at each pavilion. Kids will also want to pick up **Goofy's Epcot Guide** at the main entrance, which asks them to answer various questions around World Showcase and solve Goofy's dilemma.

Disney characters put on a show several times a day at **Showcase Plaza**, just across the bridge from Future World to World Showcase, and they also take their Character Bus on tour around World Showcase, so have those autograph books handy!

For those who enjoy new technology, World Showcase offers a morning **Around The World At Epcot** tour on the innovative two-wheeled Segway Human Transporter. It costs a hefty $80/person extra but the 2-hour tour includes full instruction and plenty of travel time on these amazing contraptions, which can go up to 12.5mph (20kph). It is open to only 10 guests at 9am each day (minimum age 16) and it's advisable to book in advance on 407 WDW TOUR.

Planning your visit

If you plan a 2-day visit, it makes sense to spend the first day in World Showcase, arriving early and going straight there while the majority stay in Future World, booking your evening meal around 5.30pm, and then lingering around the lagoon for the evening entertainment. For your second visit, try arriving in mid-afternoon and then doing Future World in a more leisurely fashion. Queues at most of the pavilions are almost non-existent for rides like Universe of Energy, Spaceship Earth and Journey Into Imagination, although Test Track, Soarin' and Mission: Space stay busy all day.

You CAN do *Epcot* in a day – if you arrive early, put in some speedy legwork and give some of the detail a miss. But, of all the parks, it is a shame to hurry this one. In the shops (almost 70 in all), try to save your browsing for when most are on the rides.

IllumiNations: Reflections of Earth

The day's big finale is an absolute show-stopper. **IllumiNations: Reflections of Earth** is a firework and special-effect extravaganza, awesome even by Disney standards. British composer Gavin Greenaway provided the original music for a 15-minute performance of vivid brilliance. Some 2,800 firework shells are launched as a celestial backdrop to a series of fire-and-water effects on the World Showcase Lagoon. The central icon is a 28ft (9m) video globe of Earth that opens in a spectacular climax of choreographed pyrotechnics. Truly magnificent. However, people start staking out the best Lagoon-side spots up to 2 HOURS in advance. The ultimate way to view IllumiNations is by private boat on

5

EPCOT with children

Here is our rough guide to the attractions that appeal to different age groups in this park:

Under 5s
Spaceship Earth, Universe of Energy, Journey Into Imagination with Figment, The Living Seas, Living with the Land, Circle of Life, El Rio del Tiempo, Soarin' (if tall enough), Kidcot stops.

5–8s
All the above, plus Body Wars, Cranium Command, Test Track, Innoventions, 'Honey, I Shrunk The Audience' (with parental discretion), Image Works, Maelstrom (Norway), The American Adventure, Miyuki the Candy Lady, JAMMitors, Kristos.

9–12s
All the above, plus Behind the Seeds tour, Mission: SPACE, Treasures of Morocco tour, Impressions de France, Wonders of China, O Canada!, Sergio, Le Serveur Amusant, Dragon Legend Acrobats, Matsuriza Drummers.

Over 12s
All the above, plus Land of Many Faces (China), Bijutsu-kan Gallery, Norway guided tours, Off Kilter (Canada), British Invasion (UK).

one of three **speciality cruises** from *Disney's Boardwalk* or *Yacht/Beach Club Resorts* (for non-residents, too). They vary from $180-258 per boat (holding 4-12 guests) and can be used for special celebrations. The Basic cruise costs $235 and the pontoon boat holds a maximum of 12 (10 adults and 2 children). It includes water, sodas and snacks. The Celebration cruise costs $258 and adds a suitable range of occasion decorations. The Classic motorboat *Breathless* then costs $179 (max. of 4 adults). Call 407 939 7529 up to 90 days in advance to book. Be aware cruises launch regardless of whether fireworks are taking place.

Behind the scenes

Epcot also has some special behind-the-scenes tours (but not for under-16s). **Dolphins In Depth** ($150, including souvenir photo, T-shirt and refreshments) is a 3½-hour delve into the backstage and research areas of the Living Seas pavilion, including a chance to meet the resident dolphins (ages 13–17 must be accompanied by an adult). **Gardens of the World** ($59) is a 3-hour tour of the park's gardens and includes tips for your own garden. **Hidden Treasures** is a 3-hour tour ($59) of the 11 countries of World Showcase. **Undiscovered Future World** is a 4½-hour journey into the creation of *Epcot*, Walt's

vision for the resort and backstage areas like IllumiNations ($49). **Dive Quest** ($140/person, ages 10 and up) is a 2½-hour experience, with a 30-minute dive into the Living Seas aquarium, plus a behind-the-scenes look at the facility at 4.30 or 5.30pm every day, and you need to have scuba certification (T-shirt and certificate for all participants; theme park admission not required). The new Aqua Seas Tour ($100/person, ages 8 and up; under 18s must be accompanied by an adult; inclusive of T-shirt and group photo; again, theme park admission is not required for this tour) is similar to Dive Quest but without the scuba diving element (daily at 12.30pm). The most comprehensive tour, **Backstage Magic** ($199; ages 16 and up), goes behind the scenes of *Epcot*, *Magic Kingdom Park* and *Disney-MGM Studios* on a 7-hour foray into little-seen aspects, such as the back-stage areas of *Disney-MGM Studios* and the tunnels below the *Magic Kingdom Park*. These tours must be booked on 407 WDW TOUR (407 939 8687).

Annual festivals

There are 2 other annual Epcot events to watch out for. The **International Flower and Garden Festival** literally puts the whole park in full bloom with an amazing series of set-pieces, seminars and mini-exhibitions from mid-April to early June. All the exhibits and lectures are free and it adds a beautiful aspect to an already scenic park. The **Food and Wine Festival** runs for 45 days from October 1 and showcases national and regional cuisines, wines and beers, with the chance to attend grand Winemakers Dinners and Tasting Events, or just sample the inexpensive offerings of more than 20 food booths around World Showcase.

The Living Seas

© Disney

Disney-MGM Studios

Welcome to Hollywood – well, the *Walt Disney World Resort in Florida* version of it. When it opened in May 1989, Michael Eisner, chairman of the Walt Disney Company, insisted it was 'the Hollywood that never was and always will be'. Sounds double Dutch? Don't worry, all will be revealed in your day-long tour of this real-life combination of theme park and working TV and film studio. The most common question about *Disney-MGM Studios* is 'Are they really working studios?', and yes, there are film and TV productions going on even while you're riding around the park peering into the backstage areas.

Rather bigger than the *Magic Kingdom* Park at 154 acres (62ha) but substantially smaller than *Epcot*, *Disney-MGM Studios* is a different experience yet again with its combination of attractions, spectacular shows (including the unmissable Fantasmic!), street entertainment, film sets and smart gift shops. Like the *Magic Kingdom* Park, the food on offer may not win awards, but some of the restaurants (notably the Sci-Fi Dine-in Theater and '50s Prime Time Café) have imaginative settings. The park also has rather more to occupy smaller children than *Epcot*, but you can still easily see all of it in a day unless the crowds are heavy.

Location

The entrance arrangements will be fairly familiar if you have already visited any of the other parks. *Disney-MGM Studios* is located on Buena Vista Drive (which runs between World Drive and Epcot Drive) and the parking fee is $8. Remember to make a note of where you park before you catch the tram to the main gates, where you must wait for the official opening hour. If the queues build up quickly, the gates will open early, so be ready for a running start. Once through the gates, you are into Hollywood Boulevard, a street of mainly gift shops, and you have to decide which of the main attractions to head for first, as these are the ones where the queues will be heaviest nearly all day. Try to ignore the lure of the shops as it is better to browse in the early afternoon when the attractions are at their busiest.

Incidentally, if you thought Disney had elevated queuing to an art form in their other parks, wait until you see how cleverly arranged they are here. Just when you think you have got to the ride itself, there is another twist to the queue you hadn't seen or an extra element to the ride that holds you up. The latter are 'holding pens', which are an ingenious way of making it seem like you are being entertained instead of queuing. Look out for them in particular at the Great Movie Ride, Twilight Zone™ Tower of Terror and Jim Henson's Muppet*Vision 3-D.

An up-to-the-minute check on queue times at all the attractions is kept on a **Guest Information Board** on Hollywood Boulevard, just past its junction with Sunset

5

Catastrophe Canyon

© Disney

Disney-MGM Studios at a glance

Location	Off Buena Vista Drive or World Drive, Walt Disney World
Size	154 acres (62ha)
Hours	9am–7pm off peak; 9am–10pm high season (Easter, summer holidays, Thanksgiving and Christmas)
Admission	Under 3 free; 3–9 $48 (1-day base ticket), $155 (5-Day Premium), $196 (7-Day Premium); adult (10+) $59.73, $193, $233. Prices do not include tax
Parking	$8
Lockers	Yes; next to Oscar's Super Service, to right of main entrance; $7 ($2 refundable)
Pushchairs	$10 and $18 ($1 deposit refunded) from Oscar's Super Service
Wheelchairs	$10 ($1 deposit refunded) or $35 ($10 deposit refunded); same location as pushchairs
Top Attractions	Twilight Zone™ Tower of Terror, Rock 'n' Roller Coaster Starring Aerosmith, Star Tours, The Great Movie Ride, Who Wants To Be A Millionaire – Play It!, Voyage of the Little Mermaid, Jim Henson's Muppet*Vision 3-D, Lights, Motors, Action!™ Extreme Stunt Show
Don't Miss	Disney Stars and Motor Cars Parade, Indiana Jones™ Epic Stunt Spectacular!, Fantasmic!
Hidden Costs	**Meals** Burger, chips and coke $8.18 / 3-course lunch $22.97 (Prime Time Café) / Kids' meal $3.99
	T-shirts $19–30
	Souvenirs $1.25–3,250
	Sundries Race 'n' Roller Coaster Starring Aerosmith ride photo $16.95; poster-size $22

Boulevard, where you can also book for the restaurants. The **Baby Center** here is located just inside the main gates on the left, next to Guest Relations, along with **First Aid**.

Disney-MGM Studios is laid out in a rather more confusing fashion than its counterparts, which have neatly packaged 'lands', so you need to consult your map often to ensure you're going in the right direction.

The main attractions

The opening-gate crowds will all surge in one of 3 directions, which will give you a pretty good idea of where you want to go. By far the 'biggest' attraction here is the **Twilight Zone™ Tower of Terror**, a magnificent haunted hotel ride that culminates in a 13-storey drop in a lift, where queues hit 2 hours at peak periods. So, if the Tower appeals to you, do it first! Head up Hollywood Boulevard then turn right into Sunset Boulevard where you'll see it at the end, looming ominously over the park. It's a FastPass (FP) ride (see page 94) like the **Rock 'n' Roller Coaster Starring Aerosmith**, at the end of Sunset Boulevard on the left, which is another huge draw, so you can get a pass for one and ride the other.

Star Tours, the great *Star Wars*™ simulator ride, and **Voyage of the Little Mermaid** are also serious queue-builders and FP attractions. If you are not up for the really big thrills, grab a FP for Mermaid (straight up Hollywood Boulevard, past Sunset, turn right into Animation Courtyard), then head for Star Tours (back across the main square past the Indiana Jones™ show). Also, the **Who Wants To Be A Millionaire – Play It!** attraction is a major draw, but sometimes has only 8 shows (holding 1,600 people a time) a day, hence FPs can run out quickly. So, if this appeals to you, head here early on (past the Little Mermaid and along Mickey Avenue).

Newly open as part of the *Happiest Celebration on Earth* is the blockbuster **Lights, Motors, Action!**™ **Extreme Stunt Show**, which plays 3–5 times a day. This is also HUGELY popular, so try to take advantage of the FastPass opportunity here.

Here's a full rundown of the attractions, in a clockwise direction:

The Great Movie Ride: this faces you (behind the hat icon) as you walk in along Hollywood Boulevard and is a good place to start if the crowds are not too serious. An all-star audio-animatronics cast re-create a number of box office smashes, including Jimmy Cagney's *Public Enemy*, Julie Andrews in *Mary Poppins*, Gene Kelly in *Singin' in the Rain* and many more masterful set-pieces as you undertake your conducted tour.

Small children may find the menace of *The Alien* too strong, but otherwise the ride has universal appeal and features some clever live twists I won't reveal (there are 2 slight variations on this ride, a cowboy and a gangster version – ask a Cast Member if you especially want to do either one). AAAA.

ABC Sound Studio 'Sounds Dangerous' Starring Drew Carey: a sound FX special which features American comedian Drew Carey in an instalment of a spoof undercover police show *Sounds Dangerous*. Most of the 12-minute show is in the dark – which upsets some children – and is centred on your special headphones as Carey's stakeout goes wildly wrong. Clever and amusing – if a bit tame for older children – you exit into the Sound Works Studio to try out some well-known sound effects. AAA.

Indiana Jones™ **Epic Stunt Spectacular:** consult your park map for the various times that this rip-roaring stunt cavalcade hits the stage. A specially made movie set creates three different backdrops for Indiana Jones'™ stunt people to put on a dazzling array of clever stunts, scenes and special effects from the Harrison Ford film epics. Audience participation is an element and there are some amusing sub-plots. Queues for the 30-minute show begin to form up to half an hour beforehand, but the auditorium holds more than 2,000 so everyone usually gets in. TTTT (FP).

Star Tours: anyone remotely amused by the *Star Wars*™ films will enjoy just queuing for one of our favourites, a breathtaking 7-minute spin in a Star Speeder. The elaborate walk-in area is full of *Star Wars*™ gadgets and gizmos that will make the long wait (sometimes up to an hour) pass quickly. From arguing robots C-3PO and R-2D2 to your robotic 'pilot', everything has a brilliant sense of space travel, and

5

DISNEY-MGM STUDIOS

1 Parade Route ... Disney Stars And Motor Cars Parade
2 Sorcerer Mickey
3 The Great Movie Ride
4 ABC Sound Studio 'Sounds Dangerous' Starring Drew Carey
5 Indiana Jones™ Epic Stunt Spectacular!
6 Star Tours
7 Jim Henson's Muppet*Vision 3-D
8 Honey, I Shrunk The Kids Movie Set Adventure
9 Catastrophe Canyon On *Disney-MGM Studios* Backlot Tour
10 *Disney-MGM Studios* Backlot Tour
11 Meet Mickey Mouse
12 Who Wants To Be A Millionaire – Play It!
13 Walt Disney: One Man's Dream
14 Voyage Of The Little Mermaid
15 The Magic Of Disney Animation
16 Playhouse Disney – Live On Stage!
17 Rock 'n' Roller Coaster Starring Aerosmith
18 The Twilight Zone™ Tower Of Terror
19 Beauty and the Beast – Live On Stage
20 Fantasmic!
21 Guest Information Board
22 Toy Story Pizza Planet
23 Lights, Motors, Action!™ Extreme Stunt Show
24 Al's Toy Barn
25 '50s Prime Time Café
26 Hollywood & Vine
27 Hollywood Brown Derby
28 Mama Melrose's
29 Sunset Ranch Market
30 Sci-Fi Dine-in Theater

DISNEY-MGM STUDIOS

the ride won't disappoint! Restrictions: 3ft 4in/101cm, no children under 3. TTTT (plus AAAAA) (FP).

Jim Henson's Muppet*Vision 3-D: the 3-D is crossed out here and 4-D substituted in its place, so be warned that strange things will be happening! A wonderful 10-minute holding-pen pre-show takes you into the Muppet Theater for a 20-minute experience with all of the Muppets, 3-D special effects and more – when Fozzie Bear points his squirty flower at you, prepare to get wet! It's a gem, and the kids love it. Queues build up through the main parts of the day, but Disney's queuing expertise makes them seem shorter. AAAAA (FP).

Honey, I Shrunk the Kids Movie Set Adventure: this adventure playground gives youngsters the chance to tackle gigantic blades of grass that turn out to be slides, crawl through caves, investigate giant mushrooms and more. However, some may turn round and say 'Yeah. A giant ant. So what?' and head back for the rides. There can be long queues here, too, so arrive early if the kids demand it (and bring plenty of film). TT (TTTT under 9s).

Lights, Motors, Action!™ Extreme Stunt Show: a direct import from the *Walt Disney Studios* in Paris is this truly amazing live action stunt spectacular, featuring cars, motorbikes and stuntmen of all kinds. It is one of the most

BRIT TIP: People begin queuing for Lights, Motors, Action!™ Extreme Stunt Show a good half-hour before seating, and the midday shows are always full. It is better to aim for the first performance, or wait until later.

remarkable shows you will see anywhere, full of genuine high-risk stunts that will leave you shaking your head in amazement. Seating starts 30 minutes prior to a show, and there is some amusing pre-show chat before the serious stuff starts. The set is based on a typical Mediterranean village and is magnificently crafted.

Once the preliminaries are completed, you are treated to a 40-minute extravaganza of daredevil stunts, with a Car Ballet sequence, a Motorbike Chase and a Grand Finale that features some surprise pyrotechnics to complete an awesome presentation (keep your eyes on the windows below the video screen at the end!). Each scene – featuring a secret agent 'goody' and various 'baddies' – is explained by a movie 'director' and the results of each 'shoot' are played back on the video screen to show how each effect was created. All the cars were specially created for the show by Vauxhall, and there are some extra

5

Lights, Motors, Action!™ Extreme Stunt Show

© Disney

BRIT TIP: If you have young children, be aware there is some (loud) mock gunfire in the Lights, Motors, Action!™ Extreme Stunt Show, which can upset sensitive ears, while the motorbike scene includes a rider catching fire, which can be frightening for them, too.

tricks in between the main scenes. The whole thing was designed by Frenchman Rémy Julienne, the doyen of film car stunt sequences, who has worked on James Bond films *Goldeneye* and *Licence to Kill* and other action-packed epics such as *The Rock, Gone In 60 Seconds* and *Enemy Of The State*.

Finally, the exit can be quite a scrum as 5,000 people have to leave together, and it can take 10–15 minutes to clear the auditorium, hence if you can sit towards the front of the grandstand, you will be out rather quicker. The fact it involves so much genuine, live co-ordination makes for a truly thrilling experience and you may well want to see it more than once, which is another reason to see it early on. TTTTT.

The Disney-MGM Studios Backlot Tour: before you board the special trams for a look at the off-limits part of the studios in this 35-minute walk-and ride tour, you are treated to some special effects (involving an amusing water tank

BRIT TIP: Do not queue up for the Backlot Tour when Lights, Motors, Action! has just let out – it will be far too crowded.

with a mock Pearl Harbor attack). The tram takes you round the production backlot and then to **Catastrophe Canyon** for a demonstration of special effects that try both to drown you and blow you up! AAA (plus TTTT). You exit into the **American Film Institute** Showcase of costumes and props from recent films.

Who Wants To Be A Millionaire – Play It!: Disney's live version of the hit TV show is based on the US programme, but is still effectively the same show. The great twist is EVERYONE gets to play – all 1,600 members of the audience. Whoever is fastest with the put-them-in-order question starts in the hot seat and, as you play along, you build up a score, with the top 10 shown on screen at various stages. Then, when a contestant loses out, the person with the highest score is next up. The hosts do a terrific job of maintaining the TV 'illusion' and there are the usual rules and lifelines, which add to the sense of reality (although you play for Disney points towards some great souvenirs). One difference is there can be no Phone A Friend. Instead, you have Phone A Complete Stranger, when a passer-by is grabbed off the street outside! It is addictive fun, and the only drawback is it is so popular the FastPass tickets run out quickly, so try to get here early. AAAAA (FP). As you come out, look for the **Meet Mickey Mouse** character greet nearby, plus **Jo Jo's Circus characters**.

Walt Disney: One Man's Dream: this interactive show-and-tell exhibit chronicles Walt himself and his lifetime of accomplishments. From archive school records to a model of the Nautilus from *20,000 Leagues Under The Sea*, the story of the man behind the Mouse comes to vivid life. The homage concludes with a preview of Disney's future developments, plus a 10-minute film encapsulating everything Walt achieved and dreamed about. AAAA.

Voyage of the Little Mermaid: a 17-minute live performance that is primarily for children who have seen the Disney cartoon. It brings together a creative mix of live actors, animation and puppetry to re-create the highlights of the film. Parents will still enjoy the clever special effects, but queues tend to be long, so go early or late. Those in the first few rows may also get a little wet. AAA (AAAAA under 9s) (FP).

> BRIT TIP: Try to sit at least halfway back in the Mermaid Theatre, especially with young children, as the stage front is a bit high for little 'uns.

The Magic of Disney Animation: an amusing and entertaining 30-minute show-and-tour through the making of cartoons. It starts with a special theatrical performance by Mushu, the Eddie Murphy-voiced dragon from the animated film *Mulan*. From there you exit into a hands-on area of interactive fun (especially for children); Ink & Paint is a colouring challenge, at Sound Stage you can try a voice-over, and You're A Character will tell you what Disney character you most resemble. From there, you have the choice of joining the Animation Academy for a tutored class in cartoon art, or exiting via the Animation Gallery, which has some fabulous gifts. Queues are rarely serious, so it's a good one for the afternoon. AAAA.

Playhouse Disney – Live On Stage!: straight out of several popular kids' TV series comes this 20-minute live show with pre-school favourites *Bear in the Big Blue House*, *Rolie Polie Olie*, *The Book of Pooh* and *Stanley*. Much of this can be seen only on cable or satellite TV in the UK, but it is still colourful and entertaining. AAA (AAAAA under 5s).

Rock 'n' Roller Coaster Starring Aerosmith: Disney's first big-thrill inverted coaster is a sure-fire draw for the high-energy ride addicts, with a magnificent indoor setting and nerve-jangling ride. It features a clever 3-D film show starring rock group Aerosmith in their recording studio. That preamble leads to the real fun, set to specially recorded tracks from the band itself and with outrageous speaker systems, as riders climb aboard Cadillac 'cars' for this memorable whiz through a mock Los Angeles setting (watch out for a close encounter with the 'Hollywood' sign!). The high-speed launch and inversions ensure an up-to-the-minute coaster experience. Go first thing or expect serious queues. Restrictions: 4ft/124cm TTTTT (FP).

The Twilight Zone™ Tower of Terror: the tallest landmark in *Walt Disney World Resort in Florida* (at 199ft/60m) invites you to experience another dimension in this mysterious Hollywood Tower Hotel that time forgot. The exterior is intriguing, the interior is fascinating, the ride is scintillating and the queues are huge! Just when you think you are through to the ride, there is another queue, so spend your time inspecting the superb detail. The ride was also revamped in 2003 to add a new, random element to the drop sequence and other special effects, while lap bars have been replaced with seat-belts for a more hair-rising experience! Restrictions: 3ft 4in/101cm. TTTTT (FP). The Twilight Zone™ is a registered trademark of CBS, Inc. and is used pursuant to a licence from CBS, Inc.

Beauty and the Beast – Live on Stage: an enchanting live performance of the highlights of this

5

BRIT TIP: Beat the crowds by booking a Fantasmic! dinner package when you enter the park (or on 407 939 3463). Just book an early-evening dinner package Priority Seating for the Hollywood Brown Derby, Mama Melrose's or Hollywood and Vine and you get VIP seating later for the show.

Disney classic will entertain the whole family for 20 minutes in the nearby Theater of the Stars. Check the schedule for showtimes (and try to catch the *a capella* singing group Four For A Dollar who perform prior to each show). AAA.

Fantasmic!: this special-effects spectacular is simply not to be missed. Staged every night in a 6,900-seat amphitheatre, it features

Rock 'n' Roller Coaster® starring Aerosmith

© Disney

the 'dreams' of Mr M Mouse, portrayed as the Sorcerer's Apprentice, through films such as *Pocahontas, The Lion King* and *Snow White*, but hijacked by various Disney villains, leading to a tumultuous battle with Our Hero emerging triumphant. Dancing waters, shooting comets, animated fountains, swirling stars and balls of fire combine in a breathtaking presentation – but beware of the giant, fire-breathing dragon! The 25-minute show begins seating up to 90 minutes in advance and it is advisable to head there at least 30 minutes before (watch out for the splash zones!). AAAAA.

Daily parade

In keeping with the park's movie-star style, the daily parade is **Disney Stars and Motor Cars**, and is another highlight. The theme is a Hollywood film premiere of the 1930s and '40s, with a series of genuine vintage cars and clever replicas being used to mount a riotous cavalcade of Disney showbiz favourites. It features 15 crazily customised cars – including a 1929 Cadillac – that provide the likes of **Aladdin, Mary Poppins, Mulan**, the **Muppets** and **Monsters Inc.** with a chance to show off in larger-than-life fashion. Watch out for the **Star Wars™** 'Land Speeder' with a radio-controlled R-2D2 in the largest parade ever staged in Disney-MGM Studios. The lead car also features any special guests at the Studios that day – or a visiting family instead. AAAA.

Disney characters are out and about along Mickey Avenue, as are performing 'actors and actresses' in Hollywood Boulevard. You can catch the Toy Story characters by Al's Toy Barn, The Incredibles at the Magic of Disney Animation and the Power Rangers at the bottom of Streets of

Hollywood Brown Derby

America at regular intervals. And, for that 'something different' factor, watch out for the classic live rock 'n' roll performances of **Mulch, Sweat and Shears**, either on Streets of America or by Rock 'n' Roller Coaster.

Places to eat

While the choice of food may not be wide, there is plenty of it and at reasonable prices. **The Hollywood Brown Derby** offers a full-service restaurant in fine Hollywood style (reservations necessary – special Early Evening Value meals 4-6pm), while **Mama Melrose's Ristorante Italiano** is a wonderful table-service Italian option (one of my favourites).

The **Sci-Fi Dine-In Theater Restaurant** is a big hit with kids as you dine in a mock drive-in cinema, with cars as 'tables', waitresses on roller skates and a big film screen showing old black-and-white science fiction clips. The **'50s Prime Time Café** is another hilarious experience as you sit in mock stage sets from

BRIT TIP: We always recommend the Sci-Fi Dine-In Theater Restaurant or '50s Prime Time Café for a main meal with a difference.

American TV sitcoms and eat meals 'just like Mom used to make'. (The waiters all claim to be your brother and warn you to take your elbows off the table, etc. Good fun.) Reservations necessary.

The fast-food eateries consist of the **ABC Commissary** (breakfast 'til 10.30am), **Backlot Express** (excellent burgers and hot dogs), **Rosie's All-American Café** (chicken, burgers, salads) and the **Toy Story Pizza Planet** (pizza, salads and drinks). More healthy fare can be found at the new **Studio Catering Co. Flatbread Grill**. A good buffet lunch (high season only) and dinner is also available at **Hollywood and Vine Cafeteria of the Stars**.

Shopping

There are 21 gift and speciality shops around the Studios – six of them along Hollywood Boulevard – worth checking out in early afternoon. Sid Caheunga's **One-of-a-Kind** (just to the left of the main gates as you enter) stocks rare movie and TV items, including many celebrity autographs. Try the **Legends of Hollywood** (on Sunset Boulevard) for some different souvenirs and **AFI Showcase Shop** (in the Backlot) with MGM logo products and movie-related gifts.

Twilight Zone Tower of Terror™

Keystone Clothiers (at the top of Hollywood Boulevard) offers some of the best apparel.

Studios at Christmas

At Christmas (in fact, from late November to January 1), one of the most amazing spectacles anywhere is the **Osborne Family Lights**, which are switched on every evening in the New York street area. The display of 5 million twinkling, themed fairy lights draws a huge crowd twice a night (try to go during a Fantasmic! performance to avoid the worst of the throngs) and is simply stunning.

Skywalker and Co.

Star Wars™ film fans will want to make a beeline for the Studios during weekends in the latter half of May and early June when the park becomes a playground for characters, film stars, photo-opportunities, competitions and other memorabilia based on anything to do with Luke Skywalker and Co. There is no additional fee to rub shoulders with (and get autographs from) various *Star Wars*™ personalities, and the Studios take on an extra (Space) dimension each weekend.

DISNEY-MGM STUDIOS with children

Here is our general guide to the rides that appeal to the different age groups in this park (and it is, possibly, the best spread of all).

Under 5s
Playhouse Disney – Live On Stage!, Voyage of the Little Mermaid, Beauty and the Beast – Live on Stage, Disney Stars and Motor Cars parade, Fantasmic!, Honey I Shrunk the Kids Movie Set Adventure, The Magic of Disney Animation.

5–8s
Voyage of the Little Mermaid, Beauty and the Beast – Live On Stage, Honey I Shrunk the Kids Movie Set Adventure, Indiana Jones™ Epic Stunt Spectacular, 'Sounds Dangerous' Starring Drew Carey, Jim Henson's Muppet*Vision 3-D, *Disney-MGM Studios* Backlot Tour, The Magic of Disney Animation, Disney Stars and Motor Cars parade, Lights, Motors, Action!™ Extreme Stunt Show, Fantasmic!

9–12s
'Sounds Dangerous' starring Drew Carey, Indiana Jones™ Epic Stunt Spectacular, Lights, Motors, Action!™ Extreme Stunt Show, The Great Movie Ride, Star Tours, Jim Henson's Muppet*Vision 3-D, *Disney-MGM Studios* Backlot Tour, The Magic of Disney Animation, Beauty and the Beast – Live On Stage, Rock 'n' Roller Coaster Starring Aerosmith, Twilight Zone™ Tower of Terror, Fantasmic!

Over 12s
Indiana Jones™ Epic Stunt Spectacular, Star Tours, The Great Movie Ride, Lights, Motors, Action!™ Extreme Stunt Show, Jim Henson's Muppet*Vision 3-D, *Disney-MGM Studios* Backlot Tour, Who Wants To Be A Millionaire – Play It!, The Magic of Disney Animation, Rock 'n' Roller Coaster Starring Aerosmith, Twilight Zone™ Tower of Terror, Fantasmic!

Disney's Animal Kingdom Theme Park

Disney's newest, smartest and most radical theme park opened in 1998 representing a completely different experience. With an emphasis on nature and conservation, it largely eschews the non-stop thrills and attractions that mark out the other parks, and instead offers a change of pace, a more relaxing motif, as well as Disney's usual seamless entertainment style – plus 2 excellent thrill attractions (3 when the under-construction blockbuster Expedition: Everest™ opens in April 2006).

The attractions are relatively few, just 5 out-and-out rides, plus 2 scenic journeys, 2 nature trails, 5 shows (including the hilarious 3-D film *It's Tough to Be a Bug!* and the full-blown theatre of *Festival of The Lion King*), an elaborate adventure playground, conservation station and petting zoo, and a Disney character greeting area. It's a far cry from the hustle-bustle of the *Magic Kingdom*

5

Disney's Animal Kingdom Theme Park at a glance

Location	Directly off Osceola Parkway, also via World Drive and Buena Vista Drive
Size	500 acres (203ha) divided into six 'lands'
Hours	9am to 5 or 6pm
Admission	Under 3 free; 3–9 $48 (1-day base ticket), $155 (5-Day Premium), $196 (7-Day Premium); adult (10+) $59.73, $193, $233. Prices do not include tax
Parking	$8
Lockers	Yes; either side of Entrance Plaza; $7 ($2 refundable)
Pushchairs	$10 and $18 ($1 refundable) at Garden Gate Gifts, through entrance on right
Wheelchairs	$10 ($1 refund) and $35 ($10 refund); with pushchairs
Top Attractions	DINOSAUR!, Kilimanjaro Safaris, It's Tough To Be A Bug!, Kali River Rapids, Festival of *The Lion King*; Expedition: Everest™ (2006)
Don't Miss	Pangani Forest Exploration Trail, Maharajah Jungle Trek, Rafiki's Planet Watch, Tarzan Rocks!, Mickey's Jamming Jungle Parade, Lucky the dinosaur, dining at Rainforest Café
Hidden Costs	**Meals** Burger, chips and coke $7.78 / 3-course meal at Rainforest Café $29.68 / Kids' meal $3.99
	T-shirts $19–39.95
	Souvenirs $1.99–750
	Sundries Caricature drawings $15, $20, $28

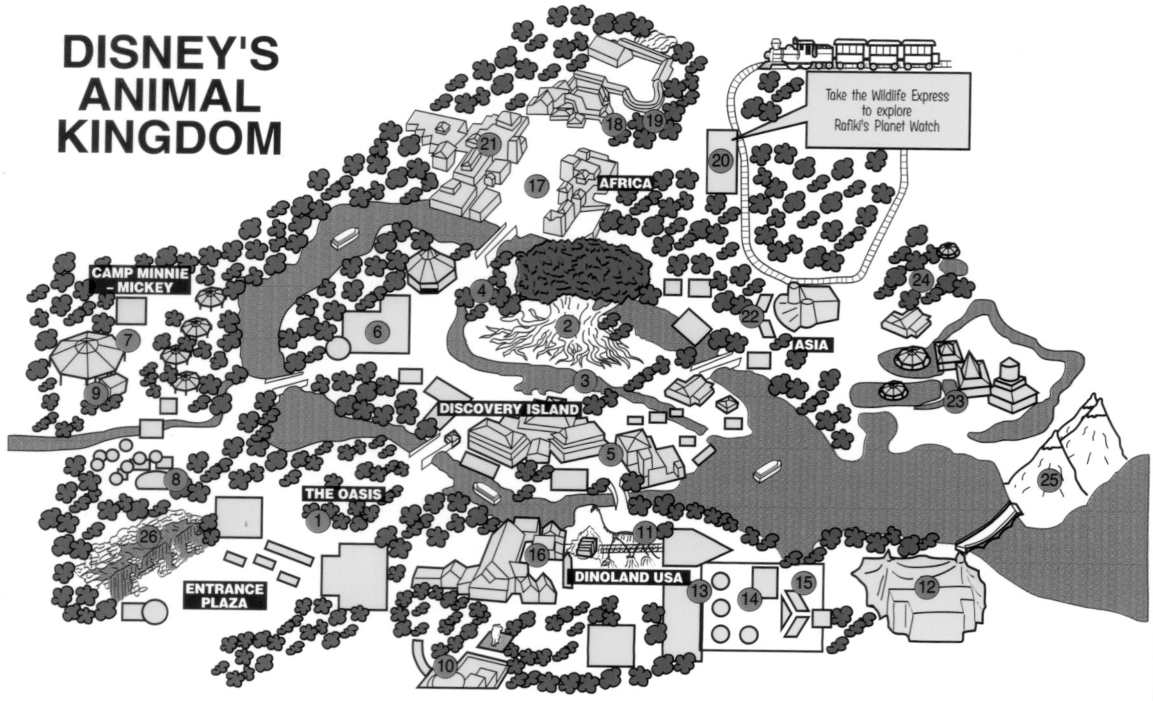

THE OASIS
1 The Oasis Tropical Garden

DISCOVERY ISLAND
2 The Tree Of Life
3 It's Tough To Be A Bug!
4 Discovery Island Trails
5 Flame Tree Barbecue
6 Pizzafari

CAMP MINNIE-MICKEY
7 Character Greeting Trails
8 Pocahontas And Her Forest Friends
9 Festival Of The Lion King

DINOLAND USA
10 Dinosaur!
11 The Boneyard
12 Tarzan™ Rocks!
13 Chester & Hester's Dino-Rama!
14 TriceraTOP Spin
15 Primeval Whirl
16 Restaurantosaurus

AFRICA
17 Harambe
18 Kilimanjaro Safaris
19 Pangani Forest Exploration Trail
20 Rafiki's Planet Watch
21 Tusker House Restaurant

ASIA
22 Flights Of Wonder
23 Kali River Rapids
24 Maharajah Jungle Trek
25 Expedition Everest
26 Rainforest Café

DISNEY'S ANIMAL KINGDOM

Take the Wildlife Express to explore Rafiki's Planet Watch

ASIA
AFRICA
DISCOVERY ISLAND
DINOLAND USA
THE OASIS
CAMP MINNIE-MICKEY
ENTRANCE PLAZA

TriceraTop Spin

Park, and it carries a strong environmental message that aims to create a greater understanding of the world's ecological problems.

It is outrageously scenic, notably with the 145ft (44m) Tree of Life and the Kilimanjaro Safaris, but it won't overwhelm you with Disney's usual grand fantasy. Rather, it is a chance to experience a part of the world that is both threatened and threatening in a safe, secure manner. It is obviously not the Real Thing but it provides a glimpse of some of the world's most majestic areas in a manner that allows ecology and the commercial world to co-exist happily and meaningfully.

The most conclusive word goes to Professor David Bellamy, who told me: 'This park has been designed and looked after by the best animal welfare people you can think of. Bad zoos are bad news and should be closed down, but good zoos are good news and the only hope for keeping about 500 species of animal alive in the future.' The park does get crowded, however, and the walkways can be congested. There are also fewer places to cool down. It is definitely a good idea to be here on time and use FastPass (FP) to minimise queuing.

Getting there

If you are staying in the Kissimmee area, *Disney's Animal Kingdom Theme Park* is the easiest to find. Just get on the (toll) Osceola Parkway and follow it all the way to the toll booths, where parking is $8. Alternatively, coming down I-4, take Exit 65, which puts you on Osceola Parkway. From West Highway 192, come in on Sherberth Road and turn right at the first traffic lights.

If you arrive early (which is advisable), you can walk up to the Entrance Plaza. Otherwise, the usual tram system will take you in, so make a note of the area in which you park (e.g. Unicorn, row 67). The Plaza is overlooked by the mountainous **Rainforest Café**, with its 65-ft (20-metre) waterfall, which is a must for breakfast, an early lunch or dinner (rarely busy). With Orlando so hot through the summer

5

Kilimanjaro Safaris

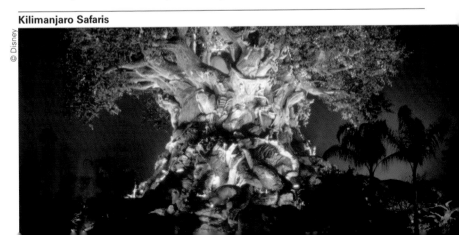

BRIT TIP: The early start is especially advised for Kilimanjaro Safaris. You will see far more animals in the first few cooler hours of the day than during the hotter afternoon.

months, you need to be here as early as possible to see the animals before they disappear into the shade.

For the early birds, here is your best plan of campaign. Once through the gates, animal lovers should head first for Kilimanjaro Safaris, through the Oasis, Discovery Island and into Africa. After the Safari, go straight to Pangani Forest Exploration Trail and you will have experienced two of the park's best animal encounters. Alternatively, thrill-seekers should turn right in Discovery Island for DinoLand USA, where the DINOSAUR! ride is the big attraction. With that one safely under your belt before the serious crowds arrive, head back through the Island to Asia and Kali River Rapids raft ride, followed by the scenic Maharajah Jungle Trek. The best combination for the first arrivals is to get a FastPass (FP) for DINOSAUR! then head straight for Kilimanjaro Safaris, and, once you have done that (and depending on your FP time), either do your DINOSAUR! ride (followed by a Kali River Rapids FP) or go straight to the Rapids. Check your show schedule for Festival of The Lion King and try to catch one of the first two performances as the later ones draw sizeable queues. The 'wait time' board at the entrance to Discovery Island is also helpful. The opening in early 2006 of Expedition: Everest™ will probably distort this picture and make this blockbuster new ride a must-do early on.

Right, those are your main tactics; here is the full rundown.

The Oasis

The Oasis Tropical Garden is a gentle, walk-through introduction to the park, a rocky, tree-covered area featuring several animal habitats, studded with streams, waterfalls and lush plant life. Here you will meet miniature deer, macaws, parrots, iguanas, sloths and tree kangaroos in a wonderfully understated environment that leads you across a stone bridge to the main open park area. AAA.

Discovery Island

This colourful 'village' is the park hub, themed as a tropical artists' colony, with animal-inspired artwork, four main shops and two eateries. Here you will also find various character meet-and-greets, plus the fun **Beatniks** percussion group.

The Tree of Life: this 145ft (44m) high arboreal edifice is the park centrepiece, an awesome creation that seems to give off a different perspective from wherever you view it. The 'trunk' and 'roots' are covered in 325 animal carvings representing the Circle of Life, from the dolphin to the lion. Trails lead round the tree, interspersed with habitats for flamingos, otters, ring-tailed lemurs, macaws, axis deer, cranes, storks, ducks and tortoises. The tree canopy spreads 160ft (49m), the trunk is 50ft (15m) wide and the roots spread out 170ft (52m) in diameter. It has 103,000 leaves (all attached by hand) on more than 8,000 branches! AAAA.

It's Tough To Be A Bug!: winding down among the Tree's roots brings you 'underground' to a 430-seat theatre and another example of Disney's artistry in 3-D

> BRIT TIP: The dark, special effects and creepy-crawlies often scare young ones in It's Tough To Be A Bug beneath the big tree.

films and special effects. This hysterically funny 10-minute show, in the company of Flick from the Disney/Pixar hit film *A Bug's Life*, is a homage to 80 per cent of the animal world, featuring grasshoppers, beetles, spiders, stink bugs and termites (beware the 'acid' spray!) as well as a number of tricks I couldn't possibly reveal. Sit towards the back in the middle of a row (allow a good number of people in first as the rows are filled up from the far side) to get the best of the 3-D effects. Queues build up from midday, but they do move quite steadily. Don't miss the 'forthcoming attractions' posters in the foyer for some excruciating bug puns on well-known films. AAAAA (FP).

Shopping is at its best here, with a huge range of merchandise, souvenirs and gifts (notably in **Disney Outfitters** and **Island Mercantile**), while the two counter service restaurants, **Pizzafari** and **Flame Tree Barbecue**, are both good choices. Indeed, provided it is not too hot, the Flame Tree is a relaxing and picturesque option, set among some pretty gardens, pools and fountains on the edge of Discovery River.

Camp Minnie-Mickey

A woodland retreat featuring gently winding paths and more of Disney's clever scenery – the benches, lighting and the gurgling stream, with Donald Duck and his nephews hiking down the side, that develops into a series of kid-friendly squirt fountains.

Character Greeting Trails: 4 trails lead to a series of jungle encounters with Disney characters such as Mickey and Minnie (naturally), Winnie the Pooh and Tigger, Chip 'n' Dale, Baloo and King Louie, Timon and Rafiki. AAAAA (for kids).

Pocahontas and Her Forest Friends: based on characters from the Disney film *Pocahontas*, this 15-minute show sees various animals – raccoons, rabbits, cranes, a skunk, armadillo and porcupine – interacting with the central actress and Mother Willow in the question of 'Who can save the forest?' However, it doesn't seem to do much for small children, there is not much shade in summer and it is standing room only once the 350 seats have been filled. AAA.

Festival of The Lion King: not to be missed, this high-powered 40-minute production brings the hit film to life in spectacular fashion with giant moving stages, huge animated figures, singers, dancers, acrobats and stilt-walkers. All the well-known songs are given an airing in a coruscation of colour and sound, and it serves to underline the quality Disney brings to live shows. Queuing begins 30 minutes in advance for the 1,000-seat theatre, so try to take in one of the earlier shows. AAAAA.

DinoLand USA

Rather at odds with the natural theming of the rest of the park, DinoLand USA is a full-scale palaeontology exercise, with this mock 'town' taken over by a university fossil dig. Energetically tongue-in-cheek (the 'students' who work in the area have the motto 'Been there, dug that', while you enter under a mock brachiosaurus skeleton, the 'Oldengate Bridge' – groan!), it still features some

5

glimpses into dinosaur research and artefacts.

DINOSAUR!: renamed after Disney's big animated film (it was initially called Countdown to Extinction), its original fast, jerky ride has been toned down a little for a more family-friendly experience (although the dinosaur menace is too scary for many young children). It is a wonderfully realistic journey back to the end of the Cretaceous period and the giant meteor that put paid to dinosaur life. You enter the high-tech Dino Institute, 'A discovery center and research lab dedicated to uncovering the mysteries of the past', for a multimedia show of dino history that leads to a briefing room for your 'mission' 65 million years in the past to view Cretaceous life. However, one of the Institute's scientists 'hijacks' your journey for his own project, to capture a dinosaur, and you go careering back to a prehistoric jungle in your 12-passenger Time Rover. The threat of a carnotaurus (quite frightening for some children; try to sit them on the inside of the car) and the impending doom of the meteor add up to a breathtaking whiz through a stunning environment. You will need to ride at least twice to appreciate all the detail, but queues build up quickly, so go either first thing or late in the day. Restrictions: 3ft 4in/101cm. TTTT plus AAAA (FP).

The Boneyard: a hugely imaginative adventure playground, it offers kids the chance to slip, slide and climb through the 'fossilised' remains of triceratops and brontosaurs, explore caves, dig for bones and splash through a mini-waterfall. The amusing signage will go over the heads of most kids, but it is ideal for parents to let their young uns loose for up to an hour (although not just after the neighbouring Tarzan show has finished). TTTT (kids only).

Tarzan™ Rocks!: and he really does. This amazing show is basically a 30-minute rock concert based on the songs from the animated film, with special effects provided by dancers, acrobats and rollerbladers, all with superb costumes and choreography. Tarzan and Jane appear only briefly, and then mainly as acrobats (ladies: no staring at that loincloth!). Its loud, high-energy style may not be everyone's cup of

Maharajah Jungle Trek®

© Disney

Carvings on The Tree of Life

tea (especially for sensitive young ears) but it is visually stunning, as are the performers. AAAA. NB: Tarzan Rocks is due to close in 2006 and the theatre will be completely refurbished.

> BRIT TIP: At Tarzan™ Rocks! try to grab a seat by the rails that divide the auditorium, as the roller-skating monkeys will come and dance by you!

Chester & Hester's Dino-Rama!: this mini-land of rides, fairground games and stalls adds a rather garish element to DinoLand USA. Its main icon is a towering Concretosaurus (!), and it is designed to have a quirky, tongue-in-cheek style reminiscent of 1950s American roadside attractions. The top rides are:

TriceraTOP Spin: another version of the *Dumbo/Aladdin* rides in the *Magic Kingdom* Park, a flying, twirling, spinning top bounces you up and down with a surprise at the top. AA (or TTTT for under 5s).

Primeval Whirl: coaster fans will definitely get a laugh out of this wacky offering that sends its riders through a maze of curves, hills and (quite sharp) drops that make it seem much faster than it actually is. It is basically a fairground lampoon of

the DINOSAUR! ride, a mock journey 'way back in time', with plenty of cartoon frippery. Extra fun is provided by the fact the cars spin, which gives an extra, unpredictable element to each 3-minute ride (plunging through the jaws of a skeleton dino at one point!). The queuing area is a riot of visual gags, but the ride itself is not recommended for anyone with back or neck problems. Height restriction 4ft/122cm. TTTT (FP).

The **Fossil Fun Games** are 6 fairground-type stalls, each costing a rather hefty $2, to tempt you into trying to win a large cuddly dinosaur, all with the larger-than-life Dino-Rama trademark. Dining options include the (you've guessed!) **Restaurantosaurus**, counter service burgers and hot dogs (presented by McDonald's, so you get McDonald's fries, Chicken McNuggets and Happy Meals but no Big Macs) and a snack bar. Shopping is centred on the huge **Chester and Hester's Dino-Rama! – Dinosaur Treasures**, the 'Fossiliferous Gift Store' with groan-inducing slogans like Merchandise of Extinction, Prehistoric Prices and Last Stop for 65 Million Years!

Africa

The largest land in the park, it re-creates magnificently the forests, grasslands and rocky homelands of equatorial Africa's most fascinating residents in a richly landscaped

Kali River Rapids

© Disney

5

setting that is part rundown port town and part savannah. In this part of the park, the outside world seems thousands of miles away and there is hardly a glimpse of it anywhere.

Harambe: a reconstruction of a Kenyan port village, complete with white coral walls and thatched roofs, is the starting point of your adventure. The Arab-influenced Swahili culture is depicted in the native tribal costumes and architecture. Here you will find 2 more shops, including the **Mombasa Marketplace/Ziwani Traders**, where you can suit up safari-style, and the counter service **Tusker House Restaurant** for rotisserie chicken, fresh fish, salads, vegetarian sandwiches and a special African dish (a healthier offering than most, but a touch expensive), plus 4 snack and drink bars, notably the **Kusafiri Coffee Shop**. The splendid **Karuka Acrobats** also perform here on select days.

Kilimanjaro Safaris: the queuing area alone earns high marks for authenticity, preparing you for the sights and sounds of the 110-acre (45-ha) savannah beyond. You board a 32-passenger truck, with your driver/guide relaying information about the flora and fauna on view and a bush pilot overhead relaying facts and figures on the wildlife, including the dangers threatening them in the real world. Hundreds of animals are spread out in various habitats, with no fences in sight – the ditches and barriers are all well

BRIT TIP: The best (i.e. the most jolting) ride with the Kilimanjaro Safaris is at the back of the truck, although there's nothing much to see from midday to late afternoon when many animals take a siesta.

concealed – as you splash through fords and cross rickety bridges, and you should get some good close-ups of rhinos, elephants, giraffes, zebras, lions, baboons, antelope, ostriches and hippos.

Halfway round, your journey becomes a race to stop elephant poachers, though the outcome is fairly obvious. Once again, the authentic nature of all you see (okay, some of the tyre 'ruts' and termite mounds are concrete and the baobab trees are fake) is quite awesome with the spread of the vegetation and the landscaping, and the only drawback is the lack of photo stops along the way (and the ride can be bumpy). The animals also roam over a wide area and can disappear from view. Not recommended for expectant mothers or anyone with back or neck problems. AAAAA (FP).

Pangani Forest Exploration Trail: as you leave the Safari, you turn into an overgrown nature trail that showcases gorillas, hippos, meerkats and rare tropical birds. You wander the trail at your own pace and visit several research stations to learn more about the animals on display, including the underwater view of the hippos (check out the size of a hippo skull and those teeth!) and the savannah overlook, where giraffe and antelope graze and the amusing meerkats frolic. The walk-through aviary gives you the chance to meet the carmine bee-eater, pygmy goose, African green pigeon, ibis and brimstone canary, among others, but the real centrepiece is the silverback gorilla habitat, in fact, 2 of them. The family group is often just inches away from the plate-glass window, while the bachelor group further along can prove more elusive. Again, the natural aspect of the trail is breathtaking and it provides a host of photo opportunities. It is best to visit early on to see the animals at their most active (and because it quickly becomes quite crowded). AAAAA.

Rafiki's Planet Watch: the little train journey here, with its peek into some of the backstage areas, is just the preamble to the park's interactive and educational exhibits. The 3-part journey starts with **Habitat Habit!**, where you can see cotton-top tamarins and learn how conservation begins in your own back garden. **Conservation Station** is next up with a series of exhibits, shows and information stations about the environment and its ecological dangers, which are aimed primarily at children. Look out for *Sounds of the Rain Forest*, the story of endangered species at the *Mermaid Tales Theater* and the Eco-Heroes (who can be quizzed on screen) trying to redress the balance, then take a self-guided tour of the park's backstage areas such as the veterinary treatment centre, the hatchery and neonatal care. You can easily spend an hour absorbing the information here, along with Disney's Wildlife Conservation Fund. Plus, youngsters can meet Rafiki and some of his animal chums. The **Affection Section**, a petting zoo of lambs, goats, donkeys, sheep and guinea pigs, completes the Planet Watch line-up. AAA.

Asia

The final 'land' of the park is elaborately themed as the gateway to the imaginary south-east Asian city of Anandapur, with temples, ruined forts, landscape and wildlife.

Flights of Wonder: another wildlife show, this portrays the talents and traits of a host of birds, built into a production of mythical proportions, as a treasure-seeking student meets Phoenix, the birds' guardian, in a crumbling, fortified town. Vultures, eagles, toucans, macaws and many other feathered friends take a bow as Phoenix reveals the treasures of the avian world. The Caravan Stage is not air-conditioned, though, and is fiendishly hot in summer. AAA.

Kali River Rapids: part thrill-ride, part scenic journey, this bouncy, raft-ride will get you pretty wet (not great for early morning in winter). It starts out in tropical forest territory before launching into a scene of logging devastation, warning of the dangers of clear-cut burning. Your raft then plunges down a waterfall (and one unlucky soul – usually the one with his or her back to the drop – gets seriously damp) before you finish more sedately, albeit with a few more watery encounters. Queues can be long through the main part of the day, so make use of FastPass here. You'll probably want to experience the ride twice to appreciate all the clever detail. Restrictions: 3ft 6in/106cm (a few rafts have adult-and-child seats allowing smaller children to ride). TTT (plus AAAA) (FP).

Maharajah Jungle Trek: Asia's version of the Pangani Forest Trail is another picturesque walk past decaying temple ruins and various animal encounters. Playful gibbons, tapirs, Komodo dragons and a bat enclosure (including the flying fox-bat, the world's largest variety) lead up to the main viewing area, the 5-acre (2-ha) Tiger Range, which includes a pool and fountains and is a popular playground early in the day for these magnificent big cats. An antelope enclosure and walk-through aviary complete this breathtaking trek (which rarely draws heavy crowds). AAAAA.

Expedition: Everest™: a major new attraction that is scheduled to open in April 2006, this roller-coaster takes you deep into the Himalayas for an encounter with the mythical Yeti. The queuing area alone will convince you of its authentic location (try to do the main queue at least once rather than

FastPass to appreciate all the fine detail) as it delivers you to an old abandoned tea plantation train station (at least, that's the clever theme). Here you undertake the ride to the foothills of Mount Everest, but you must first brave the 200ft Canyons of the Yeti to get there. Will the mythical beast be in evidence? You bet! The ride becomes a typically fast-paced coaster whiz (although with no inversions), both forwards AND backwards, as you attempt to escape from the Yeti's domain. It promises to be another fabulous new ride experience, with plenty of twists and turns, but it is also sure to draw a crowd, so make it one of the first things you do. Restrictions: 3ft 8in/115cm. TTTTT (expected; FP).

Finally, returning to the front entrance gives you the chance to sample or just visit (and shop at) the **Rainforest Café**, the second on Disney property. If you haven't seen the one at *Downtown Disney* Marketplace, you should definitely call in to witness the amazing jungle interior with its audio-animatronic animals, waterfalls, thunderstorms and aquariums. A 3-course meal will

The Boneyard®

set you back about $28 (kids' meals at $6.99), but the setting alone is definitely worth it and the food is above average. Try breakfast or an early dinner here to avoid the crowds.

Jammin' Jungle Parade

The daily highlight is a tour de force called **Mickey's Jammin' Jungle** Parade. Here, the Imagineers have created a series of fanciful 'Expedition Rovers' that give various Disney characters the chance to celebrate all the animals who live here. The parade is enhanced by stilt-walkers, puppets, mobile sculptures and different 'party animals', plus live percussionists as it snakes down a narrow path from Harambe, around Discovery Island and back. Set to a memorable musical backing, it sounds truly delightful, while 25 park guests are chosen to take part each day, travelling on the back of amusingly designed rickshaws which follow each of the character jeeps.

Finally, for a behind-the-scenes look at the park, **Backstage Safari** is a wonderful 3-hour journey into the handling and care of all the animals ($65, not for under 16s), while Wild By Design offers a 3-hour tour of the park's art, history and architecture and how it was all created ($58, not for under 14s). Book on 407 939 8687.

Dinosaur

DISNEY'S ANIMAL KINGDOM PARK with children

Here is our general guide to the rides that appeal to the different children's ages in this park.

Under 5s
Character Greetings Trails, Festival of The Lion King, Discovery Island Trails, Kilimanjaro Safaris, Pangani Forest Exploration Trail, Affection Section, Maharajah Jungle Trek, TriceraTOP Spin, The Boneyard.

5–8s
All the above, plus Pocahontas and Her Forest Friends, Habitat Habit!, Conservation Station, Kali River Rapids, Flights of Wonder, It's Tough To Be A Bug! and DINOSAUR! (with parental discretion).

9–12s
All the above, plus Expedition: Everest™ (2006), Primeval Whirl and Tarzan™ Rocks!

Over 12s
Festival of *The Lion King*, It's Tough To Be A Bug!, Kilimanjaro Safaris, Pangani Forest Exploration Trail, Kali River Rapids, Maharajah Jungle Trek, Flights of Wonder, DINOSAUR!, Tarzan™ Rocks!, Primeval Whirl, Expedition: Everest™ (2006).

5

Walt Disney World Resort in Florida at Christmas

If you can visit prior to the seriously busy days from just before Christmas Day to New Year's Day, you get the benefit of all the added decorations and atmosphere and none of the overwhelming crowds. Each of the parks takes on a festive character, with the addition of artistic artificial snow, Christmas lights and a huge, magnificently decorated fir tree.

Disney-MGM Studios also features the eye-popping **Osborne Family Lights** while, at the **Magic Kingdom** Park, Main Street USA is transformed into a Christmas extravaganza, dominated by a 60ft (18m) tree. The unmissable **Mickey's Very Merry Xmas Parade** replaces the main 3pm parade in December and is a positive delight for its lively music and eye-catching costumes. Another seasonal extra is the colourful *'Twas the Night before Xmas* show at the Galaxy Palace Theater.

Epcot is the jewel in the Christmas crown, though, with 2 outstanding features. At 6pm, the daily **Christmas tree lighting** ceremony is quite breathtaking as the rest of the park lights go out and then the World Showcase bridge and the tree itself are illuminated in dramatic stages to some grand musical accompaniment. The nightly **Candlelight Processional** also draws a crowd, with a guest narrator telling the story of Christmas to the backdrop of a large choir and elaborate candle parade. It is tasteful, dramatic and eye-catching, but you should arrive early as people start queuing almost 3 HOURS in advance. However, you can get a reserved seat if you buy the *Candlelight Processional Dinner Package* (from $30.99 to $$45.99, plus tax, depending on which World Showcase restaurant you select, and $12.99 for children 3–11), by calling well in advance on 407 939 3463 (credit card details required).

6 Five More of the Best
(or, Expanding Orlando's Universe)

It is time to leave the wonderful world of Disney and venture out into the rest of central Florida's great attractions. And, believe us, there is still a terrific amount in store.

For a start, they don't come much more ambitious than **Universal Orlando**. The area that used to consist of just the one theme park, Universal Studios, is now a fully fledged resort in its own right. A second park, Islands of Adventure, opened in 1999, hot on the heels of the CityWalk entertainment district. The first resort hotel, the Portofino Bay, made its debut in 1999, followed by the Hard Rock Hotel in 2000, and the Royal Pacific Resort in 2002.

A waterway network connects the hotels to the CityWalk hub, while the multi-storey car parks, for more than 20,000 vehicles, has done away with the need for any other transport system as it is easy to move between parks. The Orlando FlexTicket tie-up with SeaWorld and Busch Gardens, plus their purchase of the Wet 'n Wild water park, has also proved a success – not to mention great value. The addition of Islands of Adventure certainly makes this a multi-day resort and there are periodic special deals for 2- and 3-day tickets – in summer 2005, UK ticket retailers were five extra days free with the 2-Day Ticket, and an amazing 14 days with the 3-Day, effectively 11 days free! They have also introduced their Universal Express system for most rides. Similar to Disney's FastPass, it allows guests to 'reserve' one ride at a time and then another once you have done that attraction, and so on. You just present your park entry ticket at the Distribution Center next to the Universal Express ride or show of your choice, select which timeframe you want, then return at the allotted time for a 15-minute wait (instead of an hour or more at peak periods).

Universal hotel guests benefit from Express ride priority ALL DAY by producing their room key. A new feature is **Universal Express Plus**, a day pass that provides one-time access to the top rides with minimal queuing – for an extra $30 ($35 for both parks) per person. A limited number go on sale an hour after park opening and they sell fast, but they can also be bought in advance online at www.universalorlando.com or in the parks themselves for another day. NB: at peak periods, Universal hotel guests are limited to one Express ride at the five main attractions in each park until 3pm. In addition, many rides have **Single Rider** queues, which can save time if you want to go on one by yourself. Once again, any height restriction is noted and Universal Express attractions are shown by UE.

> BRIT TIP: Reader Tom Burton advises: 'If you buy an Orlando FlexTicket giving you 14 consecutive days at Universal, etc, try going to their parks a couple of times in the evenings only. There are virtually no queues this late in the day and I went on the Hulk Coaster (in Islands of Adventure) 5 times in an hour!'

Universal Studios Florida®

Universal opened its Florida park in June 1990 (its original Los Angeles site has been open to the public since before World War II) and quickly became a serious competitor to Disney. For the visitor, it means a consistently high standard and good value in everything on offer (although the choice is quite bewildering!). If you have been to the LA Universal Studios, this one is quite different. The obvious question here is do you need to do Disney-MGM Studios as well as Universal? The answer is an emphatic YES! Universal is a very different kettle of fish to Disney, with a more in-your-face style that goes down well with teens. Younger children are also well catered for in Woody Woodpecker's KidZone.

Universal Studios Florida® at a glance

Location	Off Exits 75A and 74B from I-4; Universal Boulevard and Kirkman Road		
Size	110 acres (45ha) in 7 themed areas		
Hours	9am–7pm off peak; 9am–10pm high season (Washington's birthday, Easter, summer holidays, Thanksgiving, Christmas)		
Admission	Under 3 free; 3–9 $48 (1-Day Ticket), $89.95 (2-Day Ticket), $150.90 (4-Park FlexTicket), $189.90 (5-Park FlexTicket); adult (10+) $59.75, $99.95, $184.95, $224.95; Universal Bonus Pass (5 consecutive days, online sales only) $119.50		
Parking	$9 (Preferred parking $13; valet parking $16)		
Lockers	Yes; immediately to left in Front Lot; $8		
Pushchairs	$10 and $12 (kiddie, with steering wheel), $16 and $18 (double, with steering wheel), next to locker hire		
Wheelchairs	$12 and $40 (with photo ID as deposit), same location as pushchairs		
Top Attractions	Revenge of the Mummy, Men In Black, Jaws, Back to the Future, ET Adventure, Shrek 4-D, Terminator 2		
Don't Miss	Curious George Playground (for kids), The Blues Brothers		
Hidden Costs	**Meals**	Burger, chips and coke $8.28 3-course dinner $22.70 (Finnigan's) Kids' meal $5.50–7.50 (Finnigan's and Lombard's Seafood Grill only)	
	T-shirts	$18.95–23.95	
	Souvenirs	$0.95–199	
	Sundries	Caricature drawings $15–$36	

6

PRODUCTION CENTRAL
1 Guest Services
2 Shrek 4-D
3 Jimmy Neutron's Nicktoon Blast
4 Donkey's Photo Finish
5 Monsters Café

NEW YORK
6 Twister
7 Revenge of the Mummy
8 The Blues Brothers
9 Street Breakz
10 Finnegan's Bar and Grill

SAN FRANCISCO/AMITY
11 Louie's Italian Restaurant
12 Earthquake – The Big One
13 Jaws
14 Beetlejuice's Graveyard Revue
15 Central Lagoon
16 Lombard's Seafood Grille
17 Fear Factor Live

WORLD EXPO
18 Back To The Future… The Ride
19 Men In Black – Alien Attack

WOODY WOODPECKER'S KIDZONE
20 Animal Planet Live!
21 Fievel's Playland
22 A Day In The Park With Barney
23 ET Adventure
24 Woody Woodpecker's Nuthouse
   Coaster
25 Curious George Goes to Town

HOLLYWOOD
26 Universal's Horror Make-Up Show
27 Terminator 2: 3-D Battle Across Time
28 Lucy: A Tribute
29 Mel's Drive-In
30 Café La Bamba

UNIVERSAL
STUDIOS
FLORIDA

Universal parks can also require more than a full day in high season. As at Disney, the strategies are the same: arrive EARLY (up to 30 minutes before the official opening), do the big rides first, avoid main meal times and step out for an afternoon break (try shopping, dining or visiting the cinemas at CityWalk) if it gets too crowded.

Location

Universal Studios Florida® is sub-divided into 6 main areas, set around a huge, man-made lagoon, but there are no great distinguishing features, so you need a map. The main entrance is just off the new exit of Interstate 4 (I-4) or by the Universal Boulevard link from International Drive (I-Drive) by Wet 'n Wild. Parking costs $9 in its massive multi-storey car park and there is quite a walk (with some moving walkways) from there, through the CityWalk district, to the front gates (there is also Preferred Parking, closer to the parks, for $13 and Valet parking for $16).

Once through, your best bet is to turn right on to Rodeo Drive, along Hollywood Boulevard and Sunset Boulevard and into World Expo for Back To The Future… The Ride and Men In Black – Alien Attack. From there, head across the bridge to Jaws, then go back along the Embarcadero for Earthquake and into New York for Revenge of the Mummy. This will get most of the main rides under your belt before the crowds build up, and you can then take it a bit easier by seeing some of the shows and taking advantage of Universal Express. Alternatively, try to be among the early birds flocking to the Shrek 4-D film show in Production Central and the Revenge of the Mummy in New York to avoid the queues that build up here, then use Universal Express

for the likes of Terminator 2, Back To The Future and Men In Black. Here's a full blow-by-blow guide to the Studios. For CityWalk, see Chapter 9.

Production Central

Coming straight through the gates brings you immediately into the administrative centre, with a couple of large gift stores (have a look at these in mid-afternoon) plus **Studio Sweets**. Call at **Guest Services** here for guides for disabled visitors, TDD and assisted listening devices, and to make restaurant bookings. If you are here early, you can sign up to be in the audience for one of Universal's TV shows at the **Studio Audience Center**. **First aid** is available here (and on Canal Street between New York and San Francisco), while there are facilities for nursing mothers at **Family Services** by the bank through the gates on the right. Coming to the top of the Plaza of the Stars brings you to the business end of the park.

6

Revenge of the Mummy

Shrek 4-D: this adds a whole new dimension to the genre of 3-D films as the original cast of the Oscar-winning *Shrek* movies (Mike Myers, Eddie Murphy, Cameron Diaz and John Lithgow) return for a 13-minute 'prequel' to *Shrek 2*. The evil but vertically challenged Lord Farquaad is back in ghost form to welcome visitors to his 'dungeons' and reveal his plan to ruin the honeymoon of Shrek and Princess Fiona. The amusing 7-minute pre-show leads into the 500-seat main theatre, where you don your 'Ogre Vision' 3-D glasses and prepare to enter a new world. The film is funny enough as Shrek and Donkey have to rescue the Princess, but the addition of a host of special effects (watch out for the 'spiders'!) and 'moving' seats mean this is almost a ride as much as a show, and the effect is both startling and hugely entertaining. State-of-the-art digital projection and audio systems, lighting effects, fog and smoke (plus a hilarious finale featuring an out-of-control Tinkerbell) ensure a real laugh-fest. It is a major draw, so try to go first thing in the day or expect waits well in excess of an hour. AAAAA+ (UE).

Jimmy Neutron's Nicktoon Blast: anyone not familiar with the cartoon antics of Jimmy Neutron (Boy Genius) and other members of the Nicktoon stable (Rugrats, the Fairly Odd Parents and SpongeBob SquarePants) might be bemused by this rather noisy simulator ride experience. It revolves around Jimmy tangling with the evil (but hapless) emperor Ooblar and battling to save the world, with the help of his zany inventions and cartoon friends. It is a big hit with under 10s and the ride is quite dynamic. It quickly draws a queue as it is one of the first you encounter through the gates. There is no height restriction as long as a child can sit unaided, but it is not recommended for anyone with heart, neck or back problems (although there are stationary seats). TTT (UE).

The main eating outlet here is the magnificently themed **Monsters Café**, specialising in salads, pasta, ribs, pizza and chicken. The counter-service area is done up like Frankenstein's lab, with the dining areas sub-divided into Swamp, Space, Crypt and Mansion Dining, all to the accompaniment of old black-and-white horror film clips. Shopping includes **On Location** (film, sundries, apparel, 2-way radio rentals), **Nickstuff** (Toon merchandise with Jimmy Neutron, SpongeBob SquarePants and Dora the Explorer), **Surf Hut** (the latest in beach wear) and **It's A Wrap**.

New York

From Production Central you head on to New York and some great scene-setting in the architecture and detail of the buildings and streets. It's far too clean to be authentic, but the façades are first class.

Twister: this experience, based on the hit film, brings audiences 'up close and personal' with the awesome destructive forces of a tornado. The 5-storey terror will shatter everything in its path (okay, so it's pretty tame compared with the real thing), building to a shattering climax of destruction (watch for the flying cow!). The noise is stunning, but it's a bit much for young children (parental discretion advised for under 13s). The pre-show area is almost a work of art but, unless you do it early, save this for late in the day. TTT (UE).

Revenge of the Mummy: this awesome new offering in Orlando's roller-coaster catalogue is a high-tech, high-thrill, high-fun journey into the highly successful world of *The Mummy* film series, replacing the old King Kong attraction. It features an indoor spin into Ancient Egypt that fuses new coaster technology with space-age robotics and special effects. It starts out as a 'dark ride' (a slow journey through the shadowy, curse-ridden interior of Hamunaptra, The City of the Dead) but soon evolves into something far more dynamic – with a breathtaking launch sequence.

> BRIT TIP: For the best ride experience on Revenge of the Mummy, try to sit in the back row. You are not allowed to carry anything on the ride – loose items must be left in the lockers provided.

The basic premise of the film studio becoming a fully fledged archaeological discovery is a good one, and the transition from dark ride to coaster is ingenious, with a host of special effects and eye-popping audio-animatronics as you brave the realm of *The Mummy*. The high-speed whiz into the dark (backwards to start with) does not involve any inversions but is still a thrill with its tight turns and sudden dips, while there are several clever twists that I won't reveal (the front row may get slightly damp!). It is a superb, immersive experience and, with the elaborately themed queuing area, adds a real 5-star attraction to the park. However, it is probably too dark and threatening for under 8s. Restrictions: 4ft/122cm. TTTT½ (UE).

The Blues Brothers: fans of the film will not want to miss this live show as Jake and Elwood Blues (well, pretty good doubles, anyway) put on a stormin' performance on New York's Delancey Street 4 or 5 times a day. They cruise up in their Bluesmobile and go through a selection of the film's hits before heading off into the sunset, stopping only to sign a few autographs. Terrific entertainment. AAAA.

Anyone feeling energetic can try the **Alley Climb** (rock wall) on 5th Avenue for $5. For dining, you have 2 main restaurants. **Finnegan's Bar and Grill** offers shepherd's pie, fish and chips, corned beef and cabbage along with more traditional New York fare like prime rib, burgers, fries and a good range of beers, plus Irish-tinged entertainment and Happy Hour from 4 to 7pm (half price domestic beer; 10 per cent off imported beer), while **Louie's Italian Restaurant** (and **Starbucks**) has counter-service pizza and pasta, Italian ice cream and tiramisu. For shops, you have **Sahara Traders** for *Mummy* souvenirs, as well as jewellery and toys and **The Aftermath** for Twister souvenirs. New York also boasts the inevitable noisy amusement arcade.

San Francisco/Amity

Crossing Canal Street brings you all the way across America to San Francisco/Amity and two more serious queues.

Earthquake – The Big One: this 3-part adventure gets busy from mid-morning until late afternoon. Go behind the scenes first to 2 stage sets where some of the special effects of the Charlton Heston film are explained and audience volunteers show how blue-screen filming is done (with a clip from *U-571*). Then you enter the Bay Area Rapid Transit underground and arrive in the middle of a full-scale earthquake that shakes you to your boots. Tremble as the walls and ceilings collapse, trains collide, cars fall in on you and fire erupts all around, followed by a seeming tidal wave of water. It's not for the faint-hearted

6

(or small children), while those who have bad backs, necks or are pregnant, are advised not to ride. Restrictions: 4ft/122cm (unless accompanied by an adult, with parental discretion). TTTT (UE).

Beetlejuice's Graveyard Revue: *Disney-MGM Studios* has *Beauty and the Beast* and *The Little Mermaid*, Universal goes for *Dracula, Frankenstein, The Wolfman* and *Frankenstein's Bride* in this 20-minute 'shock 'n' roll' extravaganza, compered by Beetlejuice himself. It eschews the twee prettiness of Disney's attractions yet still comes up with a fun family show with lots of laughs, as the 'Graveyard' characters perform specially adapted rock and pop anthems with a mock-horror theme in a great setting. AAAA (UE).

Jaws: the technical wizardry alone will amaze you here, and queues of an hour are common as you head out into the waters of this mini 'Amity'. This is no ordinary ride, and its 6-minute duration will seem a lot longer as your hapless boat guide steers you through an ever more spectacular series of stunts, explosions and menace from the Great White. I defy you not to be impressed – and just a little scared! TTTT (UE).

Fear Factor Live

Fear Factor Live: brand new in summer 2005 was this live action version of the popular American reality TV programme. It asks audience volunteers to take part in a series of hair-raising (and stomach-turning!) challenges, with a head-to-head competition to find the biggest daredevil. There are auditions 70 minutes before each show, and the audience is then invited in to see the chosen few battle it out, with clips from the TV show interspersed with the live action. Some of the stunts

Shrek 4-D

are distinctly off-colour (maggot milkshakes, anyone?) and may not be good viewing for young children (or anyone of a weak disposition!), but it is an extremely well-staged production. TTT (UE).

San Francisco also has the park's best dining choice, with **Lombard's Seafood Grill** the highlight (reservations accepted). Great seafood, pasta and sandwiches are accompanied by a good view over the main lagoon, and there's a separate pastry shop for desserts and coffee. **Richter's Burger Co** offers a few interesting burger variations. For a quick snack, **Chez Alcatraz** provides seafood and hot sandwiches, **Captain Quint's Seafood and Chowder House Restaurant** offers fresh chowder and coastal seafood, and the San Francisco Pastry Co serves sweet snacks and speciality coffees. For shopping, try **Quint's Surf Shack** (men's and women's clothing), **Shaiken's Souvenirs** for more upmarket mementoes and apparel, Oakley (sunglasses) and the **San Francisco Candy Factory**. An added attraction is a boardwalk of fairground games (which cost from $2-$5 to play), including a Guess Your Weight stall that usually attracts a good crowd for the fun patter of the person in charge.

World Expo

Crossing the bridge from Amity brings you to a rather nondescript area, but home to the park's other 5-star thrill attraction.

Back To The Future… The Ride: simulators just do not come more realistic than this journey through space and time in Dr Emmit Brown's time-travelling De Lorean. The queues are immense, but a lot of time is taken up by some attention-grabbing pre-ride info on the TV screens above you. Once you

reach the front, there is more information to digest and clever surroundings to convince you of the scientific nature of it all. Then it's into your time-travelling car and off in hot pursuit of baddie Biff, who has stolen another time-car. The huge, wraparound screen and violent movements of your vehicle bring the realism of the ride to a peak, adding up to a huge experience.
Restrictions: 3ft 4in/101cm.
TTTTT (UE).

Men In Black – Alien Attack: this combination thrill/scenic ride takes up where the hit film, starring Will Smith, left off. Visitors are secretly introduced to the MIB Institute in an inventive mock-futuristic setting and enrolled as trainees for a battle around the streets of New York with a horde of escaped aliens. Your 6-person car is equipped with laser zappers for an interactive shoot-out that is like a real-life arcade game, and the aliens can also shoot back and send your car spinning. The finale features a close encounter with a 30ft (9m) bug that is all mouth – will you survive? Only your collective shooting skills can save the day, and there are numerous ride variations according

6

Men In Black – Alien Attack

> BRIT TIP: For a big score in Men in Black, when you meet the Big Bug – push the big red button!

to your accuracy. Will Smith and Rip Torn are your on-screen hosts, and Will returns at the end to reveal if your score makes you Galaxy Defenders, Cosmically Average or Bug Bait! Fast, frantic and a bit confusing, this will have you coming back for more until you can top 250,000 (Defender status). Restrictions: 3ft 6in/106cm. TTTT (UE). *My best score, 265,550; reader James Home, aged 10, 301,425!*

The International Food and Film Festival here is a food court-style indoor diner offering burgers, sandwiches, meatball subs and salads (in air-conditioned comfort). For gifts, there is **MIB Gear** (apparel, jewellery, toys, sunglasses, towels) and the **Back to the Future Store**.

Woody Woodpecker's KidZone

Animal Planet Live!: this amusing show comes from the Animal Planet satellite TV channel. Several children are invited to take part and present a series of unlikely feats and stunts featuring a whole range of fairly tame wildlife, from a racoon to a snake, and on to cats and dogs. Many have been rescued from animal shelters and gone on to feature in films before finding a

> BRIT TIP: Along the lagoon in the World Expo/KidZone area is Central Park, a quiet spot where you can escape the theme park whirl for a while.

home at Universal. The big theatre provides an escape from the afternoon crowds. AAAA (UE).

Fievel's Playland: strictly for kids (and to give parents a break), this playground, based on the enlarged world of the cartoon mouse, offers youngsters the chance to bounce under a 1,000-gallon hat, crawl through a giant cowboy boot, climb a 30ft (9m) spider's web and shoot the rapids (a 200ft/61m water-slide) in Fievel's sardine can. TTTT (young uns only!).

A Day in the Park with Barney: again strictly for the younger set (ages 2–5), the purple dinosaur from the kids' TV show is brought to super-dee-duper life on stage in a large arena that features a pre-show before the 15-minute main event, plus an interactive post-show area. Parents will cringe, but the youngsters love it. NB: check out the amazing loos! AA (AAAAA under 5s) (UE).

ET Adventure: this is as glorious as scenic rides come, with a picturesque queuing area like the pine woods from the film and then a spectacular leap on the trademark flying bicycles to save ET's home planet. Steven Spielberg (Universal's creative consultant) has added some special effects and characters, and you have an individual ET greeting at the end. The masses often overlook this corner of the park, hence it is worth saving for later in the day. There is a height restriction of 4ft/122cm, but smaller children can ride with parents. AAAAA (UE).

Woody Woodpecker's Nuthouse Coaster: anchoring this excellent under-10s adventure land is this child-sized but still quite racy roller-coaster. The brilliant red 800ft (244m) track reaches only 28ft high (8m) and 22mph (35kph), but it seems the real deal to young uns. There is still a height restriction of 3ft/91cm, however. TTTT (juniors only).

Curious George Goes to Town: kids of all ages just love this amazing adventure playground and huge range of activities – and plenty of ways to get wet (bring swimsuits or a change of clothing here). It combines toddler play, water-based play stations and a hands-on interactive ball area, and is a real bonus for harassed parents. The town theme includes buildings to climb, pumps and hoses to spray water, a ball factory in which to shoot, dump and blast thousands of foam balls and – the tour de force – two 500-gallon (2,275-litre) buckets of water that regularly dump their contents on the street below. TTTTT (under 12s).

Curious George himself roams the KidZone from time to time, while other characters make regular appearances. For snacks, **Animal Crackers** offers hot dogs, chicken fingers, sausage hoagies and frozen yoghurt. Shop at the **Cartoon Store**, **Barney Store** or **ET's Toy Closet** and **Photo Spot**.

Hollywood

Finally, your circular tour of Universal brings you back towards the main entrance via Hollywood (where else?). Here, you'll find **Universal's Horror Make-Up Show** (not recommended for under 12s), which demonstrates some of the often amusing ways in which films have attempted to terrorise us, with clips from modern additions to the genre like *Van Helsing*. It's a 20-minute show, queues are rarely long and the special effects secrets are well worth discovering. AAA (UE).

Terminator 2: 3-D Battle Across Time: another first-of-its-kind attraction, this is hard to describe. Part film, part show, part experience but all action. It cost $60 million to produce and is guaranteed to leave its audience in awe. The

'Wow!' factor works overtime as you go through a 10-minute pre-show representing a trip to the Cyberdyne Systems from the *Terminator* films and then into a 700-seat theatre for a 'presentation' on their latest robot creations. Needless to say, nothing runs to plan and the audience is subjected to a huge array of (loud) special effects, including indoor pyrotechnics, real actors interacting with the screen and the audience and a climactic 3-D film finale that takes the *Terminator* story a step further. The original cast, including Arnold Schwarzenegger and director James Cameron, all collaborated on the 12-minute movie (which, at $24 million, is some of the most expensive frame-for-frame film ever made) and the overall effect is quite dazzling. However, you need to arrive early or expect queues in excess of an hour all day (parental discretion for under 12s). TTTTT (UE).

Lucy: A Tribute: the last attraction (or first, depending on which way you go round) will mean little to all but devoted fans of the late Lucille Ball and her 1960s TV comedy *The Lucy Show*. Classic shows, home movies, costumes and scripts are all paraded, but youngsters will find it tedious. AA.

If you haven't eaten by now there is a choice of four contrasting but highly enjoyable eateries. **Mel's Drive-In**, a re-creation from the film *American Graffiti*, serves all manner of burgers and hot dogs, while **Café La Bamba** offers rotisserie chicken, ribs, salad and burgers, plus Margaritas and beer (Happy Hour 3–5pm). **Schwab's Pharmacy** provides sandwiches, old-fashioned milkshakes, sundaes and ice cream and the **Beverly Hills Boulangerie** does baked breakfast treats, pastries, juices and coffee. Shop for hats in the **Brown Derby**, *Terminator* gifts and clothing in **Cyber Image**, movie memorabilia in **Silver Screen Collectible**s, and

6

BRIT TIP: Universal's trademark Halloween Horror Nights programme (see page 167) is now shared between the Studios and Islands of Adventure. Check www.universal orlando.com for updates.

Hollywood legends' jewellery in the new **Studio Styles**.

Street entertainment

Watch out for a variety of characters who appear around the park at various intervals. **The KidZone Character Bus** appears along Hollywood Boulevard and at the KidZone plaza, while the gravity-defying **Street Breakz** dancers put on shows on Park Avenue (opposite Revenge of the Mummy) in New York. Film 'doubles' for the likes of

Woody Woodpecker's KidZone

Mardi Gras

Marilyn Monroe, Charlie Chaplin, Scooby Doo & Shaggy also roam at regular intervals.

Other Universal characters appear for autographs and photo sessions, notably **Spongebob SquarePants** (inside the Nickstuff Store), and the **Star Toons** (by Fievel's Playland). **Shrek**, **Fiona** and **Donkey** can be found periodically on 8th Avenue in Production Central (just round the corner from Shrek 4-D) and are well worth catching for Donkey's amusing patter (mimicking the Eddie Murphy banter).

Special programmes

Universal Studios features some brilliant extra seasonal entertainment for **Mardi Gras**, with a hectic, bead-throwing parade, plus music, street entertainment and authentic New Orleans food each Saturday at 6pm from mid-February to late May. The evening culminates in a live concert with well-known acts (Huey Lewis & The News and Michael Bolton to name 2 in 2005), but it does draw HUGE crowds. Universal also throws a major party for **New Year's Eve** and **July 4th**,

The entrance to Universal Studios

6

when the park swings into full fiesta mode. In summer 2005 there was a **Shooting Stars** fireworks finale each night over The Central Lagoon, and they intend to do something similar in 2006.

UNIVERSAL STUDIOS with children

Our guide to the rides that generally appeal to the different age groups.

Under 5s
Animal Planet Live!, A Day In The Park With Barney, Curious George Goes To Town, Fievel's Playland, ET Adventure.

5–8s
Animal Planet Live!, Curious George Goes To Town, Fievel's Playland, ET Adventure, Woody Woodpecker's Nuthouse Coaster, Jimmy Neutron's Nicktoon Blast, Shrek 4-D, Men In Black, as well as Earthquake – The Big One (with parental discretion).

9–12s
Jimmy Neutron's Nicktoon Blast, Shrek 4-D, *Terminator 2:* 3-D Battle Across Time, Twister, Earthquake – The Big One, Animal Planet Live!, Curious George Goes To Town, Woody Woodpecker's Nuthouse Coaster, ET Adventure, Beetlejuice's Graveyard Revue, Jaws, Men In Black – Alien Attack, Back To The Future… The Ride, Fear Factor Live, plus Revenge of the Mummy (with parental discretion).

Over 12s
Terminator 2: 3-D Battle Across Time, Universal's Horror Make-Up Show, Jimmy Neutron's Nicktoon Blast, Shrek 4-D, Twister, Revenge Of The Mummy, Earthquake – The Big One, The Blues Brothers, ET Adventure, Beetlejuice's Graveyard Revue, Fear Factor Live, Jaws, Men In Black – Alien Attack, Back To The Future… The Ride.

Islands of Adventure

In May 1999, Universal's creative consultant Steven Spielberg officially opened the £1 billion Islands of Adventure, or IoA as the park is known, with the words: 'These are not just theme park rides, these are entertainment achievements beyond anything I have ever seen anywhere else in the world.' And that's only the beginning. Here is the most complete and thrilling theme park on offer. Complete, because the park offers a genuinely rounded and consistent concept, carried through to the full extent of its designers' aims. And thrilling because it contains more T-rides per square metre than almost all the others combined.

Islands of Adventure at a glance

Location	Off Exits 75A and 74B from I-4; Universal Boulevard and Kirkman Road
Size	110 acres (45ha) in six 'islands'
Hours	9am–7pm off peak; 9am–10pm high season (Washington's birthday, Easter, summer holidays, Thanksgiving, Christmas)
Admission	Under 3 free; 3–9 $48 (1-Day Ticket), $89.95 (2-Day Ticket), $150.90 (4-Park FlexTicket), $189.90 (5-Park FlexTicket); adult (10+) $59.75 $99.95, $184.95, $224.95; Universal Bonus Pass (5 consecutive days, online sales only) $119.50
Parking	$9, Preferred parking $13, Valet parking $16
Lockers	Yes; immediately to left through main gates; $8
Pushchairs	$$10 and $16; next to locker hire Kiddie w/steering wheel $12; Double $18
Wheelchairs	$8 and $40 (with photo ID as deposit); same location as pushchairs
Top Attractions	Amazing Adventures of Spider-Man, Dueling Dragons, Incredible Hulk Coaster, Jurassic Park River Adventure, Dudley Do-Right's Ripsaw Falls, Cat In The Hat
Don't Miss	Eighth Voyage of Sindbad, Jurassic Park Discovery Centre, If I Ran the Zoo playground (for toddlers), dining at Mythos

Hidden Costs		
	Meals	Burger, chips and coke $8.28 3-course lunch $29.94 (Confisco Grille) Kids' meal $5.95–$6.99
	T-shirts	$18.95–25.95
	Souvenirs	$0.99–699
	Sundries	Jurassic Park River Adventure ride photos: two 5 × 7s $20; $21.29 with frame

It has a full range of attractions, from the real adrenaline overloads to pure family entertainment. The shopping and eating opportunities are above average and it even sounds good – with some 40 pieces of original music, you can buy the CD of the theme park! Okay, so they are not really islands (the 6 themed 'lands' form a chain around the central lagoon), but that's the only illusion. And you get a lot for your money here, unless you have extremely timid children or under 5s, in which case the Magic Kingdom is still your best bet. However, Seuss Landing will keep them amused for several hours, while Camp Jurassic is a clever adventure playground for the 5–12s. The rest of the park, with its 7 5-star thrill rides and other standout attractions, is primarily geared to kids of 8-plus, their parents and especially teenagers. There are 5 elements that look truly alarming (2 of which produce moments of supreme terror), but don't be put off – they all deliver immense fun. There is also much spectator value here!

If there is one ride that sums up IoA, it is the Amazing Adventures of Spider-Man, the world's first moving 3-D simulator ride. It is sure to leave you in awe of its technological wizardry and imagination, and it is not unknown for people to applaud at the end!

Private nursing facilities, an open area for feeding and resting (with high-chairs) and nappy-changing stations, can be found at the **Family Service Facility** at Guest Services (to the right inside the main gates), while ALL restrooms throughout the park are equipped with **nappy-changing** facilities. **First aid** is provided in Sindbad's Village in the Lost Continent, just across from Oasis Coolers and in Port of Entry.

Port of Entry

You arrive for IoA as you do for Universal Studios Florida® in the big multi-storey car parks ($9, $13 and $16) off I-4 and Universal Boulevard and either walk or ride the moving walkways into CityWalk, where you continue through to the entrance plaza (head for the 130ft (40m) high Pharos Lighthouse). As with Universal Studios, you can purchase the **Universal Express Plus** pass for $30 at the Marvel Alterniverse Store, Toon Extra or Jurassic Outfitters. Once through the gates, the lockers, pushchair and wheelchair hire are all on your left as the **Port of Entry** opens up before you. This elaborate 'village' consists of shops and eateries, so push straight on until you hit the main lagoon. Later in the day, return to check out the retail experience at places like the **IoA Trading Company** and **Ocean Trader Market**. Enjoy a snack from **Cinnabon** (cinnamon rolls and pastries) or the **Croissant Moon Bakery**, or chill out with a soft drink or ice cream from **Arctic Express**. Alternatively, sit down for lunch or dinner (great steak, pasta, fish, pizza, burgers and salads) at **Confisco Grille** and grab a beverage at the **Backwater Bar** (Happy Hour 3–5pm). There is also a **Character Breakfast** at Confisco Grille (9-10.30am Thur-Sun) with various Universal characters like Spider-Man and the Cat in the Hat at $15.95 for adults and $9.95 for children (call 407 224 4012 to book).

Above all, take in the wonderful architecture, which borrows from Middle East, Far East and African themes and uses bric-a-brac from all over the world. At the end of the street, you are faced with 3 choices and this is where you need a plan of campaign. There are 5 attractions where the queues build up quickly and remain that way. If you are here for the big thrill rides, turn left into

6

PORT OF ENTRY
1 Ocean Trader Market
2 Confisco Grille

MARVEL SUPER-HERO ISLAND
3 Incredible Hulk Coaster
4 Doctor Doom's Fearfall
5 Café 4
6 Captain America Diner
7 The Amazing Adventures Of Spider-Man
8 Storm Force Accelatron

TOON LAGOON
9 Me Ship, The Olive
10 Popeye & Bluto's Bilge-Rat Barges
11 Dudley Do-Right's Ripsaw Falls
12 Comic Strip Café
13 Amphitheater
14 Toon Lagoon Beach Bash

JURASSIC PARK
15 Jurassic Park River Adventure
16 Camp Jurassic
17 Pteranodon Flyers
18 Discovery Center
19 Thunder Falls Terrace

THE LOST CONTINENT
20 Dueling Dragons
21 The Flying Unicorn
22 The Eighth Voyage of Sindbad
23 Poseidon's Fury
24 The Enchanted Oak Tavern (and Alchemy Bar)
25 Mythos Restaurant
26 The Mystic Fountain

SEUSS LANDING
27 Caro-Seuss-el
28 One Fish, Two Fish, Red Fish, Blue Fish
29 The Cat In The Hat
30 If I Ran The Zoo
31 Circus McGurkus Café Stoo-pendous
32 Green Eggs and Ham Café
33 Guest Services

ISLANDS OF ADVENTURE

The Incredible Hulk Coaster

Marvel Super-Hero Island and head straight to Spider-Man, then do Dr Doom's Fearfall and the Incredible Hulk Coaster, taking advantage of the Universal Express (UE) system. Alternatively, dinosaur fans should head straight around the lagoon to Jurassic Park, where you should be able to do the River Adventure before the majority arrive. Once you are nice and wet, you might as well go to Toon Lagoon for Ripsaw Falls and the Bilge-Rat Barges. Or, if you have younger children, turn right into the multi-coloured world of Seuss Landing and enjoy the Cat In The Hat and other family-type rides prior to the crowd build-up.

Marvel Super-Hero Island

Taking the journey clockwise, you arrive first in the elaborate comic-book pages of the super-heroes. As with all the islands, the experience is total immersion. The amazing façades of this world surround you with an utterly credible alternative reality that is one of the park's triumphs – and that's before you have tried the rides.

The Incredible Hulk Coaster: roller-coasters don't come much more dramatic than this giant green edifice that soars over the lagoon, blasting 0-40mph (64kph) in 2 seconds, and reaching a top speed of 65mph (105kph). It looks awesome, sounds stunning and rides like a demon as you enter the gamma-ray world of Dr David Banner, aka the

> BRIT TIP: At the Hulk Coaster, keep left where the queue splits up and you will be in line for the front car for an even more extreme Hulk experience.

6

Incredible Hulk and zoom into a weightless inversion 100ft (30 metres) up!

Just watching is quite mind-boggling, and the after-effects are distinctly brain-scrambling. You will need to deposit ANY loose articles (sunglasses, cameras, coins, etc) in the lockers at the front of the building as the ride is guaranteed to shake anything out of your pockets. Crowds build up rapidly, but the queues move quite quickly. Restrictions: 4ft 6in/137cm. TTTTT+ (UE).

Islands of Adventure

Dr Doom's Fearfall: stand by for one of those two moments of supreme terror we mentioned. This is where, O hapless visitor, you wander into the lair of the evil Dr Doom – arch-enemy of the Fantastic Four – and his sinister cohorts. His latest creation is the Fearfall, a device for sucking every ounce of fear out of his victims, and YOU are about to test it. Four riders at a time are strapped into chairs at the bottom of a 200ft (60m) tower, the dry ice rolls, and whoooosh! Up you go at breakneck speed, only to plummet back seemingly even faster, with an amazing split second in between when you feel suspended in mid air. Summon up the courage to do this and we promise an astonishing (if brief!) experience. Queues are substantial during the main part of the day. Restrictions: 4ft 4in/132cm, and we reckon this is way too scary for under 10s. TTTTT+ (UE).

You exit Fearfall into the inevitable high-energy video arcade, or you may prefer to calm your nerves with a meal at the Italian buffeteria **Café 4** (pizza, spaghetti, sandwiches and salads) or a burger at the **Captain America Diner**. For shopping, each ride has its own character merchandise, while the **Comic Book Shop** and **Marvel Alternative Shop** sell other souvenirs.

The Amazing Adventures of Spider-Man: just queuing is a novel experience as your visit to the *Daily Bugle*, home of ace reporter Peter Parker (or Spider-Man to his enemies), unravels into a reporting assignment in one of the 'Scoop' vehicles. Prepare for an audio-visual extravaganza as the combination of 3-D and motion simulator takes you into a battle between Spidey and arch-villains like Dr Octopus with his anti-gravity gun, culminating in a 400ft (122m) sensory drop off a skyscraper as the contest literally

hots up. There are numerous jaw-dropping special effects and you will need to ride at least twice to appreciate it all. Ride early on or leave it 'til late in the day – queues often top an hour. Restrictions: 3ft 4in/101cm. TTTTT+ (UE).

Storm Force Accelatron: this ride, aimed primarily at youngsters, puts you in the middle of a whirling, twirling battle between X-Men super-heroine Storm and arch-nemesis Magneto, with a range of special effects. It is basically an updated version of a fairground spinning-cup ride, but with some great twists (there is a 3-way rotation when the cars look set to collide at any moment!). TTT (TTTTT under 12s) (UE).

You can also meet the **Marvel Super-Heroes** for autographs several times a day.

Toon Lagoon

The thrills continue here with a watery theme and more comic-book elements as the (American) newspaper cartoon characters take a bow. Children will love to play with the fountains, squirt pools and overflowing fire hydrants, plus a purpose-built playland **Me Ship, The Olive**, a 3-storey boat full of interactive fun and games, including slides, bells and water cannons (with which to squirt riders on the Bilge-Rat Barges below) in best Popeye style. TTTT (youngsters only).

Popeye and Bluto's Bilge-Rat Barges: every park seems to have a variation on the white-water raft ride, but none is as outrageously themed and downright wet as this. It's fast, bouncy and unpredictable, with water coming at you from every direction, a couple of sizeable drops and a whirl through the Octoplus Grotto that adds to the fun. If you don't want to get wet, don't ride, because there is no escaping the

BRIT TIP: A change of clothes is often advisable after the Barges, unless it's so hot you need to cool down in a hurry. Bring a waterproof bag for your valuables.

deluge here. This is also one of the top 5 rides for queues, but it's worth the wait. Restrictions: 4ft/122cm. TTTTT (UE).

Dudley Do-Right's Ripsaw Falls: Universal's designers have again taken an existing ride concept and given it a new spin, as this becomes the first flume ride to send its passengers through the water surface and out the other side at high speed. You join guileless mountie Dudley Do-Right in a bid to save girlfriend Nell from the evil Snidely Whiplash. The action builds to an 'explosive' showdown at the top of a 60ft (18m) precipice that drops you through the roof of a ramshackle dynamite shack and into the lagoon below. Just awesome – as are the queues from mid-morning to late afternoon. Wet? You bet! Restrictions: 3ft 8in/111cm. TTTTT (UE) You can also try the Water Blasters (for 25c) on the bridge overlooking the final drop to get riders even wetter!

After drying off, walk along **Comic Strip Lane** to meet up with characters like Beetle Bailey, Hagar the Horrible, Krazy Kat and Blondie (some of whom will mean little to a British audience). Go past the **Amphitheater** on your left (home to seasonal entertainment like the amazing bikers of **Mat Hoffman's Crazy Freakin' Stunt Show**) and there is the usual array of character shops, like **Gasoline Alley** and **Toon Extra**, while you can grab a humongous sandwich at **Blondie's: Home of the Dagwood**, a

trademark hamburger or hot dog at **Wimpy's**, sample the **Comic Strip Café** food court (Mexican, Chinese, American and Italian) or grab something colder at **Cathy's Ice Cream**. Watch out for appearances at the **Toon Lagoon Character Zone** for a meet-and-greet with various characters.

Jurassic Park

Leaving the comic-book lands behind, you travel back in time to the Cretaceous age and the credible make-believe dinosaur film world. Again, the immersive experience is first class and the lavish scenery will have you looking over your shoulder for dinos.

Jurassic Park River Adventure: the mood change from scenic splendour to hidden menace is startling as your journey into this magnificent waterborne realm brings you up close and personal with the most realistic dinosaurs created to date. Inevitably, your passage is diverted from the safe to the hazardous, and the danger increases as the 16-person raft climbs into the heights of the main building – with raptors loose everywhere. You are aware of something large lurking in the shadows – will you fall prey to the T-Rex, or will your boat take the 85ft plunge to safety (with a good soaking for all concerned)? Queues usually move quite briskly here. Restrictions: 3ft 6in/106cm. TTTTT (UE). The more adventurous can then try the **Rock Climbing Wall** (just outside River Adventure) for an extra $5.

Camp Jurassic: more excellent kids' fare here with the mountainous jungle giving way to an 'active' volcano for youngsters to explore, climb and slide down. Squirt guns and 'Spitter' dinosaurs add to the fun. TTTT (children first, but parents may explore).

6

Pteranodon Flyers: the slow-moving queues are a major turn-off, especially for a fairly average ride, which glides gently over much of Jurassic Park (although at heights of almost 30ft at one point). It is designed mainly for kids, though, and the height range of 3-4ft 8in (91–142cm) requires anyone OVER the upper limit (usually 11 or older) to be accompanied by a child of the right height. TT (TTTT under 9s).

Discovery Center: this indoor centre offers various interactive opportunities, including creating a dinosaur through DNA sequencing, mixing your own DNA with a dino via a computer touchscreen, seeing through the eyes of various large reptiles and even handling 'dino eggs', plus other fun hands-on exhibits. Air-conditioned, this is a good place to visit in the hotter part of the day (open 11am–5pm). AAA.

Best of the shopping is in the Discovery Center itself, while you can chow down at the **Burger Digs** there, visit the **Pizza Predattoria** or the **Watering Hole**, or go for the rotisserie chicken at the rustic **Thunder Falls Terrace** (counter service), which boasts a great view of the River Adventure.

Jurassic Park River Adventure

The Lost Continent

This is one of my favourite lands for its theming, gentle contrast after Jurassic Park; superb attractions, great eating options and a few amusing 'extras'.

Dueling Dragons: there is no disguising the intense nature of this magnificent double coaster, with its 100ft (30m) drop, multiple loops, twists and 3 near-miss encounters.

Bilge Rat Barges

The Flying Unicorn

There is a lot more, too, as the queuing area is a real mind-boggler – 1,060yd (969m), most of it along a dark, winding path through the ancient castle that is the domain of the dragons, Fire and Ice. You are given their story while you wait, and Merlin arrives in time to cast a spell to ensure you survive. You choose which dragon to ride (the tracks differ slightly), and you can join an additional queue for the front seats. Unlike the Hulk, this is a suspended coaster, so your legs dangle free, and the initial drop is like going into free-fall (Supreme Terror moment No. 2!). Coaster aficionados rate the best ride in the back of the Ice (Blue) dragon, but it's all pretty amazing. Restrictions: 4ft 6in/137cm, and you will need to leave all loose items in the lockers provided to the left of the entrance. TTTTT+ (UE).

The Flying Unicorn: this junior-sized coaster is aimed primarily at youngsters and features a wizard's workshop, hidden in an enchanted wood, which is the gateway to a magical journey inspired by the Unicorn. There are no big drops, but it delivers a surprisingly fast-paced whirl. TTTTT (for 6-12s) (UE).

The Eighth Voyage of Sindbad: this stunt and special effects show is another marvel, as much for its elaborate staging as its performance. Mythical adventurer Sindbad and sidekick Kabob (a name that's the cue for a truly awful pun) tackle evil witch Miseria in a bid to rescue Princess Amoura, and the action springs up in surprising places. There are several loud bangs that could scare young children, but otherwise it is good, family fun. At peak times, arrive 20 minutes before showtime, but everyone usually gets in. There is also a great post-show feature where the cast reappear for photos and autographs. TTT/AAAA (UE).

6

Dudley Do-Right's Ripsaw Falls

Poseidon's Fury: a walk-through show that puts its audience at the heart of the action as you journey in the company of a hapless young archaeologist (who ignores all the various 'warnings') beneath the sea to the lost temple of Poseidon. The route passes through an amazing water vortex and your 'expedition' takes a wrong turn, awakening an ancient demon. Again, there is an element of suspense, so I won't reveal what happens, but the showdown between Poseidon and the demon is amazing. Queuing is tedious, but at least you are inside in summer. TTT (UE).

For an extra few dollars, try the **Pitch and Skill Games**, or shop at **The Coin Mint** (coins forged and struck before your eyes), or visit **Historic Families** (explore the history of your family name and coat of arms in a medieval armoury), **Pearl Factory** (pick an oyster), and **The Dragon's Keep** (dragon apparel, games and toys). **The Fire-Eater's Grill** (sausages, chips and drinks) and **Frozen Desert** (sundaes and sodas) provide the snacks, while you mustn't miss the magnificent **Enchanted Oak Tavern** (in the cool interior of a vast, sculpted oak tree) and **Alchemy Bar** for counter-service hickory-smoked chicken, ribs and salads. The elaborate **Mythos Restaurant** provides the best dining in IoA, though. Not only is the food first class (seafood, salads, grills, pizza and pasta), but the setting, inside a dormant 'volcano' with streams, fountains and clever lighting, is an attraction in its own right.

Finally, watch out for **The Mystic Fountain** in Sindbad's Village – it has the ability to get you very wet when you least expect it!

Seuss Landing

There is not a straight line to be seen in this vivid 3-D working of the books of Dr Seuss. The characters may not mean much to those unfamiliar with the children's stories, but everyone can relate to the fun here (although queues build up quickly). There is so much clever detail packed into the area, from squirt ponds to beach scenes, it can be easy to miss something, so take your time.

Caro-Seuss-el: this intricate carousel ride on some of the Seuss characters – like cowfish, elephant-birds and dog-a-lopes – has rider-activated features that are a big hit with the young ones. AAA (AAAA under 5s) (UE).

One Fish, Two Fish, Red Fish, Blue Fish: another fairground ride is given a twist as you pilot these Seussian fish up and down according to the rhyme that plays while you ride. Get it wrong and you get squirted! More guaranteed fun for the younger kids. TTT (TTTTT under 5s) (UE).

The Cat In The Hat: prepare for a ride with a difference as you board these crazy 6-passenger 'couches' to meet the world's most adventurous cat and his friends, Thing One and Thing Two. You literally go for a spin through this storybook world, and it may be a bit much for very young children. The slow-moving queues are a bit of a drag, so try to get here early or leave it until later in the day (or use the UE system). AAAA/TTT) (UE).

If I Ran The Zoo: interactive playgrounds don't get much more fun for the pre-school brigade than with the 19 different Seuss character scenarios, some of which can get them quite wet. Hugely imaginative and great fun to watch. TTTTT (under 5s only).

If you have been captivated by the land, you can buy the book at **Dr Seuss' All The Books You Can Read Store**, or visit the **Mulberry Street Store** for all the characters. **Snookers and Snookers Sweet**

Candy Cookers is a super sweet shop, while snacks and drinks can be had at **Hop on Pop Ice Cream Shop** and **Moose Juice Goose Juice**. The **Circus McGurkus Café Stoo-pendous** is a mind-boggling cafeteria for fried chicken, lasagne, pizza and spaghetti, complete with clowns and pipe organs, while **Green Eggs and Ham Café** is a must for all Seuss fans to try the meal of the same name. (And the eggs ARE green!)

Halloween Horror Nights

Now being spread between both IoA and the Studios park is Universal's massively popular Halloween celebration throughout October each year. The Horror Nights have become a real trademark and add a wonderfully bloodthirsty touch. The parks are transformed with some highly imaginative re-creations and set-pieces from various horror movies, with a parade and shows that include live (terrifyingly so, in some cases) character interaction. All the horror genres are well represented, and the Scare Houses feature some superb 'scare actors' and special effects. The rides are also all open (anyone for The Hulk and Dueling Dragons in the dark?), adding more novelty to the park experience, but this over-the-top (and occasionally downright grisly) extravaganza is definitely not for kids. It goes down a treat with adults with the right sense of humour, though, and begins every evening at 7.30pm. It is a separately ticketed event and costs $59.75 per person and it is highly advisable to book in advance on www.universalorlando.com.

And that, folks, is the full low-down on arguably the world's best theme park. Miss it at your peril.

6

ISLANDS OF ADVENTURE with children

Our guide to the rides that generally appeal to the different age groups:

Under 5s
Caro-Seuss-el, If I Ran The Zoo, The Cat In The Hat, One Fish, Two Fish, Red Fish, Blue Fish, Eighth Voyage of Sindbad, Jurassic Park Discovery Center, Me Ship, The Olive.

5–8s
All the above, plus Flying Unicorn, Pteranodon Flyers, Camp Jurassic, Amazing Adventures of Spider-Man, Storm Force Accelatron, and Jurassic Park River Adventure (with parental discretion).

9–12s
The Cat In The Hat, Flying Unicorn, Dueling Dragons, Eighth Voyage of Sindbad, Camp Jurassic, Pteranodon Flyers, Jurassic Park River Adventure, Jurassic Park Discovery Center, Dudley Do-Right's Ripsaw Falls, Popeye and Bluto's Bilge-Rat Barges, Amazing Adventures of Spider-Man, Dr Doom's Fearfall, Storm Force Accelatron, Incredible Hulk Coaster.

Over 12s
Dueling Dragons, Eighth Voyage of Sindbad, Jurassic Park River Adventure, Jurassic Park Discovery Center, Dudley Do-Right's Ripsaw Falls, Popeye and Bluto's Bilge-Rat Barges, Amazing Adventures of Spider-Man, Dr Doom's Fearfall, Storm Force Accelatron, Incredible Hulk Coaster.

SeaWorld Adventure Park

SeaWorld is firmly established as one of the most popular parks with British visitors for its more peaceful and naturalistic aspect, the change of pace it offers and the general lack of substantial queues. It is a big hit with families in particular, but also has some dramatic rides and imaginative attractions. An extensive development programme by owners Anheuser-Busch has given it the big-park treatment in recent years, with an impressive 12-acre (5-ha) entrance plaza and rebranding as an Adventure Park, and it now demands a full day's attention. The opening, in summer 2000, of sister park Discovery Cove, an exotic tropical island with dolphin, stingray and snorkelling adventures, has added still more.

Happily, the queues and crowds are more manageable here, so this is a park where you can still proceed at a relatively leisurely pace, see what you want without too much jostling and yet feel you have been well entertained (even if mealtimes do get crowded in the restaurants). SeaWorld is also a good starting point if this is your first visit to Orlando as it will give you the hang of negotiating the vast areas, navigating by the various maps and learning to plan around the showtimes. This park has a strong educational and environmental message, plus 3 1-hour, behind-the-scenes tours (book up as soon as you enter), which provide a greater insight into SeaWorld's marine conservation, rescue and research programme, as well as its entertainment resources.

The Polar Expedition provides a close-up of the penguin and polar bear environments; **Saving A Species** showcases the park's animal rescue and rehabilitation programme, with a chance to hand-feed exotic birds in the free-flight aviary ($1 of the tour fee also goes to the SeaWorld and Busch Gardens Conservation Fund); and **Predators!** offers a backstage view of Shark Encounter. You pay an extra $16 ($12 for 3–9s) for these tours, but they are worth it and, if you take one early on, it will increase your appreciation of the park. You can

Kraken

1 Information
2 Wild Arctic
3 Shamu Stadium
4 Dine with Shamu
5 Shamu Underwater Viewing
6 Blue Horizons
7 Atlantis Bayside Stadium
8 The Waterfront
9 Seaport Theater
10 Seafire Inn/Makahiki Luau
11 Sky Tower
12 Nautilus Theatre – Odyssea
13 Clydesdale Hamlet
14 Anheuser-Busch Hospitality Center
15 Manatee Rescue
16 Pacific Point Preserve
17 Sea Lion & Otter Stadium
18 Extreme Zone
19 Shamu's Happy Harbor
20 Shark Encounter
21 Sharks Underwater Grill
22 Penguin Encounter
23 Key West At SeaWorld
24 Stingray Lagoon
25 Turtle Point
26 Dolphin Cove
27 Journey To Atlantis
28 Kraken
29 Dolphin Nursery
30 Mistify
31 Mango Joe's Café
32 Mama's Kitchen

6

SEA WORLD

SeaWorld Adventure Park at a glance

Location	7007 SeaWorld Drive, off Central Florida Parkway (Junctions 71 and 72 off I-4)	
Size	More than 200 acres (81ha), incorporating 25 attractions	
Hours	9am–7pm off peak; 9am–10pm high season (Easter, summer holidays, Thanksgiving, Christmas)	
Admission	Under 3 free; 3–9 $48 (1-Day Ticket), $150.95 (4-Park Orlando FlexTicket), $189.95 (5-Park FlexTicket), $84.95 (SeaWorld/Busch Gardens Combo ticket); adult (10+) $59.75, $184.95, $224.95, $94.95	
Parking	$8, $10 preferred parking	
Lockers	Yes, by main entrance; $1.50 (also by Shamu's Emporium)	
Pushchairs	$10 and $17 ($2 refundable; from Information Center, to left of main entrance)	
Wheelchairs	$9 and $32; same location as pushchairs	
Top Attractions	Shamu Stadium, Shark Encounter, Journey to Atlantis, Kraken, Wild Arctic, Blue Horizons	
Don't Miss	Mistify at The Waterfront (high season), Manatee Rescue, Behind-the-Scenes Tours, Odyssea show, dining at Sharks Underwater Grill	
Hidden Costs	**Meals**	Burger, chips and coke $10.58 3-course lunch (Sharks Grill) $22 Kids' meal $5.69
	T-shirts	$8.99–26.95
	Souvenirs	69 cents–$6,599.95(!)
	Sundries	Face painting $8–$15

also save 10 per cent on single-day tickets if you book online at www.seaworld.com, where you print your own tickets and save waiting in a queue. Periodically, SeaWorld also offers a Second Day Free if you sign up before you leave the park – check at the information kiosk just inside the main entrance.

Four additional programmes provide other unique insights and experiences. The 6-hour **Adventure Express Tour** offers visitors their own tour guide, with back-door access to the rides, reserved seating at shows and animal feeding opportunities (an extra $89 for adults, $79 for 3–9s; book up first thing at the Guided Tours counter or call 1-800 406 2244); **SeaWorld's Marine Mammal Keeper Experience** is a new option for 2 visitors daily (aged 13 or above) to find out about the care necessary to rehabilitate injured manatees, plus bottle-feed some of them, meet the seals and walruses and prepare meals for the beluga whales. It starts at 6.30am and lasts around 8 hours for $399/person (including lunch at the Shark Encounter, T-shirt, special book, souvenir photo and 7-day

SeaWorld pass); **Sharks Deep Dive** is a totally captivating experience, a chance to suit up and dive in a specially constructed cage into the huge shark aquarium, and spend half an hour up close and personal with these amazing creatures. The 2-hour programme includes an educational induction into the world of sharks, what they are and what makes them tick (with important pointers like never wear jewellery in the sea – sharks can be attracted by the glitter, mistaking it for the reflection off fish scales). Then you are equipped for the dive with wetsuit (the water IS chilly), gloves, dive belt and a special underwater helmet that also allows communication (no scuba gear needed) for the reinforced steel cage that glides slowly from one end of the 125ft (38m) long tank to the other and back. Getting a fish-eye view of these creatures is an astounding experience, and you never tire of the underwater panorama (which includes waving to folks walking through the shark tunnel!). It is an eye-opening and addictive programme, but the best part is you get to wear a really cool wetsuit with 'Scubapro' on the front! It costs $150 (including 2-day park admission, a great souvenir T-shirt and shark book; participants must be at least 10); finally, the new **Beluga Interactive Program** (for ages 13 and up) is utterly unique, a chance to meet some of the park's biggest (but most benign) denizens in their own environment. No swimming is necessary but guests must be comfortable in the water. Touching, feeding and interacting with hand signals is all part of the programme, which is highly informative and utterly captivating (but not for expectant mothers). It costs $130 per person and runs every day, rain or shine. All the tours can also be booked online at www.sea world.com.

Location

SeaWorld is located off Central Florida Parkway, between I-4 (Exit 71 going east or 72 heading west) and I-Drive, and the parking fee is $8 ($10 if you choose Shamu's preferred parking, which gets you close to the main entrance). It is still best to arrive a bit before the official opening time so you're in good position to book one of the backstage tours or dash to one of the few attractions that draws a crowd, like Journey to Atlantis.

The park covers in excess of 200 acres (81ha), with 9 shows (10 with the nightly **Makahiki Luau** dinner show at the Seafire Inn which costs $42.95 for adults, $27.95 for 3–9s; nightly, times vary, call 407 351 3600 or book online), nine large-scale continuous viewing attractions and nine smaller ones, plus the eye-catching **Waterfront area**, relaxing gardens, a kids' play area and a smart range of shops (a noticeable feature of Anheuser-Busch parks). Their hire pushchairs (strollers) are also the most amusing – shaped like baby dolphins. Be warned, though, the size of the park requires a lot of to-ing and fro-ing to catch the various shows and can be wearing. Keep a close grip on your map and entertainment schedule and try to establish a programme to give yourself regular breaks at some of the quieter spots.

For something different, you can sign up for the free 35-minute Anheuser-Busch **Beer School** at the Hospitality Center for a glimpse into beer-making (and tasting!). New in 2004 was **Shamu and Crew Character Breakfast**, a hearty character meal with a cuddly Shamu and friends Penny Penguin and OP Otter. $14.95 adults, $9.95 ages 3–9, from 8.45–10.15am at the Seafire Inn Wed–Sun in peak season; advanced booking on 1-800 327 2420 or www.seaworld.com. There

6

is also **Dine with Shamu**, a VIP experience 'backstage' with the killer whales and their trainers. An all-you-can-eat buffet on a covered terrace alongside the main pool gives you the chance to ask questions of the trainers and watch some of their sessions. It is $34 for adults and $18 for children, is offered every day (twice daily in high season, at 4.45 and 7.30pm) and it is highly advisable to book in advance.

The main attractions

Wild Arctic: this interactive ride-and-view experience provides a realistic environment that is both educational and thrilling. It consists of an exciting simulator jet helicopter journey into the white wilderness arriving at a clever research base, Base Station Wild Arctic, where the 'passengers' are disgorged into a frozen wonderland to meet polar bears, beluga whales and walruses. This one is not to be missed (but not just after a Shamu show when the hordes descend).

Shamu the Killer Whale

Restrictions: 3ft 6in/106cm. TTTT plus AAAAA. Those who don't want to ride can just walk through to the Base Station.

Shamu Stadium: SeaWorld has long since outgrown its tag as just the place to see killer whales, but the Shamu show is still one of its most amazing sights. Watch the killer whales and their trainers pull off some spectacular stunts, as well as learn all you ever wanted to know about these majestic animals.

> BRIT TIP: Reader David Snelling from Cheshire, warns, 'Gentlemen, do not volunteer to participate in the Shamu display – it will be chauvinistically humiliating!'

There are 2 distinct shows, the more humorous *Shamu Adventure* during the day (25 minutes) and the louder, less structured *Shamu Rocks America* at night (20 minutes). Both are worth seeing, and are easily the most popular events, so make an effort to arrive early (especially as there is an amusing pre-show). Also, the first 14 rows get VERY wet (watch out for your cameras) – when a killer whale leaps into the air in front of you, it displaces a LOT of water on landing! AAAAA. All guests can then enjoy the **Underwater Viewing** area backstage.

Sea Lion and Otter Stadium: the venue for a wonderful show, *Clyde and Seamore Take Pirate Island*, it features the resident sea lions who, with their pals the otter and walrus (plus a couple of humans as the fall guys), put on a hilarious 25-minute performance of watery stunts and gags. Arrive early for some first-class audience mickey-taking from the resident pirate mime. In high season, there is a second evening show, *Clyde* *and Seamore Present Sea Lions Tonight*, which serves up a parody of other SeaWorld shows. AAAA.

Xtreme Zone: right next door is a Trampoline Jump and Rock Climbing Wall, for an extra fee (reservations required).

Blue Horizons: new in summer 2005 was this wonderful animal show with a big helping of Broadway production style about it. Replacing the old Key West Dolphin Fest, it features dolphins, false killer whales and exotic birds (including an Andean condor), but a lot more besides as the general (and rather abstract) theme of a girl's dream about maritime wildlife is brought to life. The elaborate set design is the first eye-catching element, with a 40ft-high sea-meets-sky backdrop that is also the concealed setting for a host of additional performers, from high divers to bungee performers to trapeze-like aerialists. There is no obvious interaction between trainers and animals as the show moves seamlessly from one scene to the next, both above and below the water, but there is plenty to admire as the stage is filled with graceful – and quite daring – action. The complex staging and vivid costuming (all created by Broadway designers) is also underpinned by a stirring original music score from the Seattle Symphony Orchestra. It all adds up to a magnificent 25 minutes that often draws a huge ovation. AAAAA.

Fusion: shown twice daily in the Bayside Stadium (Easter to September only), this high-energy 'surf, sand and sky' show features jet-ski stunts, 5-tiered kites, high-diving, song, dance and water-skiing, plus the wonderful frisbee-catching dog! Especially geared to a youth audience but with guaranteed family appeal, it is an eye-catching 20 minutes of music, fun and watery tricks. There is also an imaginative pre-show for children, with hula-hoops, a remote control surfer, giant beach balls and kites. AAAA.

> **BRIT TIP:** The weather may occasionally mean the outdoor entertainment is cancelled, but don't let it stop you enjoying yourself. Cheap, plastic ponchos will appear in the shops at the first sign of rain!

6

The Waterfront: not so much an attraction as a 5-acre (2-ha) 'village' at the heart of SeaWorld, offering fine dining, smart shops, several shows and street entertainment. This area forms an arc around part of the central lake, is themed like an eclectic harbour and offers three excellent eateries (the **Seafire Inn** for gourmet steak burgers, salads and coconut-fried shrimp, **Voyagers** for wood-fired pizzas, pasta and sandwiches, plus a low-carb option;

The Waterfront at SeaWorld

not cheap but quite delicious, and **The Spice Mill**, a cafeteria-style restaurant offering some succulent – and spicy – variations on soups, sandwiches, grilled chicken and jambalaya. There are also 2 snack bars (**Café de Mar** for pastries, coffees and soft drinks, and **Freezas** for frozen yoghurt and other drinks), four interlinked boutique-style shops (with some stylish souvenirs – check out **Allura's Treasure Trove** and **Under The Sun**) and some amusing street performers. Keep an eye out for the amazing percussive pots-and-pans rhythms of the **Groove Chefs**.

BRIT TIP: Grab an evening meal at The Spice Mill, head out on to their open-air terrace and you have one of the best seats in the house for the Mistify nightly finale.

New in 2004 was the unique **The Oyster's Secret** shop (with resident pearl divers who can be viewed underwater as they collect the pearl-bearing oysters on request, to be incorporated into jewellery pieces by the shop's artisans). **The Tower** is the centrepiece of The Waterfront, with a 400ft (122m) landmark offering slowly rotating rides (at an extra $3) for a bird's eye view of the park (NB: this was closed in 2005). Here you will find the **SandBar**, a water's edge cocktail bar with live musicians periodically, serving snacks and speciality drinks. It's the perfect place to watch the sun go down. Kids can also play in the area's two **squirt fountains** (remember those swimming costumes!) and the whole scene is characterised by lovely landscaping and even some clever ocean sound effects. AAAA.

Pets Ahoy!: just inside the Waterfront is the air-conditioned haven (during the hottest part of the day) of the Seaport Theater, which hosts this cute 25-minute giggle featuring the unlikely talents of a menagerie of dogs, cats, birds, rats, pot-bellied pigs and others, the majority of which have been rescued from animal shelters. AAA.

Odyssea: fans of the old Cirque de la Mer show in the Nautilus Theater will be sad to know it has gone – but happy it has been replaced by something even smarter and more captivating. Odyssea is a 30-minute fantasy featuring some mind-boggling acrobatic feats, engaging live music, clever lighting and a host of in-theatre special effects. The show tells the spectacular, if stylised, story of a seaman who falls into the ocean and descends through various levels to the sea bed, encountering an assortment of creatures along the way. Think of a watery version of Cirque du Soleil® and you are not far wrong. When it's hot or wet, this is a great place to be! AAAAA. The Nautilus Theater is also home to various weekend events through the year, notably **Jack Hanna's Animal Adventure**, the **Bud and BBQ Country Music Festival** as well as the **Viva La Musica** Latin weekends.

Clydesdale Hamlet: these massive stables are home to the Anheuser-Busch trademark Clydesdale dray horses. They make great photo opportunities when fully harnessed and there is a life-size statue outside, which makes a good backdrop. The Hitching Barn shows how the horses are prepared for the twice-daily parade, including washing, grooming and braiding. AA.

Anheuser-Busch Hospitality Center: adjoining Clydesdale Hamlet, here you can sample the company's most famous product, the world's Number 1 bottled beer, Budweiser, and its cousins. Sadly, it's only 3 small samples per visitor aged 21 or over, but you can enjoy them outside on the terrace, which provides a pleasant break from all the hustle and bustle. AA. You'll also find the **Beer School** here, while **The Deli** restaurant is an attractive proposition, serving fresh-carved turkey and beef, German sausage, sauerkraut, fresh-baked breads and delicious desserts.

Manatee Rescue: here is an exhibit that tugs at your heartstrings as you learn the plight of this endangered species of Florida's waterways. Watch these lazy-looking creatures (half walrus, half hippo?) lounge in their man-made lagoon, then walk down the ramp to the circular theatre where a 5-minute film with 3-D effects reveals the full dangers facing the harmless manatee. Then pass into the underwater viewing section, with hands-on TV screens offering more information. It's a magnificent exhibit and should invoke a strong sense of animal conservation. It is also right behind Blue Horizons, so DON'T go just after a show. AAA½.

Pacific Point Preserve: this carefully re-created rocky coast habitat shows the park's seals and sea lions at their most natural. A hidden wave machine adds the perfect touch, while park attendants provide informative talks at regular intervals. You can also buy small packs of smelt to throw to these ever-hungry mammals. AAA.

Shamu's Happy Harbor: 3 acres (1.2ha) of brilliantly designed adventure playground await youngsters of all ages here. Activities include a 4-storey net climb, 2 tented 'ball rooms' to wade through, a giant 'trampoline' tent and a splashy water maze (great on a hot day). It does get busy in mid-afternoon, but the kids seem to love it at any time. Next door is the Shamu Splash Attack (water-balloon catapults), the inevitable video arcade and some funfair games for a few extra dollars. TTTT.

Shark Encounter: the world's largest collection of dangerous sea creatures can be found here, brought dramatically to life by the walk-through tubes that surround you with more than 50 prowling sharks (including sand tigers, black tips, nurse sharks and sand bars), sawfish, tropical fish and gigantic groupers. It's an eerie experience (and perhaps too intense for young children), but brilliantly presented and, again, highly informative. You can also watch the intrepid souls in the Sharks Deep Dive cage as it traverses the aquarium (see page 171). Queues do tend to build up here at peak times, though. AAAA or TTTT.

Once you have ridden the moving walkway, head for the best restaurant in the park for another close-up at the **Sharks Underwater Grill**. Not only do you have an amazing backdrop for your meal in a clever, subterranean environment (check out the incredible bar, which is a mini-aquarium!), but the upscale, full-service restaurant features an appetising 'Floribbean'-style menu, blending local and spicy Caribbean fare. The emphasis is on seafood – and wonderful creations with scallops, jumbo shrimp (king prawns), grouper and sea bass – plus pasta, filet mignon, chicken and pork, and desserts to die for. Some refreshing (non-alcoholic) cocktails and menus for under 10s and teens complete the picture – it is a real

6

BRIT TIP: If the main adult portions look too big at the Sharks Underwater Grill – and they are pretty hefty – you can order from the Young Adults menu for smaller portions of 4 regular dishes. Check out the kids' dessert menu, too.

treat on a hot day. Open from 11am to park closing (VERY busy at lunch but quieter in late afternoon), it is advisable to book as soon as you arrive or on 407 351 3600 in advance. A 3-course meal costs around $32.

Penguin Encounter: always a hit with families (and one of the more crowded exhibits), the eternally comical penguins are brilliantly presented in this chilly showpiece. You have the choice of going close and using the moving walkway along the display or standing back and watching from a non-moving position. Both afford fascinating views of the 17 different species both above and below the water. Feeding time is highly popular, so arrive early if you want a prime spot. There is also a question-and-answer session at 2pm every day – the winner gets to pet a penguin. AAAA.

Key West at SeaWorld: a whole collection of exhibits are grouped together here under the clever Key West theme. Stingray Lagoon,

Sharks Underwater Grill

where you can feed and touch fully grown rays, includes a nursery for newborn rays, while the park's rescued and rehabilitated sea turtles can be seen at Turtle Point, which helps to explain the dangers to these saltwater reptiles. The centrepiece, the 2.1-acre (0.8-ha) Dolphin Cove, is a more spectacular, naturalistic development and offers the chance to get close enough to feed this

> **BRIT TIP:** Touching the rays and dolphins is an experience at SeaWorld you won't easily forget.

community of frisky Atlantic bottlenose dolphins. There is also an excellent underwater viewing area, while park photographers patrol here, ready to snap you at play with the dolphins, and a 2-photo framed package will set you back $22.99.

The whole area is designed in the tropical flavour of America's southern-most city, Key West, with beach huts, lifeguard chairs, dune buggies, themed shops and other eclectic elements, but it also underlines the environmental message of conservation through interactive graphics and video displays adjacent to the animal habitats, and children of all ages will find it a fun, educational experience. The selection of shops are above average, too. AAAA.

Journey to Atlantis: unique in Orlando, this terrific 'water-coaster'

Odyssea

Key West

gave SeaWorld its first 5-star thrill attraction in 1998. The combination of extra elements here ultimately makes it a one-off, with some illusionary special effects giving way to a high-speed water ride that becomes a runaway roller-coaster. The 'discovery' of Atlantis in your 8-passenger 'fishing boat' starts gently through the lost city. But evil spirit Allura takes over and riders plunge into a dash through Atlantis, dodging gushing fountains and water cannons, with hundreds of dazzling holographic and laser-generated illusions, before the heart-stopping 60ft (18m) drop, which is merely the entry to the roller-coaster finale back in the candle-filled catacombs. An amazing creation. Be ready to get soaked in the course of the ride, which is great in summer but not so clever first thing in the morning in winter. Restrictions: 3ft 6in/106cm. TTTTT. Riders exit into the **Sea Aquarium Gallery**, a combination gift shop and huge aquarium full of sharks, stingrays and tropical fish (don't forget to look up).

Kraken: this member of the coaster family is one of Florida's most breathtaking. Based on the mythical sea monster, Kraken is an innovative pedestal ride (you are effectively sitting in a chair without a floor – pretty exposed!) that plunges an initial 144ft (44m), hits 65mph (105kph), dives underground three times, adds seven inversions (including a vertical loop, a diving loop, a zero-gravity roll and a cobra roll) and a flat spin before riders

escape the beast's lair. The ride from the front row, especially down an opening drop at an angle best described as ludicrous, is positively blood-curdling, and sitting in the rear is pretty amazing, too. Restrictions: 4ft 6in/137cm. TTTTT+.

SeaWorld specials

For extra fun, there is live entertainment daily around the Key West attractions, including the trademark **Sunset Celebration** street party. Throughout the summer high season, when the park is open as late as 10pm, there are often other live elements, leading up to the big **Mistify** finale on the Waterfront lagoon. This is a wonderful piece of pyrotechnics and special effects, invoking giant sea creatures with dazzling laser images. The show mixes towering fountains (up to 100ft/30m high), mist sprays,

6

Finale of Blue Horizons

flames and unique fireworks (including some that burn under water) with an epic soundtrack. By far the largest and most spectacular evening show SeaWorld has yet produced, it doesn't quite rival Disney's Fantasmic! and IllumiNations, but it should not be missed.

As well as all the main set-pieces, several smaller ones can be equally rewarding for their more personal touch. The **Dolphin Nursery** provides close encounters with the park's (younger) dolphins, and there are the **Flamingo, Pelican and Spoonbill Exhibits**. The flamingo **pedal-boats**, which rent for $6 per half-hour (for 2 people) in one corner of the lagoon, are also fun. Look out, too, for the best photo opportunity of the day as a big, cuddly Shamu will greet the kids just inside the main entrance.

You can choose to eat at a further 9 venues, with the best of the bunch being **The Deli** (in the Anheuser-Busch Hospitality Center, see page 174), **Mama's Kitchen**, (sandwiches, salads, chilli, chicken fingers), **Smoky Creek Grill** (a Texas-style barbecue) and **Mango Joe's Café** (delicious grilled fajitas, speciality salads and sandwiches). As in the other main parks, try to eat before midday or after 2.30pm for a crowd-free lunch, and before 5.30pm if you want a leisurely dinner (or better still, book Sharks Underwater Grill or Dine With Shamu). Your wallet will also be in peril in any of the 24 shops and photo kiosks. Make sure you visit at least **Shamu's Emporium** (for a full range of cuddly toys), **Manatee Cove** (more cuddlies), **Friends of the Wild** (dedicated to animal lovers everywhere) and **The Label Stable** for Anheuser-Busch gifts and merchandise (some of it extremely smart). Your purchases can be forwarded to Package Pick-up in Shamu's Emporium, to collect on your way out, provided you give them at least hour.

Finally, non-drivers will probably want to make a note of the special daily bus service from SeaWorld (and other points on I-Drive) direct to sister park Busch Gardens (see page 183), which you can book at Guest Relations.

SEAWORLD with children

The following gives a general idea of the appeal of SeaWorld's attractions to the different age groups.

Under 5s
Shamu Adventure Show, Blue Horizons, Clyde and Seamore Take Treasure Island, Pets Ahoy!, Wild Arctic (without the ride), Manatee rescue, Penguin Encounter, Pacific Point Preserve, Clydesdale Hamlet, Odyssea, Waterfront entertainment.

5–8s
All the above, plus Wild Arctic (with the ride), Mistify, Fusion, Shark Encounter, Shamu's Happy Harbor.

9–12s
All the above, plus Kraken.

Over 12s
Kraken, Journey to Atlantis, Wild Arctic, Shark Encounter, Shamu Adventure Show, Fusion, Blue Horizons, Clyde and Seamore Take Treasure Island, Odyssea, Mistify.

Discovery Cove

Fancy a day in your own tropical paradise, with the chance to swim with dolphins, encounter sharks, snorkel in a coral reef and dive through a waterfall into a tropical aviary? Well, Discovery Cove is all that and more. The only drawback is the price. This mini theme park comes at a premium because it is restricted to just 1,000 guests a day, creating an exclusive experience, and the admission fee reflects that. The flat rate entrance fee is $239 ($259 in peak season) and the only reduction is $100 off for those not wishing to do the Dolphin Swim and for 3–5s; under 3s are free.

The Trainer For A Day programme adds an exciting opportunity to go behind the scenes into the training, feeding and welfare of the park's animals. You get to work with the experts as they interact with dolphins, birds, sharks, stingrays and tropical fish. The experience includes a behavioural training class, souvenir shirt, dolphin book and waterproof camera, and participants must be at least 6 and in good health. You need to book well ahead on 020 8668 4218 or online at www.discoverycove.com. The cost? A healthy $429, including the entrance fee.

New in 2005 was the **Dolphin Lover's Sleepover,** a chance to spend the night (from 7pm) at Discovery Cove in a tent on the beach next to the dolphin lagoon – with stories and snacks – and then be among the first to enjoy a full day in the park when you wake up. It is designed for families (but not under 6s) as it features arts, crafts and other children-friendly activities, and also provides breakfast, lunch and dinner. It costs $389/person and runs only on select Saturdays in the hotter months. Call 1800 406 2244 or go online to book.

So, just what do you get for your money at Discovery Cove? Well, as you would expect, it is a supremely personal park. You check in as you would for a hotel rather than a theme park (the entrance lobby is wonderfully impressive), and you have a guide to take you in and get you set for the day. All your basic requirements – towel, mask, snorkel, wet-jacket, lockers, beach umbrellas and lunch – are included, and the level of service is excellent. A valuable week's pass for SeaWorld or Busch Gardens is also included (valid for 7 consecutive days before or after your Discovery Cove visit; or you can upgrade to 14 consecutive days at both for $30). The lunch provided at the buffet-style **Laguna Grill** is very good, but you have to pay for further snacks and drinks around the park, while the gift shop and photographic prices reflect the entrance fee – expensive.

Location

Situated on Central Florida Parkway, almost opposite the SeaWorld entrance (open year-round from 8.30am–5.30pm. Parking is free), the whole of the 30-acre (12-ha) park is magnificently landscaped, with lovely thatched buildings, palm trees, lush vegetation, brilliant white-sand beaches, gurgling streams and even hammocks. The overall effect is as if you have been transported to a tropical paradise.

The usual tourist hurly-burly is left far behind. The 5-star resort feel is enhanced by a high staff-to-guest ratio (the lifeguards seem to outnumber guests at times). There are no queues for anything (although the restaurant may get busy at lunch) and the highlight dolphin encounter is world class. Visitors with disabilities are well catered for, with special wheelchairs that can move across the sand and into shallow water, and an area of the Dolphin Lagoon to allow those who can't enter the water still to be able to touch the dolphins.

The essence of a day here involves close encounters with all the animals – although not too close in the case of the sharks! – while the ultimate feeling is total relaxation, a veritable holiday from your holiday.

The main attractions

Coral Reef: a huge rocky pool, filled with several thousand tropical fish, offers the most amazing man-made snorkelling experience you'll find. The water teems with silverjacks, angelfish and yellowtail snapper and, even if the 'coral' is hand-painted concrete, it is a clever environment. Some of the larger stingrays inhabiting the bottom of the reef are fascinating to watch. Swimmers also come within inches of sharks and barracuda – all safely behind a Plexiglass partition – which adds another novel element. If you stay reasonably still in the water, many of the tropical fish will crowd around to inspect their latest pool-mate! AAAA.

Discovery Cove

Ray Lagoon: another carefully sculpted pool provides the opportunity to paddle among several dozen southern and cownose rays, quite harmless, but with just a hint of menace to the fascination. AAAA.

Tropical River: this 800yd (732m) circuit of gently flowing bath-warm water is a variation on the lazy river feature of many of the water parks, although with a far more naturalistic aspect and none of the inner tubes. It is primarily designed for snorkellers and features rocky lagoons, caves, a beach section, a tropical forest segment, sunken ruins and an underwater viewing window into the Coral Reef. The lack of fish makes it seem a bit bland after the Tropical Reef and Ray Lagoon, but again, it is as much about relaxing as having fun. It is

Snorkelling in Coral Reef

Dolphins at Discovery Cove

also up to 8ft deep at points, so non-swimmers are advised to use a flotation vest. AAA.

Aviary: this recently enhanced 3-part adventure is both an area in its own right and a 40yd (37m) section of the Tropical River. You can walk in off the beach or swim in through one of the two impressive waterfalls which guard each end, a beautifully scenic touch and fun for snorkellers. Some 200 tropical birds (plus tiny Muntjac deer) fill the main enclosure and, if you stand still for a while, they are likely to use you for a perch. An expansion in 2002 effectively doubled the size of the aviary by adding a small-bird sanctuary – full of finches, honeycreepers and hummingbirds – and a large-bird enclosure, featuring toucans and the red-legged seriema.

Guides will introduce you to specific birds (which you can hand-feed) and tell you about their habits, habitats and conservation issues. AAAAA.

Dolphin Swim: the headline attraction at Discovery Cove is the encounter with the park's Atlantic bottlenose dolphin community. A 20-minute orientation programme in one of the 4 thatched beach cabanas, with a film and instruction from two of the animal trainers, sets you up for this thrilling experience. Groups of 6 to 8 go into the lagoon with careful supervision from the trainers and, starting off by standing in the waist-deep (slightly chilly) water as one of the dolphins comes to you, you gradually become more adventurous until you are swimming with them. Timid swimmers are catered for and there are flotation vests for those who need them. The lagoon is up to 12ft (3.6m) deep so there is a real feeling of being in the dolphins' environment.

You will learn how trainers use hand signals and positive reinforcement to communicate with them, and get the chance to stroke, feed and even kiss (!) your dolphin. The encounter comes to a dramatic conclusion as you are towed back to shore by one of these awesome animals, which can weigh up to

6

Discovery Cove

600lb (272kg), although the activities vary according to the dolphins' own attention span. You spend around 30 minutes in the water and it is totally unforgettable. Under 6s are not allowed into the dolphin lagoon. TTTTT+.

Truly, Discovery Park is an attraction with huge style and appeal – not to mention the stuff of which cherished memories are made – but it will take a big bite from your holiday budget. A family of 4, with children old enough to do the Dolphin Swim, could pay almost $1,100 (including tax) for the day. Even with a free 7-day SeaWorld pass included, it is a massive outlay. The charge for 3- to 5-year-olds is also pretty steep, in my opinion. Your sundries add up, too. An 8 x 10 photo is $29.99. Then there are various photo packages at $29.99, $62.99 and $99.99, while the video of your experience (which includes 30 minutes of highlights of the whole park) costs $59.99 ($69.99 for a DVD). A CD with five images is $100, 11 images are $150 and 22 images are $200.

The weather can get distinctly cool in the winter months, but the water is always heated (apart from the dolphin lagoon, which remains at 72°F/22°C) and full wetsuits are also available to keep out the chill. Their attention to detail is superb and guest satisfaction ratings remain extremely high (it is hugely popular with British visitors – up to 40 per cent of the daily attendance at times). However, if any element falls below expectations, it is worth bringing it to the attention of a manager as they are always keen to rectify any oversights.

An alternative to the full day's activity is the summer **Twilight Discovery** programme – the chance to visit the park, be wined and dined in style, swim in the Coral Reef and resort pools and enjoy a shallow-water dolphin encounter. The emphasis is on a refined tropical party experience, for just 100 guests a night from 3 to 9pm (Mon-Thur). The exclusive feel is enhanced by valet parking, a festive welcome reception, tropical drinks and live, Caribbean-style music, desserts on the beach and the special dolphin interaction. It includes a 7-day pass to either SeaWorld or Busch Gardens and a 5 x 7 photo. The cost is still a hefty $259 (or $159 without the dolphin encounter) but it's another unique opportunity.

Special occasions

For that special birthday, anniversary or for somewhere completely different to propose marriage, Discovery Cove has a range of options which involve dolphin interaction and private beach cabanas. The **Platinum Ring** (an extra $474.95/couple) includes sharing your special moment with a dolphin, who delivers a specialised message buoy, a private tent on the beach, Dom Perignon champagne, a dozen roses, chocolate-dipped strawberries, disposable waterproof camera, keepsake photo and frame, and a video of the occasion. The **Golden Ring Package** ($224.95/ couple) and **Sweetheart Package** ($149.95), are scaled-down versions of the same. The **Birthday Package** ($74.95) includes dolphin activity, cake, photo and souvenir buoy, plus T-shirt and video, and a **Premium** version ($174.95) offers a T-shirt and video of the occasion. For more details, visit www.discovery cove.com. You can book online – preferably at least *3 months* in advance at busy times – or call 407 370 1280 in the US.

Busch Gardens

When is a zoo not a zoo? When it is also a theme park like the 335-acre (136-ha) Busch Gardens in Tampa. The second big Anheuser-Busch park in the area started life as a mini-menagerie for the wildlife collection of the brewery-owning Busch family (Budweiser). In 1959, they opened a small, tropical-themed hospitality centre next to the brewery and now it is a major, multi-faceted family attraction, the biggest on Florida's west coast and a little more than an hour from Orlando. It is rated among the top four zoos in America, with more than 2,700 animals representing more than 320 species of mammals, birds, reptiles, amphibians and spiders. But that's just the start.

It boasts a safari-like section of Africa spread over 65 acres (26ha) of grassy veldt, with special tours to hand-feed some of the animals. Interspersed among the animals are more than 20 bona fide theme park

Busch Gardens at a glance

Location	Busch Blvd, Tampa; 75–90 minutes' drive from Orlando	
Size	335 acres (136ha) in 11 themed areas	
Hours	9 or 10am–6 or 7pm off peak; 9am–8pm Easter, Thanksgiving, Christmas; 9 or 9.30am–10.30pm summer	
Admission	Under 3 free; 3–9 $45.95 (1-Day Ticket), $84.95 (Busch/SeaWorld Combo ticket), $189.95 (5-Park FlexTicket, including Universal Studios, SeaWorld and Wet 'n Wild); adults (10+) $55.95, 94.95, 224.95	
Parking	$8	
Lockers	Yes; in Morocco, Congo, Egypt and Stanleyville; $1	
Pushchairs	$11 and $16 ($2 gift card refund; in Morocco)	
Wheelchairs	$9 ($2 gift card refund) and $32, with pushchairs	
Top Attractions	Rhino Rally, SheiKra, Gwazi, Kumba, Montu, Congo River Rapids, Tanganyika Tidal Wave, RL Stine's Haunted Lighthouse	
Don't Miss	KaTonga, Myombe Reserve, Edge of Africa, Elephant Wash, Mystic Sheikhs band	
Hidden Costs	Meals	Burger, chips and Pepsi $9.58 3-course meal $17–24; family-style diner $11.95 and $6.95 (Crown Colony House) Kids' meal $3.99 ($5.49 with souvenir bucket)
	T-shirts	$12.99–26.99
	Souvenirs	99 cents–$1,950
	Sundries	Ride photos $9.99

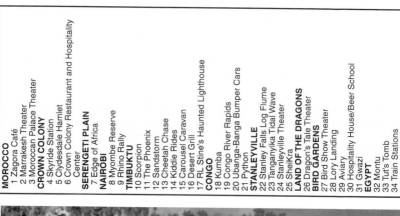

MOROCCO
1 Zagora Café
2 Marrakesh Theater
3 Moroccan Palace Theater
CROWN COLONY
4 Skyride Station
5 Clydesdale Hamlet
6 Crown Colony Restaurant and Hospitality
  Center
SERENGETI PLAIN
7 Edge of Africa
NAIROBI
8 Myombe Reserve
9 Rhino Rally
TIMBUKTU
10 Scorpion
11 The Phoenix
12 Sandstorm
13 Cheetah Chase
14 Kiddie Rides
15 Carousel Caravan
16 Desert Grill
17 RL Stine's Haunted Lighthouse
CONGO
18 Kumba
19 Congo River Rapids
20 Ubanga-Banga Bumper Cars
21 Python
STANLEYVILLE
22 Stanley Falls Log Flume
23 Tanganyika Tidal Wave
24 Stanleyville Theater
25 SheiKra
LAND OF THE DRAGONS
26 Dragon's Tale Theater
BIRD GARDENS
27 Bird Show Theater
28 Lory Landing
29 Aviary
30 Hospitality House/Beer School
31 Gwazi
EGYPT
32 Montu
33 Tut's Tomb
34 Train Stations

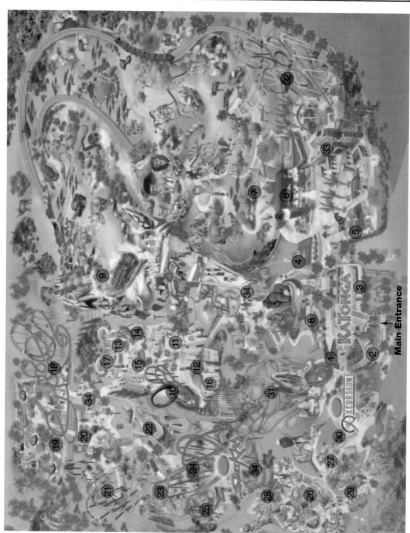

rides, including the mind-numbing roller-coasters **Kumba**, **SheiKra**, **Montu** and **Gwazi**, with guaranteed fun for coaster addicts, plus plenty of scaled-down rides for younger children. Then there are animal shows, comedians, musicians, strolling players and *KaTonga*, a family show extravaganza in the impressive Moroccan Palace Theater.

The overall theme is Africa, hence the park is divided into areas like Nairobi and Congo, and the dining and shopping are equal to most of the other theme parks. It doesn't quite have the pizzazz of *Epcot* or Universal, and the staff are a bit more laid back, but it has guaranteed, 5-star family appeal, especially with its selection of rides just for kids, and it is a big hit with British visitors. In a way, it is like the big brother of Chessington World of Adventures in Surrey, although on a much grander scale (and in a better climate). Busch Gardens is the only park to offer 1-Day Tickets with a **Rain Guarantee**, which means if you get rained out on your visit, you can return FREE within 7 days.

Location

Busch Gardens is the hardest place to locate on the sketchy local maps and the signposting is not as sharp as it could be but, from Orlando, the directions are pretty simple. Head west on I-4 for almost an hour (it is 55 miles/88km from I-4's junction with Highway 192) until you hit the intersecting motorway I-75. Take I-75 north for 3½ miles (5.5km) until you see the exit for Fowler Avenue (Highway 582). Continue west on Fowler for another 3½ miles (5.5km), then just past the University of South Florida on your right, turn LEFT into McKinley Drive. A mile (1.6km) down McKinley Drive, Busch Gardens' car park will be on your left, where it costs $8 to park.

Those without a car can use the daily **Busch Gardens Shuttle Express** bus service, which makes several round trips a day from Orlando at $10 a time (free if you have a 5-Park FlexTicket). You board the Shuttle at SeaWorld, The Mercado, Orlando Premium Outlets, Universal Studios or Old Town in Kissimmee and pick-up times range from 8–10.15am, returning at 6 or 7pm. Book at the **Guest Services** window at SeaWorld or call 1-800 221 1339.

You may think you have left the crowds behind in Orlando but, unfortunately, in high season you'd be wrong. It is still advisable to be here in time for opening, if only to be first in line to ride the amazing Rhino Rally or the dazzling roller-coasters, which all draw major queues (especially the new SheiKra).

Music show at Busch Gardens

6

The Congo River Rapids, Stanley Falls Log Flume ride and Tanganyika Tidal Wave (all opportunities to get wet!) are also prime rides. **RL Stine's Haunted Lighthouse**, a 3-D film show, is also highly popular. The queues do take longer to build up here, though, so for the first few hours at least you can enjoy a relatively crowd-free experience.

On your right as you approach the main gates is the **Tours Centre** window, and you should go there straight away (or book in advance on 813 984 4043 or e-mail Bgt.viptours@buschgardens.com) if you'd like to do the wonderful Serengeti Safari or one of their other Adventure Tours (see page 192). Busch Gardens is divided into 11 main sections, with the major rides all a bit of a hike from the main entrance.

Rhino Rally, which opened in summer 2001, is one of the prime attractions, so you should head here first (especially as the animals are more visible early in the day). Bear right through Morocco, turn left into Nairobi, pass the train station, and the Rally entrance is opposite the elephant habitat. Coaster fans flock in serious numbers to **SheiKra**, the world's highest and fastest dive coaster, and queues can hit 3 HOURS by mid-afternoon so, if you are tempted by this first, bear left through Morocco past the Zagora Café, through the Bird Gardens and up into Stanleyville. **Gwazi**, the fabulous wooden double-coaster, is another to draw a crowd relatively quickly, and you could do this en route. Then continue through Stanleyville to Congo for **Kumba**, and retrace your steps to do **Congo River Rapids**, the **Python** and the other 2 water rides. Alternatively, turn right through the main entrance and visit Egypt for **Montu**. Here is the full park layout, going anti-clockwise.

Morocco

Coming through the main gates brings you first into Morocco, home of all the main guest services and a lot of the best shops. *Epcot*'s Moroccan pavilion sets the scene rather better, but the architecture is still impressive and this version won't overtax your wallet quite as much as Disney does! For a quick meal try the **Zagora Café**, especially at breakfast when the marching, dancing, 8-piece brass band **Mystic Sheikhs** swings into action to entertain the early crowds. Alternatively, the enticing **Sultan's Sweets** serves coffee and pastries. Watch out, too, for the strolling **Men of Note**, a 4-piece *a cappella* group, and the costumed characters like TJ the Tiger and Hilda Hippo.

Turning the corner brings you to the first animal encounter, the alligator pen. Morocco is also home to two of the park's biggest shows. The Marrakesh Theater offers the 25-minute **Moroccan Roll** song and dance show, with live musicians, top-notch singers and energetic dancers all in an amusing pastiche of pop and rock with a desert theme (hence songs like *Midnight At The Oasis* and *Rock The Casbah*). AAA.

KaTonga: brand new in 2004 was this lavish Broadway-style spectacle, featuring an 18-strong cast of singers, dancers, acrobats and puppeteers. Subtitled *Musical Tales from the Jungle*, this 35-minute theatrical extravaganza celebrates African animal folklore with an ingenious mix of live actor presentation and the award-winning larger-than-life puppets of Michael Curry (who helped to create Disney's The Lion King show in London and New York). With 57 costumes, 45 puppets and troupe of stunning Chinese acrobats, it makes for a truly eye-catching performance, up to 5 times a day, that is way above usual theme park standards. It is also air-conditioned, a welcome relief in summer (you should arrive a little early as the Moroccan Palace Theater doors close right on showtime). AAAAA.

Crown Colony

This area sits in the park's bottom right corner and has 4 distinct components. Here, you can take the **Skyride** cable car (AAA) on a one-way trip to Congo (providing a great look at Rhino Rally). The **Clydesdale Hamlet** is also here, but if you've seen the massive dray horses and their stables at SeaWorld, the set-up is pretty similar (AA). Next door is the **Showjumping Hall of Fame**, which should appeal to fans of this activity (AA).

The **Crown Colony Restaurant and Hospitality Center** is a large Victorian-style building overlooking the Serengeti Plain. It offers counter-service salads, sandwiches and pizzas (downstairs) or a full-service restaurant upstairs with magnificent views of the animals roaming the plain. For a memorable meal (11.30am until an hour before park closing), head here for lunch (they don't take bookings) or, better still, come back for dinner in early evening and see the animals come down to the waterhole.

Serengeti Plain

The Serengeti Plain itself is a 49-acre (20-ha) spread of African savannah that is home to buffalo, antelope, zebra, giraffe, wildebeest, ostriches, hippos, rhinos and many exotic birds, and can be viewed for much of the journey on the **Serengeti Express Railway**, a full-size, open-car steam train that chugs slowly from its main station in Nairobi to Egypt and all the way round to Congo, Stanleyville and back. It is a good ride to take during the main part of the day when queues build up at the thrill rides. AAA.

Edge of Africa: a 15-acre (6-ha) safari experience that guarantees a close-up encounter almost as good as the real thing. The walk-through attraction puts you in an authentic setting of natural wilds and native villages (right down to the imported plants and even the smells), from which you can view giraffes, lions, baboons, meerkats, crocodiles, hyenas, vultures and even get an underwater view of a hippopotamus habitat. Look out for the abandoned Jeep – you can sit in the front cab while lions lounge in the back! Wandering 'safari guides' and naturalists offer informal talks, and the attention to detail is wonderful. AAAAA.

> BRIT TIP: Edge of Africa offers some fantastic photo opportunities but, in the hot months, come here early in the day as many animals seek refuge from the heat later.

Nairobi

Nairobi is home to the awesome **Myombe Reserve**, one of the largest and most realistic habitats for the threatened highland gorillas and chimpanzees of central Africa. This 3-acre (1.2-ha) walk-through has a superb tropical setting where the temperature is kept artificially high and convincing with the aid of lush forest landscaping and hidden water mist sprays. Take your time, especially as there are good, seated vantage points, and be patient to catch these magnificent creatures going about their daily routine. It is also highly informative, with attendants usually on hand to answer any questions. AAAAA.

Rhino Rally: this wonderfully dramatic and scenic ride starts out as an off-road Jeep safari and changes into an innovative raft adventure as your 17-passenger vehicle gets caught in a flash flood. The 8-minute whirl through the wilds of Africa includes encounters with elephants, rhinos, crocodiles, antelope and more, as the off-road part of the ride is just about as 'real' as they can make it. Your driver adds to the fun with some amusing spiel about the rally and your Land-Rover built vehicle, but it soon becomes clear your 'navigator' (the front seat passenger) has led you into a blind gully. An unused pontoon bridge is your only way out, but 'fate' has a unique twist in store, which opens the way to part two of the ride and the thrilling raging river section that is unlike any attraction we've experienced to date. Check this out (but you must get here early to beat the queues). Height restriction is just 3ft 3in/99cm. TTTT and AAAAA.

Back at **Myombe Gifts** you can buy your own cuddly baby gorilla toys and get a snack or soft drink at the **Kenya Kanteen**. This is also the place to see the Asian elephants (check the advertised times for the **Elephant Wash**) and visit the **Nairobi Field Station**, an animal nursery and care centre that houses

The Scorpion in Timbuktu

all manner of rehabilitating and hand-reared creatures. Continuing round the nursery brings you to the **Reptile House** and **Tortoise Habitat**. The **Curiosity Caverns**, just to the left of the nursery, are easy to miss but don't if you want to catch a glimpse of some nocturnal and rarely seen creatures very much at home in a cave-like setting.

Timbuktu

Passing through Nairobi brings you to the more ride-dominated area of the park, starting with Timbuktu. Here in a North African desert setting you will find many of the elements of a typical funfair, with a couple of brain-scrambling rides and two good shows.

Scorpion: a 50mph (80kph) roller-coaster, this features a 62ft (19m) drop and a 360-degree loop that is guaranteed to dial D for

Katonga

Cheetah Chase

Dizzy for a while! The ride lasts just 120 seconds, but seems longer. The queues build up here from late morning, and you must to be at least 3ft 6in/106cm to ride. TTTT.

Cheetah Chase: new in 2004, this family-orientated 'Crazy Mouse' style coaster is surprisingly energetic, rising as it does some 46ft (14m) and adding some tight turns and swift drops. Top speed is only 22mph (35kph), which won't excite Kumba fans, but it certainly seems faster and will thrill the younger lot. TTT (TTTTT for under 10s).

Other rides include **The Phoenix**, a positively evil invention, that involves sitting in a gigantic, boat-shaped swing which eventually performs a 360-degree rotation in dramatic, slow-motion style. Don't eat just before this one! Height restriction: 4ft/122cm; TTTT. **Sandstorm** is a fairly routine whirligig contraption that spins and levitates at fairly high speed (hold on to your stomach). Height restriction 3ft 6in/106cm; TTT. A series of scaled-down **Kiddie Rides** are usually a hit with the under 10s (and give Mum and Dad a break as well). The **Carousel Caravan** offers the opportunity to ride a genuine Mary Poppins-type carousel (TT), while there is the inevitable **Electronic Arcade** and a **Games Area** of side shows and stalls that require a few extra dollars.

Desert Grill is a new African-themed buffet diner here (offering large sandwiches, Italian sausage with grilled vegetables, salads and pasta, plus kids' meals in a souvenir bucket) set in a huge hall that provides some serious stage entertainment too. In summer 2005, it was the musical style of American Beats and the ABBA Celebration. AAA.

R L Stine's Haunted Lighthouse: the final element and a thoroughly fun 3-D film romp with Christopher 'Back To The Future' Lloyd that will appeal especially to children of all ages (although it may be a touch spooky for the youngest). The story centres on the 2 'ghost children' of the Haunted Lighthouse and the real children who inadvertently come to visit. Cue a riot of 3-D visuals plus many clever (and hilarious) special effects (prepare to duck when Lloyd drinks a beer!). It also uses fog and wind effects, plus strobe lighting and a few 'surprises'. Based on a story by American kids' mock-horror writer RL Stine (of *Goosebumps* fame), it is an extremely well made 22-minute movie, with full surround-sound that draws a good crowd through the main part of the day, so go early or leave it until later on. AAAA.

Congo

You're into serious ride territory here, with the unmistakable giant turquoise structure of **Kumba** looming over the area. First of all, it's one of the largest and fastest

Congo River Rapids

roller-coasters in the south-east United States and, at 60mph (97kph), it features three unique elements: a diving loop which plunges the riders a full 110ft (33m), a camelback, with a 360-degree spiral that induces a weightless feeling for 3 seconds, and a 108ft (33m) vertical loop. For good measure, it dives underground at one point! It looks terrifying close up but is absolutely exhilarating, even for non-coaster fans. Restrictions: 4ft 6in/137cm. TTTTT.

Congo River Rapids: these look pretty tame after that, but don't be fooled. The giant rubber rafts will bounce you down some of the most convincing rapids outside of the Rockies, and you will end up with a fair soaking for good measure. Restrictions: 3ft 6in/106cm. TTTT.

Ubanga-Banga Bumper Cars: they are just that, typical fairground dodgems (height restriction: 3ft 6in/106cm; TT), and you won't miss anything by passing them by for the more daring **Python**, the fourth of Busch Gardens' coasters, with this one featuring a double spiral corkscrew at 50mph (80kph) from 70ft (21m) up. Height restriction is 4ft/122cm, and the ride lasts just 70 seconds, but it's a blast. TTTT. More **Kiddie Rides** are available for the smaller visitors here while the **Vivi Restaurant** offers chicken fajitas, club sandwiches, salads and desserts, and there are 2 gift shops.

Stanleyville

You pass over Claw Island, home to the park's spectacular rare white **Bengal tigers**, to get to Stanleyville, which seems to merge into one area from the Congo. Here there are more watery rides, with the popular **Stanley Falls Log Flume** ride (almost identical to the ones at Chessington, Legoland, Thorpe

Park and Alton Towers), which guarantees a good soaking at the final drop (height restriction: 3ft 10in/116cm; TTT) and the distinctly cleverer **Tanganyika Tidal Wave**, which takes you on a scenic ride along 'uncharted' African waters before tipping you down a 2-stage drop that really does land with tidal-wave force. Height restriction: 4ft/122cm. TTTT.

BRIT TIP: Don't stand on the bridge by Tanganyika Tidal Wave or by the SheiKra splashdown unless you want to get seriously wet!

SheiKra: the park's stand-out new attraction is the giant steel structure of this monstrous coaster. A world first at 200ft (62m) tall and hitting 70mph (112kph), this is the ride to put Alton Towers' fearsome Oblivion in the shade. Higher, longer and faster, it features an initial drop at an angle as near vertical as makes no difference (with a delicious moment of stop-go balance as you teeter on the edge!), a second drop of 138ft (42m) into an underground tunnel, an Immelman loop (a truly hair-raising rolling manoeuvre) and a water splashdown over half a mile of smooth-as-silk track. The whole ride lasts 3 minutes and is almost as much fun (or terror, depending on your viewpoint) to watch as to ride. It also draws crowds like nothing else in the park, so get here early or expect to stand in line for at least an hour. Height restriction 4ft 6in/137cm. TTTTT+.

Stanleyville Theater: a good place to put your feet up as you watch the resident entertainers turn on the style. This varies seasonally; in 2005 it was the impressive percussive rhythms of Iron Beats. AAA½.

For a hearty meal (and a great view of SheiKra), visit the **Zambia Smokehouse**, where its wood-smoked ribs platter is a delight among a heavily BBQ-orientated menu (also with salads, sandwiches and kids' meals). As you leave Stanleyville behind, say hello to the muntjac deer and orang-utans (who are rarely active during the day) in the large pens either side of the train station.

Land of the Dragons

Parents will want to know about this large, wonderfully clever area of activities, entertainment, rides and attractions purely for the young uns. It features a 3-storey treehouse complete with towers and maze-like stairways, a rope climb, ball crawl and outdoor **Dragon's Tale Theater**, which presents the 15-minute show *Dumphrey's Special Day* – a birthday special with the resident cuddly dragon. It is all good, knockabout, well-supervised stuff, and some of the kiddie rides are superbly inventive, as well as offering plenty of opportunity to get wet. TTTTT (youngsters only).

Bird Gardens

Your route around the park now brings you to the most peaceful area, and the original starting point of the park in 1959, the **Bird Gardens**. Here it is possible to unwind from the usual theme park hurly-burly. The exhibits and shows are all family-orientated, too, with the 25-minute *Wild Wings of Africa* presented in the **Bird Show Theater** (AAA) and the **Hospitality Patio**, where the resident band plays a mix of musical favourites, past and present. **Lory Landing** is a desert island-themed walk-through aviary

featuring lorikeets, hornbills, parrots and more, with the chance to become a human perch and feed the friendly lorikeets (or have your ear nibbled!). A cup of nectar costs $1, but is a great investment for a memorable photo. Take a slow walk round to appreciate the lush, tropical foliage and special displays such as the walk-through **Aviary**, **Flamingo Island** and **Eagle Canyon**. AAA.

A free taste of Anheuser-Busch products is on offer in **Hospitality House**, where you can enroll for **Beer School**, a 40-minute lesson in the process of beer-making. It offers a fascinating glimpse into the brewery world, and is excellently explained, with the bonus of some tasting! You will also be presented with a Brewery Master certificate. AAA (21 and over only).

Gwazi: this is Busch's second largest roller-coaster, a massive 'duelling' wooden creation in the classic mould (i.e. no going upside down). The 2 sets of cars, the Gwazi Lion and Gwazi Tiger, each top 50mph (80kph) and generate a G-force of up to 3.5 as they career around nearly 7,000ft (2,134m) of track with 6 fly-by encounters. You get to choose your ride in the intricately themed 8-acre (3-ha) village plaza and then you are off up the 90ft (27m) lift for a breathtaking 2½ minutes. The shake, rattle 'n' roll effect of a classic coaster is cleverly re-created and the Lion and Tiger rides are slightly different, so you need to do both. Even if you don't like coasters, try this one. Height restriction: 4ft/122cm. TTTTT.

Next door is the **River Rumble** game for kids, a series of catapults that fire water-filled balloons. TTTT (for under 12s). This costs $4 for a bucket of 9 balloons (or $6 for 2 buckets). Children can also try the **bungee trampoline** and **rock-climbing wall** at $7 each or $10 for both.

Egypt

The final area of Busch Gardens is tucked away through the Crown Colony, so it is best visited either first thing or late in the day. Egypt is 8 acres (3ha) of carefully re-created pharaoh country, dominated by the roller-coaster Montu, named after an ancient Egyptian warrior god.

Montu: a truly breathtaking creation, this is one of the world's tallest and longest inverted coasters, covering nearly 4,000ft (1,219m) of track at speeds topping 60mph (97kph) and peaking with a G-force of 3.85! Like Kumba, it looks terrifying, but in reality is an absolute 5-star thrill as it leaves your legs dangling and twists and dives (underground at two points) for almost 3 minutes of brain-scrambling fun. Height restriction: 4ft 6in/137cm. TTTTT.

You can travel back in time on a tour of **Tut's Tomb**, as it was when archaeologist Howard Carter discovered it, with clever lighting, audio and even aroma effects. AAA. Youngsters can also make their own excavations in a neat **Sand Pit** (with some little 'treasures' to be found!),

Land of the Dragons

while the shopping at **Golden Scarab** takes on a high-quality air with its hand-blown glass items and authentic cartouche paintings.

You should finally return to Morocco for a spot of shopping in the area's tempting bazaars. Middle Eastern brass, pottery and carpets will all tempt you into opening your wallet yet again at **Casablanca Outfitters**, **Genie's Bottle** and **Marrakesh Market**, while there is a full range of Anheuser-Busch products and gift ideas at the **Emporium** and **Label Stable**, if you haven't already fallen prey to the array of shops and cuddly-toy outlets around the park. The new **Xcursions** is an environmentally themed gift shop, contributing to the Busch Gardens Conservation Fund.

In addition...

The **Serengeti Safari** tour is a 30-minute excursion (5 times a day, taking 20 people at a time) aboard flat-bed trucks that take you to meet the Serengeti Plain's giraffes, zebras, ostriches and rhinos close up and learn more about the park's environmental efforts. You book up at the Tour Office window just outside the main entrance, or at the kiosk in front of Casablanca Outfitters, for an extra $33.99, and places tend to fill up quickly (children must be at least 5 to take part, and 5-15s must be accompanied by an adult). New is the **Serengeti Dining Safari**, which adds dinner at the Crown Colony House restaurant for $55.49 per adult and $41.58 per child aged 5-9.

The **Guided Adventure Tours** take 15 at a time on a VIP park trek (lasting 4-5 hours), with your own guide, reserved seating at KaTonga, front-of-line access for a number of rides (including Gwazi and Rhino Rally), counter-service lunch at Crown Colony and an up-close encounter with many of the animals and their staff, including the Serengeti Safari. They cost $94.99 ($84.99 for children). The **Adventure Thrill Tours** are similar but substitute more rides – including the water rides – for the animal encounters ($74.99 and $64.93 ages 3-9). The 2-hour **Animal Adventures Tour** is a personal animal experience for 7–10 people a day. The next best thing to being a park zookeeper, it provides close encounters with the Clydesdales, black rhinos, hippos, giraffes and elephants, plus joining in animal behavioural sessions. It costs an extra $99.99/person (no under 5s).

The new **Saving A Species** truck tour is a 45-minute meet-and-greet with the park's animal specialists, learning about their work and important conservation issues, including how Busch Gardens is involved with various wildlife projects worldwide ($2 of the $44.99 fee goes to the World Wildlife Fund; no under 5s). Finally, the **Elite Adventure Tour** offers a personal, exclusive park tour, with front-of-line access to all rides, the Serengeti Safari, reserved seating at shows, free bottled water throughout, continental breakfast, lunch at the Crown Colony Restaurant, free parking and a free Fujifilm camera – all for an extra $199.99/person (ages 5 and up). Once again, all tours can be booked ahead on 813 984 4043 or online at www.buschgardens.com.

Busch Gardens is open until 10pm for the **Summer Nights** programme (June and July), which features festive food and drink, live entertainment, music and DJs. There is also a huge fireworks spectacular July 2-4. A new **Summer Twilight Ticket** offers dinner with a standard 1-day entry if you arrive after 3pm.

For a full family day out, you can combine Busch Gardens with the next-door water park **Adventure Island** (on McKinley Drive) which is particularly welcome when it hots up (provided you plaster on the sun cream). The 25 acres (10ha) of watery fun, in a Key West theme, offer a full range of slides and rides, such as the **Wahoo Run** adventure ride, the 76ft (23m) free-fall plunge of the **Tampa Typhoon** and the spiralling **Calypso Coaster**, plus a kids' playground, cafés, gift shops, arcades and volleyball, as well as the wonderful **Splash Attack** adventure, a water activity maze culminating in a 1,000-gallon (4,550-litre) bucket dump on the unwary! Adventure Island is open mid-February to late October (weekends only Feb-Mar and Sept-Oct) 10am-5pm (later in high season). Tickets are $30.95 (ages 3-9) and $32.95, and a Busch Gardens/Adventure Island combo ticket is $60.95 and $70.95.

Well, that's the low-down on all the main theme parks, but there is still more to discover…

6

Myombe Reserve

7 The Other Attractions

(or, One Giant Leap for Tourist Kind)

If you think you have seen everything Orlando has to offer by simply sticking to the theme parks, in the words of the song, 'You ain't seen nothin' yet'. It would be relatively easy to add the Kennedy Space Center to Chapter 6 because, although it's not strictly a theme park, it is adding new attractions all the time and is fast becoming a full day's excursion from Orlando to the east or 'space' coast.

Silver Springs, Historic Bok Sanctuary and a revamped Cypress Gardens all offer a taste of the more natural Florida. The Kissimmee attraction Gatorland provides a contrasting experience, with its alligators, crocs and shows (great value, too), as do the one-off venues like WonderWorks, Orlando Science Center and Ripley's Believe It Or Not. For more individual attractions, you have the unique aviation experience of Fantasy of Flight, the hair-raising haunted house walk-through of Skull Kingdom, the amazing 'sky-dive' experience of SkyVenture, plus a magnificent array of water fun parks. The choice is yours, but it is an immense selection. Let's start here with One Giant Leap for Mankind.

Kennedy Space Center

More than $120 million has been spent on revamping the Center's Visitor Complex in recent years and, while it was always a good visit in the past, now it is simply unmissable, in my opinion, for its hugely imaginative depiction of the past, present and future of NASA's space programme. The KSC also owns the nearby Astronaut Hall of Fame, and a Maximum Access pass provides entry to that as well. There are 5 continually running shows or exhibitions, 4 static showcases, a kids' play area (and a new show designed specifically for them), an art gallery, the Astronaut Encounter, 2 splendid IMAX films and a full bus tour of the

The Go Orlando Card

A new discount card for the Other Attractions was launched in summer 2005, offering 2, 3, 5 and 7 days' admission to the likes of the Kennedy Space Center, Gatorland, Water Mania, Ripleys Believe It Or Not, WonderWorks, Arabian Nights, Pirates dinner show, Morse Museum, Winter Park Scenic Boat Tour, Florida Eco-Safaris, mini-golf and Fun Spot Action Park, plus discounts at some restaurants and free shopping coupon books. You need to work hard to get full value for the Card, but some of the extras are really useful. A 2-day Card costs $99 for adults and $79 for 3-12s; a 3-day Card is $159 and $129; a 5-day is $219 and $169; and a 7-day is $279 and $199 (dinner shows available with 3, 5 and 7-day only). Cards can be picked up in Orlando free or mailed in advance (for a fee). For more info, look up www.goorlandocard.com.

Space Center, which adds up to great value for the entrance fee. In addition, there are 2 separate guided tours, while the new **Astronaut Training Experience** provides a novel element to the Center.

You enter through the futuristic ticket plaza and can spend several hours wandering around the exhibits and presentations of the 70-acre (28-ha) Visitor Complex itself. **Robot Scouts** is a walk-through display-and-show in the company of Starquester 2000, your robot host who will explain the history of NASA's unmanned space probes in a surprising and often amusing style.

Next door, the **Quest for Life** film – narrated by *Deep Space Nine* star Avery Brooks – provides another illuminating view in the Universe Theater. Head on out and see some of the hardware of space flight in the completely revamped **Rocket Garden**, which has a kids' water fountain and an Apollo space capsule gantry, to give you the feel of that last earthbound walk before the astronauts boarded the *Saturn V* rocket. Free guided tours are given twice a day. And don't forget to stop by the **Astronaut Memorial**, a sombre but moving tribute to the men and women who have died in advancing the space programme. **Shuttle Explorer** allows you to inspect a replica space shuttle, while the recently renovated **Launch Status Center** displays actual flight hardware, plus live mission briefings of rocket and space shuttle launches. Free tours are available several times a day.

Early Space Exploration is a clever and coherent walk-through trip into the recent past of the space programme, including the *Hall of Discovery*, the *Mercury Mission Control Room* – the original consoles from America's first manned space flights – and the *Hall of History*. The futuristic **Exploration in the New Millennium** exhibit provides more

appeal for youngsters, with a fun educational element from the spaceship-like *Exploring Gallery*, the *Mars Rock* exhibit and a series of interactive panels.

Children in the 7–14 age range should enjoy **Mad Mission To Mars 2025** show, a mix of educational messages and pure fun theatricals, with lots of special effects, audience participation and even its own hip-hop song, *The Newton Rap*. Also here is **Nature and Technology** (which showcases the unique balance the Center maintains with the local environment), the **Center for Space Education** (an interactive learning and Teacher Resource Center), the **Space Walk of Honor**, and **NASA Art Gallery** (space exhibits and artwork).

Perhaps the most innovative feature, though, is the **Astronaut Encounter**, with personal briefings, Q&A sessions, video footage and anecdotes from various veterans of the Mercury, Gemini and Apollo programmes, plus several Space Shuttle astronauts. It is an insightful and engrossing feature, and takes place up to 3 times a day at the Center Plaza. You can even take things a step further with **Lunch with an Astronaut** (12:30pm daily), whereby a small group gets to eat with the astronaut of the day. The featured astronaut also gives a special briefing adding extra insight into their space missions. Lunch is $19.99 adults, $12.99 for children 3-11, at 12.15pm daily, and tickets may be purchased online or by calling 321 449 4400. Youngsters have their own playground, the **Children's Play Dome**, complete with a one-fifth scale space shuttle.

The air-conditioned **Coach Tour** (departures every 15 minutes), fully narrated throughout, makes 2 important stops in addition to driving around much of the working area of the Space Center, including

7

ORLANDO'S OTHER ATTRACTIONS

A	Winter Park	T	Horse World Riding Stables
B	Downtown Orlando	U	Sleuth's Mystery Dinner Shows
C	Boggy Creek Airboat Rides	V	TD Waterhouse Center
D	Port Canaveral	W	Citrus Bowl Stadium
E	Leu Gardens	X	Osceola County Stadium/Silver Spurs Arena
F	Warbird Adventures	Y	Central Florida Zoo
G	Green Meadows Petting Farm	Z	Sak Comedy Lab
H	Sanford-Rivership Romance	A1	Pirates Dinner Adventure/Fiascos Dinner Show
I	Reptile World Serpentarium	B1	Arabian Nights
J	Osceola County Pioneer Museum	C1	Florida Eco-Safaris
K	Disney's Wilderness Preserve	D1	Disney's Fantasia Gardens Mini-golf
L	Orlando Watersports Complex	E1	Disney's Winter-Summerland Mini-golf
M	Nick Faldo Golf Institute	F1	Lake Eola
N	Kissimmee Rodeo	G1	Medieval Times
O	Richard Petty Driving Experience	H1	Mickey's Backyard Barbecue/Hoop-Dee-Doo Musical Revue
P	Black Hammock Fish Camp	J1	Skull Kingdom/Chamber of Magic Dinner Show
Q	Buena Vista Watersports	K1	Sanford Museum
R	Dolly Parton's Dixie Stampede		
S	Grand Cypress Equestrian Center		

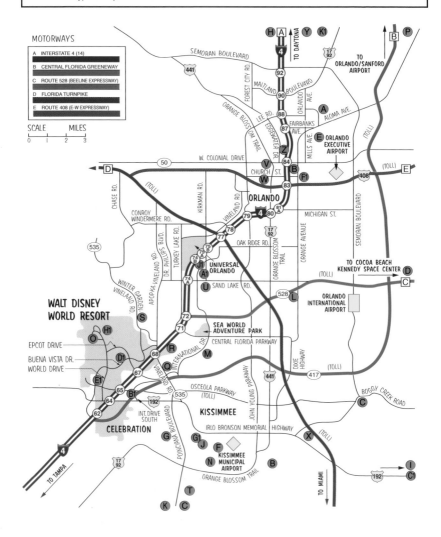

MOTORWAYS

A	INTERSTATE 4 (14)
B	CENTRAL FLORIDA GREENEWAY
C	ROUTE 528 (BEELINE EXPRESSWAY)
D	FLORIDA TURNPIKE
E	ROUTE 408 (E-W EXPRESSWAY)

SCALE — MILES
0   1   2   3

the truly massive Vehicle Assembly Building. The first stop is the **LC39 Observation Gantry**, just 1 mile (1.6km) from shuttle launch pad 39A, a combination 4-storey observation deck and exhibition centre. The exhibits consist of a 10-minute film on launch preparation, models and videos of a countdown and touch-screen information on the shuttle programme. Next is the awesome **Apollo/Saturn V Center**, one of the area's great exhibits, where you can easily spend 90 minutes. It highlights the Apollo programme and first moon landing with 2 impressive theatrical presentations on the risks and triumphs, an actual 363ft (111m) Saturn V rocket and a hands-on gallery that brings the past, present and future of space exploration into sharp focus. It is also quite a humbling experience. You should allow a good 2–3 hours to do the main tour justice. The last bus tour of the day is also at 2.20 or 2.50pm, depending on time of year.

Equally impressive back at the Visitor Complex are the **IMAX cinemas** – 55ft (17m) screens that give the impression of sitting on top of the action. The 37-minute film **The Dream Is Alive** puts you inside a space shuttle mission, while **Space Station 3-D** (narrated by Tom Cruise) is a breath-taking slice of science fact, living with the crew of the International Space Station and affording a heart-stopping look at the construction process. Both films are included in the admission price.

The Complex also has an excellent **Space Shop**, 4 restaurants, including the full-service **Mila's**, and 3 snack counters. The Apollo/Saturn V Center has its own café, too.

The latest element is the thrilling **Astronaut Training Experience (ATX)**, a full-day programme into the training required for a Shuttle mission. You progress through a sequence of simulated and hands-on preparations, with the input of various NASA veterans. The training provides a range of activities, from the multi-axis trainer and one-sixth gravity chair, to operating a full-scale Shuttle mock-up and taking the helm in Mission Control. There is an exclusive Space Center tour, with stops at the Shuttle Launch Pads, the International Space Station Center and NASA's Press Site. The ATX is limited to a few participants each day and you must be at least 14 (under 18s must be accompanied by a parent). Hard-wearing clothes and athletic shoes are advised, and 'recruits' should be free of neck and back injuries. It costs $225/person (including lunch and ATX gear), but it guarantees a memorable day for 'space cadets'. You must book in advance on 321 449 4400 or online.

Getting there: take the Beeline Expressway out of Orlando (Route 528, and a toll road, see map on page 188) for about 45 minutes, then bear left on SR 407 (don't follow the signs to Cape Canaveral or Cocoa Beach at this point) and turn right at the T-junction on to SR 405. The Visitor Complex is located 6 miles (10km) along on the right.

Admission: standard entry is $30 for adults and $20 for children 3–11, including the Bus Tour and IMAX films. The Maximum Access pass ($37 adults, $27 children) adds entry to the Astronaut Hall of Fame. Parking is free. Open 9am–6pm daily (not Christmas Day or launch

The Kennedy Space Center

days; call 321 449 4444 to check), and it is busiest at weekends. The tours and IMAX presentations start at 10am (www.KennedySpace Center.com). AAAAA.

If you want to learn more about the past and present of NASA, **Cape Canaveral: Then and Now** is a 2-hour-plus guided journey into the early days of space exploration around the older part of the facility. Highlights include the Air Force Space Museum, Mercury launch sites and Memorial, original astronaut training facility and several active launch pads, all of which are otherwise off-limits. It costs an extra $22 for adults, $16 for 3–11s.

The 90-minute **NASA Up Close** guided tour takes visitors along the astronaut's launch-day routine and includes a look at both launch pads, the VAB and the gigantic crawler transports, as well as the International Space Station Center ($22 adults, $16 for 3–11s).

BRIT TIP: Reader Les Watson advises: 'Head to Port Canaveral, and there is a recreation area called Jetty Park. It has a wooden jetty about 100yd (91m) long, brilliant for watching Shuttle launches. What an experience.'

The greatest thrill of all is watching an actual **Shuttle launch**, which resumed in July 2005, but the mission was fraught with technical problems, so the fleet has been grounded again. You can call 321 449 4400 for information and Launch Transportation Tickets to a viewing area just 6 miles (10km) from the launch pad (or buy online via the Center's website). Adult tickets cost $50 ($40 for children), including admission to the Visitor Complex. There is also viewing from the Visitor Complex and nearby Astronaut Hall of Fame ($37 and $22, including KSC admission, or $17 and $13 without). But, in the event of a launch cancellation, there are NO refunds and tickets cannot be transferred to another mission. The traffic in the area is usually horrendous, too, taking anything up to 3 hours to drive from Orlando. Alternative viewing sites are available along Highway 1 in Titusville and Highway A1A through Cape Canaveral and Cocoa Beach. Call 1877 893 6272 for launch status. To be on hand to witness a shuttle launch is certainly an awe-inspiring experience.

Astronaut Hall of Fame

While the Space Center tells you primarily about the machinery of putting men and women in space, the Astronaut Hall of Fame (on SR 405, just before the main entrance to the KSC) gives you the low-down on the people involved, with fascinating memorabilia, exhibits and engaging explanations. A chronological approach divides the Hall of Fame into 5 sections. The **Entry Experience** introduces the visions of space flight, with an 8-minute video of the astronauts as modern explorers, and leads into **Race to the Moon**, the stories of the *Mercury*, *Gemini* and *Apollo* missions. The **New Frontier** opens the way for Skylab and Shuttle missions, adjacent to the **Astronaut Hall of Fame**, the museum's heart and soul. **Simulation Station** then features a G-Force simulator and space-walk 'chairs', moon exploration, interactive computers and Mars Mission experience.

Admission: part of the Maximum Access pass for the Kennedy Space Center, or $17 adults, $13 for 3–11s on its own, it is open 10am-7pm.

There is a gift shop and refreshments are provided by the **Cosmic Café**. If you enjoyed the KSC, try to spend a couple of hours here. AAA ½.

Cypress Gardens Adventure Park

Central Florida's original theme park in Winter Haven (dating back to 1936) reopened in late 2004 after an 18-month closure, and it has had a dramatic makeover to make it more appealing for families. The new owners (who also run the Wild Adventures park in Valdosta, Georgia) have invested heavily in adding rides and shows, plus a mini water park, and it now makes a very full day out (about 45 minutes south of Kissimmee). Summer 2005 also saw a second-day-free offer, which is worth keeping an eye out for.

You enter into the **Jubilee Junction** area, a mini-village of 19 shops, restaurants and cafes, plus a Gazebo where you can kick back, enjoy a drink and listen to some live music periodically. The shops are an eclectic bunch and include Christmas-themed Kringles, The Wax Myrtle Candle Co, Jubilee Mercantile and butterfly-themed Longwings Emporium. The main dining choices are the down-home **Aunt Julie's Country Kitchen**, the barbecue flavours of **Backwater Bill's**, the food court choice of **Jubilee Marketplace** and the snacks and drinks of **Gator Bites**. This is a good place to return when it's hot to take in **Cypress Gardens on Ice**, a vibrant ice dance show, with a fully international cast (not Tuesdays).

From there, you can wander the revamped **Nature's Way**, a natural animal exhibit featuring more than 150 mammals, reptiles and birds (including Tarzan, a 74-year-old alligator that once starred with Johnny Weissmuller in the Tarzan movies, Sheba, a female jaguar, an aviary and a petting zoo) plus 6 educational shows daily (2 reptile shows, 2 birds of prey, and 2 mammal shows). **Treasure of Cypress Cove** is the area's fun-themed kids' show, full of nautical slapstick and pirate high jinks. Then you can take the **Sunshine Sky Adventure**, a massive circular arm that rises up 150ft/46m for a bird's eye view of the park. The **Cypress Cove Ferry** also runs from the Boardwalk on Nature's Way lakeside to the south end of the park.

The main **Garden** section, with some of the park's original development, has been carefully brought back to life, and now looks as smart as it did in its hey-day. Split into 2 areas, you have the Topiary Trail (watch out for the Living Garden statues here!) and Plantation Gardens, all set in front of Snively Mansion, the butterfly gardens and Wings of Wonder butterfly house. With the addition of a sparkling waterfall, the monumental topiary figures and some superb flower arrangements, this is a wonderfully eye-catching but peaceful vista, with Lake Eloise adding a sparkling backdrop. Here you will also find **Top Fun Ski Academy**, the park's long-standing tradition of spectacular water ski shows, several times daily. The boat dock here (the other end of the Cypress Cove Ferry) offers tours of Lake Eloise on the **Cypress Belle** (for a small fee), or stay after park closing for the wonderful Dinner Cruise. The original **Botanical Gardens** feature a host of exotic plants and trees (including a massive Banyan Tree) and reward the casual wanderer with myriad different paths and trails with a secluded feel.

What makes this even more remarkable is right next door is the all-new Rides area of the park (39 in all, with a 40th due to be added in 2006), split into 2 sections, plus the

7

watery fun of Splash Island (entered via a large **Midway** games arcade). **Orange Blossom Boardwalk** is the funfair-style section, with more traditional rides like the Big Wheel, bumper cars, Pirate ship and tilt-a-whirl. But it also boasts the unusual (and hugely enjoyable) **Disk'O**, a spinning, whirling platform, and **Swamp Thing**, a fast-turning suspended coaster similar to Chessington World of Adventures' Vampire. Then, the **Adventure Grove** section offers more of the big-scale rides, including steel coaster **Okeechobee Rampage**, the wildly spinning **Power Surge**, the wooden coaster thrills of the **Triple Hurricane** (in memory of the storm season of 2004!) and the junior-sized **Fiesta Express**. Then there are 2 serious water rides, the family (spinning!) raft ride of **Storm Surge** and the single-rider **Wave Runner**, with 2 separate tubes to slide down. You will also find another 9 genuine kiddie rides sprinkled between the 2 sections and the **Citrus Line Railroad**, which circles both areas. In truth, none of the rides would rate a TTTTT rating, but they do represent great fun for the 3–14 age group (and my 2 boys, aged 6 and 8, happily spent a whole afternoon there!). There are even 2 family shows in this area, the light-hearted **Farmyard Frolics** (for younger guests; not Wednesdays) and **Wild West Shenani-Guns**, a cowboy-style romp (not Mondays). A fifth coaster **Galaxy Spin** (of the Crazy Mouse type) was due to open later in 2005, and a classic wooden coaster, **Starliner**, should open in 2006.

Finally, at the furthest end of the park is the new 9-acre (4ha) **Splash Island** water park, complete with lazy river feature and beach area. It boasts a 20,000sq ft (1,856sq m) wave pool called **Kowabunga Bay** (inner-tubes available), 6 water speed slides (**Tonga Tubes**, a 40ft tall twin flume complex, and **Voodoo Plunge**, a triple slide with 2 speed tubes and a body slide), and a children's water area called **Tikki Garden** with a Polynesian Adventure wet-play structure. In addition, Cypress Gardens plays host to a variety of concerts each month, from rock to jazz and Country & Western. Check out its website for the latest acts on www.cypressgardens.com. Christmas, July 4 and Halloween see extra fun added to the park's live entertainment, with a special Christmas Wonderland theme for the festive season featuring dazzling lights and animated displays.

Getting there: From Orlando, head west on I-4 to Exit 55 for Highway 27 (Haines City) and head south for 20 miles (32km). Turn right on to SR 540 (look for signs to Cypress Gardens) and the park is 4 miles (7km) along SR 540, on the left. It is $7 to park.

Admission: open from 10am to 6, 7, 8, 9, 10 or 11pm (depending on season), it costs $34.95 for adults and $29.95 for seniors (55-plus) and children (3-9). Ask at Guest services for Second Day Free offer (within 6 days of your first visit). AAAA/TTT.

Historic Bok Sanctuary

Historic Bok Sanctuary

For those wishing to experience the genuine peace, tranquillity and floral ambience of Florida, there is no better recommendation than this national monument and natural garden centre at Lake Wales, 50 miles (80km) to the south-west of

Orlando (continue past the Cypress Gardens turn-off on Highway 27). With one of the most extraordinary attractions in the state – a majestic 205ft (62.5m) pink-and-grey marble carillon tower – set in 250 acres (101ha) of unique parkland, this is a feast for the eyes and soul. Called the Singing Tower, the 1920s-built carillon is the centrepiece of the park and recitals are given every day at 1 and 3pm. A carillon is a series of cast bronze bells played by a keyboard or clavier. There are only around 500 in the world, and Bok Sanctuary's version consists of 60 bells (crafted in Loughborough, England) ranging from 16lb (7.2kg) to nearly 12 tonnes. The park has its own resident player, or carilloneur, and his daily recitals are an undoubted highlight. The tower is also a real work of art, consisting of a neo-Gothic and art deco mix crafted from coquina stone and marble, with some stunning sculptural elements at various stages. It is wonderfully photogenic and, on a cloudless day, the combination of sight and sound is utterly captivating.

Around the tower is a wide moat, a long pond and a series of semi-formal gardens. At the highest point on peninsular Florida (all of 298ft (90m) above sea level), the view is both uncluttered and inspiring, and retains an inherent peace and solitude that persuaded founder and philanthropist Edward W Bok to grant the estate to the local people almost 75 years ago. The **gardens** themselves provide a wildlife observatory (the Window by the Pond, where you can see up to 126 species of birds, plus reptiles, butterflies, local squirrels, turtles, rabbits and armadillos, as well as the endangered gopher tortoise), nature trails, an endangered plant exhibit, butterfly and woodland gardens, and pine forests. The acres of ferns, palms, oaks and pines create a

surprisingly lush backdrop for the spectacular seasonal bursts of azaleas, camellias, magnolias and other flowering shrubs. There is even a new children's play area, plus brass rubbings, art classes.

The award-winning **Education and Visitor Center** (open 9am-5pm) illustrates the story of Edward W Bok (don't miss the orientation film about him and his impact on American society), his vision for the gardens, the carillon and tower architecture (with a close-up of the bells themselves), the landscape design and ecology of Florida. The **Carillon Café** then adds a pleasant opportunity for a light lunch and other refreshments (in the open air when it's not too hot – and there always seems to be a pleasant breeze here), while the **Tower & Garden Gift Shop** offers some unique gift and souvenir items.

For an additional fee ($5 for adults and $3 for 5–12s; Mon–Sat at 11am and 1.30pm) and Sun at 1.30pm), you can tour the **Pinewood Estate**, one of the finest examples of Mediterranean revival architecture in Florida. The 20-room mansion was built as a winter retreat for a Pennsylvania steel tycoon in the early 1930s, and has been lovingly maintained to demonstrate a real slice of period opulence.

With this genuine sanctuary being slightly off the beaten track yet an easy drive from Orlando (around

The Pinewood Estate

7

45–50 minutes), it makes a thoroughly worthwhile day out with some of the other attractions of Lake Wales.

Getting there: Historic Bok Sanctuary can be found off US Highway 27 on Burns Avenue. Take I-4 west to Exit 55, then go south on US 27 for 25 miles (40km), turn left on Mountain Lake Cutoff Road (2 traffic lights past Eagle Ridge Mall) and follow the signs.

Admission: $8 for adults, $3 for 5–12s (under 5 free), apart from occasional specially ticketed events (mainly carillon festivals and recitals). Open 8am–6pm daily (last entry at 5pm). This is also an extremely attractive wedding venue (863 676 1408, www.boktower.org). AAAA.

High on the list of Lake Wales' other must-see places is **Chalet Suzanne**, a wonderfully eclectic yet classy country inn and restaurant, quietly famous throughout Florida. This family-run delight (since 1931) is a 100-acre (40.5-ha) estate featuring 30 individual and quite charming guest rooms, a tropical sunken wedding garden, a gift shop, swimming pool and private lake, plus, wait for it, *a soup cannery*, which sent its produce to the moon! In fact, the Chalet is such a sought-after hideaway, it has its own airstrip. Its other claim to fame is its restaurant, voted one of Florida's Top 20 for more than 30 years, and a truly amazing venue. Made up of various cast-off buildings (a wing of stable here, a chicken house there) lovingly restored and melded together, the dining rooms are built on no less than 14 different levels.

Eclectic is something of an understatement. The food is another highlight, gourmet cuisine but with a semi-set menu that barely changes year by year. Specialities include broiled grapefruit, baked sugar-cured ham, Chicken Suzanne, and their own Romaine Soup – such a

favourite of Apollo 15 pilot James Irwin, he persuaded NASA to take it on the mission with them, hence it became known as Moon Soup! The set lunch starts at $29-39 a head ($15 for under 12s), while dinner varies from $59–75 ($25 for under 12s), depending on your main course selection (which includes filet mignon, lobster and crab thermidor). But, even if you don't stop to eat, or stay in one of their remarkable Swiss-style cottage rooms ($169–229 per night, plus tax), it is well worth a visit to experience the unique charm and style, learn the story of the Hinshaw family – and have a tour of that truly one-off soup cannery! Apart from anything else, a gift pack here is one of the most original souvenirs you can bring back from Florida. Call 1800-433-6011 to book (always essential) or visit www.chalet suzanne.com.

Getting there: Chalet Suzanne can be found just outside Lake Wales, off Highway 27 on Chalet Suzanne Road. AAA.

Head into the quaint town of **Lake Wales** and you will discover Spook Hill (where cars mysteriously roll uphill!), Grove House Visitor Center (home of Florida's natural fruit juice products – as fresh as it gets) and the quaint Museum and Cultural Center (set in a restored 1928 Atlantic Coast Line railroad station), as well as the world's sky-diving capital (from Lake Wales airport – every kind of parachuting known to man). For more info, call Lake Wales Chamber of Commerce on 863 676 3445 or visit www.lake waleschamber.com.

Silver Springs

Continuing the theme of natural attractions, we have Silver Springs, just under 2 hours' drive to the north of Orlando. This peaceful

7

BRIT TIP: Silver Springs and Wild Waters are both busy at the weekends, but you shouldn't encounter many queues here during the rest of the week.

350-acre (142-ha) nature park surrounds the headwaters of the crystal-clear Silver River. Glass-bottomed boats take you to watch the artesian springs (the largest in the world) that bubble up here, along with plenty of wildlife.

Expect to have some close encounters with alligators, turtles, raccoons and lots of waterfowl, while the park also contains a collection of more exotic animals such as bears, panthers and giraffes. Five animal shows, an alligator and crocodile encounter, the world's largest bear exhibit, a petting zoo, a kids' adventure playground, a new tower ride, a white alligator exhibit and a nightly water-fountain finale (peak season only) complete the attractions. To ruin a few more illusions of the film industry, this was the setting for the 1930s and 1940s Tarzan films starring Johnny Weissmuller. And, once you have absorbed the timeless tropical nature of the landscape, you will understand why they decided to save on the cost of shipping the film crew to Africa.

The park's main attraction (dating back to 1878) is the **Glass-bottomed Boat Ride**, a 20-minute tour that goes down well with all the family and gives a first-class view of the 7 different springs and a host of water life. Similarly, the **Lost River Voyage** is another 20-minute boat trip down one of the unspoilt stretches of the Silver River, with a visit to the park's animal hospital. The third boat trip, the new **Fort King River Cruise**, takes you back in time to pioneer Florida, the

Seminole wars and a reconstruction of the army Fort King. With sightings of native wildlife, an archaeological dig, movie set and Florida Cracker Farm, it is another gentle 20-minute historical perspective, with some wonderful storytelling from the boat captain as well.

As an alternative to messing about on the river, the **Wilderness Trail** is a 15-minute ride in the back of an open tram through a natural forest habitat, home to more Florida wildlife, like deer, racoons, turtles, vultures and other birds (plus a drive-through alligator pond!). Then there are the 3 **Ross Allen Island Animal Shows,** each one lasting 15 minutes and featuring an entertaining – and occasionally hair-raising – look at the worlds of reptiles, birds (including comical parrots, macaws and cockatoos) and creepy crawlies. The hair-raising part occurs only if you happen to be the victim chosen to display a large tarantula, giant cockroach or scorpion.

As you exit the animal shows, take time to wander **Big Gator Lagoon** and the **Crocodile Encounter** in a cypress swamp habitat, viewed from

Attractions no more

Here is a list of places that have closed in recent years: Hard Rock Vault (Sept 2004), Trainland Inc (Feb 2004); Splendid China (Dec 2003); SoulFire Dinner Experience (Sept 2003); Guinness World Records Experience (Apr 2002); Disney's River Country water park (Oct 2001); Masters of Magic show (Sept 2001); Church Street Station (summer 2001); Mystery Fun House (Feb 2001); King Henry's Feast and Wild Bill's dinner shows (Jun 2000); Disney's Discovery Island (Jul 1999); Terror on Church Street (May 1999).

a raised boardwalk. See the largest American crocodile in captivity, the 16-ft (5-m), 2,000-lb (900-kg) Sobek, as well as a collection of alligators, turtles and Galapagos tortoises (with gator feeding daily at 2.30pm). The **Florida Natives** attraction features a collection of snakes, turtles, spiders, otters and other local denizens. Here you will also find the new **Non-venomous Snakes** and the **Reptiles of the World** shows, which dispel various myths about these creatures. The **Botanical Gardens** then provide a peaceful haven in which to sit and watch the world go by. Other large-scale exhibits are the **World of Bears**, an educational presentation including conservation information in a 2-acre (0.8-ha) spread devoted to bears of all kinds, from grizzly to spectacled and black bears, and the **Panther Prowl**, with a unique look at the endangered Florida panther and Western cougar. Both of these have educational presentations several times daily.

Birds of Prey is a 30-minute show in the Silver River Showcase arena, highlighting the strengths, beauty and conservation issues of the park's collection of hawks, eagles, owls, falcons and vultures in a dramatic free-flight demonstration, while **Birds of the Rainforest** showcases the park's comical Macaws and Cockatoos.

Children are not forgotten, either. **The Kids Ahoy!** playland, with its centrepiece riverboat featuring slides, rides, air bounce, ball crawl, 3-D net maze, carousel, bumper boats and games, and **Kritter Korral** (with sheep, rabbits, donkeys, turkeys, and goats) are big draws for the young uns. Older children will also gravitate to the **Lighthouse Ride**, a combined carousel and gondola lift rising up almost 100ft (30m) above the park (and magnificently lit at night). At peak times, watch out for the **Fantastic Fountains Water Show**, which adds another novel element to the park's entertainment.

The usual shops and eateries are fairly ordinary here, in contrast to Orlando's slick parks, although the **Deli** offers some pleasant sandwich alternatives and the **Springside Café** is above average. In all, you would probably want to spend a good half day here, with the possibility of a few hours in the neighbouring 9-acre (4-ha) water park of **Wild Waters**, which offers slides such as the Twin Twister, a pair of 60ft (18m) high flumes, the free-fall Thunderbolt, the twin-tunnelled Tornado, the 220ft (67m) Silver Bullet and the helter-skelter Osceola's Revenge, as well as a 400ft (122m) tube ride on the turbo-charged Hurricane, a huge wave pool, and various kid-sized fun in Cool Kids Cove and Tad Pool for tots.

Getting there: Silver Springs is located on SR 40 in Ocala, 72 miles (116km) north of Orlando. Take the Florida Turnpike (it's a toll road, see map on page 12) until it turns into I-75 and, 28 miles (45km) further north, you go east on SR 40. Another 10 miles (16km) brings you to Silver Springs, just past the Wild Waters water park on your right.

Admission: $32.99 for adults, $29.99 for seniors (55+), $23.99 for children under 4ft (122cm) tall (under 3s free). A joint ticket with Wild Waters is $35.99 and $26.99. Parking is $6. Open 10am–5pm

Silver Springs glass-bottomed boat

Gatorland Jumparoo

daily (352 236 2121, www.silver springs.com). AAAA.

Gatorland

For another taste of the 'real' Florida wildlife, this is as authentic as it gets and is popular with children of all ages. When the wildlife consists of several thousand menacing alligators and crocodiles in various natural habitats and 4 fascinating shows, you know you're in for a different experience. 'The Alligator Capital of the World' was founded in 1949 and is still family-owned, hence it possesses a home-spun charm and naturalism that few of its big-money competitors can match. However, in 2005 it also invested $1million in a grand new entrance to enhance the eye-catching 'Gator Mouth' facade and added some lush tropical landscaping.

Start by taking the 15-minute **Gatorland Express** railway around the park to get an idea of its 110-acre (45-ha) expanse. This costs an extra $2 but is good for multiple rides, is fully narrated (usually in amusing style) and is especially fun for kids. You also get a good look at the native animal habitat, which features whitetail deer, wild turkey and quail. Wander the natural beauty of the 2,000-ft (610-m)

> BRIT TIP: If you have an evening flight home from Orlando International airport, Gatorland is handy to visit on your final day. Conveniently located about 20 minutes' drive away from the airport, it is the ideal place to soak up half a day.

Swamp Walk, as well as the **Alligator Breeding Marsh Walkway**, where there's a 3-storey observation tower for a close-up view of these great reptiles, who seem to hang around the walkway in the hope someone might 'drop in' for lunch.

Breeding pens, baby alligator nurseries and rearing ponds are also situated throughout the park to provide an idea of the growth cycle of the gator and enhance the overall feeling that it is the visitor behind bars here, not the animals. Many of the small-scale attractions have been designed with kids in mind and there is plenty to keep everyone amused, notably at **Lilly's Pad**, an imaginative water playground guaranteed to get kids good and wet (swimming costumes advisable).

Allie's Barnyard is a petting zoo, while you can feed some friendly lorikeets at the **Very Merry Aviary**, and view the pink inhabitants of **Flamingo Lagoon**. Other animals to see include bats, iguanas, turtles, turkey vultures, tortoises, snakes, emus, a Florida bear and deer.

7

Egret at Gatorland

BRIT TIP: If you are at Gatorland first thing, take the Swamp Walk straight away. There will be far more wildlife activity then and the peaceful ambience is quite invigorating.

However, the gators and crocs are the main attraction and it is the 3 shows that are the real draw (although you will never find yourself on the end of a queue here). The 800-seat **Wrestling Stadium** sets the scene for some real cracker-style feats (a cracker is the local term for a Florida cowboy) as Gatorland's resident 'wranglers' catch themselves a medium-sized gator and proceed to point out the animal's various features, with the aid of some daredevil stunts that will have you questioning the cowboys' sanity.

The **Gator Jumparoo** is another eye-opening spectacle as some of the park's biggest creatures use their tails to 'jump' out of the water and be hand-fed tasty morsels, like whole chickens! **Jungle Crocs of the World** features some of the deadliest animals of Egypt, Australia and Cuba, with authentic lairs and brilliant presentation, while the show element has its scare-raising moments as the knowledgeable guides enter the pens to tell you all about the inhabitants. The **Upclose Animal Encounters** is another amusing showcase of various creatures, from the obvious snakes to less obvious scorpions and cockroaches. Brave children can provide some great photo opportunities here!

Obviously, face-to-face encounters with the park's living dinosaurs are not everyone's cup of tea, but it's an experience you're unlikely to repeat anywhere else. In addition, you can dine on smoked alligator ribs and deep-fried gator nuggets (as well as burgers and hot dogs) at **Pearl's Smokehouse**, with excellent kids' meals at $3.99. The park is also home to hundreds of herons and egrets, providing a fascinating close-up of the nests from March to August. Gatorland is actually central Florida's largest wading-bird sanctuary and it adds an extra environmental aspect to this user-friendly park. Three additional programmes if you really want to get to know your gators (!) are the 1-hour **Gator Egg Collecting** in the breeding marsh, a fairly labour-intensive tour for the true adventure seeker (12 and up only, $49.95; Jun–Jul); the exclusive **Trainer for a Day**, with the chance to work behind the scenes at the park, finding out what it takes to handle such dangerous animals, behavioural training and novice gator wrangling ($100 for 2 hours for 12s and up); and the **Night Shine Tour**, a 1-hour tour of the Breeding Marsh at night (including bug spray, torch and gator food; summer hours 8.15pm, autumn and winter 6.30pm, $19 adults, $17 under 13s, reservations required).

Getting there: Gatorland is on the South Orange Blossom Trail, 2 miles (3km) south of its junction with the Central Florida Greeneway and 3 miles (5km) north of Highway 192 (see map on page 12).

Admission: adult tickets are $19.95 and 3-12s are $9.95. Open 9am–5pm (6pm in summer) daily. Parking is free (1800 393 5297, or www.gatorland.com). AAAA.

Fantasy of Flight

Another wonderful and fresh alternative on the central Florida scene is this aviation museum, which offers a 5-part adventure featuring the world's largest private collection of vintage aircraft. Even those not usually interested in the history of flight or the glamour of the Golden Age of flying will find this a fascinating experience.

You start by entering the **History of Flight**, a series of expertly recreated 'immersion experiences' into memorable moments in aviation history. The entrance alone is eye-opening – you enter the fuselage of a DC-3 Dakota as if for a parachute drop, and step out into a moonlit night. Then you visit set-pieces that include a dogfight over the trenches in World War I and a bomber mission with a Flying Fortress in World War II. Audio-visual effects and film clips enhance the experience and give everything an awe-inspiring feeling of authenticity. You exit into the **Vintage Aircraft** displays in 2 huge hangers, with the exhibits ranging from a replica Wright Flyer, to a Ford Tri-Motor, a Mk-XVI Spitfire and the world's only fully working Short Sunderland flying boat. From the museum's collection of more than 70 vintage planes, one is selected each day as the **Aircraft of the Day**, with a pilot holding a question-and-answer session about that plane before performing an aerial demonstration over Fantasy of Flight.

Two **guided tours** are given each day, one taking visitors into the Backlot and the other visiting the Restoration Shop, highlighting in detail what it takes to restore and maintain these magnificent machines. Finally, **Fightertown** features eight realistic fighter simulators that take you on a World War II aerial battle. You get a pre-flight briefing on how to handle your 'plane' (a Vought Corsair), and then climb into the enclosed cockpit to do battle with the Japanese Air Force. It's difficult, absorbing, fun and totally addictive.

The whole experience is crafted in 1930s art deco style and includes a full-service diner (the excellent **Compass Rose**; 11am-3pm) and an original gift shop. There is strong Brit appeal, too, with the exhibits of both World Wars. In addition, you can take a vintage **biplane ride** with Waldo Wright's Flying Service in an open-cockpit 1929 New Standard D-25 for $57.95/person (up to 4 passengers a time), or try the amazing hands-on 1942 Boeing Stearman PT-17 biplane trainer and take the controls! The 30-minute experience costs $189.95 (check out www.waldowrights.com). Then there is Fantasy of Flight's 3-hour **balloon ride** for $160 (up to 3 passengers). All operate seasonally and reservations are required.

Fantasy of Flight is the brainchild of American entrepreneur and aviation whiz Kermit Weeks, and I have yet to encounter an attraction put together with more genuine affection. In fact, it is as much a work of art as a tourist attraction, and the masses have yet to discover it.

Getting there: just 25 minutes west on I-4 to Exit 44 (Polk City), turn first right then left on SR 559 for half a mile, and the museum's main entrance is on the left.

Admission: $24.95 adults, $22.95 seniors (60+), $13.95 for 5–12s (under 5s free). Open 10am–5pm (closed Thanksgiving and Christmas Day) and parking is free (863 984 3500, www.fantasyofflight.com). AAAA.

INTERNATIONAL DRIVE

The 14½-mile tourist corridor of I-Drive (see maps pages 81 and 196) continues to be a fast-developing source of hotels, restaurants, shopping and, more importantly, fun. There are more than 33,000 hotel rooms, 150 restaurants and 500-plus shops, as well as 16 attractions, including 6 mini-golf courses. The **I-Ride trolley** brings it all together in transport terms and the dedicated website www.InternationalDriveOrlando.com highlights all the options. There is an Official Visitors Guide with an I-Ride map and valuable money-off **coupons**, which you can download online to get you started. There is also a new accommodation booking facility. Here's a look at the area's top attractions (see also Chapter 9 Orlando By Night and Chapter 11 Shopping to get the complete picture).

Main hangar at Fantasy of Flight

Ripley's Believe It Or Not

You can't miss this particular attraction, next to The Mercado shopping village, as its extraordinary tilted appearance makes it seem as though it were designed by an architect with an aversion to the horizontal. However, once inside you soon get back on the level and, for an hour or two, you can wander through this museum dedicated to the weird and wonderful.

BRIT TIP: Ripley's, Titanic, WonderWorks and SkyVenture are all handy retreats to keep in mind for places to visit on a rainy day.

Robert L Ripley was an eccentric explorer and collector (a real-life Indiana Jones) who for 40 years travelled the world in his bid to assemble a collection of the greatest oddities known to man. The

Biplane ride with Waldo

Orlando branch of this chain features 8,900sq ft (830sq m) of displays, including authentic artefacts, video presentations, illusions, interactive exhibits and music. The elaborate re-creation of an Egyptian tomb showcases a mummy and three rare mummified animals, while the Primitive Gallery contains artefacts from tribal societies around the world (some quite gruesome). Human and Animal Oddities, Big and Little galleries, Illusions and Dinosaurs have all received some recent updates and extra interactive elements. The collection of miniatures includes the world's smallest violin and a single grain of rice hand-painted with a tropical sunset. Larger-scale exhibits include a portion of the Berlin Wall, a two-thirds-scale 1907 Rolls-Royce built entirely out of matchsticks and a novel version of the Mona Lisa textured completely from toast! **Admission:** $16.95 for adults and $11.95 for 4-12s. Open daily 9am-1am (last ticket sold at midnight; 407 345 0501 or www.ripleys orlando.com). AAA.

Titanic – The Exhibition

Tucked away inside The Mercado is **Titanic – The Exhibition**, the first permanent exhibit to the great maritime disaster of 1912. With a mixture of genuine artefacts, re-creations of the ship's interior, clever scene-setting presentations, film memorabilia from *Titanic* and *A Night to Remember*, plus live interpretations by storytellers in period costume, you will see and hear just about everything there is to know about the *Titanic* and her tragic fate. The full experience takes at least an hour and is well worthwhile.

Admission: $17.95 for adults, $12.95 for 6-12s (under 6 free). Open 10am–10pm daily (first guided tour at 10.30am; 407 248 1166 or www.titanicshipofdreams.com). AAAA.

Skull Kingdom

The walk-through haunted house idea takes on a new dimension here. Not content with a house, this is a full-blown castle on I-Drive (opposite Wet 'n Wild) dedicated to frights, horrors and grisly goings-on at every turn. The setting and lavishness of the Kingdom of the Skull Lord marks it out as way above average, and the combination of elaborate light and sound effects, robotics and the scream-inducing live actors provides a hair-raising experience. The shock tactics are state of the art, with the best elements of horror films and haunted houses well maintained over the 2-storey spread of mazes, caverns and other demonic challenges (watch out for the monster spit!).

> **BRIT TIP:** Friday and Saturday evenings are peak periods for Skull Kingdom, with occasional half-hour queues.

The Haunted Gift Shop awaits you at the end of your 20–30-minute (depending on how much you 'enjoy' the experience!) Skull Kingdom immersion. While the fully fledged **Evening Show** is seriously intense, a new **Day Show** offers less scary guided tours through the castle, geared towards under 12s. Each child is given a torch and guests are never left without their escort. They get to explore every room and ask questions while touring (although some of it is still pretty grisly for youngsters – parental discretion is strongly advised). A new element in 2004 was the **Chamber of Magic** dinner show, with magic, laser lighting and special effects. It also has all-you-can-eat pizza, soft drinks, beer and wine (see also page 265).

Admission: Evening Show $14.04, 6pm-11pm Mon-Thur, noon-midnight Fri-Sun, with extended hours in peak season (not recommended for under 12s); Day Show $8.99, 10am-5pm; Chamber of Magic show $19.75 adults, $15.95 under 7s and seniors. Dinner show and Skull Kingdom admission $28.25 and $24.45 (407 354 1564, www.skullkingdom.com). TTTT.

Fun Spot

Here is another choice for full-scale, family-sized fun, just off I-Drive on Del Verde Way (look for the 102-ft/31-m big wheel past the junction with Kirkman Road). With 4 different and highly challenging go-

Skull Kingdom

kart tracks, bumper cars and boats, 4 daring fairground-type rides (check out the Free Fall Spring Ride and Paratrooper), an impressive 2-storey video arcade (one of the largest in Florida) and food court, plus 5 Kid Spot rides for the little ones, the 4.7-acre (2-ha) park promises several hours of fun.

Admission: free, but ride tickets are $3 each (or $22 for eight). Go-karts require 2 tickets, while other rides are a ticket apiece. For visits of an hour or longer, their 'armband' tickets are better value at $29.95 for adults (10+), which includes all-day privileges on all tracks and rides, and $9.95 for 2-9s, which allows all-day access to the six rides geared towards younger kids. The Rides Armband allows unlimited rides on the 13 Family and Thrill Rides for $19.95. It is $5.25 for an all-day ticket to the Freeplay Arcade, which contains 37 classic arcade games and a spread of more than 100 token-driven games (some of them state-of-the-art). Open 10am-midnight daily (407 363 3867 or www.fun-spot.com). TTTT.

Magical Midway

In a similar vein, **Magical Midway** back on I-Drive (just north of Sand Lake Road) offers more go-karts, games and thrill rides (including the Space Blast tower – 0 to 180ft/55m in 3 seconds!). The 2 elevated kart tracks, the double uphill corkscrew of The Avalanche (you must be at least 12 years old and 4ft 8in/147cm tall to drive, at least 16 to drive a passenger, and at least 3ft/91cm to be a passenger) and the sharply banked Alpine Jump (for which you must be at least 12 and 4ft 8in/147cm to drive, 16 to drive a passenger, and at least 3ft/91cm to be a passenger) are its signature rides. New is the Fast Track, a flat, concrete track with a 25-degree bank turn (riders must be 12 and 4ft

8in/147cm to drive; single cars only). And then there are bumper cars, a giant slide, bumper boats, 4 more fairground-type rides and a large arcade.

Admission: free, then $29.95 for All Day Armband (includes unlimited go-karts and Midway rides); $24.95 3-Hour Armband (unlimited go-karts and other rides for 3 hours); $14.95 Ride Armband (unlimited rides all day, but not go-karts, plus 10 tokens for arcade games); individual ride tickets are $6 (go-karts), $5 (Space Blast) and $3 (other rides); must be 4ft/121cm for Space Shot, Tornado and Bumper Cars, and 3ft 6in/106cm for Bumper Boats, Fun Slide, Kiddie Track. Open 10am-midnight daily (407 370 5353, www.magicalmidway.com). TTT½.

WonderWorks

I-Drive's most unmistakable landmark is this 'interactive entertainment centre, a 3-storey chamber of family fun with a host of novel elements. Unmistakable? You bet – how many buildings do you know that are upside down? That's right, all of the 82ft (25m) edifice is constructed from the roof up! The basic premise (working on the theory that every attraction has to have a story behind it) is that WonderWorks is a secret research facility into unexplained phenomena that got uprooted by a tornado experiment and dumped in topsy-turvy fashion in the heart of this busy tourist district (yeah, right!). Well, you have to give them full marks for imagination and, if the attractions aren't quite as entertaining as the exterior, there is still a lot here, especially for the 6–12s.

You enter through an 'inversion tunnel' that orientates you the same way round as the building (look out of the window to check!) and progress to chambers of entertaining and mildly educational hands-on experiences that demand several hours to explore fully. Without ever using the words 'science' or 'museum', WonderWorks steers you through five 'labs' of interactive activities, including the **Bermuda Triangle Corridor**, the **Mystery Lab** (experience earthquakes and hurricanes and see famous disasters on a bank of computer monitors), **Physical Challenge Lab** (virtual basketball, table tennis, a baseball test, health and lifestyle quizzes and the wonderfully creepy Shocker Chair, a high-voltage simulation that gives you the feeling of 2,000 jolts rather than volts – it's weird!), **Illusions Lab** (with the Bridge of Fire static electricity generator, a computer ageing process and 'elastic surgery', hall of mirrors and bubble table), plus the **WonderWorks Emporium** gift shop, souvenirs and **WonderWorks Café**. A **Lazer Tag** game on the top floor adds even more appeal for youngsters.

> BRIT TIP: WonderWorks, Fun Spot and Magical Midway are open until midnight in high season, long after most theme parks are shut, so you can have a day at the park, then let the kids loose here for a while to tire them out!

On no account miss the 2 virtual roller-coasters, a pair of amazing enclosed 'pods', that let you design and ride your own coaster. If you have already been to *DisneyQuest*, WonderWorks may seem tame, while it isn't as educational as the Orlando Science Center, but it also offers a fun dinner-show option, *The Outta Control Magic Show* (see page 263), with a good value combination ticket.

Admission: $18.95 adults, $12.95 seniors (55+) and 4-11s; $4.95 for Lazer Tag; $21.95 and $14.95 for Magic Show; $36.95 and $25.95 for WonderWorks-dinner show combo; $21.95 and $15.95 for WonderWorks–Lazer Tag; and $37.95 and $26.95 for all three. Open 9am-midnight (407 351 8800 or www.wonderworksonline.com). AAA/TTT.

SkyVenture

At the junction with I-Drive and Kirkman Road is this unmistakable blue and yellow funnel that houses one of the most fun 'rides' in town. SkyVenture is billed as a 'freefall skydiving adventure' but it is much more than that – it is a fun, addictive, difficult but exhilarating 'flying' experience, with the added bonus of being a great spectator sport! The basic premise is their huge vertical wind tunnel gives you the feeling of a freefall parachute jump, without the hassle of having to go up in a plane, find the nerve to jump out, wrestle with a parachute and possibly hit the ground too hard. The standard 1-hour programme provides a briefing of the hows and whys of skydiving, with a fully qualified instructor who puts you at ease and gets you suitably inspired for the 'jump' ahead. With the instruction over (and you are provided with all the equipment, including helmet, pads, goggles, ear-plugs and flight suit), your group of 8–12 returns to the flight deck and you get 2 1-minute 'dives' with your instructor helping you all the way. Just watching makes it seem all too easy but, as soon as you hit the tunnel yourself, you discover how fiendishly tough it is to just 'hang' in this 150mph column of air. But it soon becomes an

7

immensely fun and absorbing experience and it's almost guaranteed to make you want to try again. Non-participating members of your group are free to watch from the observation deck, while you can also turn up to see for yourself at any time – there is no fee for watching (and you may even see some sky-dive groups practising, as this is a popular venue).

Admission: standard flight, which includes a special certificate, is $38.50 for adults and $33.50 for 3–12s (although it may not suit young children); add a DVD of your flight and T-shirt for $23. There are discount coupons on their website, and you can also get $10 off a second flight within 30 days with your original ticket. You can even book 30 minutes of flight time for $350 if it becomes addictive! Open 2-11.30pm Mon-Fri and noon-11.30pm Sat and Sun (407 903 1150 or www.skyventureorlando.com; reservations recommended). TTTT.

As mentioned, there are no less than 6 mini-golf courses on I-Drive, including 4 recent ones. These latter are an 18-hole **Congo River** set-up in front of the Sheraton Studio City hotel (in addition to its 36-hole course just south of Wet 'n Wild); the 36-hole **Tiki Island Golf** behind the Salt Island restaurant just north of Sand Lake Road; a second **Hawaiian Rumble** 36 holes next to WonderWorks (its first is on Highway 535 in Lake Buena Vista);

and the indoor, glow-in-the-dark 36 holes of the **Putting Edge** at Festival Bay, at the top of I-Drive. Pirates Cove, next to The Mercado, remains the original I-Drive set-up.

DOWNTOWN ORLANDO

The last couple of years have seen a significant move towards regenerating Orlando's city centre – the 'downtown' area – with new offices, apartments, shops and restaurants. This has also brought significant tourist developments.

Orlando Science Center

Because this is Orlando, there is no such thing as a simple museum or science centre. Everything must be all-singing, all-dancing just to compete. Hence, the Orlando Science Center is more than a mere museum and far more fun than the average science centre. Here, you are given a series of hands-on experiences and habitats that entertain as well as inform, and school-age children in particular will benefit greatly from it.

The Science Center has 9 main components, plus an inviting café, a night sky observatory and a giant screen cinema. **Natureworks** is an immersion-style exhibit creating a number of typical Florida habitats (with several shows like the *Circle of Life Game* and a series of hands-on field stations). **Science City** introduces fun ways to understand and use science (including some mind-bending puzzles and challenges, notably in the Power Station), while Dr Dare's Laboratory is a new hands-on centre, with a computer guide for various experiments while Touch the Sky explores the science and math behind aviation with flight simulators, interactive displays and vintage aircraft. The **Cosmic**

Training for SkyVenture

Tourist offers a trip around our solar system with an amusing travel theme. **BodyZone** provides some fascinating insights into the human body, with an interactive element called Measure Me, which explores size, strength, flexibility, agility and sensory abilities, and a new 3-D film. **A Healthy Lifestyles** exhibit shows how bad habits like smoking affect a healthy body. Next door, **TechWorks** is a 4-part adventure into light, imaginary landscapes, showbiz science and a micro-world of microscopic investigation.

For those a bit too young for the educational element, **KidsTown** has plenty of junior-sized fun and games for under 8s. You'll be amazed at how much they learn in the course of having fun. **DinoDigs: Mysteries Unearthed** was a gift from the Walt Disney Company of their former Dinosaur Jubilee exhibit in *Disney's Animal Kingdom*. It has been re-created in the OSC as a paleontological excavation site, complete with 8 full dinosaur skeleton replicas and a number of genuine fossils. The **Darden Adventure Theater** features science-themed comedy shows and demos, like Cool Science (freezing fun with liquid nitrogen) and the audience participation of Science Spectrum.

BRIT TIP: visit the Crosby Observatory on the top of the Science Center to gaze through the region's largest publicly accessible refractor telescope. The Observatory is open Fri and Sat nights.

In addition, the Center has 2 separate programmes in the **Dr Phillips CineDome**, a 310-seat cinema that practically surrounds its audience with large-format films, digital planetarium shows (a virtual tour of the universe, anyone?). It also boasts a 28,000-watt digital sound system that makes the experience unforgettable.

Getting there: the Science Center is on Princeton Street in downtown Orlando, just off Exit 85 of I-4 (go east on Princeton, the Center is on your left but the multi-storey car park is on the RIGHT, see map on page 196).

Admission: $14.95 for adults, $13.95 for seniors (55+) and $9.95 for 3–11s ($9.95, $8.95 and $4.95 after 4pm on Fri and Sat). Parking is $3.50. Open 9am-5pm Tue-Thur, 9am-9pm Fri and Sat, noon-5pm Sun. Closed Mon (except school holidays), Easter Sunday, Thanksgiving, Christmas Eve and Christmas Day (www.osc.org). AAAA.

Orange County Regional History Center

7

This relatively recent addition offers an imaginative journey into central Florida history, from the wildlife and Native Americans to today's tourist issues and the space programme. Again, the accent is on the interactive, with hands-on exhibits and audio-visual presentations, and it is very much a journey through time, starting outside in renovated Heritage Square, complete with cypress trees and fountains. The History Center itself is in the former 1927 Orange County Courthouse, with the foyer converted into a dome featuring more than 150 icons

Garden Tomb at Holy Land Experience

BRIT TIP: Combine a visit to the History Center with lunch at the wonderfully eclectic Globe restaurant on the corner of the square.

unique to central Florida (see how many you can identify before and after your tour).

The 4-storey adventure starts at the top with the **Orientation Theater's** 14-minute multimedia presentation as you sit in rocking chairs on the 'front porch'. Then you visit the Natural Environment and First Peoples exhibits (12,000 years ago), before First Contact brings in the European element. Jump into the 1800s and visit a Seminole settlement, a Pioneer Cracker home (the first true 'cowboys'), hear tales of the old ranching days and learn about the citrus industry. The early 20th Century brings the story of Transportation, Tourism, Aviation and the great land boom, Selling Central Florida. Then witness how the region dramatically altered with the development of the Space Programme and the arrival of a certain Walter Elias Disney in The Day We Changed. From there, you move on to the beautifully restored Courtroom B for some more real-life Orlando history.

Finally, you reach the newest permanent exhibit, **Orlando Remembered** – a journey through time from the 19th Century to the edge of the 21st. This tells the story beyond the theme parks and is an inclusive history of Orlando's people, uncovering secrets of the past and unveiling some of the most significant artefacts from the collection of the Historical Society of Central Florida. An exhibit on African American history, featuring the achievements and tragedies of central Florida's African American community rounds things out, while a visit to the Historium gift shop completes your visit.

Special large-scale exhibits scheduled for 2006 include a collection of historically significant paintings on Florida's Highwaymen entitled *Legendary Landscapes* as well as *Heroes of the Sky: Adventures in Early Flight, 1903-1939*, celebrating the 100th Anniversary of flight.

Getting there: the History Center can be found off Central Boulevard and Magnolia Avenue downtown (Exit 82C off I-4, Anderson St, left on to Magnolia, right on to Central Boulevard, see map on page 196). Best parking is the Public Library multi-storey car park on Central Boulevard (History Center admission includes 2 hours' free parking if you show your ticket).

Admission: $7 for adults, $3.50 for 3–12s and $6.50 for seniors (60+), and it is open 10am–5pm Mon–Sat and noon–5pm Sun. For more information call 407 836 8500, (www.thehistorycenter.org). AAA.

Other downtown developments include the free **Lymmo** bus service that connects the central stretch along Magnolia Avenue, from South Street to the **TD Waterhouse Center** (formerly the Orlando Arena for sports and concerts) on Amelia Street, the **Downtown Arts District and Arts Market** (on Wall Street, off Orange Avenue, every Saturday; 11am–9pm Oct–April), seasonal concerts and firework shows, plus new shops and restaurants around **Lake Eola**. The Lake itself is a beautiful area to wander around, with a park, children's play area and an extremely peaceful ambience. Children can feed the birds and fish or take a Swan paddleboat ride, plus regular free open-air events such as concerts and storytelling.

The **Cultural Corridor** links the Downtown Arts District (which includes the Bob Carr Performing Arts Center and the Centroplex), with the Loch Haven area (where you find the Orlando Museum of Art, Mennello Museum of American Folk Art, Orlando Philharmonic Orchestra and the Orlando-UCF Shakespeare Festival), via the **Dr Phillips Performing Arts Center**, which is home of the Orlando Opera and Orlando Ballet. The Saturday **Farmers' Market** (8am–2.30pm) is another downtown focal point (in Heritage Square outside the History Center), with vendors now including local artisans such as glassblowers and dressmakers, as well as wonderful fresh produce. The **Thornton Park** area is currently the most happening part of Orlando, with the new Thornton Park Central (at the junction of Summerlin Avenue and Central Boulevard, just south-east of Lake Eola) offering a mix of unique boutiques and trendy restaurants. For the latest information visit www.downtownorlando.com.

The Holy Land Experience

Not so much a conventional attraction but right in the heart of the tourist mainstream is this 15-acre (6-ha) 'living Biblical museum', which sets out to re-create in detail the city of Jerusalem and its religious significance from 1450BCE to 66CE. Its aim is also to provide an explanation and celebration of the Christian faith.

The staff are all in period costume, the architecture and landscaping are impressive and the background music in both the indoor and outdoor areas is all original and suitably atmospheric (perhaps not surprising when some of the designers who worked on Universal's Island of Adventure were also involved here). From the

> BRIT TIP: Reader Peter Crumpler suggests: 'The Holy Land is an unusual cross between a theme park and an educational tour, but I'd say British Christians would find it fascinating – both for learning more about the Bible and for seeing their livelier American cousins in action.'

Jerusalem Street Market entrance to the **Qumran Dead Sea Caves**, **Calvary's Garden Tomb** (featuring *Via Dolorosa Passion*, an intense crucifixion drama) and on to the impressive **Temple of the Great King** (destroyed by the Romans in AD70), everything is portrayed in literal Biblical terms and with no little style by their actors. **Theater of Life** shows a 25-minute film, *Seed of Promise*, which 'communicates God's master plan for redeeming mankind', while the **Wilderness Tabernacle** is a theatrical portrayal of the ancient biblical ritual, featuring the Holy Ark with lasers and pyrotechnics. A huge model of **Jerusalem** – which took more than a year to build – is explained in great detail several times a day in the form of a guided tour. Recently opened is the **Scriptorium** centre for Biblical antiquities, another themed environment showcasing various rare artefacts in a 50-minute narrated tour that walks you through 4,500 years of history in fascinating fashion. At the end, **A Day In The Life Of A Monk** provides a look at those who transcribed the Bible during the Middle Ages.

Live performances include musical drama *Praise Through The Ages*, dramatic vignette *The Ministry of Jesus*, and *Centurion*, another

7

highly theatrical musical, showcasing the park's high-quality performers (look out also for *The Word Became Flesh*, a superb monologue). There is a small Kidzone, **Qaboo & Company**, with a rock-climbing wall (2–5pm daily), archaeological 'dig', misting station, books and games, plus 3 eateries, the **Oasis Palms Café** (featuring Goliath Burgers, Jaffa Hot Dogs and more healthy Middle Eastern fare), the **Royal Portico** for chicken wraps, salads and ice creams and **Simeon's Corner**, for snacks and drinks. There are also 3 major gift shops. All in all, it is a thoroughly unusual 'attraction' (although they don't call it that), a lively and literal celebration of the Christian faith, and, while it sits rather awkwardly among the main tourist offerings, it may well pique the interest of some.

Getting there: The Holy Land Experience can be found off Exit 78 of I-4, on the junction of Conroy and Vineland Roads (just north of Universal Orlando).

Admission: $29.99 for adults and $19.99 for 4-12s. Parking is $5. Open 10am-6pm Mon-Fri, 9am-6pm Sat, noon-6pm Sun (hours may vary; closed Thanksgiving and Christmas Day). Call 407 367 2065 or 1866 872 4659, or www.theholy landexperience.com. AAA.

THE WATER PARKS

If anyone has been down the slides and flumes at the local leisure centre, they will have an inkling of what Orlando's 4 big water parks are all about. Predictably, Disney has the 2 most elaborate ones, but the Universal-owned Wet 'n Wild and

Rain Forest at Water Mania

Water Mania are equally adept at providing hours of fun in a variety of styles that owe much to the flair of the theme park creators. All 4 require at least half a day of splashing, sliding and riding to get full value from their rather high prices. Lockers are provided for valuables and you can hire towels.

Disney's Typhoon Lagoon Water Park

Until *Disney's Blizzard Beach* water park opened in 1995, *Disney's Typhoon Lagoon* was the biggest and finest example of Florida's water parks. In high season, it is also the busiest, so be prepared to run into more queues. *You should definitely arrive half an hour early if possible as entry often begins before the official opening hour.* The park's 56 acres

BRIT TIP: While water parks are a great way of cooling down, it is easy to pick up a 5-star case of sunburn. So don't forget the high-factor, waterproof suntan lotion.

(23-ha) are spread out around the 2½-acre (1-ha) lagoon fringed with palm trees and white-sand beaches. *Typhoon Lagoon* is extravagantly landscaped and the walk up Mount Mayday, for instance, provides a terrific overview as well as adding scenic touches such as rope bridges and tropical flowers. Sun loungers, chairs, picnic tables and even hammocks are provided to add to the comfort and convenience of restful areas like Getaway Glen. However, you need to arrive early to bag a decent spot.

The park is overlooked by the 90ft (27m) Mt Mayday, on top of which is perched the luckless *Miss Tilly*, a

BRIT TIP: Head for Shark Reef if you want to take advantage of some of the more shaded areas.

shrimp boat that legend has it landed here during the typhoon that gave the park its name. Watch for the water fountains that shoot from *Miss Tilly's* funnel at regular intervals, accompanied by the ship's hooter, which signal another round of 6ft (1.8m) waves in the **Surf Pool** (you can hire inner-tubes to bob around on or just try body-surfing). Circling the lagoon is **Castaway Creek**, a 3ft (1m) deep, lazy flowing river that offers the opportunity to float happily along on rubber tyres.

The series of slides and rides are all clustered around Mount Mayday and vary from the breathtaking body slides of **Humunga Kowabunga**, which drop you 214ft (65m) at up to 30mph (48kph) down some pretty steep inclines (make sure your swimming costume is securely fastened!) to **Ketchakiddee Creek**, which offers a selection of slides and pools for all youngsters under 4ft (122cm) tall. In between, you have the 3 **Storm Slides**, which twist and turn through caves, tunnels and waterfalls, **Mayday Falls**, a 460-ft (140-m) inner-tube ride down a series of banked drops, **Keel Haul Falls**, an alternative tube ride that takes slightly longer, and **Gangplank Falls**, a ride on tubes that take up to 4 people down 300ft (90m) of mock rapids. The

BRIT TIP: As the busiest of the water parks, *Typhoon Lagoon* can hit capacity quite early in the day in summer. Call 407 824 4321 in advance to check on the crowds.

imaginative (but chilly) **Shark Reef** is an upturned wreck and coral reef, which you can snorkel around among 4,000 tropical fish and a number of real, but harmless, nurse sharks. Those who aren't brave enough to dive in can still get a close-up through the underwater portholes of the sunken ship (the Reef is closed during the coldest months). Substantial queues build up here from late morning, so do this early on.

BRIT TIP: 'Buy a disposable waterproof camera to tie around your wrist when you visit the water parks. We bought one cheap at Wal-Mart and have some lovely photos from *Typhoon Lagoon*,' says Judith Bingham.

7

The newest area is **Crush 'n' Gusher**, a fabulous trio of 'water-coaster' tube rides, plus a large heated pool with zero-depth entry (great for toddlers). It also has an extensive sandy beach, which makes a great place to bag a spot in the sun. The 3 different slides feature tubes for 1, 2 or 3 riders at a time that whoosh you down AND up several inclines before dropping you into the pool with a significant splash. This is also very busy from mid-day on. There are height (4ft) and health restrictions on Humunga Kowabunga and Crush 'n' Gusher (not suitable for anyone with a bad back or neck, or pregnant women). Keeping out of the sun can also be a

Disco H2O at Wet 'n Wild

problem as there's not much shade, but a quick plunge into Castaway Creek usually prevents overheating.

For snacks and meals, **Lowtide Lou's** and **Let's Go Slurpin'** both offer a bite to eat and drinks while **Typhoon Tilly's** and **Leaning Palms** serve a mixture of burgers, sandwiches, salads and ice cream. Avoid main mealtimes here if you want to eat in relative comfort. You can bring your own picnic (unlike the main theme parks), which you can eat in special scenic areas (but no alcohol or glass containers). You CAN'T bring your own snorkels, inner-tubes or rafts, but snorkels are provided at Shark Reef and you can hire inner-tubes for the lagoon. If you have forgotten a sunhat or bucket and spade for the kids, or even your swimsuit, they are all available at **Singapore Sal's**.

BRIT TIP: Ladies, please remember, down some of the whizziest slides it is advisable to wear a one-piece swimsuit rather than a bikini. Your modesty could be at stake here!

To avoid the worst of the summer crowds (when the park's 7,200 capacity is often reached), Monday morning is the best time to visit (steer clear of weekends at all costs), and, on other days, arrive either 30 minutes before opening or in mid-afternoon, when many decide to dodge the daily rainstorm. Early evening is also extremely pleasant when the park lights up.

Getting there: on Buena Vista Drive, half a mile from Downtown Disney (see map on page 12).

Admission: Adults $36.21, 3-9s $29.82 (under 3s free); included with Premium and Ultimate tickets. Parking is free. Open from 9am to dusk every day. TTTT/AAAAA.

Disney's Blizzard Beach Water Park

Ever imagined a skiing resort in the middle of Florida? Well, Disney has, and this is the wonderful result. This water park puts the rest in the shade for size as well as extravagant settings, with the whole park arranged as if it were in the Rocky Mountains rather than the sub-tropics. That means snow-effect scenery, Christmas trees and water-slides cunningly converted to look like skiing pistes and toboggan runs. It delivers a feast for water lovers and Disney admirers in general.

Main features are **Mount Gushmore**, a 90ft (27m) mountain down which all the main slides run, including the world's tallest free-fall speed slide, the terrifying 120ft (37m) **Summit Plummet**, which rockets you down a 'ski jump' at up to 60mph (97kph), **Tike's Peak**, a kiddie-sized version of the park's slides and a mock snow-beach, and **Ski-Patrol Training Camp**, a series of slides and challenges for pre-teens. **Melt-Away Bay** is a 1-acre (0.4-ha) pool fed by 'melting snow' (actually blissfully warm), and **Cross Country Creek** is a lazy-flowing half-mile river round the whole park which also floats guests through a chilly 'ice cave' (watch out for the waterfalls of ice-water!).

A ski chair-lift operates to the top of Mount Gushmore, providing a magnificent view of the park and surrounding areas. Don't miss the

BRIT TIP: You can save money at the Disney water parks by buying refillable drinks mugs – $11.95 each – when you arrive and using them all day. Return to either park and get a $6 sticker to use them again!

outstanding rides – **Teamboat Springs**, a wild, family inner-tube adventure, **Runoff Rapids**, a 1-, 2- or 3-person tube plunge, and the **Snow Stormers**, a daring head-first 'toboggan' run. **Toboggan Racers** gives you the chance to speed down the 'slopes' against 7 other head-first daredevils. All 4 go to new heights of water-park imagination and provide good-sized thrills without overdoing the scare factor. The **Downhill Double Dipper** is 2 side-by-side slides that send you down 230ft (70m) tubes in a race timed on a big clock at the bottom, and that gives you a real jolt halfway down! For those not quite up to this, the wonderfully named **Slush Gusher** is a slightly less terrifying speed slide. There is a 'village' area with a **Beach Haus** shop and **Lottawatta Lodge** fast-food restaurant, offering diners a grandstand view of Mount Gushmore and Melt-Away Bay beach. Snacks are also available at **Avalunch** (ouch!), the **Warming Hut**, **Polar Pub** and **Frostbite Freddie's Frozen Refreshments**.

Getting there: just north of Disney's All-Star Resorts off Buena Vista Drive (see map on page 12).

Admission: Adults $36.21, 3-9s $29.82 (under 3s free); included with Premium and Ultimate tickets. Parking is free. Open from 9am to dusk every day. TTTTT/AAAAA.

Adjacent to *Disney's Blizzard Beach* is the amazing **Winter Summerland Miniature Golf Courses** (where Santa's elves hang out!), with two wonderfully elaborate courses that provide children with a great diversion. Watch out for a riot of visual gags, as well as some tricky mini-golf.

> BRIT TIP: Avoid the weekends and from mid-morning onwards on Wednesday to Friday when the crowds are massive.

Wet 'n Wild

If Disney scores highest for scenic content, Wet 'n Wild, the world's first water park in 1977, goes full tilt for thrills and spills of the highest quality. This park will test the material of your swimsuit to the limit!

Wet 'n Wild is one of the best-attended water parks in the country, and its location in the heart of I-Drive makes it a major draw. Consequently, you will encounter some crowds here, although the 16 slides and rides, **Lazy River** attraction, an elaborate kids' park (with mini versions of many of the slides), **Surf Lagoon** and restaurant and picnic areas manage to absorb a lot of punters before queues develop. Amazingly, waits of more than half an hour at peak times are rare, but it is busiest at weekends, with July attracting most crowds.

You are almost spoilt for choice with main rides, from the highly popular group inner-tube rides of the **Surge** and **Bubba Tub**, through

> BRIT TIP: The Children's Playground at Wet 'n Wild was built especially for those under 4ft (122cm) tall – right down to having the only junior wave pool in the world.

the more demanding rides of **The Blast** to the high-thrill factor of the 2-person **Black Hole** (like the *Magic Kingdom*'s Space Mountain, but in water!), **Blue Niagara** (also enclosed, but this one's a body slide) and **Mach 5**, to the terror of **Der Stuka** and the **Bomb Bay**. The latter duo are definitely not for the faint-hearted. Basically, they are 2 76ft (23m) body slides with drops as near vertical as makes no difference. Der Stuka is the straightforward

7

BRIT TIP: For all the
water parks, it is a good
idea to bring a pair of deck
shoes or sandals that can be
worn in water.

slide, while the Bomb Bay adds the
extra terror of being allowed to *free
fall* on to the top of the slide. For
some reason, only 15–25 per cent of
the park's visitors pluck up the
courage to try it! There are
4ft/122cm height restrictions on
Bomb Bay, Der Stuka and Blue
Niagara, while older kids can get
their own excitement on the huge,
inflatable **Bubble Up**, which
bounces them into 3ft (1m) of water.

The thrilling toboggan-like **Flyer**
takes 4 passengers in 8ft (2m) in-line
tubes that whoosh down more than
450ft (137m) of banked curves and
straights, and the bungee-like **Hydra
Fighter** is a 2-person swing
equipped with a large fire-type hose
that sends the contraption into mad
gyrations as you increase the water
pressure! **The Blast** is a 1- or 2-
passenger thrill ride that surprises
you with sudden twists and turns,
explosive pipe bursts and drenching
waterspouts that lead up to a final
waterfall plunge. And don't miss
The Storm, a pair of identical
circular slides billed as 'body
coasters' – the enclosed tubes
(complete with storm sound and
light effects) send the rider plunging
into a circular bowl, around which
they spin at high speed before
landing in the splash-pool below.
Huge fun. New in 2005 was **Disco
H2O**, a superbly-themed family raft
ride which plunges down an
enclosed tube into a madly-swirling
'disco bowl' (featuring lights and a
mirror ball!) before spitting you out
through a waterfall. It is all
accompanied by 1970s-style music
and commentary to add to the fun.

This draws quite a queue by midday, though.

For those under 4ft (122cm) tall,
the recently renovated **Kids Park** has
a full range of junior-sized slides, plus
a new sandcastle structure with 2
semi-circular water-slides and a giant
bucket that fills and tips up at regular
intervals. Uniquely, the children can
use speciality tubes, beach chairs and
tables that have been designed
specifically for their height.

The neighbouring lake is also part
of the fun (although not in winter
when it's too chilly), adding the
options for cable-operated **Knee
Ski**, **Wakeboarding** and (for a
nominal fee) the **Wild One** (large
inner-tubes tied behind a speedboat).
Alternatively, take a breather in the
slow-flowing **Lazy River** as you
float leisurely through palms and
waterfalls, or abandon the water
altogether for one of several picnic
areas (although they are popular).
The energetic can also play beach
volleyball. Lockers, showers, tube
and towel rentals are all available
but, if you bring your own floating
equipment, you must have it
checked by one of the lifeguards.

For food, **Bubba's Bar-B-Q**
serves chicken, ribs, fries and drinks,
the **Surf Grill** features burgers, hot
dogs, chicken and sandwiches and
another 7 snack bars offer similar
fast-food fare, including a pizza bar.
Picnics can also be brought in,
provided you don't include alcohol
or glass containers.

Getting there: Wet 'n Wild is
half a mile north of I-Drive's
junction with Sand Lake Road at the
intersection with Universal
Boulevard (see map on page 12).

Admission: $33.95 for adults,
$27.95 for 3–9s and free for under
3s; alternatively, it is included with
the Orlando FlexTicket. Tube
rentals are $4 ($2 deposit), towels $2
and lockers $5 ($2 deposit), or $9 for
all 3 ($4 deposit). Parking is $7.
Open year-round (with heated pools

in the cooler months) from 9am in peak periods (10am at other times) until variously 5, 6, 7, 9 or 11pm (www.wetnwildorlando.com). TTTTT/AAA.

Water Mania

If Wet 'n Wild attracts the serious thrill seekers, Kissimmee's version, Water Mania, is more family-orientated and laid back, with the crowds greatest at weekends when the locals flock in. That's not to say this park doesn't have its share of scary slides (or Wet 'n Wild doesn't cater for families), it's just their emphasis is slightly different and those looking to avoid the crowds often end up here. Where this 36-acre (15-ha) park scores over its rivals is in the provision of 3 acres (1ha) of wooded area where you can enjoy your own picnic (no glass items, though).

Eight different slides, including a patented non-stop surfing challenge called **Wipe-Out**, the usual **Cruisin' Creek**, a 720,000-gallon (3,276,000-litre) **Wave Pool** (waves every 15 minutes, up to 4ft/122cm high) and 3 separate kids' areas provide the main attractions – plenty to keep you occupied for at least half a day. Top of the list for those daring enough to throw themselves down things like Der Stuka is the **Screamer**, an aptly named 72-ft (22-m) free-fall speed slide, and the **Abyss**, 380ft (116m) of enclosed-tube scary darkness. The **Anaconda** and **Banana Peel** both feature family-sized inner-tubes down long, twisting slides, while the **Double Berzerker** offers 2 different ways to

> BRIT TIP: Kids are again extremely well catered for, and Water Mania can even host birthday parties in Mr Kool's Party Land. Call 407 396 2626 for details.

be whooshed along and spat out into a foaming pool at the bottom. However, the outstanding feature, for both trying and watching, is the **Wipe-Out**, one of only two such attractions in the world. The challenge is to grab a body board and try to ride the continuous wave, risking going over the edge into another pool if you stray too wide, or being sent flying backwards if you lose your balance. A real blast!

When it comes to pint-sized fun for the children, Water Mania is one of the best. The **Pirates Lagoon** is designed for the 2–10s, with a 5,000sq ft (464sq m) pool ranging from 3in (7cm) to 2ft (60cm) deep and featuring a selection of mini-slides, fountains and water guns, all arranged around a wonderful large-scale pirate ship, with more chances to climb, jump and generally swashbuckle. Other recent additions are the **Rain Train**, a near life-size locomotive that sprays water out of its stack in the centre of a shallow pool, with other interactive play features and more slides, and **Tot's Town** for the toddlers (and parents who want to relax), a playground with sand beach and paddling area, added shade and refreshment hut. In addition to the cooling picnic areas, there are several snack bars, a mini-golf course, rock-climbing wall (small fee), volleyball and basketball courts, a games arcade and a large shop.

Getting there: On Highway 192, a mile (1.6km) east of the I-4 intersection (see map on page 12).

Admission: $29.95 and $26.95 for 3–9s; parking is $6. Open 10am–5pm early Mar to end Sept, 11am–5pm Thur–Sun only in October, closed Nov-Feb (hours subject to change) (407 396 2626, www.watermania-florida.com). TTTTT/AAA.

So that sums up the large-scale attractions, but now let's explore some alternatives to the mass-market experience…

Off the Beaten Track

(or, When You're All Theme-Parked Out)

A fter several days in the midst of the hectic tourist whirl of mainstream Orlando, you may be in need of a break from the non-stop theme park activities. Or you may be a repeat visitor looking for a different experience. If either is the case, this chapter is for you.

Hopefully, you will already have noted the relatively tranquil offerings of Silver Springs and Historic Bok Sanctuary in the previous chapter but, to get away from it all more completely and to enhance your view of the area further, the following are guaranteed to take you well off the beaten tourist track. This chapter should really be subtitled 'A Taste of the Real Florida', as it introduces the areas of Winter Park and Seminole County, nature boat rides, eco-tours and journeys by airboat, balloon, ship, train and plane (for the best maps, see page 59).

Winter Park

Foremost among the 'secret' hideaways is this elegant northern suburb of Orlando, little more than 20 minutes' drive from the hurly-burly of I-Drive yet a million miles from the relentless commercialism. It offers renowned museums and art galleries, fabulous shopping, numerous restaurants, pleasant walking tours, a delightful 50-minute boat ride around the lakes and, above all, a chance to slow down.

The central area is **Park Avenue**, a classy street of fine shops, restaurants, 2 museums and a wonderfully shaded park. At one end of the avenue is Rollins College, a small but highly respected arts education centre that houses the **Cornell Fine Arts Museum**, with the oldest collection of paintings, sculpture and decorative arts in Florida (open 10am–5pm Tue–Fri, 1pm–5pm Sat–Sun, closed Mon and main holidays, admission free) and the **Annie Russell Theater** (www.Rollins.edu).

The **Morse Museum of American Art** is a must for admirers of American art pottery, American and European glass, furniture and other decorative arts of the late 19th and early 20th Centuries, as it includes one of the world's foremost collections of works by Louis Comfort Tiffany. The dazzling chapel restoration from the 1893 Chicago World Expo is now on display in its original form for the first time since the late 19th Century and is worth the entrance fee alone. The museum is open 9.30am–4pm Tues–Sat and 1–4pm Sun, admission $3, under 12s free, plus free admission 4–8pm every Friday Sept–May. (www.morse museum.org).

The **Albin Polasek Museum and Sculpture Gardens** are also worth a look for culture buffs and for the serene setting devoted to this Czech-American artist. Open 10am–4pm Tue–Sat, 1–4pm Sun (closed July and August), admission is $5 for adults, $4 for seniors, under 12s free, and it is also a superb setting for weddings (www.polasek.org).

The **Scenic Boat Tour** (started

in 1938) is located at the east end of Morse Avenue and offers a charming, narrated 12-mile (19-km) tour of the 'Venice of America' around the lakes and canals for a fascinating glimpse of some of the most beautiful houses, boat houses and lakeside gardens (properties in the area start around $1 million and several top $5 million!). Tours run 10am–4pm daily and cost $8 for adults and $4 for children 2–11, and it is one of the most relaxing hours you will spend in Orlando (www.scenicboattours.com).

You can also take the **Park Avenue Walking Tour**, with useful free maps provided by the Chamber of Commerce on New York Avenue.

The shops of Park Avenue are a cut above most you will encounter and, while you may find the prices equally distinctive, just browsing is an enjoyable experience with the charm of the area highlighted by the friendliness hereabouts. For shops that are both unique and fun, look out for **Park Avenue Jewelers**, **Park Avenue Gallery** (art), **Kendyl's Kloset** (children's clothes and toys) and **The Doggie Door** (for pets). Recent additions are sports store **Golf Almighty**, **Olive This Relish That** (a wonderful gourmet food store with Mediterranean specialities), superb Italian menswear store **Milano's** and **Peter Brook Chocolatier**. Regular pavement craft fairs and art festivals add splashes of colour to an already inviting scenario, plus live jazz in Central Park once a month on Sundays in summer.

In addition to **Park Plaza Gardens**, which specialises in Continental cuisine (see Chapter 10, page 288), you can sample French, Italian and Thai cuisines, among others. The new **East of Paris** receives rave reviews from the locals for its sparkling continental and tapas-style menu. **Allegria Café and Cucina** is another fine romantic, Italian-flavoured choice, while **310 Park South** offers the epitome of elegant, European-style café culture. You can also try the pavement bistro offerings of **Briar Patch** or the five-star French fare of **Jardins du Castillon**, which is wonderfully romantic. Street parking usually allows 3 hours free, but the SunTrust Building on the corner of Comstock and Park Avenue is a better bet. And keep an eye out for the **Sidewalk Art Festival** every March and the Autumn Art Festival in October.

The **Central Park** area alongside Park Avenue, notable for its fountains and flowers, is due to be expanded in the near future, which should enhance things still further. Check out www.wpfl.org and www.parkave-winterpark.com for more info.

Another high point of a visit to Winter Park is the **Kraft Azalea Gardens** on Alabama Drive (off Palmer Avenue at the north end of Park Avenue), 11 acres (5ha) of shaded lakeside walkways, gardens and hundreds of magnificent azaleas. The main focal point, the mock Grecian temple, is a beautiful setting for weddings.

To get to Winter Park, take Exit 87 from I-4, Fairbanks Avenue. Turn right on to Fairbanks and head east for 2 miles (3km) until it intersects with Park Avenue and turn left.

Midway between Winter Park and downtown Orlando is another botanical gem, **Leu Gardens**, a 50-acre (20-ha) retreat featuring formal gardens, peaceful walks and a boardwalk overlooking Lake Rowena. **The Leu House Museum** is open 10am–4pm (closed in July) with tours every 30 minutes (last tour at 3.30pm). The gardens are open daily from 9am–5pm (9am–8pm in summer) and cost $5 for adults and $1 for under 13s (also free entry from 9am–12 noon every

8

Monday). You will find them on the corner of Forest and Nebraska Avenues, via Mills Avenue and Princeton St from Exit 85 on I-4 (www.leugardens.org).

Airboat rides

The thrill of airboat rides can be experienced on many of Florida's lakes, rivers and marshes. An airboat is a totally different experience to any boat ride you will have had before, as it is more like flying at ground level. As much a thrill as a scenic adventure, it has the advantage of exploring areas otherwise inaccessible to boats.

Airboats simply skim over and through the marshes, to give you an alternative, close-up and very personal view. Travelling at up to 50mph (80kph) means it can be loud (hence you will be provided with headphones) and sunglasses are also a good idea to keep stray flies out of your eyes. However, it is NOT the trip for you if you are spooked by crickets, dragonflies and similar insects that occasionally land in the boat! In summer months, a good insect repellant is also advisable.

Several operations offer airboat rides in the area, from 'you-drive' boats that do barely 5mph (8kph) to much bigger ones, but for the most quality-conscious operation my tip goes to **Boggy Creek Airboat Rides**. Its airboats can be found at its main site on Lake Toho at peaceful Southport Park (all the way down Poinciana Boulevard, off Highway 192 between Markers 10 and 11, and across into Southport Road – about a 30-minute drive) and at a

Boggy Creek airboat ride

> BRIT TIP: Look out for discount coupons in tourist literature offering up to $3 off airboat rides.

secondary location on East Lake Toho. For the latter, you either take Exit 17 off the Central Florida Greeneway (417) and go south on Boggy Creek Road, then right into East Lake Fish Camp; better still, take Osceola Parkway all the way east until it hits Boggy Creek Road. Go left and then turn right at the Boggy Creek T-junction, then right into East Lake Fish Camp after 2 miles (3km).

The **East Lake Fish Camp** is itself a little gem, offering a variety of boating and angling opportunities (407 348 2040) as well as the wonderfully authentic rural Florida charm of the **restaurant and gift shop** (open 8am–9pm every day). If you are heading for a morning airboat ride, consider arriving early for a huge all-day breakfast at the fish camp first, where the more adventurous will want to try the local delicacies – catfish, frogs' legs and gator tail. For another great slice of local eating, try the Friday buffet and Saturday night seafood buffet, fabulous value at $10.95 and $12.95 each on an all-you-can-eat basis.

> BRIT TIP: Best time for an airboat ride is first thing on a weekday morning when the wildlife is not hiding from the weekend boaters.

Boggy Creek's **half-hour ride** features the most modern 18-passenger airboats in Florida, skimming over the local wetlands for a close-up view of the majestic cypress trees and wildlife that can include eagles, ospreys, snakes and turtles, as well as the ever-present gators. The Southport Park site tends to be the quieter of the two, with more wildlife – especially in the spring – but involves a longer drive than East Lake Fish Camp.

You do not need to book, just turn up, as boats go every half-hour (9am–5.30pm daily), and rides cost $18.95 for adults and $14.95 for children 3–12 (don't forget the sunscreen as you can really burn out on the water). They also do a 1-hour **Night Tour** ($29.95 for adults, $24.95 for 3–12s, Mar–Oct only) for a completely different and exhilarating experience (gator eyes glow red in the dark!), but you must book at least 3 days in advance. New in 2005 at the Southport Park location was a **Swamp Buggy Adventure**, offer a fascinating close-up of the lakeside flora and fauna in a purpose-built, giant-wheeled vehicle that chugs effortlessly through the local marshes. The 40-minute ride itself costs $20.95 (adults) or $15.95 (children 3–12) or there is a combo ticket for both swamp buggy and airboat ride at $35.91 and $27.18. The addition of this extra element also makes this a highly worthwhile half-day adventure.

Finally, it offers a 45-minute **private tour** in its 6-passenger boat ($45/person), which provides an even more personal view of this amazing area. Call 407 344 9550 or visit www.bcairboats.com for more info and a money-off coupon.

> BRIT TIP: If you are staying in or visiting Seminole County, visit Black Hammock Fish Camp for its version of the wonderful airboat adventure (see page 232).

Also in Kissimmee, **Aquatic Wonders Boat Tours** were closed for much of 2005 following damage from the previous year's hurricanes, but it does plan to start up again, with a new mix of nature tours around the extensive lakes and waterways. Captain Ray Robida is a mine of information on the local flora and fauna, and his plans include some longer tours, including overnight stops. Find out more on www.florida-nature.com or 407 846 2814.

Balloon trips

Florida is one of the most popular areas for ballooning and, if you are up early enough in the morning, you will often see several. The experience is a majestic one. If Orlando represents the holiday of a lifetime, then a balloon flight is the ride of a lifetime. The utterly smooth way in which you lift off into the early morning sky is breathtaking in itself, but the peace and quiet of the ride, not to mention the stunning views from 2,000ft (600 metres) above ground, are quite awesome. It is not a cheap experience, but it is equally appealing to all but the youngest children or those who have vertigo or a fear of heights. It is a highly personalised ride, taking up to 6 people. Some baskets take up to 12, but it's a squeeze!

Blue Water Balloons

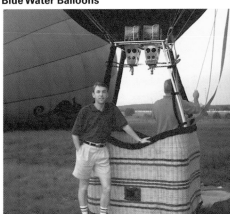

Orange Blossom Balloons is one of the premier companies in central Florida, with over 20 years' experience and a wonderful laid-back style that stems from its British-owned operation. You meet in the restaurant at **La Quinta Inn Lakeside** (which is due to become a Best Western in the near future) on Highway 192 (5 traffic lights WEST of the main entry to Disney) at 6am – the best winds for flying are nearly always first thing in the morning – and then transfer to the take-off site, where you help the crew members set up one of their 4 balloons (for 4, 8, 10 or 12 passengers in new compartmentalised baskets), one of which is disabled-accessible.

BRIT TIP: Dresses are not advisable for balloon trips and hard-wearing shoes for the set-up and landing areas are essential.

Owner-operators Richard Ornstein and Jonathan Robinson, and their team of Jeff, Mike, Bob, Pat and Donna are a real hoot, and you are soon up, up and away in awe-inspiring style, floating serenely up into the sky or sinking down to skim the surface of one of the many lakes (disturbing the occasional gator or deer). After about an hour you come back to earth for a traditional champagne landing ceremony and return to La Quinta for a full breakfast and your special balloonist's certificate. The full experience lasts 3–4 hours and costs $175 per adult (inclusive of tax) and $95 for 10–15s (under 10s go free with their parents). Hotel pick-up is also available at $10/person round trip, or you can pay $20 to be part of the chase crew and just enjoy the champagne landing and breakfast. Call 407 239 7677 for reservations

(they do book up well in advance, even though they fly every day, weather permitting) or go to www.orangeblossomballoons.com.

Alternatively, check out **Blue Water Balloons** for a more small-scale experience, finishing with a breakfast and champagne picnic out in the peaceful wilds of Florida where you land. Owner-operator Don Edwards and his team are also a pleasure to fly with and have thousands of hours' flying experience plus a wealth of stories to pass on (they have flown in more than 30 US states and piloted the Energizer Bunny – the largest shaped balloon in America!). The picnic includes fresh fruit, cheeses, pastries and nachos and salsa, plus champagne and fresh orange juice. Don says: 'We have asked our passengers over the years if they would prefer a restaurant breakfast or our traditional picnic, and the answer is usually "We can eat in a restaurant anytime, this is much more personal and intimate".' Each passenger receives a Flight of Ascension certificate and a souvenir balloon-etched champagne glass. The price is $175 for adults and $90 for children 10 and under, while you can also book a private flight for 2 for $475 or $200/single, and buy gift certificates at $155 and $190. Wedding flights are available on request. Visit www.bluewater balloons.com for a $10 discount voucher. Call 407 894 5040 or 1-800 586 1884 to book.

Everglades and the Bahamas

Day trips are increasingly common from Orlando to the Everglades, Miami, the Florida Keys and the Bahamas and, if you are prepared to put up with a long day out (up to 16 hours) you can see a lot of the state this way. However, if the primary attraction is the half-hour airboat ride, you are better off going to Boggy Creek Airboats and avoiding the long journey.

Real Florida Excursions and **International Divers** are 2 companies worth recommending.

Real Florida has a variety of tours, from an Orlando Shopping Bonanza excursion to a new 2-day **Grand Bahama Getaway**. This latter is a real paradise island getaway, with a morning flight from Orlando International airport to Nassau and then an overnight stay at the **Nassau Beach Hotel**, with neighbouring **Crystal Palace Casino**. You have the best part of 2 full days to enjoy the resort and its beaches and watersports, while there are optional island tours, the local **Dolphin Encounter** or a trip to the world famous – and quite stunning – **Atlantis Resort** on Paradise Island. The Getaway costs $239 per adult and $199 for children 2–12 (plus $89/person in hotel and local departure tax). Its newest trip is a night-time limo ride to **Planet Hollywood, Mickey's Hollywood Magic**, which includes a full meal at the movie-themed restaurant and the chance to meet a variety of Disney characters ($89 for adults and $69 for children 3–9).

Another Real Florida 2-day trip is the **Clearwater Getaway**, which provides luxury coach transport to the Gulf coast, overnight accommodation at a 3-star hotel with beach access, plus a dolphin encounter cruise and optional boat excursions. The trip itself costs $95 for adults and $29 for 3–9s (plus $12/person hotel tax). Alternatively, a 1-day **Clearwater Beach** trip ($52 and $31) provides ample time on the beach, with lunch included and optional speedboat, dolphin cruise, pirate cruise and fishing excursions.

Real Florida's **Naples-Everglades Adventure** trip provides a taste of Florida in just a day (although a greater proportion of time is spent on the coach), with a 30-minute airboat ride through the Everglades to a Native American reservation, including lunch. The afternoon is given over to visiting beautiful Naples, with a cruise along the coastal waterways and some beach time. This costs $109 (adults) and $80 (3–12s).

A relatively new offering is its limo evening out to Universal's CityWalk, with dinner and a pass for the clubs. Called **Be A Star in a Great Big Car**, it involves a return trip from your hotel to CityWalk in a stretch limo, and is proving highly popular at $80 for adults and $65 for 3–12s. A **Kennedy Space Center** day trip costs $72 and $56 (including admission), and there is a **Kennedy Eco Tour** and an airboat ride ($83 and $63). The **Shopping Bonanza** (including an all-you-can-eat buffet breakfast and visits to Wal-Mart, Premium Outlets and Mall at Millenia) will set you back $34 for adults and $26 for 3–9s. Call Real Florida Excursions on 1-866 266 5733 or visit www.real floridaexcursions.com.

International Divers offers an increasingly diverse range of memorable excursions, although it is best known for its swim-with-dolphins tours to the Florida Keys. It is also a *Brit's Guide* Partner (see inside back cover), which means our readers qualify for a *12½ per cent discount* on all its tours. Take your pick from: **The Fast & The Furious**, an all-day adventure to Daytona, including the morning at either Daytona USA Raceway or a 95-minute Trolley Duck Amphibious Ride around the city and inland waterway, followed by lunch and an afternoon trip to New Smyrna Beach to include either bike hire, beach chair or umbrella hire or boogie board for the kids. It leaves between 7 and 8am and costs $99 for adults and $79 for children (3-9);

8

Sun, Sand and Scales, an excellent value all-day trip to Cocoa Beach leaving at 9am, with time to enjoy Ron Jon's Surf Shop before heading off to the Airboat Outpost for an animal show and barbecue with unlimited food and drink, followed by a night-time airboat ride in search of gators ($89 and $59); **Clearwater Screamer**, leaving at 7.45-9.30am, a beach day plus a speedboat ride (an hour-long trip on the huge *Sea Screamer* – watch for the dolphins), including lunch at the Hilton Resort and plenty of time to enjoy the sugar-white sands ($99 and $79); **Florida Everglades Adventure**, a chance to see the REAL Florida on an all-day getaway, with an exhilarating airboat ride, gator wrestling, native wildlife exhibits, a visit to Tarpon Cove 'Millionaires Club' for lunch, a boat cruise around Naples Bay and even some time for the beach. The tour leaves between 6.45 and 8.30am but doesn't return until around 11pm ($109 and $64); **Manatee Interactive Tour**, another all-day adventure (and its No 1 Florida attraction) this features an all-you-can-eat breakfast buffet, a 2-hour boat trip on the picturesque Crystal River (with snorkel and mask provided to check out where the manatees swim at close quarters!). There is also a picnic lunch, an airboat ride and a trip to Homosassa State Wildlife Park, plus an educational briefing on the manatees and a chance to see them being fed from the special underground viewing area. It departs between 7.30 and 8.30am ($109 and $79). Then there are their two trademark **Swim With the Dolphins** tours, a 1-day excursion to the beautiful Florida Keys with a 2-hour dolphin programme (and the choice of either an organised or unstructured dolphin swim), or the grand 2-day trip, including resort accommodation with its own private beach, dolphin swim, island-style evening meal, Everglades airboat ride, alligator and snake-handling show (interactive!), and a half-day to see Miami with shopping at the Bayside plaza or a boat tour along the inland waterways. The dolphin programme includes a full briefing and then about 30 minutes in the water, with dolphin contact guaranteed. It leaves between 6.15 and 7am, returning around 7.30pm the next day ($199 for adults, $179 7-9s, $99 2-6s; plus dolphin swim $135/person). You can also arrange deep-sea **scuba-diving** trips every Saturday to the likes of Key Largo and Fort Lauderdale (check online for details), or try out its **American Football** day-trips to see the Jacksonville Jaguars ($99/person, Sep-Dec). For more info, call on 407 352 4646 or look them up at www.floridadolphintours.com. To enjoy the special *Brit's Guide* discount, just call up and quote '12½% off with the *Brit's Guide*, please!'

International Divers also has its own limo and transportation service, which can be tailor-made to provide airport transfers, wedding cars or just a special night out. Look up www.skyylimousine.com or call 407 352 4644. Skyy also offers the *Brit's Guide* discount, so don't forget to ask!

Flying Tigers Warbird Air Museum

This vintage aeroplane museum on Hoagland Boulevard in Kissimmee was forced to close most of its operations after the hurricanes of 2005. It was still open to casual visitors, but its trademark guided tours and the secrets behind its

Flying Tigers Warbird Adventures

amazing aircraft restoration had ceased. However, as we went to press, there was hope of new ownership, with scope for the museum to re-open later in 2005. Please visit www.askdaisy.net/orlando for the latest info.

Warbird Adventures

Anyone even slightly interested in World War II aviation should certainly consider a trip to Kissimmee to try out the Warbird Adventures. *This is the best ride in town, bar none, guaranteed.* Not only do you get to fly in one of their 3 1945 T-6 Harvard fighter-trainers, but also, after a period of getting used to the front seat of this vintage 2-seater… you get to fly it! And you don't just handle the controls, your instructor will get you doing loops, barrel rolls and all manner of aerobatics. This is simply the most exhilarating ride I have ever done, enhanced by in-flight video and wingtip camera to record every moment. It is the only place where you can walk in off the street and, 20 minutes later, be flying a plane with no previous experience at all.

My instructor was the excellent Thom Richard and, despite my initial reluctance, he eventually had me doing the full aerobatic business before long. Roller-coasters? They're for wimps! Mind you, this is not cheap – a 15-minute flight costs $170, a 30-minute trip is $280 and an hour $510. Aerobatics (on 30- or 60-minute flights only) cost $30, while the PAL video is $50 (or DVD for $60) and the stills $20 (or all three 'extras' for $95). Nevertheless, this is a memory to last a lifetime, and the thought of it still thrills me to bits. They also operate a 1966 Bell 47-G M*A*S*H helicopter for flights and instruction (407 870 7366, www.warbird adventures.com). You can find

Warbird Adventures just off Hoagland Boulevard, half a mile (1 km) south of Highway 192 on the left.

Green Meadows Petting Farm

From one extreme to another, here is guaranteed fun for kids aged 2 up to about 11 and their parents (don't forget your cameras). It's the ultimate hands-on experience as, on the 2-hour guided tour, kids get to milk a cow, pet a pig, cuddle a chick or duckling, feed goats and sheep, meet a buffalo, chickens, peacocks and donkeys and learn what makes a farm tick. There are pony rides and a play area for the young ones and tractor-drawn hay rides for all, plus the Green Meadows Express steam train that takes you on a scenic chug around the farm.

BRIT TIP: Reader Lynda Letchford says: 'Wear enclosed shoes to Green Meadows, which my 2-year-old really enjoyed. When you are in the pens with the animals, they nibble your toes and you step in all sorts! Also take some hand wipes for extra hygiene.'

8

Kayaking in Wekiva Springs State Park

The shaded areas, free-roaming animals and peaceful aspect all contribute to another pleasant change of pace, especially as Green Meadows is barely 10 minutes from the tourist hurly-burly of Highway 192 (south on Poinciana Boulevard). It is open 9.30am–5.30pm daily (last admission at 4pm) and costs $19 ($16 for seniors, under 2s free); allow 3–4 hours for your visit. Drinks, snacks and gifts are available, but it is also the ideal place to bring a picnic (407 846 0770, www.green meadowsfarm.com).

Osceola County Pioneer Museum

Only just off the beaten track in Kissimmee but a delightful discovery is this small-scale homage to 19th-century Florida life, with a preserved cracker (cowboy) homestead portraying how the original settlers lived in the 1890s. The fascinating little museum traces the history of Osceola County, and includes a cattle camp, nature walk, country store and information centre with library. But the real highlight is provided by the volunteers who take you round, providing a fascinating view of life here more than 100 years ago. Situated on N Bass Road (turn off Highway 192 right by the big Wal-Mart Supercenter next to Medieval Times), it is open 10am–4pm Tue–Fri and noon–4pm Sat and Sun and admission is by $2 donation per adult and $1 per child (407 396 8644).

Reptile World Serpentarium

Another throwback to an earlier time in Florida (albeit only BD – Before Disney) is this wonderfully kitsch roadside attraction in St Cloud. Florida is actually home to a wide variety of snakes, both

BRIT TIP: If you are brave enough to volunteer during the venom show, you won't actually be asked to help in this genuinely dangerous activity, but you will get the chance to stroke a boa constrictor afterwards.

venomous and non-venomous, and all of them can be seen here. In all, there are more than 60 species of worldwide reptile featured in the clean, indoor exhibits (including the Australian Taipan – rated the world's deadliest snake), but the standout feature is the twice-daily (at midday and 3pm) 'milking' of venom from some of the more hazardous residents – cobras and vipers – for snake research. Snakes are their stock-in-trade, but you will also meet turtles, gators and iguanas. Out on the eastern stretch of Highway 192, just past St Cloud, it is open 9am–5.30pm Tue–Sun and costs $5.50 for adults, $4.50 for 6–17s and $3.50 for 3–5s (407 892 6905).

Disney and cruising

Taking a cruise is fast becoming a regular option with an Orlando stay and, with the introduction of *Disney Cruise Line* in 1998, you will now see a lot of publicity for these competitively priced 2-, 3-, 4- and 7-day sailings out of fast-developing Port Canaveral.

Although a relative newcomer to cruising, Disney has a couple of breathtaking ships, the 83,000-ton *Disney Magic* (1998) and *Disney Wonder* (1999), with their own dedicated cruise terminal. Classic design plus the usual Disney Imagineering have produced these two huge vessels, incorporating special features for kids, teenagers AND couples without children.

Both ships are a destination experience in their own right, each with 4 restaurants, a 1,040-seat theatre, cinema, nightclub complex, choice of bars and a full health spa, while they sail to the Bahamas, Caribbean and Disney's stunning private island. It is not a cheap option and the 3- and 4-night cruises can feel a little frenzied, but the 7-night Caribbean cruises – either to St Maarten and St Thomas or Key West, Grand Cayman and Cozumel in Mexico – offer a genuinely relaxing style that is hard to beat. They boast some novel touches with superb on-board entertainment, Disney character interaction and wonderful features like the adults-only champagne brunch. Many tour operators offer *Disney Cruise Line* packages but you can also book cruise-only at great rates with Dreams Unlimited Travel (see page 28).

The ships are identical in practical terms, and the week-long cruises allow you to enjoy fully the wide range of facilities. The impact of the 4-restaurant set-up (where you dine in a different one each night, including the amazing black-and-white *Animator's Palate* which comes to life all around you), the fabulous entertainment 'district', the vast array of kids' facilities (including Buzz Lightyear's Cyberspace Command Post) and the picturesque beaches of Disney's Castaway Cay island is just superb. When you add in some scintilating theatrical performances, all with the high-quality Disney hallmark, this really is as complete a package as you will find anywhere at sea.

Other Port Canaveral options (www.portcanaveral.org) include the glitzy **Carnival Cruise Lines** (all-modern hardware, party atmosphere; call 1-866 299 5698 in the US or 020 7940 4466 in the UK) with 3- and 4-day Bahamas voyages on the *Fantasy*, alternating

7-day cruises to the east and west Caribbean on one of its biggest ships, the *Carnival Glory*, and 7-day cruises from Port Canaveral to the Bahamas and New York on one of its newest vessels, *Carnival Miracle*. **Royal Caribbean International** (3 more modern, glamorous ships; call 1-866 562 7625 in the US or 0800 018 2917 in the UK) have similar trips to Nassau and its private island of Coco Cay, alternating 7-day Caribbean cruises on mega-ship *Mariner of the Seas* and 7-day voyages taking in Baltimore, the Bahamas and Key West. **NCL** is another bright, quality-conscious brand (call 1-800 625 5306 in the US or 0845 658 8010 in the UK) and features the magnificent *Norwegian Dream* year-round from Port Canaveral to Miami, the Bahamas and New York (it actually pioneered the Big Apple route). There are even 2 casino ships daily from Port Canaveral, **Sterling Casino Lines** (1-888 783 2212 or www.sterlingcasino lines.com) and **Suncruz Casinos** (1-800 474 3423 or www.suncruz casino.com) with 5- and 6-hour round-trips if you feel the need for a flutter in style. For more advice, consult another of my publications, *World of Cruising* magazine (www.woconline.com or 0870 429 2686) or specialist UK travel agent, **The Cruise Line Ltd**, on 0870 112 1102. In Orlando, try **Cruise Planners** on 1-877 772 7847 or www.gocruiseplanner.com.

For a smaller and more low-key approach, the **Rivership Romance** (daily out of downtown Sanford) is a great choice, especially for the lunch cruises on the wildlife-rich St John's River. The old-fashioned steamer can take up to 200 in comfort and adds a fine meal, live entertainment and a river narration, as well as providing a relaxing alternative to the usual tourist rush. Choose from the 3-hour lunch cruise (11am–2pm

Wed, Sat and Sun) at $36.75 a head, the 4-hour cruise (11am–3pm Mon, Tue, Thur and Fri) at $47.25 or an evening dinner-dance voyage (7.30–11pm Sat) at $52.50. New in 2004 was the **Special Event Show**, a themed dinner show that might feature a madcap wedding, a haunted holiday or something equally offbeat to keep you amused and involved while you eat (7–9.30pm Fri; $45). To book, call 407 321 5091 or visit www.rivership romance.com. Its dock can be found off Exit 101A of I-4, east into Sanford, then left on Palmetto Avenue.

Seminole County

Having arrived in the historic town of Sanford, the heart of Seminole County, it is worth pointing out the possible diversions of a day or two in this area that will get you well off the beaten track. The **Central Florida Zoological Park** is a private, non-profit-making organisation that puts a pleasant, natural accent on the zoo theme and is set in 116 wooded acres (47 ha) of unspoilt Florida countryside with boardwalks and trails around all the attractions. These include more than 100 species of animals, weekend feeding demonstrations, educational programmes, a picnic area, pony rides and a butterfly garden, plus the Zoofari Outpost gift shop. It's good value, too, at $8.95 for adults, $6.95 for seniors (60+) and $4.95 for 3–12s (half-price admission 9–10am Thur), and the park (off Exit 104 of I-4) is open every day (except Thanksgiving Day

Riding in the Florida countryside

> **BRIT TIP:** Visit Central Florida Zoo at the weekend and you will be offered a series of educational Animal Encounters (ranging from gators and snakes to hedgehogs).

and Christmas Day) 9am–5pm. A 2004 update enlarged several exhibits and added whole new animal habitats, including an Australian section with emu and kangaroos. (www.centralflorida zoo.org).

St John's River Cruise, at Blue Spring State Park, features a 2-hour nature tour of this historic waterway, with interactive narration of the history, flora and fauna (which includes manatees in winter months). This immensely personable, family-run tour costs $16 for adults, $14 for seniors (60+) and $10 for 3–12s and leaves from Orange City marina several times a day (take Highway 17/92 north from Sanford to French Avenue and head west for 1 mile (1.6km). Call 407 330 1612 to check times and book.

One of the most fun and entertaining of the area's airboat rides is to be found at the **Black Hammock Fish Camp and Restaurant** (off Exit 44 of the Central Florida Greeneway, take SR 434 east, turn left on Deleon St and left on to Black Hammock Road). This peaceful backwater on beautiful Lake Jesup is home to Captain Joel Martin, a Frenchman who enjoys his Florida boating, and his 1-hour tours will take you into every nook and cranny of either the east or west lake (and this really is a great lake to explore, positively crammed with gators, including some of the biggest I've seen in the wilds). It is an eye-opening adventure, and Captain Martin even keeps his own gators, large and small, back at the Fish Camp. Rides are $35.95 for adults and $29.95 for under 10s, (30-minute rides available for $23.95 and $19.95) and you should book in advance on 407 365 1244.

Afterwards you can grab lunch or dinner at the **Black Hammock Restaurant** (fine local delicacies, especially the catfish and gator tail, plus other dishes and a kids' menu; 11am–10pm Sun and Tue–Thur, 11am–midnight Fri and Sat, with Happy Hour 4–6.30pm; call 407 365 2201) or visit the **Lazy Gator Bar** (open 3pm Tue–Fri, noon Sat and Sun) for karaoke (Sat) and live music (Fri–Sun), with Happy Hour all night on Wed. You can even rent canoes or fishing boats and enjoy another view of this unspoilt corner (www.theblackhammock.com).

Alternatively, **Bill's Airboat Adventures**, on the St John's River east of Sanford, offers 90-minute tours in the company of conservationist and river historian Captain Bill Daniel for $35 ($20 for under 14s) on his 6-person boat, subject to a $90 minimum (407 977 3214, www.airboating.com).

Dana's Fishing and Scenic Tours can take you out on to Seminole County's lakes and waterways for some brilliant bass fishing or guided scenic tours (by appointment only, call 407 645 5462 or check out www.fishingincentralflorida.cc).

Of course, you can just head for one of the splendid **State Parks** in this area and take your own tour of the well-marked trails. **Wekiva Springs State Park** offers hiking, canoeing and swimming, plus picnic areas and shelters and most recently started offering bike rentals, while **Little Big Econ** state forest has 5,048 acres (2,045ha) of scenic woodlands and wetlands.

Sanford itself is a fascinating city (more of a town by UK standards) on the south shore of Lake Monroe

and a designated historic centre, full of brick-paved streets, antique shops and an 'artists' colony' at the heart of a major regeneration project. It is very much small-town America, having lost the growth battle with Orlando many years ago, but it makes a peaceful diversion with some lovely walks, notably the new **Riverwalk** project and First Street renovations.

Head for the **Sanford Museum** (520 East First Street) to get the full historic overview of the city's growth from its incorporation in 1877, under the patronage of pioneering lawyer and diplomat Henry Sanford, as a hub destination on the St John's River, the 'Nile of America'. The museum (open 11am–4pm Tue–Fri, 1–4pm Sat; admission free) beautifully illustrates the life and times of the city's founder, its growth into the 'celery capital of the world' and its modern history as a US Naval Air Force base.

From there, head on to **First Street** and check out the turn-of-the-19th-century buildings, stop for a bite at Morgan's Gourmet Café and finish up by wandering down to the river.

Sanford also harbours **The Rose Cottage Inn**, a wonderful tea room, restaurant and quaint B&B. It is one of the prettiest settings for lunch, tea or dinner in Florida, serving a mouth-watering array of soups, sandwiches, pastas, salads and quiches, as well as fabulous fruit teas. This little treasure (open 11am–3pm daily) can be found on

8

Deep-sea fishing

Park Avenue, 13 blocks out of Sanford city centre (dinner reservations are advisable on 407 323 9448). Its B&B features a full English breakfast and 5 completely individual rooms, all with a real turn-of-the-last-century country cottage style.

Or you could try the equally stylish and Victorian **Higgins House** (on South Oak Avenue and 5th Street; 407 324 9238, www.higginshouse.com).

For more info on things to do and see in Seminole County look up www.visitseminole.com or call in at one of its **Visitor Centers** at Orlando Sanford airport (in the Welcome Center as you exit the main building) and at 1230 Douglas Avenue in Longwood (one block west of Exit 94 on I-4; 407 665 2900).

Finally, if you enjoy hiking, biking or in-line skating – literally getting off the beaten track – then Seminole County boasts miles of trails and other recreational pursuits. **Spring Hammock Preserve** offers 1,500 acres (607ha) of wilderness to explore, while the **Lake Proctor** wilderness area is home to 6 miles (10km) of hiking, biking and equestrian adventures. There are more trails to explore in the **Econ River Wilderness Area**, along the Econlockhatchee River, while Chuluota boasts 625 acres (253ha) and the **Geneva Wilderness Area** 180 acres (73ha) including the **Ed Yarborough Nature Center** (407 665 7352, www.co.seminole.fl.us/trails).

> BRIT TIP: Need a hotel in Seminole County for a night or several? Look up www.NorthOrlandoHotels.com for a great selection of short-term accommodation at good prices.

If you enjoy the Seminole County experience and want to travel a bit further afield, head out to the Gulf Coast, just north of Homossasa Springs, and visit the **Crystal River State Park**, which offers another wildlife fiesta. The Crystal River is home to the endangered manatee, and it is possible to go swimming with these wonderful creatures. **Orlando Dive and Snorkel Tours** (407 239 3573, www.dive orlando.com) offers magical opportunities to see them (Manatee Dive $74, Manatee Snorkel Encounter $40).

Eco-tourism

Genuine eco-tourism is still in its infancy, in general terms, in central Florida, but there are 2 major exceptions worth knowing about.

Florida Eco-Safaris at Forever Florida is, for my money, one of the most outstanding, non-theme park attractions. It is both a 4,700-acre (1,900-ha) wilderness preserve and a working ranch. As well as a close-up of Florida's flora and fauna and its conservation issues, you get a taste of the original cowboy life, cracker style (crackers were the original cowboys, pre-dating their Western counterparts by 50 years), which is a fascinating slice of history. Eco-safaris, covered wagon tours, horse rides, bike trails, nature walks and, for the kids, pony rides and a free petting zoo, are the highlights, as well as the magnificent **Cypress Restaurant** and **Visitor Center**, which offers an essential 30-minute orientation programme into the conservancy's creation.

Beginning as a dream of gifted young biologist and ecologist Allen Broussard, Forever Florida was completed after his death (from complications of Hodgkin's disease) by his parents, Dr William and Margaret Broussard. They continue to give their time and energy to developing the wilderness as a non-profit-making memorial to their son. The education element alone is awesome, and tours feature a strong conservation message in this tranquil, untouched corner of Florida. The **Guided Eco-Safaris** (2 hours, including lunch, at $29.50/person) are their stock-in-trade, a tranquil trundle around much of the woods, swamp and prairie that make up the ranch and conservancy in a large-wheeled, open-sided buggy. An education co-ordinator provides the low-down on the history and environmental issues of the ecosystems. You are likely to encounter alligators (at a safe distance), whitetail deer, armadillos and a host of bird life – including bald eagles – and leave with a good understanding of the real Florida. The **Rawhide Roundtrip** is a full half-day ranch experience, again including lunch ($89), while its 1-, 2- and 3-hour **Guided Horseback Safaris** ($37.50, $57 and $73) are offered daily and reservations are recommended. **Pony rides** are available, too, at $8.

Forever Florida is a good 80-minute drive out of Orlando, 40 miles (64km) east on Highway 192, through St Cloud as far as Holopaw, then 7½ miles (12km) south on Highway 441, but it is well worth the journey.

Call 1-866 854 3837 at least a day in advance to check availability and make reservations (www.floridaeco-safaris.com).

On an equally authentic scale is **Disney's Wilderness Preserve**, run by the Nature Conservancy (the

> BRIT TIP: The **Kissimmee Convention and Visitors Bureau** (see page 49) publishes an excellent eco-guide.

world's leading private international conservancy group) in Poinciana, south of Kissimmee. This restoration of a 12,000-acre (4,860-ha) preserve is a work in progress and allows visitors in for various (well-marked) hiking trails, with a 1-hour guided tour on Saturdays (at 9.30am) and 2-hour buggy tours on Sundays (1.30pm).

The preserve's pine and scrubby flatwoods, dry and wet prairies, freshwater marshes and forested wetlands are home to more than 300 wildlife species, including bald eagles, Florida scrub-jays and sandhill cranes, Sherman's fox squirrels, eastern indigo snakes and gopher tortoises, plus more than 50 butterfly species. Come here for a chance to unwind and enjoy the peace and quiet of the real Florida countryside. Admission is $3 for adults and $2 for children, while the buggy tours are an extra $7 and $5. Located at the end of Pleasant Hill Road (follow Hoagland Boulevard south off Highway 192), the preserve is open daily 9am–5pm Oct–May, Mon–Fri Jun–Sept (407 935 0002, http://nature.org/wherewework/northamerica/states/florida/).

Beach escapes

When it comes to beaches, you are again spoiled for choice. The sea, sand and surf of **Cocoa Beach** is only an hour's drive from Orlando (east on the Beeline Expressway – 528 – then south on Highway A1A) and offers some good shopping (including the unmissable **Ron Jon's Surf Shop**, a massive neon emporium of all things water related) in addition to the 2 main public beaches. As it's the Atlantic, the sea can be pretty chilly from November to March, but Cocoa Beach is rapidly developing into a major coastal resort, so the facilities are excellent.

Its more famous neighbour, just to the north, is **Daytona Beach**, which is still only an hour away from Orlando if you take I-4 all the way east. This is the prime site of the Atlantic coast scene, with an array of good beaches (some of which you can even drive on – for a $5 toll, speed limit 10mph/16kph), boating and fishing trips, sightseeing – including the **Ponce de Leon Inlet Lighthouse**, a formidable 203 spiralling steps to the top of this magnificently preserved monument, but well worth it for the view (10am–5pm daily, $5 for adults, $1.50 for children), and surprisingly smart shopping and dining at the redeveloped **Ocean Walk Village**, next door to the main beach, pier and boardwalk area. Here you will find **RC Theatres' Ocean Walk 10 Cineplex**, the serious film-themed fun of **Bubba Gump's Shrimp Company**, the **Mai Tai** bar and **Adobe Gila's Margarita Fajita Cantina** (check out its near-lethal range of cocktails!). Recent additions inclue **Maui Nix Surf Shop**, **Harley-Davidson Apparel**, **Candle Gallery**, a **Johnny Rockets** diner, **Starbucks** and **Planet Smoothie**. This is also where you can pick up Daytona's great **Trolley Boats**, an amphibious 75-minute ride around all the main local sights, both on land and in water, fully narrated to cover all the area's history, from the Native Americans to NASCAR ($21 for adults, $19 for seniors, $15 for children 6–15 and $5 for 2–5s). Check out more on www.daytonatrolleyboattours.net and www.oceanwalkshoppes.com. The newest attraction, in May 2005,

was **Daytona Lagoon**, a combination water park, go-kart track, mini-golf course, arcade and laser tag centre (also with a rock-climbing wall and elaborate ball pool for the young uns). The water park consists of a wave pool and lazy river, 10 different flumes and an area purely for toddlers ($19.99 for those over 4ft (122cm) tall, $16.99 for those below). There are 3 9-hole courses for the mini golf (from $4.99), single and double go-karts (from $5.99), while the laser tag (must be above 3ft 6in (108cm) tall, $5.99) and rock climbing (from $4.99) and ball play ($4.99) are also separate items. Look up more at www.daytona lagoon.com. Then there is the lively **Riverfront Marketplace** along historic Beach Street.

More family-orientated fun can be found at the **Marine Science Center** (just around the corner from the lighthouse at Ponce Inlet), which showcases whale, mangrove, mosquito and sea turtle exhibits, plus a new seabird sanctuary, along with turtle rehabilitation facilities and a 5,000-gallon (22,750-litre) artificial reef aquarium, as well as static and interactive educational displays. A boardwalk and nature trail system extends throughout the park, which also has a gift shop. Open 10am–4pm Tue–Sat and noon–4pm Sun (closed Mon) and costs $1 for 5–12s and $3 for 13 and older, under 5s free (www.echotourism. com/msc).

The **beaches** are a lively affair around Spring Break (pre-Easter college holiday) but fairly quiet otherwise. Other highlights include cruising the intra-coastal waterway to see the dolphins at play – check out **A Tiny Cruise Line** (386 226 2343, www.visitdaytona.com/ tinycruise/) for details of its 4 cruises, $11.03–18.85 with tax, which include a lovely Sunset/City Lights tour from April to October.

Riverfront at Daytona Beach

The **Riverfront Marketplace** is the heart of downtown Daytona Beach, with a museum of local history, restaurants, nightclubs, coffee bars and a performing arts theatre, all in a quaint riverside setting. Dining opportunities are many and inviting along the beaches, with **Inlet Harbor** and **Lighthouse Landing** among the best. The tide can retreat by up to 500ft (150m) and the beaches are open to the public year-round.

> BRIT TIP: Check out the **Lighthouse Landing** in Lighthouse Point Park for lunch or dinner for a truly eclectic piece of Floridian restaurant life.

Lighthouse Point Park is especially worthy of note, a 52-acre (21-ha) stretch of nature trails, fishing, observation deck, swimming and picnicking (open 8am–9pm, $3.50/vehicle).

For the latest on all Daytona Beach has to offer, call 020 7935 7756 in the UK or visit www.daytonabeach.com. And of course, one of the biggest attractions is the Daytona USA racetrack (see page 250).

To the west you have the **Gulf Coast**, which is a good 90 minutes' drive down I-4 from Orlando and through Tampa on I-275 south to **St Petersburg Beach** (105 miles/

> BRIT TIP: During the summer the locals all get the urge to head for the beach at weekends, so unless you leave before 9am and come back after 8pm you will encounter serious traffic queues.

169km) or **Clearwater Beach** (110 miles/177km; see also page 238), while heading further south offers a string of equally beautiful cities and resorts, all of which feature stunning white-sand beaches, great fishing, watersports and far fewer crowds than you would imagine. The sea is also a touch warmer and calmer on this side of Florida, so it is more suitable for small children.

Around 2 hours-plus brings you to the artsy **Bradenton/Sarasota** area (down I-4 then I-75), which features the superb beachfronts of **Anna Maria Island** (charming and secluded beaches), **Longboat Key** and **Venice** ('the shark tooth capital of the world' and great for fossil hunters). Go further south (about 170 miles/272km) and you have **Charlotte Harbor**, Florida's second-largest bay after Tampa Bay, and home to the more low-key destinations of **Punta Gorda**, **Port Charlotte**, **Englewood** and **Boca Grande**. From here, the **Fort Myers/Sanibel** area is only a short drive. This is part of the mini tropical paradise of the **Lee Island Coast**, immediately south of Charlotte Harbor, featuring the history and nature-rich city of **Fort Myers** and funky **Pine Island**, plus the barrier islands and dazzling beaches of **Fort Myers Beach**, **Sanibel Island**, **Captiva Island** and **Bonita Beach**, all renowned for sea shells, quirky shops and great nature tours. Continue south (about 230 miles/368km) and you have the magnificent **Naples** and **Marco Island**, 2 of Florida's less well-

Extreme games in St Petersburg

Florida's Beach: St Pete/Clearwater

The huge stretch of beaches and 'cities' from St Pete Beach to Clearwater (collectively known as Florida's Beach) represent the heart of the Florida Beach experience, with a wonderful array of attractions as well as 35 miles (56km) of lovely white sands and an average 361 days of sunshine a year. **St Petersburg** itself, just across the Howard Frankland Bridge from Tampa, is a bright, attractive city, with a range of developments, both recent and historical, which makes a visit worthwhile. Take time here for the wonderful **Dali Museum** (open 9.30am–5.30pm Mon–Sat, 12 noon– 5.30pm Sun, to 8pm on Thur; $13 for adults ($11 for seniors, $7 for 5–9s), and the **Bay Walk** complex of shops, restaurants and a 20-screen cinema. An additional assortment of museums (notably the elegant **Museum of Fine Arts**, the newly expanded **St Petersburg Museum of History** right on the Pier, the exceedingly child-friendly **International Museum** and the fascinating **Great Explorations** – look up more at www.stpete.org/museums/, pedestrian-friendly steets and the Pier all provide plenty of interest, while fan-friendly **Tropicana Field** hosts the Tampa Bay Devil Rays baseball team – April to September – for another slice of highly recommended local fun (tickets from $5; www.devilrays.com).

Out in the **Beaches**, from the 800-acre (324-ha) Fort De Soto Park in the south to stunning **Caladesi Island** in the north, there is plenty to do, too, with the likes of Treasure Island, Sand Key and St Pete Beach all receiving the Blue Wave Award for cleanliness and safety. **Fort De Soto Park** offers free walking tours of its Spanish-American War era fort and wilderness areas and has one of the prettiest beaches (voted America's No 1 beach in 2005, ahead of locations in Hawaii and California).

John's Pass Village and Boardwalk is an unusual shopping district full of art galleries and restaurants (and home to the fun Pirate Cruise daily – a replica sailing ship that offers a 2-hour party cruise around the waters of Treasure Island; $30 for adults and $20 for children, inclusive of beer, wine

known seaside treasures. Naples is both a fresh, modern city with plenty of attractions (notably the Museum of Art, plus great shopping) and a major beach destination while Marco Island is more seaside splendour as well as a major national wildlife refuge. This is also a great base from which to explore the wonderful Florida Everglades. For more info, check out www.visitflorida.com/destinations/.

> BRIT TIP: An early-morning tee-off in the summer can provide some peaceful and scenic golf.

SPORT

In addition to virtually every form of entertainment known to man, central Florida is one of the world's biggest sporting playgrounds, with a huge range of opportunities either to watch or play your favourite sport, whether it's on the water, up in the air or on good old terra firma.

Golf

Without doubt, the number one activity in Florida is golf, with some 168 courses within an hour's drive of Orlando. The weather, of course, makes it such a popular pastime, but some spectacular courses – many of them designed by world-famous and soft drinks; 727 423 7824), while **Dolphin Landings** in St Pete Beach is another big draw for its dolphin-watch cruises, Shell Island day trips and sunset sailings (the dolphin cruise is a real highlight for its guaranteed close-up encounters along the calm inland waterway; the 2-hour yacht voyage costs $30 for adults and $20 for children (727 367 4488, www.dolphinlandings.com).

Along at Indian Shores, you must not miss America's largest wild bird hospital, the **Suncoast Seabird Sanctuary**, usually caring for more than 500 injured patients. **Clearwater Beach** boasts the Marine Aquarium and Pier 60, where the daily sunset celebration, complete with craft stalls and music, is held. Reaching **Caladesi Island** brings you to one of the world's most picturesque beach spots and another Top 10 American location.

For those wishing to take it easy, rather than drive, the **Suncoast Beach Trolley** is the perfect transport link both along the beaches and into St Petersburg ($1.23/ride or $3 for an all-day pass; 727 530 9911, www.psta.net).

A suitably wide choice of accommodation is available, too. A range of **Superior Small Lodgings** combines desirable beachfront locations with small-scale, personalised service (check out the Seahorse Cottages and Apartments on Treasure Island Beach as the perfect example – with weekly rates from $450 for a 1-bedroom cottage; 727 367 2291, www.beachdirectory.com). Of course, there are upmarket hotels, too, witness the superbly equipped **Tradewinds Beach Resorts** (a 1,100-room complex of three resorts that combine their wide range of facilities; 727 562 1221, www.tradewindsresort.com) on St Pete Beach and the huge (and hugely impressive) **Sheraton Sand Key Resort** at Clearwater Beach, a 10-storey edifice with 10 acres (4ha) of private beach and facilities ranging from floodlit tennis courts to a fitness centre, children's pool and playground (with supervised programmes in summer). Rates $149–299 (727 595 1611, www.beachsand.com). The area also boasts some 2,000 restaurants. For general info, visit www.floridasbeach.com.

8

names such as Greg Norman, Tom Watson, Arnold Palmer and Jack Nicklaus – add to the attraction, and there are numerous holiday packages geared towards keen golfers of all abilities. With an 18-hole round, including cart hire and taxes, from as little as $40 on some courses (and they average around $75), it is an attractive proposition and quite different for those used to British courses.

If you go in for 36-hole days, it is possible to save up to $30 by replaying the same course, while it is cheaper to play Monday to Thursday than Friday to Sunday.

Sculpted landscapes, manicured fairways and abundant use of spectacular water features and white-sand bunkers add up to some memorable golfing. The winter months are the high season, hence the most expensive, but many courses are busy year-round. Be aware also that some courses pair up golfers with little thought for age, handicap, etc. So, if 2 of you turn up, the chances are that you will play with 2 complete strangers ('A little frustrating when you get paired with 2 middle-aged ladies from Switzerland who have only just taken up golf,' says *Brit's Guide* reader John Cartlidge).

Virtually every course will offer a driving range to get you started, plus lockers, changing rooms and showers, while the use of golf carts is universal (and many include the amazing GPS positioning system which gives the yardage for every shot, plus the ability to order drinks or even lunch while you're on the course!). They all feature comforts like iced water stations and drinks carts that circulate the course (don't forget to tip the trolley drivers). Some have swimming pools, and all offer a decent bar and restaurant for that all-important 19th hole.

Your best starting point is to visit one of the 5 **Edwin Watts** golf shops around Orlando to pick up a free copy of the *Golfer's Guide* or the *Guide To Golf* for a handy introduction to most of the courses available (and even pick up a new set of clubs at the Watts National Clearance Center just south of Wet 'n Wild on I-Drive; 407 352 2535, www.edwinwatts.com). Alternatively, Tee-Times USA (1-888 465 3356) offers an excellent advice and reservation service. The Visit Florida organisation publishes an *Official Golf Guide* (850 488 8374, www.flasports.com, as does Daytona Beach (1-800 881 7065, www.golfdaytonabeach.com).

For a unique and personable touch, you can't beat the all-in-one golf instruction service of **Professional Golf Guides of Orlando**, led by owner/operator and PGA member Phillip Jaffe, who is a mine of golfing lore and knowledge, as well as great company. They take up to 3 golfers at a time around some of the area's finest courses, and can supply

transport and high-tech (graphite and titanium) clubs if required. The playing lesson is of the highest quality and includes full on-course instruction, course management strategies, full game analysis, game improvement suggestions, shot-making demos and a wrap-up lesson that will leave you with the knowledge and skills to take your game to the next level. It is an eye-opening experience to play alongside Phillip and his staff of PGA professionals (hey, he even managed to get me hitting the green from some way off, which is no mean feat!) and well worth it for the keen golfer who wishes to improve his or her game in one round. (Call 407 227 9869 for rates or visit www.progolfguides.com.)

Alternatively, the **Nick Faldo Golf Institute** on the lower portion of I-Drive (1-888 463 2536) is a great place to visit if you just want to hit a few golf balls.

Walt Disney World Resort in Florida has been quick to attract the golf fanatic, with five championship-quality courses, including the 7,000-yd (6,400-metre) **Palm**, rated as one of *Golf Digest's* top 25 (and reputedly the 18th here is one of the toughest holes in America), plus a 9-hole par-36 course, **Oak Trail**. Fees vary from $99–174 for Disney resort guests and $119–179 for visitors, with half-price reductions after 3pm. Call 407 939 4653 for tee-times. Private and group lessons are available under PGA professional guidance, with video analysis and a great range of club rentals. The rolling **Osprey Ridge** (up to 7,101yd/6,493m) and the visually intimidating **Eagle Pines** (up to 6,772yd/6,192m) are the 2 newest – introduced in 1992 – designed by master architects Tom Fazio and Pete Dye respectively.

Another luxury experience is available at the nearby **Hyatt Grand Cypress** on Vineland Road (407

Golf at Reunion Resort

239 1904, rates from $130–170 depending on season). It has 3 elegant 9-hole courses and a superb 18-hole links-style offering (all designed by golf legend Jack Nicklaus), which present a truly magnificent challenge.

MetroWest Country Club, on South Hiawassee Road to the north of Universal Studios (407 299 1099; $89–129), is a 7,051-yd (6,447-metre) masterpiece designed by Robert Trent Jones Snr and features elevated tees and greens, with pleasant rolling fairways and expansive bunkers.

The superb **Keene's Pointe** in Windermere to the north of *Disney* is Nicklaus's newest and most exciting course, measuring 7,173yd (6,559m) if played off the pro Bear tees (there are always 5 tees for the various handicaps, ladies and seniors). Surrounded by lakes, it has a truly impeccable look and outstanding facilities, including a pool (407 876 1461; $80–125).

The **Legacy Club at Alaqua Lakes** is a masterpiece of conservation and tranquillity (it is part of the Audubon preservation and restoration scheme) as well as a tour de force of lush fairways and weird and wonderful greens (a signature feature of Tom Fazio). Winding through some spectacular forest in the suburb of Longwood in Seminole County, it is a serious challenge for serious golfers (407 444 9995; $45–79).

Also in Seminole, **Magnolia Plantation** is another wonderful contrast, a heavily wooded and peaceful haven that feels miles from the theme park world and yet is less than half an hour away up I-4. Woven among the lakes and ponds of the Wekiva River basin, Phillip Jaffe rates it a 'must play' course (407 833 0818; $40–80).

Falcon's Fire in Kissimmee is an outstanding course, too, featuring the 'ProShot' digital caddy system

BRIT TIP: Some of the best tee times at the *Walt Disney World Resort in Florida* golf courses are reserved for Disney resort guests.

and water coolers on all golf carts. Plenty of water around the course assures a testing 18 holes, but it is very picturesque (407 239 5445; $77–147).

The **Orange Lake Country Club** is a huge vacation resort in Orlando (just 4 miles/6km from Disney) with two 18-hole courses, a 9-hole course and a par-3, floodlit 9 holes. The new **Legends at Orange Lake** course (designed by Arnold Palmer) is their top-of-the-range offering (407 239 1050; $57–119). **Kissimmee Oaks** features some majestic moss-draped oaks and local wildlife as well as 18 holes of memorable lakeside golf, all just 3½ miles (6km) south of Highway 192 in Kissimmee in the Oaks Community off John Young Parkway (407 933 4055; $50–80).

Down on I-Drive, the former International Golf Club opposite the Faldo Golf Institute has been renamed **Marriott's Grande Pines**, with new greens that run fast and true. However, its strategic location close to the Convention Center means it books up early. You can get cheaper for similar quality further out and rates vary widely with the season, but its 7,012-yd (6,412-metre), par-72 style is hard to beat this close to the centre of things (407 239 6909; $60–130).

Legends at Orange Lake golf course

No less than four new courses
were built in 2003, with pride of
place going to **Grande Lakes
Orlando**, the amazing hotel/resort
complex just off John Young
Parkway. This Greg Norman-
designed masterpiece offers 18 holes
of genuine Florida nature with the
added benefit of a caddie-concierge
service (call for rates, 407 206 2400).
The monstrous **Harmony Golf
Preserve** in the town of Harmony in
Osceola County (out on the east
stretch of Highway 192, past St
Cloud) is an incredible 7,428yd
(6,792m) at its longest, designed by
Johnny Miller and with terrific
associated recreation facilities (407
891 8525; $40–100). The rolling and
aptly named **Victoria Hills** in
DeLand (mid-way between Orlando
and Daytona Beach, Exit 116 off I-
4) gets a big thumbs up from Phillip
Jaffe ('A great track – very
challenging!'), with a par-72 course
designed by Ron Garl and a superb
practice facility (386 738 6000;
$39–75).

The extravagant **Reunion Resort
and Club** (in Davenport, just to the
south of Disney, Exit 54 off I-4) is
still being developed as they
complete the massive resort around
the three courses – a Watson,
Palmer, Nicklaus collaboration, with
18 holes designed by each. Watson's
7,257-yd (6,636-metre)
Independence Course is possibly the
most challenging, with a style not
dissimilar to the famous Augusta

National (1-888 300 2434; $50–85).
However, golf here is restricted to
those who own property in the
resort or are staying here (highly
recommended; see page 86). The
main clubhouse is positively 5-star
in its design and facilities and each
course is quite superb just to look at,
never mind play. It certainly gets the
Jaffe seal of approval ('great
conditions, great layout').

New courses continue to spring
up all the time, notably **Mystic
Dunes**, just off the beaten path of
Highway 192 near the *Disney World*
entrance. This course winds through
native oaks and other vegetation and
is a real test of golf. The clubhouse
has a wonderful menu and is stocked
with the latest fashions and
equipment (407 787 5678; $42–95).
Shingle Creek (www.shinglecreek
golf.com) is a beauty from great
local architect Dave Harman, set in
dense oaks and pines along the
historic Shingle Creek, the
headwater that leads to the
Everglades. Located within a mile of
the Convention Center it is a world
class facility at the heart of what will
be a major convention resort in
2006 (407 996 9933; $63–110). The
Legends Golf and Country Club
is just 25 minutes from Disney, away
on Highway 27 towards Clermont,
and offers an extremely pleasant
layout with rolling hills (unsual for
Florida; 188 246 4843; $36–45).
Forest Lake Golf Club has quickly
become one of the best in the
region, ('One of my favourites,' says
Phillip Jaffe), with no houses to be
seen, just pure Florida. Just up the
Florida Turnpike (www.floridalake
golf.com) some 30 minutes from
Disney (407 654 4653; $43–83).
Again up to the north in Seminole
County, **Rock Springs Ridge
Golf Club** (another Jaffe
recommendation) offers 27 holes of
great golf in a contrasting, natural
setting (407 814 7474; $30–55). Not
a new course but one that has

gained recent prominence as host of the finals of the PGA Tour Qualifying event is **Orange County National** (www.ocngolf.com), an awesome 36 holes just to the north of Disney off Highway 545, with a 1-mile (1.6-km) circumference driving range and many target greens (407 656 2626; $80–120).

When you book, check on the club's dress code, as there are a few differences from course to course. Typically, you need a collared shirt, Bermuda shorts and no denim. There are also dozens of other choices; this is only a sample.

Mini-golf

Not exactly a sport, but definitely for holiday fun, are the many quite extravagant mini-golf centres around Orlando. They are a big hit with kids and good fun for all the family (if you have the legs left for it after a day at a theme park!). Several attractions and parks offer mini-golf as an extra, but for the best, try out the self-contained centres, of which there are a large variety.

Predictably, Disney has come up with some terrific courses of their own. **Disney's Fantasia Gardens Miniature Golf Courses**, next to the Swan Hotel just off Buena Vista Drive, is a 2-course challenge over 36 of the most varied holes of mini-golf you will find. Hippos dance, fountains leap and broomsticks march on the 18-hole crazy, golf-themed **Fantasia Gardens** – its style is taken from the Disney classic *Fantasia*, meaning lots of cartoon fun as the park's Imagineers challenge you with a riot of visual gags as well as some diabolically difficult mini-golf. Watch out for *Toccata and Fugue in D Minor* where good shots are rewarded with musical tones, and *The Nutcracker Suite*, where obstacles include dancing mushrooms!

Fantasia Fairways is a cunning putting course, complete with rough, water hazards and bunkers to test even the best golfers. The 18 holes range from 40ft (12m) to 75ft (23m), and it can take more than an hour to play a full round. Each course costs $10.65 (adult) and $8.52 (child), and they are open 10am–11pm every day.

The 36-hole **Winter-Summerland Miniature Golf Courses** are located at the entrance to *Disney's Blizzard Beach* water park. Divided into two 18-hole courses, these mini works of art feature a 'summer' setting of surf and beach tests (watch out for squirting fish), and a 'winter' variety of snow and ice-crafted holes, all with a welter of visual puns as befits the vacation resort of Santa's elves (yes, that's the theme, and kids love it – you can even see the marks where Santa landed his sleigh!). An adult round is $10.65 (3–9s $8.50), a double round is half price. Open 10am–11pm. You do not need Blizzard Beach admission for the mini-golf.

Elsewhere, **Pirate's Cove** has a twin-course set-up at Lake Buena Vista (by the Crossroads shopping plaza) and at I-Drive (just south of The Mercado), with mountain caves, waterfalls and rope bridges to test your skill and please the eye. The I-Drive location is one of the premier sites around here; the Captain's Course costs $8.95 for adults and $7.95 for children, while Blackbeard's Challenge is $8.49 and $7.49, with a 36-hole adventure at $12.49 and $11.49. Open 9am–11.30pm daily year-round (407 352 7378).

Tiki Island Golf is new on I-Drive (behind the smart Salt Island restaurant), another 36-hole set-up with enthusiasts able to putt through a 4-storey volcano and among tiki statues, caves, paddleboats and waterfalls. Similarly, the new **Hawaiian**

8

Rumble is a tropical fiesta, with 36 holes of ornate South Pacific icons surrounding the obligatory volcano and other unique 'hazards' (in 2 locations, on I-Drive next to Wonderworks and on Vineland Road, Highway 535, a mile south of I-4; $9.95 and $7.95, or $14.95 and $11.95 for 36 holes. **River Adventure Golf** (on Highway 192, almost opposite Medieval Times) offers a Mississippi River adventure with rolling rapids, waterfalls and an authentic water wheel. **Bonanza Miniature Golf and Gifts** (next door to the Magic Mining Co restaurant on west Highway 192) has an imaginative – and tricky – 36 holes with a gold mining theme. **Pirate's Island** (further east along Highway 192) is another spectacular 36-hole spread, while arguably the most impressive of the lot is the **Congo River Golf and Exploration Co.**, which has courses on Highway 192, I-Drive and Highway 436 in Altamonte Springs. They could almost be Disney-inspired, they are so artificially scenic. The Kissimmee location also has paddleboats, while I-Drive has go-karts, and all have games and video arcades. Charges are $8.95 for a single round and $14.95 for a double (look out for money-off coupons on www.congoriver.com).

Open 10am–11pm Mon–Thur, 10am–midnight Fri and Sat (weather permitting).

Freshwater fishing

Freshwater fishing on Central Florida's abundant rivers and lakes (St John's River, Kissimmee Chain of Lakes, and Lake Tohopekaliga, for example) attracts enthusiasts worldwide. In addition, many visitors find a quiet day of fishing provides a highly enjoyable and welcome change of pace. The primary draw for most out-of-towners is the opportunity to catch giant Florida bass – which often grow to record-breaking size in the area's grassy waters – and to view some of the local and plentiful wildlife in its natural environment.

To fish in a freshwater lake, river, or stream you need a Florida Freshwater Fishing License, which you can buy online from the Florida Fish and Wildlife Commission (http://myfwc.com/license/index.html – have your credit card handy). You will be issued a temporary licence number within minutes, which enables you to fish right away. A permanent licence will be mailed to you within 48 hours. The cost of a 7-day licence is $17.

Fishing at Clearwater

It is also advisable to book a reservation for a guided trip 2 or more weeks in advance, especially in holiday periods. **Cutting Loose Expeditions** is operated by A Neville Cutting, one of America's leading fishing adventurers. Cutting, who maintains high standards with his guides, can organise fresh or seawater expeditions and arrange hotel pick-up if necessary. Rates start at $200 for a half-day's bass fishing (2 fishermen per boat with a licensed guide). Bait and licence are included. Other trips, including offshore fishing for marlin, can be arranged. Call 407 629 4700, or write to Cutting Loose Expeditions, PO Box 447, Winter Park, Florida 32790-0447.

Want to catch giant Florida bass, virtually guaranteed? Then look for **AJ's Freelancer Bass Guide Service**, the oldest continuously operating guide service in central Florida. Freelancer specialises in trophy bass fishing on Lake Tohopekaliga, just minutes from Disney. Toho is rated the best big bass lake in the USA, and AJ's holds the record for largemouth bass here – 16lb 10oz! Saltwater guide trips are also offered. *The Freelancer* is owned and operated by Captain A James Jackson, one of the top professional fishing guides in the country. Jackson is featured in fishing magazines and a book on fishing around the world (*Adventure Fishing* by H Gilbey, Dorling Kindersley). Anglers rate Freelancer guide trips as one of the greatest fishing experiences anywhere, providing a highly personalised service to both experienced and novice fishermen. All guides are experienced, full-time professionals and run trips of 4, 6 and 8 hours. For rates, services, photos, testimonials and seasonal fish reports, check out Jackson's excellent website at www.orlandobass.com. For reservations call 407 348-8144 or e-mail capjackson@aol.com.

Seminole County has its share of fishing action, too. Check out **Spotted Tail** for a good range of angling adventures with fly and light tackle (407 977 5207, www.spottedtail.com).

Water sports

Florida is mad keen on water sports of all types. So, on any area of water bigger than your average pond, don't be surprised to find the locals water-skiing, jet-skiing, knee-boarding, canoeing, paddling, windsurfing, boating or indulging in any other watery pursuits.

Walt Disney World Resort in Florida offers all manner of boats, from catamarans to canoes and pedaloes, and activities, from water-skiing to parasailing, on the main **Bay Lake**, as well as the smaller **Seven Seas Lagoon Crescent Lake** and **Lake Buena Vista**. Parasailing (from *Disney's Contemporary Resort* – see page 64) comes in 2 price categories, a Regular flight which goes up to 450ft (137m) for 8–10 minutes, and a Premium flight up to 600ft (183m) for 10–12 minutes. It costs $85–105 solo or $135–155 tandem, while boat rentals (from a range of resorts) vary from $8/hour (14-ft/4-metre sailboats and catamarans) to

Disney's Winter-Summerland mini-golf

© Disney

8

$66.04/hour (21-ft/6-metre pontoon boats). For reservations, call 407 939 7529.

Various other locations can provide a variety of watersports, and two worth trying are **Buena Vista Watersports** (for jet skis – $45/half-hour – waterski, wakeboard and tube rides – $70/half-hour) on Little Lake Bryan next to the Holiday Inn Sunspree on Highway 535 (www.bvwatersports.com) and **Orlando Watersports Complex** just off the Beeline Expressway (528) near Orlando International airport (www.orlandowater sports.com). This latter is a highly elaborate teaching facility featuring wakeboarding and waterskiing, by boat and suspended cable, for novices and experts alike. It has a huge range of classes and options, for individuals, groups and even birthday parties. Check out its website, call 407 251 3100 or try International Divers (www.swim dolphins.com) for some interesting tours and packages.

Horse riding

Orlando is home to one of the foremost equestrian centres in America – the **Grand Cypress Equestrian Center**, which is part of the 1,500-acre (608-ha) Grand Cypress Resort, and all its rides and facilities are open to non-residents. This stunningly equipped equine haven offers a dazzling array of opportunities for horse enthusiasts of all abilities.

A full range of clinics, lessons and other instructional programmes are available, from half-hour kids' sessions to all-summer academies, plus a variety of trail rides. Serious horse riders will note this was the first American equestrian centre to be approved by the British Horse Society, and it operates the BHS test programme. Inevitably, this 5-star

facility does not come cheap but it is a worthwhile experience, especially for children. Private lessons are $55/half hour or $100/hour, while a package of eight 1-hour group lessons is $280. Young Junior Lessons (15-minute supervised rides for ages 3–7) are $25, while the Western Trail Ride (a 50-minute excursion for novice riders, minimum age 10) is $45 per person.

The Center is open 8.30am–6pm Mon–Fri, 8.30am–5pm Sat and Sun, and can be found by taking Exit 68 on I-4 on to Route 535 north, turning left after half a mile (1km) at the traffic lights and then following the road north for a mile (1.6km) past the entrance to the Grand Cypress Hotel, and it's on the right (407 239 1938, www.grandcypress. com/equestrian_center).

On a smaller scale and none the less charming is the **Horse World Riding Stables** on Poinciana Boulevard, just 12 miles (19km) south of Highway 192. This gets you more out into the wilds and you can spend anything from an hour to a full day enjoying the rides and lessons on offer. The 3 main rides are the Nature Trail ($39), a walking-only tour of 45–50 minutes, for beginners aged 6 and up, through 750 acres (304ha) of untouched Florida countryside, the Intermediate Trail (10 years and up) for nearly 1 hour ($47), and the Advanced Private Trail, a 75- to 90-minute trip for advanced riders with private guide ($69). There is also a picnic area with fishing pond, playing fields, pony rides for under 7s ($7) and farm animals to pet. Riding lessons are $49/hour for group or private lessons. A 3-hour Children's Horse Camp (for 8–14-year-olds) is available on Saturdays at 9am (call for prices). There is no charge for just looking, and the stables are open 9am–5pm daily (407 847 4343, www.horseworldstables.com).

Spectator events

When it comes to spectator events, Orlando is not quite as well furnished as other big American cities, but there is always something for the discerning sports fan who would like to see a local big match. There are no top-flight American football or baseball teams here, but there is an indoor version of gridiron (American football) called Arena Football, plus Spring Training (pre-season) for several baseball teams (notably Atlanta in *Disney's Wide World of Sports*).

The main sport is **basketball** and the team is Orlando Magic of the National Basketball Association (NBA). The season runs from November to May (with exhibition games in October), and the only drawback is the 16,000-seat **TD Waterhouse Center** where they play (on Amelia Street, Exit 83B off I-4, turn left, then left again) is occasionally fully booked. Contact the Center's box office (407 649 3245) to see if there are any tickets left, although you will need to call in person to buy them (from $10 up in the gods to $100 courtside), or you can call TicketMaster on 407 839 3900 for credit card bookings.

The Orlando Predators, one of America's top **Arena Football** teams, are also popular at the same venue (from February to June, $10–50; call several days in advance to see one of their lively home games that feature some great entertainment as well as their fast, hard-hitting version of indoor gridiron).

For the real thing in gridiron terms, the nearest teams in the **National Football League** are the Tampa Bay Buccaneers, 75 miles (120km) to the west, the Miami Dolphins, some 3–4 hours' drive to the south, down the Florida Turnpike, or the Jacksonville Jaguars way up the east coast past Daytona, a 3-hour drive up I-4 and I-95.

Again, TicketMaster can give you ticket prices ($30–60) and availability (Sep–Dec; and the Buccaneers sell out early these days). Local excursion company (and *Brit's Guide* partner) International Divers also runs a limited number of trips to Jacksonville each season, and these are well worth seeking out (see pages 227–228).

A Spring Training **baseball** opportunity can be seen at Osceola County Stadium in Kissimmee, where the Houston Astros take up home for the month of March. Being part of the audience here is to experience a genuine slice of Americana. Call 321 697 3201 for more details, or TicketMaster to book tickets on 407 839 3900. In truth, the best opportunity here is to take in a Tampa Bay Devil Rays' game in St Petersburg, as tickets are nearly always available and their indoor stadium is superb (see page 249).

Disney's Wide World of Sports Complex™

The best all-round sports facility in the area is inevitably a Disney project, although there are only a handful of genuine spectator events here. *Disney's Wide World of Sports Complex™* is a 220-acre (86-ha), state-of-the-art complex, featuring 30 sports and is quite awesome to wander round even when no one is playing. The complex's main features are a 7,500-seater baseball stadium, a softball quadraplex, an 11-court tennis complex, sports field and the **Official All Star Café®** with a massive array of sports memorabilia and even themed food. The Cracker Jack Stadium is home for spring training of baseball's mighty **Atlanta Braves**, and the crowds flock in for pre-season games in March (highly recommended).

The complex is also home from

mid July for a month to the NFL's **Tampa Bay Buccaneers** as they begin their pre-season training, and it is an eye-opening experience to watch these amazing athletes in action, even if it is only in practice. A 20-acre (8-ha) expansion in 2004 added more fields for soccer, lacrosse and American football, plus four extra baseball and softball fields. Standard admission is $10.50 for adults and $7.75 for 3–9s, but it is also an optional extra with all Premium and Ultimate tickets (excluding special events). *Disney's Wide World of Sports Complex*™ can be found off Osceola Parkway, on Victory Way. Call 407 939 4263 for details of events and prices.

The **Walt Disney World Marathon** is a major annual sporting event and its 12th running will be on January 8, 2006. Some 13,500 runners take part – including some of the world's leading athletes – drawing huge crowds, as the route takes in all four theme parks. Be aware the parks face some serious disruption but, as with the London Marathon, the Disney version also serves up a great spectacle. The annual **Half-Marathon** takes place on the same weekend (www.disney worldsports.com).

Bronc riding

Fitness centres

You may decide you can't spend a full 2 weeks here and not go to the gym at least once (as if walking all round the parks won't keep you in trim!). So here, especially for the health-conscious, is a quick guide to your fitness centre choice: **Ritz-Carlton Spa**, 4012 Central Florida Parkway (407 206 2400; Guest Pass $25; Spa and Fitness Center included in daily guest pass); **The Orlando Fitness and Racquet Club**, 825 Courtland St (407 645 3550; 6am–9pm Mon–Fri; 7am–8pm Sat and Sun; guest fee $10; full service fitness centre with childcare); **World Gym**, 5600 West Colonial Dr (407 447 5800; 8am–10pm Mon–Fri, 8am–6pm Sat and Sun; guest fee $15; childcare); **Paramount Health Clubs**, 2317 North Orange Ave (407 898 4884; 6am–9.30pm Mon–Thur, 6am–8pm Fri, 9am–5pm Sat, noon–5pm Sun; guest fee $5; childcare); **Ladies' Workout Express**, 12086 Collegiate Way (407 243 9835; 8am–8pm Mon–Fri, 10am–5pm Sat; guest fee $10; women only); **Creative Health and Fitness**, 1218 South John Young Parkway (407 933 1300; 6am–10pm Mon–Fri, 8am–7pm Sat, 9am–2pm Sun; guest fee $10; childcare).

Rodeo

An all-American pursuit straight out of the Old West, the **Silver Spurs Rodeo** is staged twice a year at the brand new, 8,300-seat Silver Spurs Arena. The biggest event of its kind in the south-east, it is held in mid-October and the last week in February. However, it sells out fast so book well in advance on 407 677 6336 or www.silverspursrodeo.com. The event features classic bronco and bull riding and attracts top competitors from as far away as Canada. The new arena is part of the $84-million **Osceola Heritage**

Park, which includes Osceola County Stadium (for baseball) and the Kissimmee Valley Livestock Show and Fair Pavilion. The **Silver Spurs Arena** is a state-of-the-art facility that can also be used for concerts, and there is not a bad seat in the house. The ease with which they convert it from the rodeo venue and back again, with truckloads of dirt, is quite amazing.

On a slightly smaller scale, the **Kissimmee Rodeo** is held every Friday at 8pm (except when the Silver Spurs is on) at the Kissimmee Sports Arena, on Hoagland Boulevard 2 miles (3km) south of Highway 192. Events include calf roping, steer wrestling and bull riding, and admission is $18 for adults and $9 for children 12 and under. Kids love the live action, which can be surprisingly rugged (if not dangerous), and there is even a kids' contest – grab the ribbon from the calf's tail! The **Catch Pen Saloon** lounge is open 8pm–2am Fri and Sat, and 6pm–2am Sun, with line dancing 6pm–8pm and $1 drinks (407 933 0020, www.ksarodeo.com).

Motor sport

For the guaranteed ultimate in high-speed thrills, *Walt Disney World Resort in Florida* has its own speedway oval where **Richard Petty Driving Experience** is based (in the

> BRIT TIP: Race fan Alan Rogers, of Chester, rates Daytona USA highly: 'Try the hands-on Pit Stop Live, the excellent *Daytona 500* movie and the 30-minute tour of the track. It's a real thrill.'

car park for the *Magic Kingdom*, NOT at the *Wide World of Sports Complex*™). Here you can experience one of their 650-bhp stock cars as either driver or passenger at up to 145mph (233kph). The programmes have been devised by top NASCAR driver Richard Petty and offer the three-lap **Ride-Along Experience**; a 3-hour **Rookie Experience** (with tuition and 8 laps of the speedway); the **Kings Experience** (tuition plus 18 laps); and the **Experience of a Lifetime** (an intense 30-lap programme).

The Ride-Along Experience will probably appeal to most (16 and over only) – 3 laps of the 1.1-mile (1.8-km) circuit with an experienced, race-proven driver lasting just 37 seconds a lap but an unbelievable blast all the way. Your initial take-off from the pit-lane takes you 0–60mph (97kph) in a couple of seconds and you are straight into Turn One with your

8

Disney's Wide World of Sports Complex

brain some distance behind. It is a bit like flying at ground level, it is hot and noisy and you must wear sensible clothes (you have to climb in through the window), but it is definitely the Real Thing in ride terms and a huge thrill.

You don't need to book for the Ride-Along Experience, which is available daily and there is no admission fee, so you can come along just to watch (8am–1pm). The 3 driving programmes (not Tue or Thur) all require reservations, while the track is occasionally closed for race testing from October to April. However, before you get carried away, wait for the prices: $99 for the Ride-Along Experience; $379 for the Rookie Experience; $749 for the Kings and $1,249 for the Lifetime Experience – you must be 18 or over for the last 3 (407 939 0130, www.1800be petty.com).

Race fans will also want to check out **Daytona International Speedway** just up the road in Daytona (take I-4 east, then I-95 and Highway 92) for lots more big-league car and motorcycle thrills. It hosts more than a dozen race weekends a year, including stock cars, sports cars, motorcycles, go-karts and trucks, and highlights are the **Daytona 500** (February 20, 2005), and **Pepsi 400** (first Sunday in July). The big events attract more than 200,000 devotees and provide some of the most colourful sport anywhere in the world (386 253 7223, www.daytonainternational speedway.com).

Daytona USA, an interactive motor sport-themed attraction, is here as well, offering a series of hands-on exhibits, rides and films to give you a taste of all the high-speed action. Change tyres in a timed pit stop, design and video test a racing car, commentate on a race and experience the *Daytona 500* film. Other elements include Acceleration Alley (for an additional fee), with full-size NASCAR simulators combining motion, video and sound to capture the thrills of head-to-head racing at more than 200mph (322kph), and Daytona Dream Laps, another elaborate motion simulator to put riders inside the Daytona 500 itself. The history and great moments of speedway are well detailed and there is a good gift shop. A half-hour, open-sided tram tour of the speedway stops in Pit Road, giving a real close-up of this amazing arena. New in 2004 were *NASCAR 3-D: The IMAX Experience* and *Daytona 500: The Movie* at the **Pepsi IMAX Theater**.

Open 9am–7pm (not Christmas Day) it costs $21.50 for adults, $18.50 for seniors (60+) and $15.50 for 6–12s (under 6s free with adult), while the Speedway tour on its own is $7.50/person (386 947 6800, www.daytonausa.com).

The Richard Petty Driving Experience is available here too (for those aged 16 and over) and the $125 fee for 3 laps of the world-famous, steeply banked 2½-mile (4-km) tri-oval also includes entrance to Daytona USA.

Okay, that's the full daytime scene, now let's check out everything there is to know about the night-time entertainment...

Orlando by Night
(or, Burning the Candle at Both Ends)

Hands up those who still have plenty of energy left! Right, this chapter is especially for you. If we can't wear you out at the theme parks and Florida's other attractions, we'll just have to resort to a full-frontal assault on your sleep time.

For, when it comes to night-time fun and frolics, Orlando again has a dazzling collection of possibilities, from its purpose-built entertainment complexes, through its range of evening dinner shows and on to a full array of bars and nightclubs. The choice is suitably widespread and almost always high in quality.

Unfortunately, the development that started the evening entertainment ball rolling has now closed down. **Church Street Station**, in the heart of the downtown area, shut in 2001 and there is still no firm news of what will take its place. The site formerly occupied by Rosie O'Grady's, the Cheyenne Saloon, the Orchid Room, Apple Annie's Courtyard, Phineas Fogg's and Lili Marlene's is now home to a comedy club – **Orlando Improv**, a mini (non-smoking) theatre with a separate bar/dining area – and **GameTime** sports bar and grill (open 4pm until midnight Wed–Sun; 321 281 8181). Orlando Improv features stand-up comedians from various American TV shows (DEF JAM, BET and Comic Review) but plays to a largely adult audience, i.e. 21 and over only, except for Friday nights, when it's 18 and up. Shows run at 7 and 8pm

Wed–Sun – smoke-free on Thur and Sat – with a 9:30 and 10.30 performance on Fri and Sat. Admission price varies but is usually around $22; (321 281 8000, www.orlandoimprov.com).What used to be Crackers Restaurant is now **Louis'**, an equally upscale fine dining experience. There are plans afoot to redevelop the Station for offices, retail and more restaurants, but they have still to confirm any concrete timescale for renovation.

Disney joined the big evening entertainment concept in 1987 with **Pleasure Island**, an imaginative range of clubs, discos and restaurants, and it is continuing to refine the formula to keep it fresh and appealing. **Disney's BoardWalk Resort**, which opened its doors in 1996, has added more to their night-time options.

International Drive (I-Drive) caught up with this process in 1997 when **The Pointe Orlando** opened. Although its prime focus is shopping and restaurants, it has a strong evening entertainment component with the big Muvico 21-screen cinema centre, its lively bars and two good nightclubs.

Finally, Universal Orlando got with the beat in late 1998 with the opening of **CityWalk**, possibly the most elaborate and sophisticated centre of the lot. They all represent yet another slick opportunity for you to be dazzled and relieved of your cash in the name of holiday fun. However, you should try to experience at least one.

DOWNTOWN DISNEY

The large-scale development of what is now *Downtown Disney* (the old Village Marketplace and *Pleasure Island*) has evolved into a 3-part complex (*Downtown Disney* Marketplace, *Pleasure Island* and West Side) doubling the size of the old site and providing 2 key evening entertainment sources.

Pleasure Island

This is the traditional nightclub zone, which packs in the locals as well as the tourists and where every night is New Year's Eve. You must be 18 or over to enter (unless accompanied by a parent), while you must be at least 21 to enter 2 of the clubs (see below). *Pleasure Island* (which forms the centrepiece, or linking part, of *Downtown Disney*) consists of 7 original club venues and just about every music type you can think of, plus several novel twists. The **Rock 'n Roll Beach Club** is a multi-level live music venue featuring 40 years of classic rock (mainly the 1980s and 1990s) with a resident cover band and DJs. It also boasts pool tables, arcade games and several bars. Serious clubbers head for **Mannequins Dance Palace** (21 and over), a huge, popular disco, with a revolving dance floor, mirrored walls, dry ice and lasers, plus a pounding sound system and superb lighting. At the **Comedy Warehouse**, the highly talented and quick-witted Improv Co gives

Fun at Arabian Nights

© Disney

Downtown Disney® West Side

periodical shows with guest 'volunteers' (beware sitting near a phone – you WILL end up in the show!). Queuing can begin up to half an hour before a performance, which lasts for around 45 minutes and is guaranteed to be different every time. For a touch of retro groovin', **8Trax** is a homage to 1970s music, dance and styles (right down to the lava lamps) and usually draws a lively crowd of all ages.

The unmissable **Adventurers' Club** is a personal favourite, a 2-storey entertainment lounge, in 1920s Gentleman's Club style, which comes to life around you (watch the animal heads and masks!) and the stars of the shows mix with the guests. Again an element of comedy improvisation is mixed in with the scripted action and, if the cast happens to pick on you, don't try to win a battle of wits – they have the microphone, remember!

The **BET Soundstage Club**™ (21 and over) is a totally modern offering, with an interactive VJ/DJ and featuring the best of R & B, soul and hip-hop sounds. **Motion**

BRIT TIP: Taking a form of photo ID is essential for *Pleasure Island*, even if you happen to be the 'wrong' side of 30. No ID equals no alcohol, and there are no exceptions.

(formerly the Wildhorse Saloon) is a cavernous dance club, featuring Top 40 to Alternative music, animated DJs and a giant TV screen. This is another happening club, and is especially popular with the locals at weekends (18 and over only). In addition, the outdoor **West End Stage**, which hosts *Pleasure Island's* resident band and occasional big-name acts, is the focus for the street party and fireworks at midnight, because, of course, every night is New Year's Eve…

As well as the clubs, *Pleasure Island* has a range of 6 shops, including **Reel Finds** for film memorabilia, **DTV**, an up-scale Disney fashion store and **Changing Attitudes**, offering some stylish men's and women's clothing. You can also grab a snack at the **Missing Link Sausage Co** (hot dogs, burgers, sandwiches and fries). New in summer 2005 was Raglan Road, an Irish-themed pub, with lively musical entertainment, matching food and a genuine Emerald Isle style where you really can enjoy the craic.

For a full-scale meal, the neighbouring **Portobello Yacht Club** offers excellent northern Italian cuisine in smart, lively surroundings. Of course, you can also visit the many eating outlets elsewhere around *Downtown Disney*, including **Planet Hollywood**® (the largest of this world-wide movie-themed chain, and the busiest restaurant of the lot), *Brit's Guide*

BRIT TIP: If you need to escape the *Downtown Disney* hurly-burly, head upstairs in the Virgin™ Megastore, where their great coffee/ sandwich shop is a relative oasis of calm offering a good range of snacks and drinks, usually queue-free.

favourite **Wolfgang Puck's Café and Dining Room**, **Cap'n Jack's Restaurant** (for great chowder, crabcakes, shrimp or the trademark 'fishbowl' margaritas), and **Fulton's Crab House** (for some of the best seafood in Orlando – see page 287). Lunch is served from 11am–4pm and dinner from 5–11pm.

As ever, to make an **Advanced Dining Reservation** booking for a Disney restaurant, call 407 939 3463 (see page 64). *Pleasure Island* is open from 7pm–2am daily and there is no charge to wander the shops and restaurants. However, there is a $9.95 charge to enter any of the clubs, or you can purchase a 1-night Club Pass for $20.95. It is also included as a Plus Pack Option with all Premium tickets and included for the full 2- or 3-week duration with Ultimate tickets. Single club tickets can be purchased only at *Pleasure Island* itself or at *Downtown Disney* Guest Services.

West Side

This is the newest element of the Downtown Disney expansion and incorporates the AMC® Pleasure Island 24 Theaters Complex with 24 screens and 6,000 seats in state-of-the-art surroundings, as well as the…

9

Pirates Dinner Adventure

Cirque du Soleil®

The most eye-catching part of West Side is home to the greatest show on earth (or at least, the greatest we've seen anywhere in the world), the Cirque du Soleil® production *La Nouba*™. Twice a day, five times a week, the company's purpose-built, 1,671-seater theatre stages the most stupendous combination of dance, circus, acrobatics, comedy and live music in a 90-minute show that involves more than 60 performers. Anyone familiar with the unique styling, outrageous costumes and captivating sounds of the world-famous Cirque company will know what to expect, but even they will be left in awe by this multi-dimensional assault on the senses. It features trampolines, trapezes, balancing acts and even mountain bikes, woven with innovative dance routines, comedy (watch out for the inspired clowns) and spell-binding music, all with the most magnificent staging.

Words alone do not do it justice – go and see it. It is not cheap, but I believe it is worth every cent. Booking is vital and can be done up to 6 months in advance on 407 939 7719. Shows are at 6pm and 9pm Tue–Sat but try to be early for some excellent pre-show fun. There are 3 pricing groups: Cat. 1 (front centre seats) at $87 for adults and $65 for children (3–9); Cat. 2 at $75 and $56; and Cat. 3 at $59 and $44 (but there is hardly a bad seat in the house).

More venues

The other *Downtown Disney* elements are a fantastic mix of live music, fine dining, unique shopping and *DisneyQuest*, the ultimate in interactive game arcades.

The cavernous **House of Blues**®, a combination live music venue and restaurant in backwoods Mississippi style, is a must for anyone even vaguely interested in blues, rock 'n' roll, R & B, gospel and jazz and some top-name bands play here (407 934 2583, www.hob.com), while their trademark **Gospel Brunch** on Sundays serves up some fabulous food with a full gospel show (10.30am and 1pm; $30 for adults, $15 for 3–9s). 'Praise the Lord and pass the biscuits', is their slogan, and it is a lot of fun.

The 500-seat restaurant next door to the concert hall also offers some fine fare, including catfish, jambalaya and a host of other delicious Cajun dishes, with more good, footstompin' live music, free, in the **Blues Kitchen** (Thur–Sat). The inevitable gift shop also stocks some quality merchandise.

Bongos Cuban Café™ (co-owned by Gloria and Emilio Estefan) brings the sights, sounds and tastes of Old Havana to another imaginative setting, with red-hot Latin music and some excellent Cuban fare. **The Wolfgang Puck**® **Café** offers a rich experience from the renowned Californian chef, with no less than four dining options: the Café, gourmet food in a casual setting; Wolfgang Puck Express, the fast-food version; B's Bar for sushi, seafood, pizzas and micro-brew beers; and the Dining Room, an upscale restaurant featuring the best of the group's international cuisine (407 938 9653). They cater for just about every taste (the sushi is to die for) and are extremely friendly, with excellent kids' menus and games.

The West Side shopping is also original and engaging, from the basic sweet shop **Candy Cauldron**, which resembles a fairytale dungeon, through the one-off outlets such as **Sosa Family Cigars**, **Celebrity Eyeworks** and the wonderfully stylish glass and ceramics of **Hoypoloi Gallery**, to the predictable souvenir stores and the truly mega **Virgin**™ **Megastore**, the largest music store in Florida, with more than 100 listening stations, a full-service café, hydraulic outdoor stage and a mean sound system!

DisneyQuest

The most unusual element to *Downtown Disney, DisneyQuest* opened in June 1998 and brought yet another novel idea to life. It is described variously as 'an immersive, interactive entertainment environment', the latest in arcade games, a series of state-of-the-art adventure rides or, as one Cast Member told me, 'a theme park in a box'. It houses 11 major adventures, such as CyberSpace Mountain (design and ride your own roller-coaster), Invasion – An Alien Encounter (a fun virtual-reality rescue mission), Virtual Jungle Cruise (shooting the rapids, prehistoric style) and Aladdin's Magic Carpet (more virtual-reality riding in best cartoon fashion), a host of old-fashioned video games in the Replay Zone, the latest sports games, a test of your imagination in Animation Academy and 2 futuristic cafés, Wonderland Café with computers and internet tables, the other, Food Quest, straight out of a space-age comic book (both operated by the excellent Cheesecake Factory).

Two additional highlights are Radio Disney SongMaker (a computer-generated professional audio system that creates a CD with you as the star!) and Pirates of the Caribbean: Battle for Buccaneer Gold (an amazing 3-D immersion in a swashbuckling, cannon-shooting

BRIT TIP: You can buy a combined annual pass for *DisneyQuest* and Disney's water parks at $137.39 for adults and $105.44 for 3–9s that can work out better value for multiple visits.

adventure for pirate treasure). The newest attraction, Ride the Comix! is another virtual-reality battle, this time with super-villains. You enter via the clever 'Cybrolator', which brings you to Ventureport, and you then have 4 main areas to explore: Score Zone (for most of the game-playing), Create Zone (hands-on activities to be your own 'Imagineer'), Replay Zone (a 'moonscape' of classic games and rides) and Explore Zone (a mix of virtual reality games and role-playing).

DisneyQuest is open 11.30am–11pm Sun–Thur, 11.30am–midnight Fri and Sat but, if you want to avoid the queues (the building admits only 1,500), go during the day. A 1-day ticket costs $32.02 ($26.63 for 3–9s, although it is a bit too elaborate for most youngsters) and teenagers love it.

Finally, the whole of *Downtown Disney* West Side is characterised at night by outstanding lighting effects and a vibrant, thrilling, almost intoxicating atmosphere.

Disney's BoardWalk

Disney's other big evening entertainment offering is part of their impressive **Disney's BoardWalk Resort**, where the waterfront entertainment district contains several notable venues (not counting the excellent micro-brewery and restaurant of the Big River Grille and Brewing Works, the thrilling ESPN Club for sports fans and the 5-star Flying Fish Café). **Jellyrolls** is a variation on the duelling piano bar, with the lively pianists conjuring up a humorous and often raucous evening of audience participation songs ($8 cover charge; 21 and over only; 7pm–2am).

The **Atlantic Dance** club features mainly modern dance music (it started life as a classic 1930s dance club and also moved through a

9

Latin phase) with both house and guest DJs, plus occasional live music, all with a huge dance floor and a great bar service and ambience. It is especially popular on Friday and Saturday nights (perhaps because there is no cover charge any more; 9pm–2am; closed Mon). It is strictly 21 and over, so remember your ID (no ID, no entry here). *Disney's Boardwalk Resort* also features some amusing stalls and live entertainers, which add to the carnival atmosphere, while the ESPN Club features regular celebrity (American) sports guests.

UNIVERSAL'S CITYWALK

As part of the big Universal Orlando development – and in direct competition with *Downtown Disney* – this 30-acre (12-ha) spread has just about everything in the world of entertainment. The resort's hub is a busy, bustling expanse of shops, restaurants, snack bars, open-air events and nightclubs. It offers a huge variety of cuisines, from fast food to fine dining, an unusual mix of speciality shops and a truly eclectic nightclub mix, from reggae to rock 'n' roll to salsa to jazz and high-energy disco. Unlike *Pleasure Island*, there is no overall entry fee, but you do pay a cover charge ($5–7) at the 7 clubs. You can also buy a **CityWalk Party Pass** ($9.95 plus tax) or **Party Pass with Movie** (one free film at the 20-screen Universal Cineplex; $19.95) for entry to all 6 (except one-off concerts at Hard Rock Live), while the FlexTicket includes a Party Pass.

The area splits into 3, with the main plaza featuring shopping and restaurants. Among the most original (and amusing) of the 13 shops are **Endangered Species**, with products designed to raise eco-awareness; **Quiet Flight**, for radical surf and beachwear; the retro-American decor

BRIT TIP: Park in Universal's multi-storey car park where there is no charge after 6pm for all the CityWalk venues. For more info on the complex, call 407 363 8000 or visit www.citywalkorlando.com.

of **Fossil** for leather goods, watches and sunglasses; the **Universal Studios Store** for park merchandise; and **Cartooniversal**, dedicated to cartoon-based gifts and toys featuring Spider-Man, Scooby-Doo and SpongeBob SquarePants.

For eating, you have the **NASCAR Café** (a must for motor-racing fans, 10am–late) with full-size stock cars and racing memorabilia, videos and interactive games while you dine on burgers, ribs, steaks and popcorn shrimp. **Pastamore** is a delightful indoor/outdoor Italian diner, with the choice of full-service dining (5pm–midnight) for pizza, pasta, grilled chicken and steaks or the **Pastamore Café** (8am–2am) for sandwiches, pastries and ice cream. **Emeril's** restaurant is at the 5-star end of the range, a sophisticated and vibrant journey into the cuisine of New Orleans master chef Emeril Lagasse. Fine wines and a cigar bar both add to Emeril's Creole-based gourmet creations, and if you don't try the Louisiana oyster stew here, you have missed a real treat (lunch 11.30am–2pm; dinner 5.30–10pm Sun–Thur, 5.30–11pm Fri and Sat). It also books up well in advance at weekends, so try weekdays (call 407 224 2424 to book). **Jimmy Buffet's Margaritaville** (11am–2am) is an island homage to Florida's laid-back musical hero, with 'Floribbean' cuisine (a mixture of Key West and Caribbean), live music and 3 bars, including the Volcano Bar, which 'erupts' margarita mix (!) when the blender needs filling. There is a cover charge ($5) after 10pm when their live band hits the stage.

Across the CityWalk waterway is the **Lagoon Front** location of another huge dining experience, the 2-storey **NBA City**, which is sure to thrill basketball fans with its Cage dining room, interactive playground area and Club lounge where you can watch live and classic games (11am–10.30pm Sun–Thur; 11am–11.30 pm Fri and Sat). Next door is the massive mock-Coliseum architecture of **Hard Rock Live**, a 2,500-seat concert venue with state-of-the-art staging and sound. Big-name bands and performers are on stage several times a week (Robbie Williams and Oasis have both played here) in this slightly retro rock 'n' roll theatre (407-351-LIVE, www.hardrocklive.com). Of course, you can't miss dining at the **Hard Rock Café** here, the world's largest example of this international chain, with its collection of rock 'n' roll memorabilia (including a pink 1959 Cadillac). It remains hugely popular, so try to get in early for lunch or dinner (11am–2am) to sample their classic diner fare. Collectors of Hard Rock souvenirs will also find prices in the excellent gift shop friendlier here than the UK.

Finally, you come to the **Promenade** area, which offers a choice of nightclubs and some more fine dining (notably in the case of Latin Quarter), plus the ubiquitous Starbucks coffee house. The **Decades** bar and diner (formerly the Motown Café) closed down in summer 2005, with word that Bubba Gump's Shrimp Factory (themed after the film *Forrest Gump*) was the likely replacement. The lower level consists of a large games arcade (open 11.30am–11pm Sun–Thur, 11.30am–2am Fri and Sat). **Bob Marley – A Tribute to Freedom** is a clever re-creation of

BRIT TIP: CityWalk too crowded? Can't get in any of the restaurants? Jump on one of the boats to the Hard Rock Hotel or Portofino Bay Hotel and you can usually dine without a wait at The Kitchen (Hard Rock) or Trattoria del Porto or Mama Della's (Portofino Bay).

Marley's Jamaica home, turned into a courtyard live music venue, restaurant and bars. The bands are excellent, the atmosphere authentic and the place really comes alive at night (4pm–2am, 21 and over after 10pm; cover charge $5 after 8pm).

Next up is **Pat O'Brien's**, a faithful reproduction of the famous New Orleans bar and restaurant (4pm–1am), with its Flaming Fountain courtyard, main bar and special duelling piano bar (6pm–2am, cover charge $5 after 9pm, 21 and over with passport ID). Excellent Cajun food and world-famous Hurricane cocktails are the order of the day, but don't drink too many and expect to walk home!

CityJazz is a real contrast, a hip, upmarket centre combining history, education and live music from a series of local and international musicians, with tapas-style food.

Hard Rock Café

Visually it is stunning, with good sound quality and, if you're keen on the live music, which varies from swing and R & B to pure jazz (8pm–1am Sun–Thur, 7pm–2am Fri and Sat, cover charge $5), you can easily spend all night here. From Thur–Sat, CityJazz becomes Bonkerz Comedy Club, with some outstanding stand-up comedy acts at 8pm (cover charge $7, but still included with CityWalk PartyPass).

For younger, club-minded visitors, **the groove** is the next generation in disco entertainment, a vivid, pounding, high-energy dance venue designed like a Victorian theatre but with the latest in club music, lighting and special effects (9pm–2am, cover charge $5; 21 and over only).

Finally, completing the Promenade tour is the **Latin Quarter**, a wonderful venue/restaurant that serves up a genuine slice of Latin American style in its atmosphere, music, dance, decor and cuisine. The food is outstanding – a combination of beef, fresh fish and poultry with tangy fruit sauces, spicy salsas and mouth-watering marinades (don't miss their version of rack of lamb) – the ambience is mesmerising and the sounds are so wonderfully vibrant and alive, you can't help dancing, even in your seat. From Cuba to Chile, here is a great experience, with the live bands whipping up a samba and salsa storm. Drop in for a meal or just check out who's playing the music on Thur, Fri and Sat (5pm–2am Mon–Fri, midday–2am Sat and Sun; cover charge $7 after 10pm). There is even a Latin Quarter Express dining window if you'd like a quick bite on the go.

Breathless yet? Well, there's still the **Universal Cineplex**, a 20-screen cinema complex with a 5,000 capacity and the latest in stadium seating, curved-screen visuals and high-tech sound systems.

The Pointe Orlando

This eye-catching development on I-Drive, almost opposite the Convention Center, is a mix of unique shops, cinemas, restaurants, the **WonderWorks** science centre (with its magic-themed dinner show), an arcade-style entertainment centre and two nightclubs. It is open all day but has plenty of evening appeal, too. It was due to undergo a major renovation in 2005–06 to add more dining options.

The big-name stores (open 10am–11pm) are all upscale and include some imaginative touches that make them stand out from the crowd (see page 295). The collection of bars and restaurants strive to be different too. On the main ground level you have **Johnny Rockets**, a highly entertaining 1950s-style diner with an indulgent burger-and-milkshake menu (and waiters and waitresses who perform dance routines if the right song comes on the jukebox!). **Dan Marino's Town Tavern** is a surprisingly elegant sports-themed diner (check out the football-shaped bar), with a mix of lively and intimate areas and a well-balanced menu from this former American football star. Head upstairs to the second level and you find **Lulu's Bait Shack** leading the way for New Orleans-style cuisine and entertainment (it looks like an old shack blown in from Bourbon Street). Then there is **Adobe Gila's**, a fine Mexican *cantina* featuring more than 70 tequilas (!) and some south-of-the-border dining delicacies (try the Gila Wraps), and the 'soon to be relatively famous' wings, burgers and seafood of **Hooters** (with its equally famous 'Hooter Girl' waitresses). Lulu's and Adobe Gila's are especially popular with locals and are often packed at weekends, as they stay open until 2am, while they feature live outdoor music and DJs several days a week. On a Friday or Saturday, the atmosphere should be kicking from 6.30pm, while on weekdays it is more likely to be from 8.30pm.

The big redevelopment means there will be more shopping and restaurant choice in 2006, so be sure to check www.askdaisy.net/orlando for the latest details.

The 21-screen **Muvico** cinema, with its wonderfully vast and cleverly themed entrance foyer, boasts state-of-the-art stadium seating and sound systems, and you can often see a newly released film here several months before it gets to the UK. By the way, American cinema popcorn is almost invariably of the SALTED variety!

Entertainment venue **Pacman Café** offers 3 floors of fun and games where you can 'dine, dance and defend the world'. An appealing restaurant (try its excellent burgers, salads or brick oven pizzas) occupies the ground floor, and you ride the escalator up to the entertainment levels. Here, you will find more than 100 interactive games and attractions (including a virtual-reality roller-coaster, rock-climbing challenge, several state-of-the-art shoot 'em up games, a new role-playing horse-race game, some arcade-style prize games and high-speed internet access), fully stocked bars, live music with resident DJs and two roof terraces that enjoy views over I-Drive. For the games, you can get Time cards for 1 or 2 hours ($22 or $28) or buy a Cash card for any amount. It is open 11.30am–midnight Sun–Thur, and 11.30am–1am Fri and Sat, and is also an ideal place for lunch (www.pacmancafe.com).

The Pointe also boasts 2 popular recent additions to the nightclub scene: **Matrix** (open 9pm–2am, Wed–Sun), a high-tech, high-energy, high-volume club, pulses to the techno beat for much of the time and has a kind of future-surreal decor that appeals to the younger (18–25) crowd. Age restrictions are strictly 18 and up (apart from Tue, when it's over 21). The dance floor is huge and is ringed by two video walls, 16 TV screens and a multi-million dollar light show, while the lounge features art deco loungers, chairs and loveseats. Thursday is Ladies' Night (with 3-for-1 drinks until midnight), Saturday is Inferno (top DJs, BreakBeats and Hip-Hop; 21 and over only) and Sunday is Latin Night.

Metropolis (open 9pm–2am Thur–Sun) offers a more sophisticated atmosphere, with retro Top 40 music in a plush disco environment. It has 7 Victorian billiards tables in the lounge area, various TV and video screens, and another large dance floor, and it tends to attract a slightly older crowd (25–35). It is 21 and over here only for men (18 and up for ladies; 25 and over only on Fridays), except for college night on Thursdays. At both clubs, the cover charge (after 10pm) varies per night (from $5–15, free for ladies over 21 on Fridays). Stylish dress is required (no jeans, baseball caps or trainers).

For more on The Pointe, call 407 248 2838 or visit www.pointeorlando.com.

DINNER SHOWS

Another source of evening entertainment comes in the many and varied dinner shows that are a major Orlando phenomenon. From murder mysteries to full-scale medieval battles, it's all wonderful imaginative fun, even if the food is usually quite ordinary. As the name suggests, it is live entertainment coupled with dinner and unlimited free wine, beer and soft drinks in a fantasy-type environment, where even the waiters and waitresses are in costume and taking part.

They always have a strong family appeal and you are usually seated at large tables where you can get to know other folks, too, but, at $35–45 for adults, they are not cheap (especially with taxes and tips). Beware, too, the attempts to extract more dollars from you with photos, souvenirs, etc.

Disney shows

Walt Disney World Resort in Florida's offerings here are often overlooked by visitors unless they are staying at one of the hotel resorts. For an excellent night of South Sea entertainment, try **Disney's Spirit of Aloha** (at the Luau Cove at *Disney's Polynesian Resort*). It's a bit expensive at $50.22 for adults (including tax and tip), and $25.43 for under 12s, but it is still good value as the 2-hour show features some splendid entertainment, varying from the fun to the thrilling (Hawaiian sounds, singers, dancers and other Polynesian acts, including the amazing Samoan fire juggler, all with a strong family story). You need to come hungry for this show, too, as the food is plentiful, with salad, roast chicken, ribs, rice and vegetables, plus a fresh fruit dessert (or peanut butter and jam sandwiches, macaroni cheese, chicken fingers and hot dogs for the kids). Beer, wine and soft drinks are all included, and shows are Tue–Sat at 5.15 and 8pm.

The **Hoop-Dee-Doo Musical Revue** at *Disney's Fort Wilderness Resort & Campground* is an ever-

Pirates of the Caribbean battle for Buccaneer Gold at DisneyQuest®

© Disney

popular nightly dinner show that maintains the resort's impressive cowboy theme, and has great food (all-you-can-eat ribs, fried chicken, corn on the cob, baked beans and strawberry shortcake, plus unlimited beer, sangria and soft drinks). Especially loved by children, it features the amusing song and dance of the Pioneer Hall Players in a merry American hoedown-style show. Okay, it's corny and a tad embarrassing to find yourself singing along with the hammy action, but it is performed with great gusto, and you're on holiday, remember! The Revue plays nightly at 5, 7.15 and 9.30pm at the Pioneer Hall, $50.22 for adults (inclusive of tax and tip), $25.43 for under 12s, and lasts almost 2 hours. Reservations are ALWAYS necessary but can be made up to 2 years in advance.

If you can't get enough of the Disney characters, **Mickey's Backyard Barbecue** could be for you. A twice-weekly dinner show (usually Tue and Thur) from Mar-Sept at 6.30pm at *Disney's Fort Wilderness* resort, it features Mickey and the gang in a country buffet-style dinner under an open-air pavilion with picnic tables, with live music, line dancing, rope tricks and other entertainment, and plenty of character interaction (great for younger children). The all-you-can-eat buffet offers BBQ pork ribs, baked chicken, hot dogs, burgers and salads with all the trimmings. Like all Disney dining, this is a no-smoking environment, but it may be cancelled if bad weather threatens. It costs $39.01 for adults and $25 for children 3-11.

To book for all 3 Disney dinner shows, call 407 939 3463.

An alternative is the nightly (and free!) **Electrical Water Pageant** which circles Bay Lake and the Seven Seas Lagoon, passing by each of the *Magic Kingdom* Park resorts in

BRIT TIP: Most dinner shows can feel quite cool, especially those involving animals such as Arabian Nights, Medieval Times and Dixie Stampede, so bring a jacket or sweater to beat the air-conditioning.

turn from 9pm. It lasts just 10 minutes so it is easy to miss, but it is almost a waterborne version of the SpectroMagic parade, with thousands of twinkling lights on a floating cavalcade of boats and mock sea creatures. The usual schedule is 9pm at *Disney's Polynesian Resort*, 9.15pm at *Disney's Grand Floridian Resort and Spa* (and you get a grandstand view in Narcoossee's restaurant), 9.35pm at *Disney's Wilderness Lodge* , 9.45pm on the shores of *Disney's Fort Wilderness Resort & Campground*, and 10.05 at *Disney's Contemporary Resort*. It can also be seen from the boat jetties outside the *Magic Kingdom* Park.

Arabian Nights

This lovingly maintained, family-owned attraction is a real large-scale production and one of the most popular with locals as well as tourists. It's a treat for horse lovers but you don't need to be an equestrian expert to appreciate the spectacular stunts, horsemanship and marvellous costumes as some 70 horses, including Arabians, Andalusians, Belgians and Walter Farley's famous black stallion, perform a 20-act show. Loosely based on a tale of Princess Scheherezade returning to her rightful place on the throne and finding the Prince of her dreams, the show is staged in the huge arena at the centre of this 1,200-seater 'Palace'. Daring gypsy acrobats,

magical genies, square-dancing cowboys and a thrilling chariot race all add up to a memorable show that kids, especially, adore. The recent addition of new characters (notably the comic Gaylord Maynard and his Appaloosa stallion Chief Bear Paw), costumes and special effects, including some breathtaking magic, have given Arabian Nights a real boost and help to keep its appeal fresh. A special Christmas Holiday show takes over for the winter season, and there is also some impressive pre-show entertainment, featuring acrobats, a magician and exotic dancers. The food (salad, a choice of prime rib, grilled chicken breast, vegetable lasagne, chicken tenders or chopped steak, and dessert) is above average, too.

Located just half a mile east of I-4 on Highway 192 (on the left, just to the side of the Parkway shopping plaza, or just past Water Mania if you are coming from the east end of 192), Arabian Nights runs every evening at 6 or 8.30pm (often having both), with occasional matinees. It lasts almost 2 hours, and tickets ($47 for adults and $29 for 3–11s) may be purchased at the box office from 8am-10pm or by credit card on 407 239 9223 (visit www.arabian-nights.com for a saving offer or free upgrade). A 'VIP' upgrade ($15 for adults, $13 for children) adds a souvenir poster, pre-show drink in the VIP area, priority seating (in the first 3 rows) and the chance to meet the stars before the show.

9

Unicorn, Arabian Nights

Pirate's Dinner Adventure

This show (which has been revamped several times since it opened in 1997) features one of the most spectacular settings, with the Spanish galleon pirate ship centrepiece being 150ft (46 metres) long, 60ft (18 metres) wide, 70ft (21 metres) tall and 'anchored' in a 300,000-gallon (1,365,000-litre) lagoon. It also delivers good value with its pre-show elements, plentiful (if ordinary) food and drink, and the imaginative after-show Buccaneer Bash disco (until 10.30pm), plus the Pirate's Maritime Museum, which guests are free to wander around. Coffee is also served at the Buccaneer Bash, and there are kids' meals if the main choice of beef and chicken with rice and mixed veg does not appeal. The basic premise of the audience being 'hi-jacked' by the wicked 18th-century pirates is a clever one, even if the actual storyline is occasionally hard to follow. Chaos and mayhem ensue, with the local princess being abducted by the villainous crew of Captain Sebastian (boo! hiss!), and swashbuckling abounds, with sword fights, acrobatics, trapeze artists and boat races. There are plenty of stunts and special effects (plus

BRIT TIP: When there are two shows of The Pirate's Dinner Adventure in one night, opt for the second one if you want the disco bash afterwards. A new Pirate's Preferred seating upgrade provides front row priority and guaranteed cast interaction for a small extra cost (407 248 0590, www.orlandopirates.com).

audience participation, which the kids love) and tickets are $49.95 for adults and $29.95 for 3–11s (look out for discount coupons). The show is located on Carrier Drive between I-Drive and Universal Boulevard, and runs daily from 6, 7.30, 8 or 8.30pm, with appetisers served for 45 minutes until seating begins.

Medieval Times

Eleventh-century Spain is the entertaining setting for this 2-hour extravaganza of medieval pageantry, sorcery and robust horseback jousts that culminate in furious hand-to-hand combat between 6 knights. It is worth arriving early to appreciate the clever mock castle design and the staff's costumes as you are ushered into the pre-show hall before being taken into the arena itself. The weapons used are all quite real and used with skill, and there are some neat touches with indoor pyrotechnics and other special effects. You need to be in full audience participation mode as you cheer on your knight and boo the others, but kids (not to mention a few adults) get a huge kick out of it and they'll also love eating without cutlery – don't worry, the soup bowls have handles! The elaborate staging takes your mind off the unexciting chicken dinner, but there is positively heaps of it and the serfs and wenches who serve you make it a fun experience. Prices, which include the Medieval Life exhibition (see below), are $48.95 for adults and $32.95 for 3–11s (again, check its website for discounts). A Royalty Package upgrade for $10 per person includes preferred seating, Knight's cheering banner, a behind-the-scenes souvenir DVD and commemorative programme member. Doors open 90 minutes prior to showtime. Times vary with the season, so call 1-800 229 8300 or visit www.medievaltimes.com for more details and reservations.

For those who have been before, the **Knights of the Realm** show made its debut in January 2003, with a new storyline and characters (although much of the fast-paced action is the same), plus a musical score by the Prague Symphony Orchestra and the addition of a superb black Friesian stallion, which contrasts with the snowy Andalusian horses ridden by most of the cast.

The castle is on Highway 192, 5 miles (8km) east of the junction with I-4. If you have 45 minutes to spare pre-show, the **Medieval Life** exhibition makes an interesting diversion ($3.50/person on its own). This mock village portrays the life and times of 900 years ago, with artisans demonstrating pottery and tool-making, glassblowing, spinning and weaving, plus a wonderfully gruesome dungeon and torture chamber that is definitely not for young children.

Sleuth's Mystery Dinner Shows

This is a real live version of Cluedo acted out before your eyes in hilarious fashion while you enjoy a substantial meal (with a main course choice of honey-glazed Cornish hen, prime rib or lasagne) and unlimited beer, wine and soft drinks. You can choose between 3 theatres and no less than 11 different plot settings (several of which have amusing British settings), including *Joshua's Demise*, *Roast 'Em, Toast 'Em* and *Lord Mansfield's Fox Hunt Banquet* (mayhem at an annual English banquet), that add up to some elaborate murder mysteries. The action takes place all around you and members of the audience can take part in some cameo roles. The quick-witted cast keeps things moving and you guessing during the

theatrical part of the 2½-hour show, then during the main part of dinner you can think up some questions for interrogation (but be warned, the real murderer is allowed to lie!). If you solve the crime you win a prize, but that is pretty secondary to the overall enjoyment – this is a show we enjoy a lot. Prices are $47.95 for adults and $24.95 for 3–11s and again show times vary, so call 407 363 1985 for details or visit www.sleuths.com.

Purely for children is **Sleuth's Merry Mystery Dinner Adventure**, with a special kids' dinner, dessert and unlimited soft drinks. Designed primarily for 6–12-year-olds (mainly on Saturday afternoon), it features one of two adventures, *The Faire of the Shire* and *The Magical Journey of Juniper Junior* costing $28 for adults and $16 for 3–12s.

Sleuth's Mystery Dinner Shows moved to a new location in 2005, the Goodings Plaza on International Drive next to the Mercado with 3 different theatres, a smart pre-dinner bar area and expanded gift shop.

WonderWorks: The Outta Control Magic Show

On a smaller scale but no less fun, this show is offered at WonderWorks on I-Drive (on one corner of The Pointe Orlando). A novel mixture of improvised comedy and clever, close-up magic, the show is accompanied by all-you-can-eat pizza, beer, wine and coke. Set in the intimate Shazam Theater, it features live music, special lighting effects and some slick magic tricks from illusionist Tony Brent and sidekick Danny Devaney. The tricks are all fairly routine, but the show is served up in style and involves plenty of audience participation. There are also a couple of terrific running gags throughout the fast-paced show, but beware of sitting too close to the stage – you WILL end up as part of the act! Performed twice nightly at 6pm and 8pm, it costs a reasonable $21.95 for adults and $14.95 for children and seniors. Alternatively, a Magic Combo ticket for the show and unlimited access to WonderWorks afterwards (open until midnight, see page 210) costs $36.95 and $25.95 (407 351 8800, www.wonderworks online.com).

Dolly Parton's Dixie Stampede

The biggest development in Orlando dinner shows for many a year opened in June 2003, when Country and Western queen Dolly Parton unveiled the fourth venue for her Dixieland extravaganza of music, comedy, horsemanship and ostrich races(!). The show features a high-energy cowboy competition (with lots of audience participation) between north and south, with various contests, speciality acts, song, dance and a huge southern-style feast. Indeed, the food is a major part of the experience – which has been a big hit elsewhere in America – as you chow down on vegetable soup, whole rotisserie chicken, corn on the cob, home-made biscuit (that's a savoury scone to us), barbecue pork loin, jacket potato and apple pastry. Your unlimited drinks are Pepsi, tea and coffee (with some excellent non-alcoholic cocktails available pre-show). Alcohol is limited to 2 glasses of beer or wine per meal.

Sleuth's Mystery Dinner Show

BRIT TIP: You can visit the stars of Dolly Parton's Dixie Stampede – the horses – for free from 10am until showtime. You'll find them along the horsewalk outside the venue.

The quality of the entertainment is high and the $28 million development provides a spectacular venue, with an elaborate pre-show (featuring the trick riding and cowboy rope and whip tricks of Greg Anderson – beware being one of his chosen audience 'victims' as you'll be in for a real test of nerve!) in the Carriage Room before the audience moves into the 1,000-seat, 35,000-sq-ft (3,255-sq-metre) main arena. Here the headlining abilities of the 32 horses and 30 riders are demonstrated over a series of tests and races, from Roman-style riding to trick riding and fast-paced barrel racing. Spectacular costumes, ostrich races, pig races and a feature buffalo 'stampede', plus a rousing, patriotic finale, American-style, with doves, flags and Dolly's closing anthem (penned after September 11) complete the picture.

Sadly, Dolly herself does not make an appearance, apart from on screen, but it all adds up to 5-star family fun. A separate **Christmas show** is staged from November 1 to January 1, featuring a live Nativity scene, snow and other seasonal festivities (the show contest pits the North Pole v South Pole instead!). In many ways this is a more novel and theatrical performance and, if you have seen one, you should definitely see the other.

Dixie Stampede operates once or twice a night, depending on the season, at either 5.40pm or 7.40pm (with the main show at 6.30pm or 8.30pm), and lasts almost 2½ hours, including the pre-show, plus browsing time in the inevitable gift shop. It's billed as Orlando's 'Most Fun Place To Eat', and it is hard to argue. Tickets are $46.99 for adults and $19.99 for 4–11s and it is located right next to Orlando Premium Outlets, just off I-4 at Exit 68, or via I-Drive (407 238 4455, www.dixiestampede.com).

Chamber of Magic Show & Dinner

Hidden away in the depths of wonderful Skull Kingdom on International Drive is this offering with an interactive magic show theme. Accompanied by as much pepperoni and cheese pizza as you can eat, plus beer, wine and soda, the small-scale dungeon theatre setting is all part of the act as the resident magicians stage a well-crafted hour-plus of sleight of hand, set-piece trickery and amusing banter, with plenty of chance to involve the audience in their antics. The acts change from time to time, hence there is plenty of variety, although there is also regular input from the resident 'ghost' hosts.

It is good, family fun (with shows at 6 and 8pm nightly) and makes a welcome bonus with a trip round Skull Kingdom itself or just as a stand-alone show (with the chance to peek into part of the Castle). It is usually a walk-up show at quiet times of the year, but it is advisable to book during the main holiday seasons on 407 354 1564 or at www.skullkingdom.com. The Magic Show alone costs $19.75 for adults and $15.97 for children, while a combo Skull Kingdom-Magic Show ticket is $28.25 and $24.45. We at the *Brit's Guide* are suckers for this well-paced, knockabout magic fun, and both the Chamber of Magic and the Outta Control Magic Show at WonderWorks are highly

worthwhile shows, especially with children.

Fiascos

Almost impossible to describe but a new institution on the dinner-show scene is this terribly British and wildly unpredictable offering from West Country impresario 'Grumpy' Joe Weston-Webb, who is best known for his spectacular failures to leap the river Avon. Billed as a 'Circus and Magic Dinner Show,' it is more like a live Monty Python episode, mixed in with some Benny Hill (cue John Thomas and his Mighty Organ) and Tommy Cooper. You know you are in trouble when the main sponsor is Itchy Bum Beer, the chef is down with food poisoning and the trapeze artist is afraid of heights! Joe's self-deprecating (bordering on manic depressive) MC leads the way into a chaotic series of pre-show acts (including goldfish racing and a group of anarchic dogs) before guests move to the ramshackle main theatre where anything can and will go wrong. They apologise in advance for the bad food, poor service and regular mishaps, while the main acts include a singer who thinks he's Neil Diamond, a sozzled organist and a magician who'd rather be a pop star. It all adds up to a wonderfully silly 2½ hours of carefully unscripted comedy, complete with popcorn fights and a 'goody bag' that includes a madcap bingo game and some worrying rain ponchos!

Chamber of Magic

9

The food choice is actually an amazing 100-item menu, much of which comes from local takeaways, but the main choices of fish and chips, other English dishes and an extensive American selection are all cooked on site and washed down with copious amounts of their free drinks (which also, unusually, extend to the pre-show). Prices are $45 for adults and $25 for children, and Fiascos theatre can be found in Republic Plaza on the junction of Universal Boulevard and Carrier Drive (just off International Drive). The show starts each evening from 6.30pm and usually finishes around 9.15, but 'these times are approximate and depend on how badly the show goes'! You can call them on 1866 4634 2726 or visit www.fiascos.us.

THE NIGHTCLUB SCENE

Orlando is blessed with a huge variety of nightlife, from regular discos to elaborate live music clubs and 'duelling piano' bars. The majority are situated in the downtown area, away from the main tourist centres. The *Orlando Sentinel* has a Friday supplement, *Calendar*, which has all the local entertainment listings, while www.orlandocitybeat.com details the nightspots, events, happy hours and other essential info. The free *Orlando Weekly* (available from supermarkets and tourist centres) is also a valuable guide, or visit www.orlando weekly.com.

Bars and discos come and go at an amazing rate, so don't be surprised if you go to a nightclub you have visited before to find it has had a complete change of name and personality. The basic distinctions tend to be **live music clubs**, **mainstream nightclubs**, with the occasional live band, and **bars** with evening entertainment.

Live music clubs

The following should give you a representative taste of the most popular venues (in most cases for those aged 21 and over only).

Country music fans (and others in search of the 'in' crowd) will definitely need to check out **:08 Seconds**, a huge, multi-level entertainment centre. It earns its 'unique' tag by hosting live bull riding (!) on the first Saturday every month, as well as having a huge dance hall with live bands, line dancing lessons, 12 bars ($2 for all alcoholic drinks on Saturday, a real bargain), a pool hall, games room and classic country barbecue. The atmosphere is both authentic and infectious, right down to the well-priced gift shop. This is one of our favourite clubs in town. On West Livingston Street in the heart of downtown, it has bags of style, but call 407 839 4800 for the latest details (Fridays feature Bike Night, with free admission for riders, plus stunt shows and live entertainment, and $20 all-you-can-drink admission; and Saturdays offer free line dancing lessons at 8pm, mechanical bull riding and their 'ultimate party night' style). By the way, the :08 seconds refers to the average time a bull-rider stays on his bull! Check out www.8-seconds.com for more.

While Hard Rock Live at CityWalk and House of Blues at *Downtown Disney* are the 2 main regular live music venues in town, **The Social** is the next best option in size terms, and offers a far more intimate and 'clubby' atmosphere, along with a great range of local bands, up-and-coming acts and the occasional bigger name (Supergrass, The Killers and Billy Bragg, among others) looking for a more offbeat venue. Situated in the heart of the city's downtown area (on North Orange Avenue, right next to Tabu),

The Social features the full spectrum of blues, rock, jazz and Latin sounds, with great house and guest DJs in between. The small main auditorium and bar still holds up to 400, and the secondary bar provides an excellent hideaway at the back of this well-run club. Its website – www.thesocial.org – offers the chance to listen to some of the forthcoming acts and buy tickets in advance, generally from $7–20, with free entry and special price drinks most Tuesdays. For more info, call 407 246 1419. Check out the local hangout of the **Bar BQ Bar** next to The Social for cheap drinks.

For pure, relaxed jazz and other live music, check out the Bosendorfer Lounge at the **Westin Grand Bohemian hotel** (see page 78), also on South Orange Avenue. Usually from 6–10pm every evening (plus Saturday Jazz Brunch 10.30am–2.30pm), the sounds of their $250,000 Bosendorfer piano are well worth travelling to hear.

As a complete alternative to the music scene, **Sak Comedy Lab** (on West Amelia Avenue in the Theater Garage) is like a live version of the TV show *Whose Line Is It Anyway?* Fast-paced and funny (and with a 'no obscenity' rule for concerned parents), the Sak performers do a mix of competitive ad lib comedy, with every show offering something different and the young performers living on their wits. Consistently voted Florida's best live comedy, see for yourself Tue–Sat (with 2 different shows Fri and Sat), admission $5–13. Their Lab Rats show (Tue) features Sak's 'students' and costs just $2. Booking is advisable on Fri and Sat (407 648 0001, www.sak.com).

Mainstream nightclubs

In addition to the mainstream DJ dance centres at *Downtown Disney's Pleasure Island* and Universal's CityWalk, **Tabu** (formerly the Zuma Beach Club on North Orange Avenue, just up from Church Street) appeals widely to the young, disco crowd with regular nightly line-ups, guest DJs and special events, usually of a fairly raucous nature! $7–12 (21 and over) Wed–Sun (407 648 8363).

Cairo has quickly become a haunt of the younger set on South Magnolia Avenue, with three rooms featuring dance music, reggae and out-and-out disco – high energy, top 40 and hip-hop every Fri and Sat; alternative sounds from the 1980s and 1990s Sun; old school and house Wed; ladies don't pay $5–10 cover charge and drink free until 11.30pm on Fri (407 422 595).

The Independent (formerly Barbarella) on Orange Avenue on the corner of Washington Street, offers alternative and new wave music 9pm–3am Wed–Sat. Again, it offers more of a techno-dance sound, but features various retro-progressive, old wave and Video Go-Go nights. Friday is ladies' night, and the club has three contrasting levels, including an area with pool tables. Cover charge $5–10 (407 839 0457).

The Club at Firestone is also hard to categorise but scores well with the alternative/progressive crowd. It ranges from mainstream disco to acid jazz lounge, with something different each Thur, Fri and Sat. Two venues inside the club– the Den and the Glass Chamber – feature dance, house, jungle and hip-hop, with their Latin night, El Club Caliente, usually on Fri. About half a mile north of Church Street on the corner of Orange Avenue and Concord Street, The Club is open 10pm–3am with cover charge $10 – or $20 on Open Bar Saturdays (407 872 0066, www.theclub-online.com).

The **Blue Room** (West Pine Street) is another lively offering, although more intimate, drawing a

9

more diverse crowd with its mixture of art, music and style. Completely remodelled for reopening in 2004, it features live DJs and drink specials Wed–Fri (9pm–3am), it mixes hip-hop, dance and R&B in a highly successful style, with the special mixing of DJ Gerry LeBorge each Saturday. A smart, stylish 2-level venue, this should please even the most ardent of clubbers. Cover charge usually $10 (407 843 2583, or visit www.blueroomorlando.com).

For the 'in' crowd, **Club Paris** is definitely the place to be seen. New (in January 2005) in the old Orchid Ballroom of Church Street station, this is a joint venture with hotel heiress and celebrity girl Paris Hilton (she even puts in an occasional appearance), designed with an eye for her favourite styles (lots of pink). With Latino Night (Wed), Ladies' Choice (Thur), Prize Fridays and House Party Saturdays, plus drink specials Wed–Fri, it is the hot place to party. Open variously from 4.30 and 7pm to 3am, cover charge is $5–15, with extra VIP levels. Check out more on www.clubparis.net or 407 832 7409.

For the gay scene, **Parliament House** (on North Orange Avenue) and **Southern Nights** (Bumby Avenue and Anderson Street) remain the most happening venues, while the **Cactus Club** (on North Mills Avenue), **Faces** and **Studz Bar** (both on Edgewater Drive) and **Wylde's** (out at 3535 South Orange Blossom Trail) are also popular.

La Nouba™ by Cirque du Soleil®

© Disney

BARS

With live entertainment, extrovert barmen, sports-themed bars and raw bars (offering seafood, often by the bucket!), the choice is, as ever, wide-ranging. Bars of all types simply abound in Orlando. The area around Church Street is the core of this development (even since much of Church Street Station closed), with a terrific range of restaurants and bars. Look out in particular for the raucous **Mako's** and **Antigua** (DJ house music). Upstairs from the latter is **Ybor's Martini Bar**, an upscale cigar and cocktail emporium. Also on this floor (and easy to overlook next to Antigua) is the highly recommended **Big Belly Brewery** with a micro-brewery and an impressive range of other beers (as well as an outrageous collection of wall art), and above that is roof-top bar **Latitudes**.

Travel out past Church Street into Orange Avenue and Pine Street and you are into real locals' territory with the likes of **One-Eyed Jack's**, which has a party pop atmosphere and live music singalongs, and is connected to the **Loaded Hog** and **Wall Street Cantina**, which are packed at weekends (there is often a queue to get in, but, once in, you can roam between all 3). New bars spring up on N Orange all the time, and others to watch out for are **Alpha Bar** (with an old school club vibe), **Eye Spy** (a high-tech bar with inside and outside seating), **Sky 60** (Miami-style rooftop bar), **Room 39** (a cool lounge that likes to groove) and **Lizzy McCormack's** (just one of downtown's Irish pubs). Turn left on to West Central Boulevard and you find **Kate O'Brien's Irish Pub** for more lively bar entertainment (and a great beer garden), the similarly Irish-themed **Scruffy Murphy's** is a block further north on Washington Street. There is no cover charge and it has a real good-time atmosphere.

South on Orange, the underground **Tanqueray's Bar and Grille** offers live music (Fri and Sat).

On Pine Street you have the **Pine Street Bar and Grill** (11am–2am Mon–Fri, 8pm–2am Sat and Sun) for one of the best bar-restaurants in the area, ideal for a late-night snack, with pool and billiards, and the fun Hawaiian style of **Maui Jack's Draft House and Raw Bar**. The **AKA Lounge** is where Orlando's hottest DJs come to spin, while **Back Booth** is a top bar for live music and imported beers.

The eclectic duo of **Slingapour's** and **The Globe** (the latter an off-the-wall 24-hour diner) are also worth seeking out for a lively drink or three on Wall Street, just off Orange, boasting a range of bars, a pool hall and live music, as well as The Globe's fun eating style. More new style can be found here at the handy **Monkey Bar** (a Martini lounge with food) and the **Waitiki Retro Tiki Lounge** (nightlife with a Polynesian flavour!). Other new bars to watch for are **Rhythm & Flow** (an upscale lounge bar with high-end cocktails), **Matador** (Spanish-styled) and **Cleo's** (a lounge with DJs at the weekend).

Sports bars

Finally, with the multitude of sports bars that are another particularly American speciality, **Friday's Front Row Sports Grill** on I-Drive (just south of the Sand Lake Road junction) really sticks out as a major tourist trap that even the locals enjoy. Here you can catch ALL the action (and, yes, they do show soccer) on 84 TV screens, plus enjoy some 100 beers from around the world – the bar features $1 domestic 12oz drafts! – as well as try out their basketball nets, pool tables and shuffleboard, and rub shoulders with local sports stars from time to time.

The food is standard American diner fare and there is plenty to keep the kids amused, too (paper tablecloths to colour and video games). The atmosphere varies according to the time of day and which sports event it is (pretty rowdy for Orlando Magic basketball games), so call 407 363 1414 for up-to-the-minute info. Open 11am–2am daily.

Other choices for the sports bar experience include the massive **Players Sports Pub** on Curry Ford Road; 87 TV screens, with 12 big-screens, open 11am–2am every day (407 273 7363) and **Headlightz Sports Bar** on East Colonial Drive, which also offers live music (407 273 9600). Our favourite is the **Orlando Ale House** group, with a fine example on Kirkman Road, just opposite Universal Studios (407 248 0000). With more than 30 TVs, a raw bar and great seafood, it also has an above-average range of beers.

Walt Disney World Resort in Florida can boast the excellent **ESPN Club** at *Disney's BoardWalk Resort*, a full-service restaurant with sports broadcast facilities, video games, more than 70 TV monitors, giant scoreboards and even a Little League menu for kids. No sports fan should miss it. Equally, **NBA City** (for basketball fans) at Universal's CityWalk, and the **Cricketers' Arms** and **Orlando George & Dragon** (for British sport) in The Mercado and next to Wet 'n Wild should not be overlooked, especially for TV addicts (www.cricketersarms.pub.com and www.britanniapubs.com).

Now, you will also want to know a lot more about where, when and how to tackle that other holiday dilemma – where to eat. Read on…

9

Hoop-Dee-Doo Musical Review

10 Dining Out
(or, Man, these portions are HUGE!)

Eating is a Big Deal in America. Consequently, dining out is a vital component of their entertainment business. Whether it be breakfast, lunch or dinner, the experience needs to be well-organised, filling and good value. To say Americans take mealtimes seriously would be the understatement of the year!

It is sometimes hard to dispel the notion that food is the 'be all and end all' of some Americans' holiday experience, as the options for dining are seemingly omnipresent and large scale. However, this is all good news for us Joe Tourists.

Variety

The variety, quantity and quality of restaurants, cafés, fast-food chains and snack bars is in keeping with the American tradition of eating as much as possible, as often as possible. At first glance, the full selection is overwhelming. Cruising along either I-Drive or Highway 192 will quickly reveal a dazzling array of eateries, the choice of which can be quite bewildering.

As a general rule, food is plentiful, relatively cheap, available 24 hours a day and nearly always appetising and filling. You will encounter an increasing number of fine-dining possibilities, but the basic premise remains that you will get good value for money and are unlikely to need more than 2 meals a day. Put simply, portions tend to be large, and of a steak, chicken or pizza-based variety, with service of an efficient, friendly character. It is actually hard to come by a bad meal. The one real exception is if you like fresh veg. The US diet often seems to overlook this staple, but if you look up the vegetarian options lower down or check out one of the outlets of **Chamberlin's**, notably at the Market Place on Dr Phillips Boulevard and in the new Winter Park Village, you will find a healthy, balanced choice.

Exceptional deals

In keeping with the climate, most restaurants tend towards the informal (T-shirts and shorts are usually acceptable) and cater readily for families. This also leads to 2 exceptional deals for budget-conscious tourists, especially those with a large tribe. Many hotels and restaurants offer 'kids eat free' deals, provided they eat with their parents. The age restrictions can vary from under 10s to under 14s, but it obviously represents good value for money. The second item of interest is the 'all-you-can-eat' buffet, another common feature of the chain restaurants. This means you can probably eat enough at breakfast, to keep you going until dinner! A few establishments also offer 'early bird' specials, a dinner discount if you dine before 6pm (quite often, you may have to wait for a table if you want dinner between 6 and 8pm; you need to arrive by 5 or after 8.30pm to beat the typical dinner rush).

BRIT TIP: As portions are so large, you can save money by sharing an entrée, or main course, between 2. Your waiter or waitress will be happy to oblige (provided you keep their tip up to the full rate).

Don't be afraid to ask for a doggy bag if you have leftovers (even if you haven't brought the dog). The locals do it all the time and, again, it is highly wallet-friendly. Just ask for the leftovers 'to go'. And don't hesitate to tell your waiter or waitress if something isn't right with your meal. Americans will readily complain if they are not happy, so restaurants are keen to make sure everything is to your satisfaction.

And, *please*, don't forget to tip. The basic wage for waiters and waitresses is low, so they rely heavily on tips to supplement their income – and they are taxed on the tips, whether they receive them or not. Unless service really is shoddy, in which case you should mention it, the usual rate for tips is 10 per cent of your bill at buffet-style restaurants and 15 per cent at full-service restaurants. It is worth checking to see if service is already added to your bill, although this is not common in the US.

With Orlando being the world's favourite holiday destination, and with the city springing up from such eclectic roots, you will encounter a

BRIT TIP: Don't worry about eating 'dolphin', it's not a mammal related to Flipper but a different species called dolphin-fish or mahi-mahi.

monumental array of food types. Florida is renowned for its seafood, which comes at a much more reasonable price than in the Mediterranean. Crab, lobster, shrimp (what we would call king prawns), clams and oysters can all be had without fear of breaking the bank, as well as several dozen varieties of fish, many of which you won't have come across before.

Cuban, Cajun/Creole and Mexican are other more local types of cooking that are well represented here, and there is plenty of Asian fare from Chinese and Indian to Japanese, Thai and Vietnamese. The big shopping malls offer a good choice in their food courts, which are often particularly good value. Cracker (cowboy) cooking is original Floridian fare, and the more adventurous will want to try the local speciality – alligator meat. This can be stewed, barbecued, smoked, sautéed or braised. Fried gator tail 'nuggets' are an Orlando favourite. Of course, you must try the traditional Key Lime Pie, a truly decadent dessert. Look for the stall in *Pleasure Island* selling it at $1 a slice – true heaven!

How to order

Ordering food can be an adventure in itself. The choice for each item is often the cue for an inquisition of exam-type proportions from your waiter or waitress. You can never order just 'toast' – it has to be white, brown, wholegrain, rye, muffin or bagel; eggs come in a baffling variety of ways (order them 'sunny side up' for a traditional British fried egg; 'over easy' is fried both sides but still soft); an order of tea or coffee usually brings the response 'Regular or decaf? Iced, lemon or English?' and salads have more dressings than the National Health Service. Whenever I've finished ordering,

10

BRIT TIP: American bacon is always streaky and crisp-fried and sausages are chipolata-like and slightly spicy.

I'm tempted to say, 'Have I passed?' Ask to see a restaurant's menu if it isn't displayed. It is no big deal to Americans and they won't feel insulted if you decide to look somewhere else.

Vegetarian options

In a country where beef is culinary king, vegetarians often find themselves hard done by. However, there are a couple of bright spots, plus a handy hint when all seems lost. Firstly, there are 2 speciality vegetarian restaurants in Orlando, the Indian cuisine of **Woodlands** on the South Orange Blossom Trail (407 854 3330) and the **Chinese Garden Café** on West Colonial Drive downtown (407 999 9799), while the tapas-style **Café Tu Tu Tango** on I-Drive serves a good variety of veggie dishes.

However, most of the upscale restaurants should be able to offer a vegetarian option and will be happy for you to ask in advance. *Walt Disney World Resort in Florida* is slightly more enlightened in that the

California Grill (in *Disney's Contemporary Resort*), **Citricos** (*Grand Floridian Resort and Spa*), **Le Cellier** (Canada pavilion in *Epcot*) and **Spoodles** (*Disney's BoardWalk*) feature vegetarian dishes, while the seafood-orientated **Flying Fish** (*Disney's Boardwalk*) and **'Ohana** (*Disney's Polynesian Resort*) can also serve up decent veggie fare if asked (thanks to Kaylee Robbins for that tip via www.wdwinfo.com). Most full-service restaurants (notably **Bongos Cuban Café**™ and **Wolfgang Puck's® Café** in *Downtown Disney*) and even some of the counter-service ones are usually keen to try to cater for non-menu requests. It is always worth asking.

BRIT TIP: An excellent section of the *Unofficial Walt Disney World Information Guide* website lists places that cater for special dietary needs, including veggie, at www.allearsnet.com/din/special.htm

Sweet Tomatoes is a salad buffet restaurant (distinctly vegetarian-friendly) with possibly the best meal deals in central Florida. On I-Drive (by Kirkman Road junction), it offers an astonishing all-you-can-eat choice for just $7.50 at lunch ($8.99 at dinner, after 4pm) that includes a vast salad spread, a choice of soups, pizza, pasta, bread and pastries, plus fruit and frozen yoghurt. Drinks are $1.69 (with free refills) and kids' meals are $1.79 for under 6s and $4.99 for 6–12s. Open 10.30am– 9pm Sun–Thur, 10.30am–10pm Fri and Sat, the restaurant should be sought out by all value- and health-conscious eaters. **Chamberlin's Market and Café** (with 8 Orlando locations) is another more enlightened choice,

Wolfgang Puck's Café

with homemade soups, vegetarian chilli, sandwiches, salads and blissful fresh fruit smoothies (www.chamberlins.com). The **Panera Bread** chain also offers some decent vegetarian soups and sandwiches (plus free wireless internet).

Eating 24/7

It is not unusual to find restaurants that never close – you can eat around the clock, or 24/7 as the Americans say. So, especially for those who can't sleep on their first night in the USA (plus those who just like to eat!), here is a guide to where you can go for a snack or even tuck into a full-scale meal at 4 in the morning:

Chain restaurants: Denny's, Waffle House, Steak & Shake.

Individuals: B-Line Diner (Peabody Hotel, I-Drive), Mickey D's (world's largest McDonald's, Sand Lake Road; high season only), The Globe (downtown Orlando), Planet Java (Gaylord Palms Resort), Baskervilles (Grosvenor Resort), Tubbi's Buffeteria (Disney's Dolphin Hotel) and the Village Inn (in St Cloud).

Drinking

The biggest complaint of Brits on holiday in the USA is about the beer. With the exception of a handful of English-style pubs (see pages 277–78), American beer is always lager, either bottled or on draught, and ice cold. It goes down great when the weather's hot, but it is generally weaker and fizzier than we're used to.

Of course, there are exceptions and they are worth seeking out (try Killian's Red, Michelob Amber Bock or Samuel Adams for a fuller flavour), but if you are expecting a good, old-fashioned British pint, forget it (although **The Cricketers Arms** in The Mercado, the **Orlando George & Dragon** on

> BRIT TIP: If there are several of you, ordering a pitcher of beer will work out cheaper than buying it by the glass.

International Drive and the **Rose & Crown** at *Epcot*'s UK pavilion come close if you don't mind paying more than $6 a pint. You should also look out for **The Big River Grille** at *Disney's Boardwalk Resort*, **Big Belly Brewery** in downtown Orlando or any of the excellent new **Hops Bar & Grill** chain, which are all micro-breweries. Spirits (always called 'liquor' by Americans) come in a typically huge variety, but beware ordering just 'whisky' as you'll get bourbon. Specify if you want Scotch or Irish whiskey and demand it 'straight up' if you don't want it with a mountain of ice.

> BRIT TIP: Most Orlando supermarkets don't sell spirits, just beer and wine (and some liqueurs, like Kahlua). If you want whisky, gin, etc, you need to seek out a 'Liquor store' like the ABC chain.

10

If you fancy a cocktail, there is a massive choice and most bars and restaurants have lengthy Happy Hours where prices are very consumer-friendly. Good-quality Californian wines are also better value than European.

Nine Dragons Restaurant at Epcot®

© Disney

BRIT TIP: Tourist brochures often include money-off coupons for many restaurants so you can make useful savings. See www.floridacoupon.com.

If you are sticking to soft drinks (sodas) or coffee, most bars and restaurants give free refills. You can also run a tab in the majority of bars and pay when you leave. And a few words of warning: Florida licensing laws are stricter than ours and **you need to be 21 or over to enjoy an alcoholic drink in a bar or lounge**. You will often be asked for proof of age before you are served (or allowed into entertainment complexes like *Disney's Pleasure Island*), and this means your passport or new-style driving licence with a photo. It's no good arguing with a reluctant barman. Licensing laws are strict and they take no chances. No photo ID, no beer! No one under the age of 21 may sit or stand near a bar either.

Right, that gives you the inside track on HOW to eat and drink like the locals, now you want to know WHERE to do it, so here's a guide to that veritable profusion of culinary variety. At the last count there were more than 4,000 restaurants in the Orlando area, with new ones being added and some biting the dust all the time and, while it would be a tall order to list every one, the following section covers the main areas and groups.

The Chain Gang

The first thing you need to do is make sense of the vast number of chain restaurants over here. Knowing your Perkins from your Chevys is vital tourist info, while new outlets like Smoky Bones and Bahama Breeze are well worth knowing about.

Of course, you will find all the main American brands we have in the UK. If you are a **McDonalds** fan, there are no less than 66 outlets in the greater Orlando area, from small drive-in types to a mega, 24-hour establishment on Sand Lake Road, **Mickey D's** (near the junction with I-Drive), that also has the biggest play area for kids of any McDonald's in the world and a number of differently themed eating areas. **Burger King** is well represented, with 45 outlets, as is another familiar US franchise, **Wendy's**, which has 25 restaurants. **KFC** has 25 branches in the area, and you will also find **Pizza Hut** and **Domino's**, both of which deliver locally (even to hotel rooms).

However, if you've come all this way, do you *really* want to have exactly the same thing you can have

The Best Burgers

Getting a burger in Orlando is no problem; getting a really good burger takes more doing. Here is our guide to the Top 10:

Beaches & Cream, the classic diner at Disney's Yacht Club.

Jimmy Buffet's Margaritaville, the stylish Universal CityWalk venue.

Smokey Bones, any one of their succulent BBQ diners.

Sam Snead's, a speciality restaurant in downtown Orlando.

Fuddrucker's, a national chain now at Festival Bay on I-Drive.

Orlando Ale House, where all the bar food is done just right.

Steak 'n Shake, simple diner style with classic burgers.

B-Line Diner, the Peabody Hotel's 24-hour speciality.

Back Yard Burgers, a fast food eaterie just north of Florida Mall.

TGI Fridays, a good standard choice at this big chain option.

back home? At the very least, you should seek out some of the local variations on the fast-food theme, like **Checkers** or **Hardees** for burgers, **Popeye's Famous Fried Chicken & Biscuits** or **Chik-fil-A** as a KFC alternative, **Taco Bell**, if you'd like the cheap and cheerful Mexican food option, or **Arby's**, for a range of hot roast beef sandwiches that make a nice change from burgers. **Dairy Queen** offers a mix of burgers, hot dogs, pork sandwiches and ice cream dishes, while **Papa John's, Little Caesar's** and **Hungry Howie's** make a decent alternative to Pizza Hut. A particularly American form of take-away is the 'sub', or torpedo-roll sandwich. This is what you will find at any branch of **Subway, Sobik's, Quiznos** or **Miami Subs**. They're a healthier option than yet another Big Mac and offer some imaginative fillings.

An even better bet is the health-conscious **Tijuana Flats** chain, which started in central Florida and now has some 25 outlets, most notably on E Central Boulevard downtown near Lake Eola. Its Tex-Mex style is geared around fresh, hand-made products in a lively, convivial atmosphere (McDonalds eat your heart out!). Check out its burritos, quesadillas, enchiladas, tacos and salads, and you will struggle to spend more than $9 a head (www.tijuanaflats.com).

Many of these establishments will also have a drive-through window, which will be fun to try at least once on your visit. Simply drive around the side of the building where indicated and you will find their take-away menu with a voice box to take your order. Carry on around the building (don't wait by the voice box!) and you pay and receive your food at a side window. You will probably find your car has a slide-out tray from the dashboard area that will take a cup, too.

Another variation on this theme is **Sonic**, a modern version of the old American drive-in diner, where you stay in your car and the 'Carhop' waiter or waitress comes to your window, takes the order and then delivers it all while you sit behind the wheel. The fare – burgers, hot-dogs, wraps, salads and sandwiches – won't win any awards, but the style is great fun. Check out its newest location on International Drive just north of Kirkman Road (7am-11pm).

And, if you *are* hooked on burgers and similar fare, we suggest you still give McDonalds a miss – in favour of the **Steak 'n Shake** chain. This classic diner-style option is open 24 hours and cooks everything to order, with both counter and table service, plus a drive-through. They also serve proper hand-dipped milkshakes and malts that are worth going in for on their own!

Family restaurants

After the welter of fast food choices, there is then a range of restaurants that specialise in more family-style fare, still with a predominantly American theme (naturally) but with greater variety. None of them is licensed (hence no alcoholic drinks), but without fail they offer some of the best breakfast fare in town, and at wallet-friendly prices, too. Here you will also find many of the famous all-you-can-eat buffets.

The most popular are the **Ponderosa Steakhouse** and **Sizzler** restaurants. Whether it's breakfast,

10

BRIT TIP: A buffet breakfast at Ponderosa or a similar establishment should keep you going until tea-time and is a good way to start a theme-park day.

lunch or dinner, you'll find consistent if unspectacular food (we have had a few reports of poor quality in recent years, but by and large they turn out great quantity and, therefore, value for money). You order and pay for your meal as you enter and are then seated, before being unleashed on some huge buffet and salad bars. Ponderosa has the rather flashier style (and the better reputation in town) but you'd be hard pushed to tell whose food was whose. Expect to pay about $4–6 for the breakfast buffets and $7–10 for lunch and dinner (there IS a difference in price depending on location, with the I-Drive area tending to be a dollar or two dearer). Standard dinner fare includes chicken wings, meatballs, chilli, ribs, steaks and seafood, while their immense salad bars are also a big draw. Both open from 7am until late evening and can be found in all the main tourist spots.

However, the breakfast buffet theme is served rather better by 3 other local chains, **Golden Corral**, **Black Angus** and **Shoney's**, where you may pay a dollar or two more but the extra quality is undeniable. Golden Corral especially impresses for its clean, fresh style (open 7.30am-10pm) and delicious Carver's Choice of roast meats plus the usual buffet deals, an excellent vegetable selection and a terrific dessert bar. Shoney's (7am-11pm) has an extensive à la carte menu as well as its excellent buffets, all with a Southern-tinged accent. Black Angus (7am-11.30pm) is the odd one out in that it is a full-service (i.e. with a bar) steakhouse for the

Bahama Breeze

rest of the day after breakfast.

If you want the true American touch (especially for breakfast), you should also consider the following selection, with a more homely touch and equally good value for money. For a hearty breakfast at any time of day, **International House of Pancakes** (aka IHOP) and the **Waffle House** are both a good bet. You will struggle to spend more than $7 on a full meal, whether it be one of their huge breakfast platters or a hot sandwich with fries. Waffle Houses are open 24 hours a day, while IHOPs open 6am–midnight. Another traditional 24-hour family restaurant is **Denny's Diner**, the nearest thing to our Little Chef. Again, they make a traditional bacon-and-egg breakfast seem ordinary with their wide selection, and do an excellent range of toasted sandwiches and imaginative dinner meals, like grilled catfish, as well as a Senior Selections menu, featuring smaller portions at reduced prices for over 55s. **Perkins Family Restaurant** has a lookalike menu (with some branches open around the clock). For a really hearty breakfast try Perkins Eggs Benedict (2 eggs and bacon on a toasted muffin with hash browns and fresh fruit), while its bread-bowl salads are equally satisfying. The **Friendlys** chain is another cheerful breakfast-based diner, with a mouth-watering array of typically hearty American fare, plus a delicious range of ice cream-based desserts.

The *Brit's Guide* recommendation in this category, though, goes to **Cracker Barrel** and **Bob Evans**. If you are travelling on the major highways of Florida and you see one of the 50 branches of Cracker Barrel, stop and check out its delightful Old Country Store style, with mountainous breakfasts, well-balanced lunch and dinner menus, Kid's Stuff choices and an old-fashioned charm that is a nice change from the usual tourist frenzy (6am-10pm Sun-Thur, 6am-11pm Fri and Sat). The Bob Evans chain is also notable for its friendly, country style, hearty menus (plus low-carb options) and mouth-watering desserts (6 or 7am-10pm). It also offers a take-away and country store selection that is well worth trying.

Home cooking is also the trademark of the **Boston Market** restaurants (11am-10pm), although they don't serve breakfast. They specialise in freshly-carved meats, rotisserie chicken, decent vegetables (praise be!) and excellent value if you have a hungry brood to feed. A new one-off restaurant getting rave reviews is the **Whistle Junction Buffet & Grill** on International Drive, just south of Festival Bay. Its lunch and dinner buffets (and breakfasts at weekends) are always fresh and well presented, and feature a huge range of dishes, from salads, steak and barbecue to salmon, roast turkey and crisp-fried chicken, with plenty of fresh veg and a good range of desserts options (11am-10pm Mon-Fri, 7.30am-10pm Sat and Sun).

Two recent additions worthy of note for any time, but especially breakfast, are the mushrooming chains of **Panera Bread** (wonderful pastries and fresh breads, salads, soups and sandwiches, with some good vegetarian selections; 7am-10pm) and **First Watch**, specialising in breakfast, brunch and lunch (all manner of egg dishes, gluten-free and low-carb choices, plus great coffee and pastries, served double-quick; 7am–2.30pm). Panera's also offer something of a rarity in the US – decent bread. As with a good number of their foodstuffs, American bread tends to be on the stodgy and sweet side (corn bread in particular is more like cake), but Panera specialise in a range of crusty, fresh-baked loaves that appeals more to European palates.

Finally for this section, a popular one-off restaurant is **Captain Nemo's** on Highway 192 opposite Fort Liberty. It serves breakfast 8am-noon, lunch until 3pm and dinner until 11pm, and its seafood and steak menu means mum and dad can try oysters, lobster, salmon, swordfish or grouper while the kids get their burger fix. Prices are budget-orientated, with daily specials, and Happy Hour 3–7pm.

Home from home

Having extolled the virtues of the American-style family diners, it is appropriate to note the handful of British pubs that will appeal to UK visitors. All offer a predictable array of pub grub and imported British beers. You'll find the odd Brit or two working behind the bars and you can happily take the kids into them, providing they don't sit at the bar. The **Cricketers Arms** in The Mercado on I-Drive (midday–2am) has become a favourite haunt of British visitors due to the large selection of beers, appetising food, live evening entertainment and (soccer fans take note) live Premiership and other domestic matches. It gets busy in the evenings, its live music is usually good, and many of the staff are Chelsea fans, but we won't hold that against them! NB: There is usually a cover charge for footy. Relatively new on I-Drive (in a small plaza immediately south of Wet 'n Wild) is the **Orlando George & Dragon**,

10

Emeril's Tchoup Chop

another all-British operation that also serves a hearty traditional breakfast as well as typical pub fare for lunch and dinner. Open 9am-2am (kitchen until 11pm), it stocks Guinness, Boddingtons, Stella, Fosters, Newcastle Brown, Bass and Carlsberg (among others), and also feature darts, pool, karaoke, Sky Sports and live entertainment on their outdoor patio. This is also the place to come if you're looking for a traditional Christmas turkey dinner with all the trimmings, while they celebrate St George's Day (April 23) in style, too.

> BRIT TIP: Orlando
> George & Dragon puts
> most British chippies to
> shame!

Highway 192 in Kissimmee sports a few fairly derivative pubs, all keen to appeal to the home market. The best are **Harry Ramsbottom's** at Fort Liberty (between Markers 10 and 11), which also has a fish 'n' chippie, and the well-kept **Stage Door**, 6 miles (10km) west of the junction with I-4 (and west of Marker 4, just past Lindfields Boulevard). *Coronation Street* fans should make a beeline for **The Rovers Return** on the Vine Street stretch of 192, then there is the **Fox and Hounds**, **Queen Victoria Tavern** and **The Albert**, all of which are British owned and run. Up in Winter Park, **Fiddlers Green** (on Fairbanks Avenue) is possibly the best Irish pub in the area. With Happy Hour 4-7pm, live jazz Sunday evenings, 20 beers on tap and a fully Irish-tinged menu, it's a winning formula (11.30am-2am Mon-Sat, 11.30am-midnight Sun; www.fiddlersgreenorlando.com). **Raglan Road** is the latest Irish-themed bar-restaurant in *Downtown Disney*, but we hadn't had a chance to review it before we went to print.

American diners

For full-service American restaurants, Orlando is blessed with about every type you can imagine, while some chains even originated here and have gone on to national fame (like the Olive Garden restaurants). All feature a bar if you just prefer a drink and many have multiple TVs. Children are well catered for with their own menus and activity packs in many cases. This section is limited to the main tourist areas, plus a few one-offs worth sampling. Unless specified, they are in multiple locations in Florida. The $ price listings are intended only as a rough guide for a 3-course meal:

$	=	$10–15
$$	=	$15–20
$$$	=	$20–25
$$$$	=	$25–30
$$$$$	=	$30-plus

Steak and Ale is a popular, basic diner (11.30am–10pm Mon-Thur, 11.30am–11pm Fri, noon–11.30pm Sat, noon–10pm Sun; $$). It does some great steaks and ribs, plus tempting seafood and chicken dishes, with early bird specials of a 3-course set meal 4–7pm (4–6pm Nov–Mar), and 2-for-1 drink specials. The **Bennigan's** chain (11am–2am; $$) is a *Brit's Guide* favourite for its friendly, efficient service, smart decor and tempting menu, especially at lunchtime. It has a bar atmosphere straight out of the TV programme *Cheers*, and its Irish flavour comes into its own on St Patrick's Day (March 17). Happy Hour(s!) are 2–7pm and 11pm–midnight. Similarly, **Houlihan's** is a classic bar-restaurant with plenty of style, cheerful service, an extensive and appetising menu (look out for its Down Home Pot Roast in particular) and some seriously large portions (but also a mini-desserts selection; 11am–1am; $$$).

Anyone familiar with the **TGI Fridays** chain will know what to expect from this group, and Orlando boasts several of the newest design (notably on I-Drive just north of The Pointe Orlando), which refines its loud, eclectic style a little. A drinks menu the size of a book (with more specials than you can shake a cocktail stick at) and a main menu that is heavy on wings, ribs, burgers and steaks (11am–2am; $$$). Equally lively, **Hooters** makes no bones about its style. 'Delightfully tacky yet unrefined' they say, and this is a relatively simple establishment, especially popular with the younger, beach-party crowd – and for the famous Hooter Girl waitresses (11am–midnight Mon–Thur, 11am–1am Fri–Sat, noon–11pm Sun; $$). The entertaining menu features seafood, salads and burgers, plus Hooters Nearly World Famous Chicken Wings in 5 strengths: mild, medium, hot, 3 Mile Island or Wild Wing. You have been warned!

Uno Chicago Grill is the place to go if you're bored with Pizza Hut, as it specialises in deep-dish pizzas plus pastas, chicken dishes, steaks and salads (11am–midnight; $$), while **Applebee's** calls itself the 'Neighborhood bar and grill,' and offers a rather more health-conscious menu with excellent salads and Weight Watchers choices as well as a tempting array of steaks and chicken dishes (11am–midnight, $$). **Hops** puts the accent on its in-restaurant breweries, with 4 standard 'house' beers (all of which are well worth trying) and seasonal specials, while it also serves a good selection of casual dining menu items (steaks, chicken, pastas and seafood in its own signature sauces and marinades) in a pleasant, airy restaurant (11am–11pm; $$$). A Florida speciality is the **Orlando Ale House** chain, one of the most

pub-like of the local bar-restaurants, with pool tables and a host of TV screens for the latest (American) sports. With a friendly, efficient style and a surprisingly varied menu for a basic diner-type establishment, this is a great place to hang out with friends, bring the family or just pop in for a drink (11am–2am; $$).

Cowboy style

These add a cowboy flavour to the typical bar-diner style. The **Lone Star Steakhouse** takes you to Texas for its mesquite-grilled steaks, ribs, chicken and fish, with a typical friendly Lone Star state welcome and a Roadhouse ambience (and suitably large portions!). Kids also eat free with parents on Tuesdays (11am–11pm; $$$). **Cattleman's Steak House** also goes for the cowboy approach, with a neat saloon bar, early bird specials (4–6pm) and the Little Rustlers' Round-up menu for the kids. Steaks are the order of the day, but you can also try chicken, seafood and its Heavenly Duck (4–11pm, saloon open until 2am; $$$).

Perhaps more fun is **Logan's Roadhouse** where the funky, rustic atmosphere is enlivened with masses of peanuts in their shells, which end up all over the wooden floor. Burgers, chicken, steaks and ribs are its stock-in-trade, while it also offers an Express lunch selection (11am–10.30pm Sun–Thur, 11am–11.30pm Fri and Sat; $$$). The hugely popular **Outback Steakhouse** has an Australian slant on the theme, and with some of the best fare (and biggest portions). Its thick, juicy well-seasoned steaks, ribs and seafood selections are all above average, while its trademark is the Bloomin' Onion, a large fried onion with a special dipping sauce. It also features a good kids' menu (4–10.30pm Mon–Thur, 3.30–11pm Fri and Sat, 3.30–10.30pm Sun; $$$$).

10

Chili's restaurants take you into Tex-Mex territory, an Americanised version of Mexican cuisine that originated in Texas, but with the emphasis more on steak and ribs and less on tortillas and spices. Service is frighteningly efficient and, if you are looking for a quick meal, you'll be hard-pushed to find a quicker turnaround (11am–1am Mon–Sat, 11am–11pm Sun; $$). Similarly, **Chevy's** offers a healthy slice of Mexicana, while still providing some reassuring American selections. Their salsa is always fresh made every hour, and the tortilla chips, guacamole and tortillas are equally appetising (4–11pm Mon–Thur, 4–midnight Fri, 11am–midnight Sat, 11am–11pm Sun; $$). A more elaborate Mexican offering is the **Don Pablo's**. Clever theming, lively atmosphere (especially around the Cantina bar) and a classic, well-explained menu add up to a fun experience (11.30am–10pm Sun–Thur, 11.30am–11pm Fri–Sat; $$).

BBQ blitz

Looking for good barbecue? Orlando again has it aplenty in the next selection. At **Wild Jack's** (on I-Drive, just north of Sand Lake Road), the magnificent wood-smoked aroma hits you as you walk in the door. The huge interior features a big, open-pit barbecue where you can watch your food being cooked. Steaks, ribs, chicken and turkey represent the main choices and they are all served with bags of panache. Happy Hour is 4–7pm and kids eat free with a full-paying adult (11.30am–11pm; $$$). Another good choice that also pulls in a lot of positive reader feedback is **Key W Kool's Open Pit Grill** on Highway 192 (just opposite the now-closed Splendid China). Choice cuts of meat, mouth-watering steaks – prime rib, daily specials and the succulent,

BRIT TIP: Don't miss Wild Jack's Jalapeño Mashed Potatoes, Dynamite Chicken Wings, Cowboy Baked Beans and the Jack Daniels Chocolate Cake for dessert!

inviting aroma add up to an outstanding dining choice (4–11pm; $$$). **Sonny's Real Pit Bar-B-Q** is a national chain with no great pretensions, just masses of food of the barbecue persuasion served up in friendly, let's-get-messy style. Ideal for families, with a good kids' menu, try the ribs and the own-recipe coleslaw (11am–10pm; $$). Out of the same log-built mould is **JT's Prime Time** (just past Orange Lake Country Club on West Highway 192), with another heavily barbecue-orientated menu, good kids' choice (plus a games room), and a slice of old pioneer style. It is also popular at weekends (noon to 11pm; $$).

We also recommend **Tony Roma's**, which rightly pronounces itself 'famous for ribs'. The airy but relaxing decor and ambience, clever kids' menu (the Roma Rangers Round-up, full of puzzles and games), junior meals, and melt-in-the-mouth ribs make a winning combination. You can still get chicken, burgers and steaks, but why ignore a dish when it's done this well? (11am–midnight Sun–Thur, 11am–1am Fri and Sat; $$$). A new favourite is **Smokey Bones**, which also goes for the log-cabin touch, with rustic, mountain lodge décor and some of the most succulent, deep-smoked BBQ in town. It also does fish, chicken, burgers and salads, but we heartily recommend the barbecue platters. Sports fans are also well served here with a huge array of TVs through the bar and restaurant (11am–11pm; $$$).

Italian touch

Good Italian family-style dining has 4 excellent chains to recommend hereabouts. The **Olive Garden** restaurants are one of America's big success stories as they brought Italian food into budget, mass-market range, and its first outlet was right here on I-Drive. The light, airy dining rooms create a relaxing environment and, while it doesn't offer a huge choice, what it does, it does well and in generous portions. Pastas are the speciality, but it also offers chicken, veal, steak, seafood and great salads, plus unlimited refills of salad, garlic breadsticks and non-alcoholic drinks (11am–10pm Sun–Thur, 11am–11pm Fri–Sat; $$). Similarly, the **Macaroni Grill** chain offers a wonderful slice of family dining Italian style. Its spacious restaurants are stylish, comfortable and well served, with excellent à la carte and family-style menus (serving 8–10). The pasta and wood-oven pizzas are first class and the wine list is impressive, to (11.30am–10pm Sun–Thur, 11.30am–11pm Fri and Sat; $$–$$$).

Carraba's comes direct from Sicily, with more casual-but-elegant dining in a warm, festive atmosphere. House specialties include crispy calamari, chicken marsala, tender filet, unique pasta dishes and handmade pizzas in a wood-burning oven. The children's menu is one of the best and the style is extremely child-friendly (4–10pm Sun–Thu, 3–11pm Fri and Sat; $$$). Possibly the most elegant of this section is **Brio Tuscan Grille**, a real slice of La Dolce Vita and some superb taste sensations. The menu emphasis is on prime steaks and chops, pasta specialties and flatbreads prepared in an authentic Italian wood-burning oven. The interior décor is also well above average, but so is the price tag (11am–10pm Sun–Thur, 11am–11pm Fri and Sat; $$$–$$$$).

Antonio's (an impressive local chain), goes completely into the upmarket, 5-star area with 3 restaurants (including one with a café, deli and superb wine shop) that all feature an individual, exclusive style as well as outstanding cuisine – sensational risottos are a signature dish while veal and New York strip steak are an equally wise choice (5–10pm Mon–Sat; $$$$$).

Seafood specials

The choice of seafood eateries is equally wide, from the standard identikit type to some excellent individuals. **The Crab House** should be self-explanatory. Garlic crabs, steamed crabs, snow crabs, Alaskan king crabs, etc. You can always try its prime rib, pasta or other seafood, but it would be a shame to ignore the house speciality (11.30am–11pm Mon–Sat, noon–11pm Sun; $$-$$$). Part of the same chain family is **Joe's Crab Shack**, more fun and inventive but less seafood based (despite the name). Distinctly family-friendly with its Sand Lot play area, this is ideal if you don't want to go the whole shellfish hog (11am–10pm Sun–Thur, 11am–11pm Fri and Sat; $$-$$$). **Landry's Seafood** is from the same company, but with a more elegant touch, if still a theatrical style. There is a fresh catch of the day, seafood platters and an excellent salad bowl with every dish, and the staff really know their menu (11am–10pm Sun–Thur, 11am–11pm Fri and Sat; $$$).

Red Lobster is part of the Olive Garden chain, and is for the family

The Olive Garden

market, with a varied menu, lively atmosphere and one of the best kids' menu/activity books. While lobster is the speciality, the steaks, chicken, salads and other seafood are equally appetising, and it does a variety of combination platters (11am–10pm Sun–Thur, 11am–11pm Fri–Sat; $$$). **Boston Lobster Feast** is the place for a real blowout, with an unlimited lobster and seafood buffet. There are excellent-value early-bird specials 4.30–6pm Mon–Fri, 2–4.30pm Sat–Sun, and, while it is not gourmet fare, its 40-item Lobster Feasts are guaranteed to stretch the stomach (4.30–10pm Mon–Fri, 2–10pm Sat–Sun; $$$$).

Of the one-off restaurants, **Ocean Grill** (on I-Drive, just north of the Sand Lake Road junction) offers good seafood at moderate prices. Daily specials, including early-bird from 4–6pm, jostle with fried clams, south-western swordfish, fried catfish, shrimp Creole and seafood lasagne and, for the hearty appetite, the surf 'n' turf is great value (5–11pm; $$$). **McCormick and Schmick's** is easily the most quality-conscious of the seafood chains, but there is nothing mass-produced or identikit about its style. The chef creates a daily menu based on product, price and availability (with a prominent listing of what's fresh). Oysters are a speciality, along with soups and salads, and you will be hard-pushed to find better shrimp, scallops and Atlantic salmon (11am–11pm Mon–Thur, 11am–midnight Fri and Sat, 11am–10pm Sun; $$$$-$$$$$).

Steaks and more steaks

Just about every restaurant you visit will feature steak on the menu, but there are a handful that make it their speciality. **Charley's Steak Houses** cook over a specially built woodfire pit and consistently earn high marks from meat-lovers

> BRIT TIP: Visit McCormick and Schmick's during daily Happy Hour (5–7pm) and all appetisers are just $1.95 if served as bar snacks.

throughout the US. All their meat is specially aged, hand-cut and seasoned, making for a superb array of steaks and chops and, while they also offer fine seafood, you'd be foolish to overlook their stock-in-trade (5–11pm; $$$$$). Another imaginative option is one–off **Vito's Chop House** (in front of the Castle Hotel on I-Drive). Its choice beef cuts – check out the Tuscan T-Bone – are aged for 4–6 weeks and cooked over wood fires. Pork chops, seafood and pasta are also available, as well as an extensive wine list (5pm–10.30pm Sun–Thur, 5pm–11pm Fri–Sat; $$$$).

Ruth's Chris Steak House, another major chain, also offer prime beef in a mouth-watering variety of choices is the order of the day. It isn't cheap, but you'll be hard-pushed to get a better steak. Simply seared, seasoned and served, there is a good reason why it has more than 80 locations worldwide (5–11pm Mon–Sat, 5–10pm Sun; $$$$$). **Morton's of Chicago** has a more upmarket (sometimes pretty smoky) style, with a lively ambience that adds to the enjoyment of its trademark steaks, which are cooked on an open range. It does not come cheap, especially as vegetables are extra, but it is a memorable experience (5pm–midnight Mon–Sat, 5pm–11pm Sun; $$$$$). Similarly, **Shula's Steak Houses** are both expansive (on your waistline) and expensive. The porterhouse and prime rib are outstanding, and this chain (owned by famous ex-American football coach Don Shula) is highly popular with locals (5–11pm; $$$$$).

Our Top 10

Susan and I frequently try to compile our list of favourites from this long Diner section, which is hard (but fun!) with the ever-changing restaurant scene. At the time of writing, here's how we would present our top 10:

1) **Café Tu Tu Tango** – an ideal combination of novel entertainment and great tastes.
2) **Macaroni Grill** – one of our 'locals' and a consistent, friendly choice.
3) **Outback Steakhouse** – great value and hard-to-fault food with a few neat twists.
4) **Smokey Bones** – fresh, inviting style and a superb barbecue selection.
5) **Hops** – worth trying just for its excellent array of home brews.
6) **Sweet Tomatoes** – terrific value from its buffet spread, and wonderfully healthy, too.
7) **Steak 'n Shake** – good fun for a quick burger and milkshake
8) **Bob Evans** – guaranteed down-home breakfasts with fun counter seating.
9) **Olive Garden** – great (and filling) lunch for a quick soup and salad.
10) **Bahama Breeze** – just gotta love that eclectic Caribbean style.

Novel dining

Next, we come to a series of restaurants where a lively menu is matched by equally upbeat décor and service. Step forward the **Bahama Breeze** restaurants, appealing for their striking Caribbean styling (which includes an outdoor patio bar with live music) and food that puts most diner fare to shame. Try West Indies Patties, Black Pepper Seared Tuna or the Cuban beef stew Ropa Vieja. Service is in keeping with its personable style and there is a pleasing individual touch (4pm–2am Mon–Sat, 4pm–midnight Sun; $$$). Also well worth visiting is the **Cheesecake Factory**. While it makes a feature of desserts (with more than 30 varieties of cheesecake), the rest of the huge menu is impressive in an eclectic, high-tech setting. Mexican dishes jostle with pizza, pasta, seafood, burgers, steaks and salads, and they also offer a great brunch selection – you really need to come hungry here (11am–11pm; $$$$).

Another restaurant with Brit appeal is **Café Tu Tu Tango**. The accent is artist-colony Spanish, with a really original tapas-style menu,

live entertainment and artwork all over the walls that changes daily. Vegetarians are well catered for here, and you can try some particularly succulent pizzas, seafood, salads and paella. Mexican and Chinese dishes are also on offer, along with a thoughtful kids' menu. The fun atmosphere complements the rich array of dishes perfectly (11.30am– midnight; $$-$$$).
B-Line Diner, inside the Orlando Peabody Hotel on I-Drive, is an amazing art deco homage to the traditional 1950s-style diner, faithful in every detail, including the outfits of the staff. You sit at a magnificent long counter or in one of several booths, with a good view of the chefs at work and with a rolling menu that changes four times a day. The food is way above usual diner standards, but the prices aren't. Desserts are displayed in a huge glass counter and we dare you to

10

BRIT TIP: Bahama Breeze restaurants do not take reservations and are very popular, so there can be quite a wait from 6–8pm.

ignore them (open 24 hours, $$-$$$).

Planet Hollywood can also be found here (next door to *Downtown Disney Pleasure Island*) and is a pure fun venue. The food is fairly predictable, although everything is served with pizzazz, but the cavernous interior lends itself to a party atmosphere, complete with film clips and a stunning array of movie memorabilia. Some memorable house cocktails, too, but visit either mid-morning or mid-afternoon to avoid the serious queues (11am–2am; $$$). Disney also has 2 versions of the eco-aware **Rainforest Café** chain (outside the *Animal Kingdom Theme Park* and in *Downtown Disney*), one with a huge waterfall exterior and the other topped by a 'volcano', and they have to be seen to be believed. You don't dine, you go on a 'safari adventure' in a rainforest setting amid audio-animatronic animals (including elephants and gorillas), thunderstorms, tropical birds, waterfalls and aquariums. It is great for kids and the food is above average, too. Unless you arrive before midday, you'll have a wait, but that's no hardship given their locations. Beware the huge gift shop! (11am–11pm; $$$).

Hard Rock Café is a fairly worldwide chain, but its Orlando outlet (at Universal's CityWalk) is a bit special. With tall, statuesque pillars, it stands like a Coliseum of rock and boasts more music memorabilia than any other location. If you have never tried the loud, lively style, this would be worth a visit. The food – salads, burgers, steaks, ribs, chicken and sandwiches, including the trademark pulled pork speciality – won't win any awards, but, like Planet Hollywood, it is consistent and hearty (and plentiful!), although it doesn't cater quite so well for youngsters (11am–midnight; $$$). An unmistakable landmark on I-Drive is the super-charged, super-large restaurant of **Race Rock**, packed with rare motor-racing memorabilia and eye-catching machines of all kinds. Two giant car transporters line the entrance, which also boasts a giant-wheeled buggy, 2 dragsters and a hydroplane, welcoming you into the circular, 20,000sq ft (1,860sq m) restaurant. Giant TV screens and a host of regular TVs, video games, virtual reality racing machines and loud music, plus chequered flag tables, complete the atmosphere, while the central bar sports an upside-down racing car circulating as the world's biggest ceiling fan! The food is traditional diner fare given a few tweaks like Start Your Engines (the starter selections), Circle Tracks (pizza), Stock and Modified (burgers and sandwiches), Pole Position Pastas and The Main Event (ribs, chops, chicken and salmon), and children are well catered for here (11.30am– midnight; $$).

International flavours

Your restaurant choice extends beyond the obvious to an array of international cuisines. **Chinese** food is well established in America and well represented in Orlando, although many outlets are pretty uninspired, not to mention downright insipid.

Bill Wong's Famous Super Buffet (yes, they really do call it that) on I-Drive offers a cross between Chinese and diner-type fare. The all-you-can-eat buffet features jumbo shrimp (and that

Race Rock

means JUMBO!), as well as crab, prime rib, fresh fruit and salad. Think cheap and cheerful and that's Bill Wong's (11am-10pm; $$). Similarly, the **Sizzling Wok**, on Sand Lake Road just across from the Florida Mall, offers an opportunity to get stuck into a massive Chinese buffet at a very reasonable price (11am–10pm Sun–Thur, 11am–10.30pm Fri–Sat; $$). The **China Café** on I-Drive (at the corner of Kirkman Road) is also above average, with a lunch buffet from 11am–3pm and a well presented array of dishes (the crispy duck is outstanding). Daily specials also feature (11am–11pm; $$). Tucked away in a plaza off Apopka-Vineland Road, just past the Crossroads shops near *Downtown Disney*, is the **Dragon Court Buffet** (look for it behind the IHOP). This locals' favourite serves a magnificent spread of fresh, appetising dishes at a terrific lunch price. With more than 50 items on offer, including a genuine sushi selection, this is well worth trying (11am–midnight; $-$$).

Ming Court on I-Drive, just south of King Henry's Feast, is the Rolls-Royce of local Chinese restaurants. With a magnificent setting and live entertainment, you can easily convince yourself you have been transported to China itself. The menu is extensive and many dishes can be had as a side order rather than a full main course to give you the chance to try more (11am–2.30pm and 4.30pm–midnight; $$$). Arguably the best of the bunch, though, is the latest 'chain' offering, **PF Chang's China Bistro**, which mixes classic Chinese fare with an American bistro style that makes fans of virtually all who sample it. Seek out the Spicy ground chicken and eggplant, the Cantonese roasted duck or Oolong marinated sea bass for dishes with real distinction. There is also a good vegetarian selection (5–11pm; $$$).

Japanese

The more adventurous (and those already familiar with their cuisine) will want to try one of the fine Japanese restaurants here. **Shogun Steakhouse** is a national chain ideal for those a little unsure whether to go for the full Japanese experience straight away. The service is Teppanyaki-style, at long, bench-like tables with the chef cooking in front of you, but you can still order a no-nonsense steak or chicken. The full Japanese menu is well explained and demonstrated by the chefs, however, and it is heartily recommended (6–10pm Mon–Thur, 6–10.30pm Fri–Sun; $$). **Kobe** brings a touch of Americana to its dining content. With 4 locations in the area, Kobe goes for the mass market but still achieves individuality with the chef preparing your food at your table in a style that is as much showmanship as culinary expertise (11.30am–11pm; $$).

Ran-Getsu, on I-Drive opposite The Mercado, does for Japanese cuisine what the Ming Court does for Chinese – it's stylish, authentic and as much an experience as a meal, and still reasonably priced. The setting is simple and efficient, and you can choose to sit at conventional tables or at the long, S-shaped sushi bar as many Americans do (5pm–midnight; $$$). **Benihana** restaurants offer another memorable experience, with everything again cooked Teppanyaki-style in front of you by expert chefs. Their steaks are also among the most tender you will experience (5–10.30pm; $$$).

Indian

If you have come all this way and still fancy a curry, believe it or not you can still get a decent chicken tikka masala and naan bread (although it tends to be more

10

expensive than in your local High Street). In fact, there are more than a dozen Indian restaurants in the Orlando area, but some are distinctly better than others. For a medium-range restaurant, **Passage to India** (on I-Drive and Highway 192) gets the locals' top vote and is a cut above the average, with unusual and exotic chicken dishes and vegetarian Sabzi Dal Bahar. It is a *Brit's Guide* favourite for its attentive service and relaxed atmosphere, and you'll probably find yourself dining with a few fellow Brits (11.30am–midnight; $$$). A recent addition is **Essence of India** on West Sand Lake Road (at the junction with Universal Boulevard). Its style again aims to be traditional rather than avant garde and it offers a superb value lunch buffet ($7.99 a head) in addition to the à la carte choice, which features some tasty vegetarian dishes (11.30am–2.30pm Mon–Fri, noon–3pm Sat and Sun; 6–11pm nightly; $$$).

Others worth considering are **Flavours of India** (on S Kirkman Road, just south of International Drive; 11.30am–10.30pm, $$-$$$), **Memories of India** (on Turkey Lake Road, just south of Universal; 11.30am–10pm Mon–Sat, 11.30am–9pm Sun; $$-$$$), the **New Punjab Restaurant** (on I-Drive, just north of Sand Lake Road; 11am–11pm Tue–Sat, 5pm–11pm Sun and Mon; $$) and **Shalimar** (in a similar location; 11am–11pm, $$).

Thai and more

For other types of Oriental cooking, the **Siam Orchid** (on Universal Boulevard, round the corner from Wet 'n Wild) offers exceptional Thai food in a pretty setting overlooking Sandy Lake (5–11pm; $$$). **Little Saigon** (on East Colonial Drive) will introduce you to Vietnamese cuisine and a whole new array of soups, barbecue dishes, fried rice variations and other interesting treats (10am–9pm; $$). The **Red Bamboo** (on S Kirkman Road just north of I-Drive) is a wonderful mix of authentic Thai and contemporary, clean decor. Its soups and curries are to die for, while the house speciality Smokey Pot is a heavenly stew of marinated shrimp, vegetables, and glass noodles in chilli (11am–2.30pm Tue–Fri, 5–10pm Sat, noon–10pm Sun, closed Mon; $$$).

Cuban

Cuban food is a Floridian speciality and you'll find some of the best examples at **Rolando's** (on Semoran Boulevard, in the suburb of Casselberry; head east from I-4 Exit 92). Try the red snapper or pork chunks and find out why the Orlando Sentinel rates this the best Cuban food north of Havana (11am–9pm Tue–Thur, 11am–10pm Fri–Sat, 1–8pm Sun; $). However, the **Samba Room** on West Sand Lake Road is the 5-star experience, an elegant lakefront restaurant full of Latin ambience. The menu exhibits a wonderfully exotic touch, with the likes of Mango-barbecued ribs, Cachaca-smoked boneless chicken and Sugar cane beef tenderloin, and its range of cocktails is suitably Cuban-laced (with lots of rum and martini). Extremely popular, so reservations are advised (407 266 0550; 11am–midnight Mon–Sat, noon–10pm Sun; $$$$$).

Continental

A somewhat unlikely but highly worthwhile discovery is **Gain's German Restaurant**, on the South Orange Blossom Trail (just past Oakridge Road going north), both for food and an excellent selection of bottled and draught beers. The friendly welcome, authentic

Bavarian decor and tempting menu come as a real surprise in the heart of tourist Orlando (11.30am–2.30pm and 4.30–10pm Tue–Thur, 4.30–11pm Fri and Sat, 4.30–10pm Sun; $$–$$$). Another unusual but welcome choice is **The Melting Pot** chain. As the name suggests, this is fondue territory and an extremely quality-conscious version of the genre. Its *Fondues for Two* feature a cheese fondue, salad course and entrée (a main fondue with one of 3 meat selections in a choice of 4 cooking styles). You can still order from a standard entrée list (including chicken, shrimp and steak), but that would be to miss the point (5.30–9.45pm Sun–Fri, 5.30–10.45pm Sat; $$$$).

Splashing out

Finally, if you fancy really splashing out, here are some notable suggestions where both the food and ambience are way above average, albeit with prices to match. Fine dining is on the increase in Orlando and long may it continue – we certainly enjoy the research! Most notably, the area of Sand Lake Road immediately to the west of I-4 (the Fountains and Venezia Plazas) has become a gourmet's delight. These top restaurants are so popular it's advisable to book well in advance.

The wonderfully trendy **Seasons 52** is the most upmarket offering of the Darden group (Bahama Breeze, Olive Garden, Red Lobster). The restaurant's name refers to the fact every week, different products come into season, which is reflected in the menu. New items feature weekly, with some seriously creative cuisine choices. It is also designed to be totally health-conscious, with a balanced approach to carbohydrate/fat content. All appetisers, side salads and soups range from 100-250 calories, the majority being either grilled or oven-roasted, and all entrées are in the 300-475 calorie range. Your server can offer bags of advice – not least with an extensive wine list – and the whole contemporary, bustling atmosphere makes for a really refreshing experience (Plaza Venezia, 407 354 5212; 4.30–11pm; $$$$).

Another great place for seafood (in the Fountains Plaza on West Sand Lake Road) is the splashy **Moonfish**, a true individual in both decor and menu terms. You could make a feast of its appetisers alone, while its sushi and sashimi is inspired. It also has a raw bar with a superb array of oysters. Many restaurants that go for the avant garde look often fail to deliver the goods, but Moonfish does not fall into that trap. It also makes a good romantic excursion for 2 (but not at the tables nearest the bar). Dare to be different could be the motto here (407 363 7262; 11.30am–10pm; $$$$$).

A third notable restaurant in this vicinity (the Plaza Venezia) is **Timpano Italian Chophouse**, a richly decorated upscale classic diner, with cuisine and service to match. The dark, elegant interior lends itself to a romantic occasion and the 1950s New York Italian accent is carried through with great style. And, from its trademark martinis to the tiramisu dessert, everything is served up with panache and taste. Menu highlights include filet mignon, pork chops and Maine lobster, plus linguini, baked ziti and their homemade foccacia bread. If the modern restaurant touch is somehow too brash, Timpano will be a soothing antidote (407 248 0429; 11am–10pm Mon–Fri, noon–11pm Sat, noon–10pm Sun; $$$$$).

Good seafood is not hard to come by in Orlando, but *great* seafood is the preserve of a handful – like **Fulton's Crab House** in *Downtown Disney*'s Marketplace, which is a wonderful choice. This mock riverboat has 6 differently themed

10

dining rooms (albeit with the same menu), plus the Stone Crab Lounge, which features a complete raw bar (and always seems to be busy). Nautical props, photos and lithographs fill the interior, giving it a wonderfully eclectic, period atmosphere, but the real attraction is the food – some of the freshest and most tempting fish, crab and lobster dishes in Florida. The Alaskan king crab is a rare treat, the snow crab claws are as succulent as they come, as is the tuna filet mignon, but there are fresh specials every day (the air shipping bills for which are posted in the main hall), as well as a children's menu. Fulton's features an extensive wine list, micro-brewed beers and its own specialities, but the dining rooms often have a queue as early as 6pm, so it is advisable to book (407 394 2628). The Stone Crab Lounge serves lunch and dinner 11.30am–midnight, while the restaurant is open for dinner only (5–11pm; $$$$-$$$$$).

The **Flying Fish**, at *Disney's Boardwalk Resort*, is also a 5-star seafood experience. The menu is not overburdened with choice, but what it does it does with great flair wonderful presentation. Its 'Peeky Toe' Crab Cake starter melts in the mouth, while the Wood-Fired Mahi Mahi and Spice-crusted Yellowfin Tuna are outstanding. Steak and veal, plus a vegetarian option, are also available (4–11pm Mon–Sat, 4–10pm Sun; $$$$$).

Sticking with the Disney theme, returning to *Downtown Disney* (and next to Fulton's Crab House), is the **Portobello Yacht Club**. It's easy to

miss in its tucked-away location but don't, for this is an Italian experience of great richness and taste sensations. From the complimentary glass of Italian sangria and fresh-baked bread with oven-baked garlic to the classically elegant menu and full wine list, this is a restaurant to be savoured in relaxed style. If nothing else, come in just for the wood-roasted Portobello mushroom starter – absolute heaven for the tastebuds. You can then choose from something as simple as pizza or a classic Caesar salad to proscuitto and sage-wrapped yellow fin tuna, with fine steaks, rack of lamb, veal and pastas all vying for your attention. It all adds up to one of the most enjoyable dining options anywhere in *Walt Disney World*, and reservations are not always necessary (407 934 8888; 11.30am–midnight; $$$$).

The **Park Plaza Gardens** is part of the Park Plaza Hotel on Park Avenue, Winter Park, and this beautiful courtyard restaurant gives you the feel of outdoor dining with the air-conditioned comfort of being indoors. Attentive service is coupled with an elegant, versatile menu that offers a relatively inexpensive lunch or a 3-course adventure featuring escargots, pasta with salmon, medallions of beef or several tempting fish dishes. Cuisine is distinctly 'nouvelle' rather than American and its setting becomes even more intimate and charming in the evening with lights scattered among the foliage. Enjoy Happy Hour in the lounge (5–7pm, with complimentary buffet Thur and Fri), while its popular 3-course Sunday brunch features unlimited champagne and live jazz (407 645 2475; 11.30am–3pm Mon–Sat and 11am–3pm for Sunday brunch, 6–10pm Mon–Thur, 6–11pm Fri–Sat, 6–9pm Sun; $$$$).

A highlight of the Renaissance Orlando Resort is the **Atlantis**

Fulton's Crab House

seafood signature restaurant. This wonderfully elegant, even intimate, corner of an equally smart hotel offers not only fine dining in the normal course of events, but also a scintillating range of daily fresh Floridian seafood specials that just demand to be sampled. A fine wine list complements the full à la carte dinner menu (5–10.30pm; $$$$$). For another meal with a difference check out the **Renaissance's Sunday Brunch**, which is something of an Orlando tradition. Not so much a buffet as a 100-item banquet, it costs $35.95 for adults, $17.50 for 4–12s. Try this and brunch will never be the same again, while it is perfect for a special occasion or group gathering – look out for the chocolate fountain for dessert! (407 351 5555; 10.30am–2.30pm).

The opening of Universal's Hard Rock Hotel brought with it the **Palm Restaurant**, the latest in an upscale nationwide chain that has a big celebrity following. Founded in New York in 1926, it is famous for prime-aged steaks and jumbo lobsters, served in spacious, elegant surroundings and with personable, knowledgeable service. The house speciality, Jumbo Nova Scotia lobster, is spectacular. Its steaks are a bit special, too (check out the Double steak, a 36-oz/1kg+ New York strip for 2 at $65), plus you can choose swordfish, crab, salmon, pork, veal and pasta. All this decadence is reflected in the prices, and vegetables are extra, but the lunch menu shows a more modest touch while maintaining the quality (407 503 7256; 11am–11pm Mon–Sat; noon–10pm Sun; $$$$$).

Salt Island Chophouse and Fish Market is not only an unusual name on International Drive (just north of Sand Lake Road), it is a wholly unusual place to find a true fine dining establishment. It is also a complete original, from its tiki-

Flying Fish Café at Disney's Boardwalk Resort

torch-lit outdoor terrace and complimentary valet parking to the unusual aquatic interior décor (complete with large aquariums) and live jazz lounge. The comprehensive (if rather expensive) wine list superbly offsets the heavily steak and seafood dominated menu, while service is suitably refined and efficient. All the dishes are well explained and even demonstrated, and you will be hard-pushed to choose between the likes of their oak-grilled steaks, trademark blackened grouper and daily seafood specials. For a romantic occasion, try to get a table in their Waterfall dining room (407 996 7258; 5–11pm; $$$$$).

A great favourite of ours is the lovely **Jiko** at *Disney's Animal Kingdom Lodge*, possibly its most imaginative and impressive culinary offering to date. Maintaining the hotel's African theming with its decor and lighting, Jiko ('The

10

Cooking Place') features twin wood-burning ovens, a masterful menu and an exclusive selection of South African wines sure to please any connoisseur. The menu reflects influences from India and Asia as well as Africa, with dishes like Banana-leaf steamed sea bass, Whole roast papaya stuffed with spicy minced beef and Oven-baked garlic chicken tagine with grapefruit, olives and herbs. The personal service and ethnic ambience underline the adventure of eating here and make it a real highlight, while it is the perfect setting for a romantic meal *a deux* (407 939 3463; 5–11pm; $$$$$).

Old Hickory Steakhouse is another hotel-based offering in the Gaylord Palms on I-Drive South. The elaborate Everglades theming gives it an extra dimension, but the steak needs few gimmicks as the house speciality certified Black Angus beef is aged for 21–35 days and cooked to perfection. Side dishes are extra, but the attentive service and alternatives such as oven-roasted swordfish and Maine lobster provide a memorable experience. Watch out, too, for its artisanal cheese course, imported by trendy New York chef Terrance Brennan. If you are fortunate enough to be staying at this amazing hotel, Old Hickory should definitely be on your to-do list. Otherwise, it is a great excuse to pay the Gaylord Palms a visit (5–10.30pm Mon–Fri, 5–11pm Sat, 5–10pm Sun; $$$$$).

Returning to Disney (as everyone does), **Wolfgang Puck's** is an unusual mix of styles and restaurants (4 of them) under one roof, but it represents some of the best family dining in *Downtown Disney* – and a great couples option in the upstairs Dining Room. The main Café is smart enough (and an ideal choice for lunch with children in tow), while the Sushi Bar turns out some truly superb sushi; everything they do here has a fresh, inviting style that complements the bright décor. But head upstairs to the gourmet restaurant and you are in seriously romantic territory, with a great view of *Pleasure Island* at night and service to match. The contrast with the fun hubbub below is striking, while the menu is thoughtful and wonderfully varied – try the braised duck papardelle or the 'chinois' rack of Colorado lamb for a different taste sensation. Whatever the occasion, Wolfgang Puck has it covered (407 938 9653; 6–10.30pm; $$$$$).

When it comes to one of the hippest new places in town, **bluezoo** (at the *Walt Disney World Dolphin Hotel*) not only looks the part, it easily serves up some of the finest food in the Disney realm. Celebrity chef Todd English has made a name for himself in America by creating individual and contrasting restaurant experiences in places as diverse as Seattle and the new *Queen Mary 2* cruise ship – and bluezoo is another gem. With an under-the-sea themed decor that benefits from superb lighting (dine here later rather than earlier for the full effect), it has a wonderfully soothing effect, whether you are just at the bar or in one of the 3 main areas of the restaurant. Both the service and the waiting staff's knowledge of the cuisine and wine list (which is extensive) are impeccable, so feel free to let them steer you around a mouth-watering menu. For starters choose between Steamed mussels in a red curry broth, Teppan seared sea scallops and crab gnocchi, or individual pieces from its raw bar. Fish is the signature dish (although it still offers rotisserie chicken, beef filet and slow-roasted pork chop) and seafood lovers will struggle to narrow down the choice here: Miso-glazed Chilean sea bass, Spit-roasted swordfish, Rare yellowfin tuna, Cantonese lobster, and more, or you could just opt for bluezoo's Dancing fish – your choice of freshly caught fish, whole-roasted over its special rotisserie. With so much quality on offer you will want to linger over every morsel as you admire the creativity that has gone into both the restaurant and the food (3.30–11pm daily; $$$$$).

Finally, we have saved the best for last with what we consider the most amazing and enjoyable restaurant experience currently in central Florida. **Tchoup Chop** (pronounced 'chop chop'), at Universal's Royal Pacific Resort, is the latest establishment in the gourmet stable of New Orleans master chef Emeril Lagasse, and it offers Asian–Pacific fusion cuisine in the most eye-catching setting. The huge central pond is a tribute to feng shui, and you can easily sit and study the interior for much of the meal and still notice new things at the end. Service is a team effort at each table (which can be off-putting), but the superb menu is well presented and explained. And oh, that menu! Taking some of the most aromatic and flavoursome elements of Thai, Chinese, Japanese, South Seas and other Pacific Rim cultures, Lagasse has conjured up a mouth-watering array of dishes, all immensely tempting and tasting as good as they sound. Start with Homemade dumpling box (with a fresh port and ginger filling, hand-rolled, steamed and served with sake soy dipping sauce) or the Polynesian crabcake (with ginger scallion aioli and papaya salsa), then graduate to superb entrees like Macadamia-nut crusted Atlantic salmon (served with ginger soy

BRIT TIP: For a special occasion (particularly a romantic one), bluezoo, Jiko and Tchoup Chop are the pick of a rich crop.

butter sauce, steamed rice and stir-fried vegetables), Tchoup Chop's Clay pot of the day (served with steamed rice and seasonal vegetables) or the Hawaiian dinner plate including smoked ribs, kahlua pork, teriyaki-grilled chicken, chorizo potato hash and baked macaroni. If that does not set your tastebuds trembling, nothing will!

Dinner here is exceptionally busy, so try lunch if they cannot squeeze you in (407 503 2467; 11.30am–2pm; 5.30–10pm Sun–Thur, 5.30–11pm Fri and Sat; $$$$$).

Best of the rest

There are at least another 10 restaurants worthy of a passing mention here. They are: **Everglades**, the smart steak and seafood-orientated dining room inside the Omni Rosen Center hotel on International Drive; **Sunset Sam's**, the Gaylord Palms' Key West-style restaurant inside its magnificent resort; **Roy's**, a hugely upscale gourmet choice in the Plaza Venezia on West Sand Lake Road; **Zen**, a wonderfully stylish new Asian-fusion restaurant at the Omni resort at Champions Gate; the **Venetian Room**, the surprising upscale dining venue at the Caribe Royale Resort on World Center Drive; **Boheme Restaurant**, a quite magnificent menu in this tucked-away gem at the Grand Bohemian hotel in downtown Orlando; **Le Jardin du Castillons**, a small but eye-catching French restaurant just off Park Avenue in Winter Park; **Norman's**, the feature restaurant of celebrity chef Norman Van Aken at the Grand Lakes Resort; **Texas de Brasil**, an unusual but delicious Brazilian-style steakhouse; and **Citrico's**, the most chic of *Disney's Grand Floridian Resort* restaurants.

Now on to another of our favourite topics – shopping…

10

11 Shopping
(or, How to Send Your Credit Card into Meltdown)

As well as being a theme park wonderland, the vast area that constitutes metropolitan Orlando is a shopper's paradise, with a dazzling array of specialist outlets, malls, flea markets and discount retailers. It is also a vigorous growth market, with new centres springing up seemingly all the time, from the smartest of malls to the cheapest of gift shop plazas – and you can hardly go a few yards in the main tourist areas without a shop insisting it has the best tourist bargains of one sort or another.

With the exchange rate so favourable for UK visitors in recent years, shopping has, in fact, become as much an attraction as the theme parks! You will be bombarded by 'retail therapy' opportunities wherever you go, and the only danger is you will seriously exceed your baggage allowance for the return flight – or your Duty Free allowance. **Your limit in the catch-all duty category of 'gifts and souvenirs' is still only £145 per person**, and it is easy to exceed that by a distance. Paying the duty and VAT can still be cheaper than buying the same items at home, but remember to keep your receipts and go back through the red 'goods to declare' channel.

You pay duty (which varies depending on the item) on the total purchase price (i.e. inclusive of Florida sales tax) once you have exceeded £145, plus VAT at 17.5 per cent. You CANNOT pool your allowances to cover one item that exceeds a single allowance. Hence, if you buy a camera that costs £200, you have to pay the duty on the full £200, taking the total to £213.20, and then VAT on that figure. However, if you have several items that add up to £145, and then another which exceeds that, you pay the duty and VAT only on the excess (and the customs officers usually give you the benefit of the lowest rate on what you pay for). Duty rates are updated regularly and vary from 2.7 per cent (golf clubs) to 15 per cent (mountain bikes). For more info, contact the Customs and Excise National Advice Service on 0845 010 9000 or visit www.hmce.gov.uk. Your ordinary duty-free allowances from America include 200 cigarettes and 1 litre of spirits or 2 litres of sparkling wine and 2 litres of still wine. Alligator products, which constitute an endangered species, require a special import licence, and you should consult the Department of the Environment first.

When it comes to the fun part of shopping (and American stores are genuinely fun to just browse, let alone splash out in), you can expect to pay in dollars what you pay in pounds for items like clothes, books and CDs, and real bargains are to be had in jeans, trainers, shoes, sports equipment and cosmetics. Virtually everywhere offers free, convenient parking, while American shop assistants couldn't be more polite

ORLANDO'S SHOPPING CENTRES

A Downtown Disney
B The Mercado
C The Pointe Orlando
D Old Town
E Belz Festival Bay
F Prime Outlets
G Wal-Mart SuperCenter
H Prime Outlets
I The Loop
J Lake Buena Vista Factory Stores
K Orlando Premium Outlets
L Flea World
M Osceola Flea And Farmers' Market

N Florida Mall
O Shops of Celebration
P Altamonte Mall
Q Seminole Towne Center
R 192 Flea Market
S Plaza Venezia
T Mall At Millenia
U Park Avenue
V Winter Park Village
W Kissimmee Historic District/Farmers' Market
X Goodings International Plaza
Y Crossroads Plaza
Z Fountains Plaza

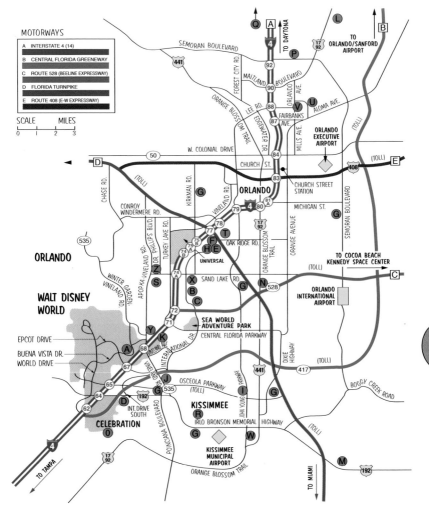

MOTORWAYS

A	INTERSTATE 4 (14)
B	CENTRAL FLORIDA GREENEWAY
C	ROUTE 528 (BEELINE EXPRESSWAY)
D	FLORIDA TURNPIKE
E	ROUTE 408 (E-W EXPRESSWAY)

SCALE   MILES
0   1   2   3

11

> BRIT TIP: Pick up the *Orlando Sentinel* newspaper on a Sunday and you will get the full local lowdown on all the great SALES for the coming week.

and helpful. Be aware, though, of the 'hidden extras' of shopping costs. Unlike our VAT, Florida sales tax is NOT part of the displayed purchase price, so you must add 6 or 7 per cent (depending on the county) for the final price.

If those are the mechanics of shopping, here is a rundown of the main attractions and the sort of fun and bargains to be had.

Downtown Disney

The heart of *Walt Disney World* in many ways is its *Downtown Disney* district, split into three linked sections: *Marketplace*, *Pleasure Island* and *West Side*. This is typical Disney, a beautiful location, imaginative building and landscaping and a host of one-off elements that make shopping a pleasure, with no less than 51 shops and dining opportunities.

In the *Marketplace* (9.30am–11pm), don't miss the **World of Disney** store, the largest of its kind, the **Lego Imagination Center** (an interactive playground and shop), the amazing **Art of Disney** and **Team Mickey's Athletic Club**. **Once Upon A Toy** is a gigantic toy

> BRIT TIP: Don't buy electrical goods in the US – they will not work in the UK without an adapter. Some games systems (notably the Nintendo Gamecube) are NOT compatible with UK players.

emporium complete with a host of classic games, many with a Disney theme, for kids to try. Other worthwhile one-offs are the blissful **Basin** (for hand-carved soaps, bubble baths and shampoo bars) and **Disney's Wonderful World of Memories** (for all scrapbook fans, plus the only place to get a Disney postmark for your postcards home!). Those keen on the Disney hobby of pin trading should check out **Pin Traders**, while **Summer Sands** offers an excellent range of swimwear and casual clothing.

Dancing fountains and squirt pools (where kids tend to get seriously wet), the lakeside setting and boating opportunities all add to the appeal here. Restaurants include the superbly themed **Rainforest Café**, **McDonald's**, **Wolfgang Puck Express** and the casual waterfront setting of **Cap'n Jack's Restaurant**, while ice cream and chocolate fans should check out **Ghirardelli's** for cool sundaes and super shakes. For a British touch, opt for the speciality hot sandwiches at the **Earl of Sandwich**, a joint venture between Planet Hollywood and Lord John Montagu, the 11th Earl of Sandwich himself. For an upmarket touch, we rate **Fulton's Crab House** and **Portobello Yacht Club** (see Chapter 10 Dining Out).

The shops of *Pleasure Island* (7pm–1am) add the smart streetwear of **Changing Attitudes**, movie memorabilia at **Reel Finds**, the sports-themed **DTV** and the seemingly omni-present style of **Harley-Davidson**, plus the new **Raglan Road**, an Irish-themed pub and restaurant, with live music daily.

Continuing to *Downtown Disney West Side* (10.30am–11pm) gives you the superb **AMC 24** cinema complex and the world's largest **Virgin Megastore,** plus another 18 retail and dining outlets. The **Hoypoloi Gallery** is one of our favourites for an eclectic range of artwork, from metal to glass, while **Magic Masters** (all kinds of magic tricks and souvenirs, with demonstrations), **Sunglass Icon**, **Guitar Gallery** and **Magnetron** are all highly original. The dining choice is again superb, with **Planet Hollywood**, **House of Blues**, **Bongo's Cuban Café** and our favourite, **Wolfgang Puck** – a 4-part restaurant with something for everyone.

Downtown Disney can be found off Exits 67 and 68 of I-4 and is well signposted (Exit 68 can be congested at peak periods).

International Drive

This core tourist area is simply awash with shopping of all kinds, from the cheapest and tackiest plazas, full of 'Tourist Gift Shops', to clever, purpose-built centres. Some of the shops just north of the Sand Lake Road junction are best avoided, while the northern end of I-Drive is undergoing a major redevelopment. Typically, this area has been renowned for discount outlet shopping – a local speciality, offering name brands in large quantities at heavily reduced prices to clear. However, there had been a noticeable downturn in business (and in the quality of the outlets as a result) in recent years, leading to the sale of the well-known Belz Discount Outlet World and Belz Designer Outlet Center in summer 2005. **Prime Outlets** are the new owners, and there are plans for a long-overdue redevelopment of the 2 extensive shopping plazas. However, no new building will take place until early 2006, and then the full 'extreme makeover' will take 3 years with parts of the outlet centre closing while others remain open, and with new shops coming in. The former Belz Designer Outlet Center a little further down I-Drive is also part of this process, and will be incorporated into the full Prime

> BRIT TIP: Need a proper British breakfast? Head for The Mercado food court and check out **Best of British** for the full Monty in brekkie terms, plus lunch and dinner specialities. Run by Brits Paul and Lorna Hunjan, it is a rare gem.

Outlets refurbishment.

Equally, **The Mercado**, one of the original speciality complexes in the heart of I-Drive, has hit financial trouble in recent years, with many units closing and attractions like Guinness World Records Experience and Hard Rock Vault also failing. At the time of writing, there remain 16 speciality shops, 5 restaurants (the fine Italian of **Bergamo's**, the seafood-orientated **Mahi Mahi Bistro**, buffet-style **La China,** the authentic Mexican of **Guadalajara Grill and Cantina** and the excellent steaks of **The Butcher Shop**), the all-British **Cricketers' Arms** pub (see also page 277) and an increasingly unappetising food court (with the one bright spot of **Best of British**).

The Mercado is open 10am– 10pm daily (from 8am in the food court and until 11pm at the restaurants), and also offers live evening entertainment in its Courtyard (www.themercado.com).

Another major I-Drive shopping complex is also undergoing a sea change, with **The Pointe Orlando** beginning a $30 million, 18-month redevelopment in summer 2005. The dramatic rebuild will see the demolition of the huge FAO Schwarz toy store (whose parent company went bankrupt in 2003) and the opening of a new entrance plaza directly from I-Drive, as well as adding new shops and restaurants. However, the rest of The Pointe

11

The Mercado

WILL remain open, meaning there are still 36 smart shops and 9 restaurants and cafés to enjoy. You can indulge your passion for fashion at places like **Victoria's Secret**, **Armani Exchange**, **Image Leather**, **Chico's**, **Gray Fifth Avenue** and the **Everything But Water** swimwear store, or stock up on gifts and souvenirs at **Bath & Body Works**, **Yankee Candle** (highly recommended), **Glow**, **Sunglass Hut** and the excellent **Tharoo & Co** jewellery.

You can also still visit the state-of-the-art, **Muvico Pointe 21** cinema complex, and finish up with a meal at lively **Johnny Rockets** American diner, **Hooters** (wings, ribs, chicken and the famous Hooters girls), **Adobe Gila's** (Mexican style, with a killer range of margaritas!) or **Lulu's Baitshack** (New Orleans-flavoured cuisine). Our favourite is **Dan Marino's Fine Food & Spirits**, a stylish sports-themed bar and restaurant with an excellent range of salads, sandwiches, seafood and meat dishes. The **Pac Man Café** arcade-and-restaurant then offers the chance to let the kids play on a vast array of video games and simulators while mum and dad take time to do the shops in peace (it's also great for desserts!). Parking is in its multi-storey car park, but several shops and restaurants will redeem your parking ticket if you spend money there. The Pointe is open 10am–10pm Mon–Sat

and 11am–9pm Sun (later at the bars and restaurants; www.pointeorlando.com).

The latest centre is **Belz Festival Bay**, right at the top of I-Drive. Its mix of shops and entertainment is quite unusual, and many of the stores will be unfamiliar to Brits – but don't let that put you off as there is much to discover here. The main entrance is graced by a huge fountain and multi-coloured tiling, while it also features **Ron Jon's Surf Shop** battling for prominence with **Fuddruckers** diner (superb burgers), the eclectic golf-themed **Murray Bros Caddyshack** and the new **Dixie Crossroads** seafood restaurant. Step inside the mall doors (for it is mainly an enclosed centre) and you discover a huge water feature and another 57 stores and restaurants, plus **Vans Skate Park** and the superb **Cinemark 20-screen Movie Complex**, arguably the fanciest cinema in Orlando (featuring state-of-the-art stadium seating). The massive **Bass Pro Shops Outdoor World** is worth checking out for its range of outdoor clothing and equipment (fishing, boating, hunting, hiking) as well as the amazing themed decor, while **Shepler's Western Wear**'s range of apparel, boots and other footwear has to be seen to be believed (all at great prices, too). **Steve & Barry's University Sportswear** is another unusual clothing store (especially for the value-conscious), while **Hilo Hattie's** is a wonderful emporium of all things Hawaiian. Other notables include **Candle Time**, **Charlotte Russe** (trendy women's clothing),

> BRIT TIP: The new *Festival News* carries a good range of UK publications if you need to stay in touch with home news.

Zirbes Emporium (an eclectic gift-and-furniture store) and **Swim Smart**, plus a unique, glow-in-the-dark mini-golf course, the **Putting Edge**, which is a great place to occupy the kids for a while.

Vans Skate Park is the perfect opportunity to unleash anyone with a skateboard or roller-blade obsession (visit www.vans.com, then Skateparks, then Orlando), offering 6 2-hour sessions a day (10am–midnight) as well as a full range of safety equipment and board rentals, plus a chill-out lounge. Due in summer 2006 is **Ron Jon's Surf Park**, a unique $10m, 100,000sq ft facility that will offer the chance to surf and body-board on 3 open-air wave pools. Designed for beginners or experts, the main Pro Surf Pool will feature 8ft (2.5m) waves, but there will also be lessons for novices in the 3ft (1m) waves of the Boogie Pool. Add a Surf Shop, Ron Jon Restaurant and spectator seating and you should have an amazing facility.

The emphasis of Festival Bay is as much on entertainment as on shopping, and the relaxing, village street style is aimed at the casual wanderer. There is no food court, but there are small dining outlets dotted around, notably **Long John Silver's**, **Asian Café**, **Auntie Anne's**, **Cold Stone Creamery** (superb ice cream), **Subway, Villa Pizza Cuccina** and **Rocky Mountain Chocolate Factory**. The 3 feature restaurants are all great choices for a meal or just a post-shopping snack. **Fuddruckers** is a highly tempting counter service diner offering all manner of burgers (including ostrich, turkey, salmon

BRIT TIP: Visit Charlotte Russe's clothes shop for a free Advantage card offering $200 in savings throughout Festival Bay.

and vegetarian options), salads, soups and desserts; **Murray Bros Caddyshack** offers a varied mix of salads, steaks, seafood, barbecue, pasta and pizza (one of the best all-round menus in town); and the new **Dixie Crossroads** is a must for seafood lovers, specialising in rock shrimp, Maine lobster, snow crab and scallops. Festival Bay is open 10am–9pm Mon–Sat and 11am–7pm Sun (www.belz.com/realestate/retail/festival).

Kissimmee

Kissimmee's version of the purpose-built tourist shopping centre is **Old Town**, an antique-style offering in the heart of Highway 192, with a tourist-friendly mix of shops, restaurants, bars and fairground attractions, all set out along brick-built streets. The 75 shops range from standard souvenirs, novel T-shirt outlets and Disney merchandise to sportswear, motorbike fashions and other collectibles (check out the **General Store** for a step back in time, or the **Old Town Portrait Gallery** for period style). The **International Space Station** offers a host of NASA-inspired gifts and games, while **Black Market Minerals**, **Andean Manna** and **Magic Max** are great for novel gift ideas.

There are 17 restaurants or snack bars and some amusing diversions, like the 5-storey **Haunted House of Old Town** ($10 for adults, $6.75 for children) and the **Hollywood Wax Museum and Tower of London Experience**, a novel and

11

Shops for the boys in Old Town

well-constructed attraction with both a waxworks and a fairly grisly torture chamber replica (probably too graphic for young children). It costs $5/person (under 5 free) or $15 for a family of 5 (2 adults, 3 children). Those in need of some pampering or a massage should head for the **Time For Pleasure Day Spa** (open 10am–10pm daily).

Old Town then features 23 out-and-out rides, from the standard and rather tame bumper cars, go-karts and 60ft (18m) **Century Wheel** to the **Windstorm** roller-coaster, **Turbo Force** (a crazy version of the big wheel) and the immense **Old Town Slingshot** – a 365ft (110m) bungee catapult! There is a **Kids' Town** area of junior rides and tickets are sold separately for most rides (at $1 each), but if you plan to do several, go for the Valuepak at $20 for 22 tickets or $30 for 35. There is also an All You Can Ride Wristband at $15 (Mon–Thur) and $20 (Fri–Sun). The Slingshot ($25), bumper cars ($5), go-karts ($6) and Turbo Force ($10) have separate fees. **Damon's Grill** restaurant is an excellent dining choice, with great ribs, burgers and salads (plus sport on their big screen TVs) but the **Blue Max Tavern** is a fun alternative.

Allow up to 4 hours here and try to take in the weekly **Saturday Nite Cruise** at 8.30pm, a drive-past of 300-plus vintage and collector cars (the biggest in America) that has become a real trademark here and celebrated its 15th anniversary in June 2005. A **Friday Nite Cruise** features cars built from 1973–87, plus live music and prizes. Every Thursday is **Motorcycle Nite** from 6pm, and the place can get fairly raucous later on, with plenty of alcoholic libations (witness the **Sun on the Beach** bar). Parking is free and Old Town is open 10am–11pm daily (rides open from noon–11pm; www.old-town.com).

Right next door to Old Town you will also find the amazing **SkyCoaster** ride and its partner speed demon **G Force**. SkyCoaster is a 300ft (90m) tower that sends up to 3 riders at a time on a free-fall plunge that turns into a giant swing – at 85mph (136kph)! The air-powered G Force sees 2 dragster cars race side-by-side at up to 120mph (192 kph) (0–110mph (176kph) in 2 seconds!) for a grand total of 11 seconds. An intense – if brief – thrill. A single rider flight on SkyCoaster costs $40, while it is $70 for 2 and $90 for 3 (noon–midnight daily), while G Force costs $30 as the driver and $10 as passenger (noon–11.30pm daily). Its website – www.skycoaster.cc – offers a discount coupon for either ride and a combo ticket for both at $50.

Kissimmee is short of quality shopping otherwise, as the Kissimmee Manufacturers' Outlet Mall and Osceola Square Mall are in urgent need of refurbishment. However, new development **The Loop** helps redress the balance. This imaginative open-air plaza (at the junction of Osceola Parkway and John Young Parkway, opened in 2005) offers a unique mix of shops and restaurants, plus a 16-screen Regal Cinema, in a pleasant, pedestrian-friendly landscaped setting, with the shops grouped around the large car park. Many of the shops may not mean much to UK visitors but are worth visiting, notably **Ross** (a huge discount warehouse of clothes, shoes, linens, cosmetics and more), **Kohl's** (a well-priced department store), **Bed, Bath & Beyond** (a huge range of household wares), **Pac Sun** (beach and casual wear), **Old Navy** (clothing), **Michaels** (arts and crafts), **Sports Authority** and **Famous Footwear** (discounted shoes and trainers). In addition, there is a hairdresser, nail salon,

BRIT TIP: If you are into scrap-booking or other arts and crafts, you should definitely seek out one of the 8 Michaels stores as a scrap-booking heaven!

chemist (CVS) and a superb line-up of 10 restaurants and cafés. Look out in particular for **Mama Fu's** Asian-fusion cuisine, the excellent Italian style of **Macaroni Grill**, the gourmet Mexican of **Chipotle Grill** and the more hearty fare of **Panera Bread** (excellent soups, salads and sandwiches). Once fully completed, The Loop will have more than 40 stores and cafés, open 10am–9.30pm Mon–Sat, 11am–6pm Sun (later at the restaurants and cinemas; www.attheloop.com).

Lake Buena Vista

The Lake Buena Vista area has 2 of the best discount outlet centres, with a range of goods to make even the most jaded shopper salivate – and prices to match!

High on your list of 'must visit' shops should be **Orlando Premium Outlets**, which are a huge hit with UK visitors. With a fresh look and style, and a legion of big-name designers (from the likes of Nike, adidas and Gap to Ralph Lauren, Hugo Boss, Versace and Zegna) they can be found on Vineland Avenue between I-Drive and I-4 (just south of SeaWorld; or Exit 68 off I-4). In all, they offer 115 stores of well-known brand names (like Timberland, Reebok, Banana Republic, Fossil and Calvin Klein) in a semi-covered pedestrian plaza, with easy parking and the convenience of being at the south end of the I-Ride Trolley (Main Line). Recent additions include Samsonite Company Store,

Wedgewood/Waterford, Ecco Unltd (upscale T-shirts, jeans and sportswear), Fendi (stylish women's clothing and signature handbags), Little Me (baby/toddler clothes), Rack Room Shoes (a mini-warehouse of footwear fashion) and KB Toys (a huge discount choice for kids of all ages). Also under construction in summer 2005 was a large Gap Outlet store.

Watch out also for big Disney bargains at the **Character Premiere** store and Universal items at **Universal Studios Outlet Store**. Even the food court is above average, with 11 outlets from JR's Steakery and Max Orient to Starbucks and Subway. Open 10am-10pm Mon-Sat (10am-11pm in summer), 10am-9pm Sun (407 238 7787, www.premiumoutlets.com). For those without a car, there is a daily shuttle service at $6/person round trip from hotels in the Lake Buena Vista area and $9/person from Highway 192 in Kissimmee. Call 407 390 0000 for reservations. The Lynx bus service also stops here (407 841 2279) or you can try Star Taxi (407 857 9999).

BRIT TIP: Try to shop at the big Outlet centres during the week or in the evening – they can draw big crowds at the weekend and public holidays.

The recently expanded **Lake Buena Vista Factory Stores** offer another range of big-name products at discount prices, from Fossil, Sony, Reebok and Tommy Hilfiger and Ralph Lauren) to a budget-priced Disney Character Corner, OshKosh B'Gosh Superstore and (the better-priced) Carter's Childrenswear. This centre is another open-air plaza, with almost 50 stores spread over 6 acres (2.5ha) and with plentiful,

11

convenient parking. It is slightly off the beaten track and therefore not quite as busy as some of the others. New shops are being added all the time, and 2005 saw the addition of Eddie Bauer, Waterford/Wedgwood and Nike. There is also a decent food court (now serving beer in deference to British requests!) and a kids' playground. Some of the stores and brand names may not be well-known to us, but the likes of **Old Navy** (excellent value casual clothing), **Perfume Smart** (heavily discounted fragrances and other cosmetics), **SAS Shoemakers** (think Hush Puppies, only cheaper!), **Welcome Home** (home furnishings and accessories) and **Rack Room Shoes** (big names at serious savings) are well worth discovering. Other notable shops are **Borders Books Outlet** (bargain books) and the quirky **Notable & Notorious** (film and rock music memorabilia). **World of Coffee** is both an internet café and one of the most pleasant places you will find to sip a speciality coffee and enjoy a cake or pastry, with its outdoor terrace and bird cages.

> BRIT TIP: Go online at www.lbvfs.com for up to $400 in discount coupons.

Other services include an office of **Florida Leisure** vacation home management and their Cruise Planners agency, plus the main Welcome Centre for **Travel City Direct**. The Factory Stores can be found on SR 535 (2 miles/3km south off Exit 68 on I-4) and are open 10am– 9pm Mon–Sat, 10am–6pm Sun. Its shuttle service picks up at various hotels and condos units in a 10-mile (16km) radius (407 238 9301; www.lbvfs.com).

Kids Town in Old Town

Malls

If the discount outlets often represent the best value, the choice and style of the area's malls are unarguable, and well worth adding to your holiday agenda. They boast a huge range of shops and, if you can take advantage of their periodic sales, you will be firmly on the bargain trail. The top 2 locally are the Florida Mall and the Mall at Millenia, and both offer a contrasting shopping experience.

The **Florida Mall** is the largest in central Florida and features 264 shops, with 6 large department stores and an excellent food court with a choice of 16 outlets, plus the lively bar-restaurant **Ruby Tuesday** and the excellent **California Pizza Kitchen**. Located on the South Orange Blossom Trail, on the corner of Sand Lake Road, this spacious and extremely smart mall is open 10am-9pm Mon-Sat, 12pm-6pm Sun. Highlights are the department stores, led by the upmarket (but expensive) Saks Fifth Avenue and Macy's (formerly

> BRIT TIP: Need a good book? Make a beeline for Barnes & Noble, on West Sand Lake Road in the Venezia Plaza or on the S Orange Blossom Trail opposite the Florida Mall, for a magnificent array of titles and a great coffee shop.

Burdines), plus JC Penney, Sears and Dillard's. New in October 2002 was Nordstrom (which also has a sit-down café), another upscale department store. Other shops worth looking out for are Bath & Body Works, Williams Sonoma ('the place for cooks' – and how!), PacSun (beachwear and more) and (for kids) Build-a-Bear Workshop, KB Toys and Playmobil Fun Park.

You can also benefit here from a discount coupon packet (from Guest Services) that includes a handy International Size Chart to help you deal with American clothes sizing. Additional services include free wheelchair use, pushchair rental and a video arcade in the food court. There are even spa and beauty treatments available in the Lancôme Institut de Beauté in Dillard's, the JC Penney styling salon and day spa, and the Elizabeth Arden salon at Saks Fifth Avenue. You can also visit the smart Florida Mall Hotel for their **Le Jardin** restaurant and bar. For more info, visit www.simon.com.

> BRIT TIP: Kids – let your parents take you to the Florida Mall, then insist on visiting the huge Toys R Us store right in front!

If the Florida Mall is the biggest shopping venue in town, the **Mall at Millenia** (which opened in October 2002) is the smartest. Located just off I-4 to the north of Universal Orlando (Exit 78), it is the most upmarket, dramatic and technologically advanced shopping complex in Florida, with New York's most famous department stores – Bloomingdale's, Neiman Marcus and Macy's – among a select number of other top-name boutiques such as Tiffany and Louis Vuitton. The entrance features a 60ft (18m) glass rotunda with a flowing water garden theme and a helpful concierge desk

> BRIT TIP: Visit the Concierge office at Mall at Millenia, fill out their marketing questionnaire and receive a free gift.

(valet parking is also available). Then you can head out in one of 4 directions over the marble and terrazzo floors or go upstairs to the refreshing, high-quality, 12-outlet food court, the Orangerie Cafés, where the only difficulty is deciding which of the tempting (and health-conscious) eateries to choose. Look out in particular for **Bistro Sensations** (wonderful salads, pastas, pittas and wraps), the authentic Mandarin-style of **Chinatown**, the fresh taste of **Nori Japanese Grill** (beef and chicken teriyaki and excellent sushi, all prepared on the spot) and the **Southwest Grill** (succulent chicken, barbecue beef and salads), as well as the **Tango Grill**, an Argentinean-style café (steaks, chicken and signature crêpes).

The grand architecture is also focused on 5 separate courts along a flattened, serpentine 'S' shape, topped by a flowing, arched glass roof like some gigantic conservatory. On 2 airy levels (3 in Macy's and Bloomingdale's) and with 8 'Juliet' balconies connecting the 2 sides, the mall consists of a colossal amount of glass, plus a stunning Grand Court, featuring a dozen 20ft (6m) columns capped by curved plasma video screens. And, while around 20 per cent of the 150 outlets are upscale and exclusive (Cartier, Chanel,

11

The Mall at Millenia

Lacoste, Jimmy Choo, Tiffany & Co, Bang & Olufsen, etc, plus the luxury of Neiman Marcus for brands like Gucci and Prada), the other 80 per cent comprise more mainstream shops like Gap, Banana Republic and Victoria's Secret. Several outlets provide a distinctive shopping experience – Metropolitan Museum of Art, Z Gallerie, People's Pottery and Rocks Fine Jewellery – without the price tag to go with it.

The 4 main restaurants are also first class: heavenly **Cheesecake Factory**, gourmet seafood **McCormick & Schmick**, **PF Chang's China Bistro** and **Brio Tuscan Grille**. On top of that (AND the **Orangerie Cafés**), you have the excellent fresh bread and sandwich style of **Panera Bread**, the **California Pizza Kitchen** and a **Johnny Rockets** 1950s-style diner. This is also the only mall to have a US Post Office inside (NB: standard postcards back to the UK cost 70c, 80c for large ones). The **First Friday** of each month also sees a free concert in the Orangerie, from 5–8pm, featuring some outstanding performers, from jazz and blues to rock and soul. Also new in 2005 was the chic **Blue Martini**, a speciality martini bar, sushi/tapas restaurant and live music venue. With more than 29 unique martinis, plus an extensive wine and spirits list, premium cigars and some appetising menu samplers, this is the current trendy hangout, on either its outdoor terrace or indoor stage room. There is live music – jazz and R&B – from 7.30–11.30pm, then dance music with the house DJ. Hours are 4pm–2am Mon–Fri and 1pm–2am Sat and Sun (Happy Hour 4–7pm; see more on www.blue martinilounge.com). It takes the shopping experience to a new level in Florida and is open from 10am–9pm Mon–Sat, 12am–7pm Sun (www.mallatmillenia.com).

Three alternatives to these popular (and busy – especially at weekends) malls are the **Altamonte Mall**, on Altamonte Avenue in the suburb of Altamonte Springs (take Exit 92 off I-4 and head east for half a mile on Route 436, then turn left), **Seminole Towne Center**, just off I-4 to the north of Orlando on the outskirts of Sanford (Exit 101C off I-4) and **Oviedo Mall**, to the east of Orlando (right off Exit 41 of the Central Florida Greeneway, 417). The Altamonte Mall is above average and slightly off the beaten tourist track, featuring 118 speciality shops, 4 major department stores – Macy's, Dillard's, JC Penney and Sears – a 19-outlet food court and 4 more restaurants, including **Ruby Tuesday** and the **Orlando Ale House**. A major refurbishment in 2003 added an 18-screen cinema, a remodelled food court and children's soft-play area. Open 10am–9pm Mon–Sat and 11am–6pm Sun, and it offers a VIP savings book to visitors at the Customer Service Center (www.altamontemall.com). Seminole Towne Center offers a 2-storey wonderland of 100 designer shops and boutiques and 5 department stores, as well as craft stalls, food court and 6 full-service restaurants (including **Orlando Ale House**, **Olive Garden** and **Red Lobster**). It makes a handy place to while away your last few hours if you have a return flight from nearby Orlando Sanford airport and is open 10am–9pm Mon–Sat, and noon–6pm Sun (www.simon.com). **Oviedo Marketplace** is on a slightly smaller scale, albeit still with a distinctive range of shops, and the department stores of Sears, Macy's and Dillards. You will also find a Footlocker Superstore, Bed, Bath & Beyond, Chamberlin's Market & Café (a health food choice), a food court and the quaint Bill's Elbow South Restaurant & Bar, plus the Regal Cinemas 22 cineplex.. New in 2005 was RJ Gators Florida Sea Grill &

Bar. Open 10am-9pm Mon-Sat and noon-6pm Sun (www.oviedo marketplace.com).

Flea markets

The locals also have a passion for flea markets, highlighted by **Flea World,** America's largest covered market, with 1,700 stalls spread over 104 acres (42ha), including three massive (air-conditioned), themed buildings and a 7-acre (2.8-ha) amusement park, **Fun World** (rides cost about $2 each). It is open Fri, Sat and Sun only, 9am–6pm, and can be found a 30-minute drive away on Highway 17/92 (best picked up from Exit 90 on I-4) between Orlando and Sanford (to the north). The stalls include all manner of market goods (nearly all new or slight seconds), from fresh produce to antiques and jewellery, while there is a full-scale food court and a 300-seat pizza and burger eatery, the **Carousel Restaurant**, plus free entertainment on the Fun World Pavilion stage. Call 407 330 1792 or look up www.fleaworld.com.

On a smaller scale is the **Osceola Flea and Farmers' Market** at the eastern end of Highway 192 in Kissimmee (8am–5pm Fri–Sun), offering food, clothing, household and kitchen supplies, electronics, sporting goods, collectibles and handicrafts (call 407 846 2811 for more details). In downtown Kissimmee, Toho Square is home to a small **Farmers' Market** every Thursday (7am–1pm) with everything from fresh produce to jewellery and candles for sale. Nearby, **Susan's Courtside Café** offers delicious sandwiches, pizzas, salads, smoothies and coffees (7am–8pm Mon–Fri). The **192 Flea Market**, in the heart of Highway 192 just past Medieval Times and the Wal-Mart Supercenter, is more convenient for the main tourist area and is open 7 days a week (9am–

6pm), with 400 booths from apples to timeshare, plus as many cheap Disney T-shirts as you can carry!

Traditional shopping

The attractions and possibilities of Winter Park's **Park Avenue** have already been detailed in Chapter 8 (see page 222), but the area also has the **Winter Park Village**, a small, upscale, open-plan development of boutique shops, larger speciality stores like Borders Books, and some fine restaurants. The Village is on North Orlando Avenue – Exit 87 off I-4, head east on Fairbanks Avenue, then north on Highway 17/92, North Orange Avenue, for 2 miles (3km), and it is on the right. It offers a nice change from the usual malls and plazas – as well as some excellent dining at **PF Chang's China Bistro** (their spicy Szechuan chicken is delicious), **Brio Tuscan Grille** (fine Italian fare) and the gorgeous **Cheesecake Factory** (www.shopwinterpark village.com).

More traditional shopping can also be found in the revamped **Historic District of Kissimmee** on Broadway, 2 blocks south of Highway 192 on Route 17/92, along Main Street and Broadway. These are a number of restored turn-of-the-century buildings featuring craft and gift shops, a children's boutique, country store and 7 restaurants (including **Azteca's** for fine Mexican fare), plus antiques, Western and sportswear. The Historic District shops are open 9am–5.30pm weekdays, 9am–3pm Sat.

Also off the beaten tourist path but worth a visit are the shops and restaurants of Disney's town of **Celebration**, a unique collection of speciality stores, an ice cream and candy shop, restaurants, cinemas, lakeside dining and a Saturday Farmers' Market, plus boat and bike rentals and the superb Celebration Hotel (see page 78). Follow the

11

signs to downtown Celebration along Celebration Avenue, just off Highway 192 (a quarter of a mile east of I-4). The shops are open 10am–9pm Mon–Sat, noon–6pm Sun. This is a re-creation of the 1950s 'ideal' town, complete with white picket fences, and there are some lovely walks round the main lake. The dining options – notably the stylish Spanish-Cuban ambience of the **Columbia Restaurant**, the Italian **Café D'Antonio** and the New England seafood of the **Celebration Town Tavern** all on Market Street – are superb.

Supermarkets

Apart from the big chemist chain stores, **CVS** (formerly Eckerd) and **Walgreens**, which both sell a huge range of goods (including basic groceries), there are any number of supermarkets in Orlando these days. High on many people's lists is **Wal-Mart**, the warehouse-like American supermarket that sells just about everything. There are no less than 20 Wal-Marts in central Florida, 15 of which are the open-24-hour Supercenter kind. The main tourist area stores are on Highway 27 (just north of 192), Highway 192 by Medieval Times, Osceola Parkway (at Buenaventura Lakes), John Young Parkway (at Sand Lake Road), on Kirkman Road (north of Universal) and a new Kissimmee store by Highway 535 and Osceola Parkway. There is plenty of choice for supermarkets, though, and you will find better quality produce at the likes of **Publix** (throughout the main tourist areas, notably on Highway 192 and 27), **Goodings** (on International Drive and the Crossroads plaza near *Downtown Disney*), **Winn-Dixie** (a major US chain) and our favourite **Albertson's** (mainly Orlando and to the north – the store at Dr Phillips Boulevard is close to International Drive).

For clothes, DIY, home furnishings, souvenirs, toys, electrical goods, household items and groceries, check out **Target** (its new superstores on Highway 192 just west of Highway 535 and near Mall at Millenia are fine examples) and **Kmart**.

> BRIT TIP: Wal-Mart offers 1-hour processing at great savings on UK prices, as do all branches of Walgreens.

Specialist shops

Keen shoppers will want to check out other individual outlets that might not mean much at first glance. **Ross** (11 in Orlando – see www.rossstores.com) carries a huge range of discounted brand name clothes, shoes, linens, towels and other goods (9.30am–9.30pm Mon–Sat, 11am–6pm Sun), and **Marshalls** (5 in Orlando – www.marshallsonline.com) and **TJ Maxx** (also 5 – www.tjmaxx.com) are similar. For jeans and more, **World of Denim** (and **Denim Place**) have 6 shops in the main tourist areas (good for Tommy Hilfiger, DKNY, Calvin Klein, Polo, Lee and more), while **The Sports Authority** and **Sports Dominator** both offer all manner of sporting goods and apparel. Golfers should definitely visit one of the 5 **Edwin Watts Golf** shops, including their national clearance centre on I-Drive (www.edwinwatts.com), or any of the 5 **Special Tee Golf & Tennis** shops. You can pick up some great deals on golf clubs in particular. By the same token, anglers can stock up on the latest gear at bargain prices at **Bass Pro Shops Outdoor World** (Festival Bay).

Now the shopping's done, it's time to think about the journey home…

Going Home

(or, Where Did The Last Two Weeks Go?)

A nd so, dog-tired and lighter in the wallet but (hopefully) blissfully happy and with enough memories to last a lifetime, it is time to deal with that bane of all holidays – the journey home.

If you have come through the last week or 2 relatively unscathed, here's how to avoid any last-minute pitfalls.

The car

Returning the hire car can take time if you had to use an off-airport car depot so allow half an hour. The process is much slicker with the firms who operate directly from the airports. Most airlines require you to arrive 2–3 hours before an international flight, so don't be tempted to leave your check-in until the last minute. Virgin and Travel City Direct's check-in facilities at Downtown Disney and Lake Buena Vista Factory Stores are a major bonus in this respect for their passengers.

BRIT TIP: You are advised to leave all luggage unlocked (no combination locks or padlocks) when you check in for your return flight as the TSA security open a LOT of bags at their screening process and they have the right to open ANY case, locked or unlocked.

Now you probably have some time to kill, so here is a detailed guide to the 2 main airports.

Orlando International airport

Orlando International is 46 miles (74km) from Cocoa Beach and 54 miles (87km) from Daytona Beach on the east coast, 84 miles (135km) from Tampa and 110 (177km) from Clearwater and St Petersburg to the west, 25 miles (40km) from *Walt Disney World* and 10 miles (16km) from Universal Orlando; so always allow enough time for the return journey, plus check-in (the Beeline Expressway can get quite congested in the afternoon, for example).

This modern airport is the third largest in size terms in the USA, the 14th for number of passengers (No 1 in Florida) – and the top-rated for passenger satisfaction. It hit 31.1 million passengers in 2004 for the first time (some 80,000 a day on average), putting it level with Gatwick and Tokyo, and with half the traffic of Heathrow. It can get busy at peak times, but its 854-acre (345-ha) terminal complex usually handles the crowds with ease, and this is one of the most comfortable airports you will find. It boasts a great range of facilities, and its wide, airy concourses feel more like an elegant hotel (one end of the terminal is taken up by the airport-owned Hyatt Regency Hotel).

Ramps, restrooms, wide lifts and large open areas ensure easy wheelchair access, and features like TDD and amplified telephones, wheelchair-height drinking fountains, braille lift controls and companion-care restrooms are there to assist travellers with disabilities. Should you have more than 3 hours to spare, it is worth taking the 15-minute taxi ride to the Florida Mall, or checking in early, keeping the car and visiting Gatorland about 20 minutes away (see page 205).

In keeping with the Orlando area, the international airport is always engaged in staying a step ahead, and a major 2004 renovation added a major food court, extra restaurant options and some superb shops. Construction of a second major terminal building is also going on beyond the Hyatt Hotel end of the terminal.

Landside

As with all international airports, you have a division between LANDSIDE (for all visitors to the airport) and AIRSIDE (where you need to have a ticket). Orlando's Landside is divided into 3 levels: **One** is the recently enhanced area for ground transportation, tour operator desks, parking, buses and car rental agencies; **Two** is for Baggage Claim (which you negotiated on your arrival) and for private vehicles meeting passengers; **Three** is where you should enter on your return journey as it holds all the check-in desks, shops and restaurants. Level Three divides into 5 inter-connected sections: **Landside 'A'** is the check-in for **Gates 1–29** and **100–129**. Here you will find Aer Lingus, American Airlines, ATA (American TransAir), Continental, Southwest, JetBlue and AirTran. **Landside 'B'** has check-in desks for **Gates 30–99** and airlines such as Spirit, Northwest, United, US Airways, BA, Delta, Icelandair and Virgin.

Once you have checked in, you can explore both the **East** and **West** sections of the main concourse on Level Three. These house a good mix of shops and restaurants, plus currency exchange, information desks and ATM machines (cash dispensers), while the Hyatt Hotel is also in the East Hall. The East and West Halls are then linked by the shops, restaurants and services of the **North** and **South Walks.** In all, there are 40 places to shop and eat, plus a smart food court, and it is almost like being in a high end shopping mall. There is the Alien Attack arcade, a Suntrust bank, post office and even the relaxing D-parture Spa and Salon (get a massage before you fly!). Many shops feature outstanding design and even photo opportunities – see the 2 Disney stores, Harley-Davidson, SeaWorld/Busch Gardens and Kennedy Space Center. Other notable shops are the blissful bath products of Lush, the natural cosmetics of L'Occitane, Borders Books (with its Seattle's Best coffee bar), the Key West-themed Mel Fisher's Treasures, Florida Market and the fashion jewellery of Bijou Terner. There are also 2 newsagents.

Dining here is also a pleasure. The 8-counter **Food Court** features McDonalds, Sbarro, Krispy Crème and Nathan's Hot Dogs, as well as the healthier options of Zyng's Asian Noodlery, Fresh Deli Delights and Chick-Fil-A. **Macaroni Grill** is a tasty Italian option, while **Fox Sports Bar** adds a multi-screen TV set-up and both counter and table service, while upstairs at the West Hall is **Chili's Too**, a cheerful, quick-service Tex-Max bar-diner. The **East Hall** tends to be quieter and more picturesque as it is dominated by the 8-storey Hyatt Hotel atrium. Up the escalator (or lift) is the main entrance, and if you fancy seeing out your visit in style, **McCoy's Bar and Grill** (up and turn right) is a smart bar-restaurant with a grandstand view of the airport runways. All flight timings are shown on TV monitors. To go really upmarket, take the lift to the 9th-floor **Hemisphere Restaurant** (breakfast and dinner only). Not only do you have an even more impressive view, its superb continental cuisine and wine tasting evenings offer some of the best fare in the city. It's pricey, but the service and food are 5-star.

Airside

Once it is time to move on to your departure gate, you have to be aware of the 4 satellite arms that make up the airport's AIRSIDE. This is where you will probably need to queue as the security screening takes time, and you should allow at least HALF AN HOUR for this. The 'arms' are divided into **Gates 1–29** and **30–59** at the west end of the terminal, and **60–99** and **100–129** (American domestic flights) at the east. ALL the departure gates are here, plus duty-free shops and more restaurants.

The 4 satellites are each connected to the main building by an automated tram, so you need to be alert when it comes to finding your departure gate. There are no tannoy announcements for flights, so you should check your departure gate and time when you check in. However, there are large monitors in the terminal that display all the departure information. As a rule, British Airways, Virgin, Icelandair and Delta use Gates 60–99. Spirit, Air Canada, Northwest, United and US Airways usually use Gates 30–59, while Aer Lingus, ATA, American and Continental depart from Gates 1–29. Airlines using Gates 100–129 include low-cost carriers Southwest, JetBlue and AirTran.

Although there isn't quite so much choice as the main terminal,

you should find the Airside areas just as clean and efficient, with the bonus of 3 duty-free shops. As you pass through the ticket and baggage check at the west end of the terminal, you will find the **Alpha Retail Duty Free** on your right. This is the biggest of its 4 shops and is open only to departing international passengers, so you need your boarding card. Your purchases are delivered to the departure gate for you to collect as you board.

At **Gates 1–29**, you will find another duty-free shop, a newsagents (the Keys Group News and Gifts), 2 **Café Azalea** lounge bars, **Pepito's Cuban Café**, and a mini food court featuring **Burger King**, **Cinnabon** and **TCBY** (which stands for The Country's Best Yogurt). **Gates 30–59** also have **Café Azalea** and **Pepito's Cuban Café**, plus the **Floribbean Court** (with **Miami Subs**, **Villa Pizza**, **Freshens Yogurt** and the **Manatee** bar/lounge) and **Hudson News**. **Gates 60–99** (the main satellite for UK flights) offer another duty-free shop, a currency exchange, newsagents, the speciality **Mindworks** shop, **The Grove** snacks and candy and a mini play area. A food court contains **Burger King**, **Nathan's Hot Dogs**, **Starbucks** and **Fresh Attractions** deli, plus the excellent table service of the **Outback Steakhouse Outpost** and bar.

Gates 100–129 offer 2 **Johnny**

BRIT TIP: Save some film for the excellent photo opportunities at the airport shops – outside the Disney stores, the 2 Harley-Davidson shops and the Kennedy Space Center outlets.

12

Rivers Smokehouse Express outlets, a food court with **The Coco Oasis Bar & Lounge**, **McDonald's** and **Sbarro Pizza**, plus four shops. For more details on Orlando International airport, visit www.orlandoairports.net, which features 'live' departure and arrival information.

Orlando Sanford International airport

Returning to what is now the main Orlando gateway for British charter flights should be a relatively simple experience, providing you retrace your route on the Central Florida Greeneway (following signs for Orlando *Sanford* airport, NOT Orlando International) and come off at **Exit 49**. Turn first right at the lights, then first right again on to Lake Mary Boulevard and follow it to the airport. The efficiency of Alamo and Dollar's car rental return adds to the simplicity.

Orlando Sanford was created as a full international airport in 1996, as an initiative between the airport authorities and several British tour operators. And so MyTravel (Airtours), Thomson (Thomsonfly), Monarch, Thomas Cook, the burgeoning Travel City Direct and First Choice (First Choice Airlines), plus the new Orlando operations of Air Scandic and Excel, all now go for this simpler option. With its small, uncomplicated design (straight off the plane into Immigration, one baggage carousel and then a walk across the road to the Dollar or Alamo offices), it can get you mobile quickly. Of course, you are further north, so your journey time is 30–35 minutes longer and you have to pay an extra $2–3 in tolls compared with the journey to and from Orlando International but, providing you follow the simple directions to the main tourist areas, you can save time overall.

And, while this charter gateway is smaller than Orlando International, it boasts a spacious check-in area and works hard to make the departure as painless as the arrival process, especially with its Guest House facility. **Terminal B** opened in 2001 and Thomas Cook, Monarch, Air Scandic and Excel all use it for check-in. The other UK airlines check in at **Terminal A** but all passengers still use the same international departure lounge. It continues to grow with both domestic and international traffic, and has recently finished a major facility upgrade, notably in Terminal B and the Guest House.

There are no food or beverage outlets at the check-in level at Terminal A, but you can walk across to Terminal B where there is a new **Ritazza Café** and snack counter. Once checked in, you need to pass through Security to reach the International Departure Lounge. Here you have **Chadwick's Pub**, which serves a decent range of food as well as British beers, and the completely revamped (in 2003)

Duty-free delight

For those who can't resist a bargain, it is worth saving some shopping time for the Duty Free stores at both airports. Prices are up to 60 per cent cheaper than in the UK, better even than the local malls. Here is a guide to some of the guaranteed savings on offer (based on exchange rate of £1=$1.75):

Perfumes – Calvin Klein 45%, Chanel 25%
Cosmetics – Clinique 40%
Alcohol – 45%
Tobacco – 60%
Watches – Gucci 25%, Tag Heuer 35%

ORLANDO INTERNATIONAL

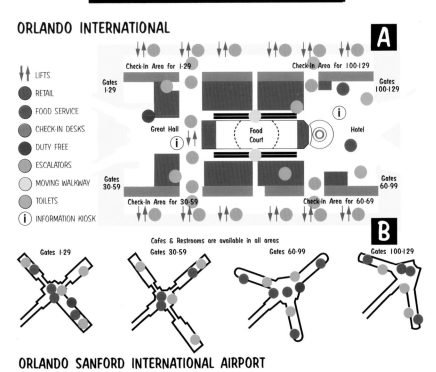

Cafes & Restrooms are available in all areas

ORLANDO SANFORD INTERNATIONAL AIRPORT

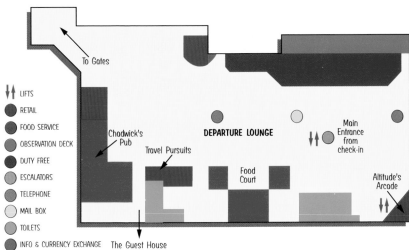

Food Court. The four-part outlet offers American Grill (burgers and fries), Daily Specials (shepherd's pie, chicken pot pie, lasagne and more), Sweet Endings (baked goods and pastries) and the aptly named Grab-N-Go (soft drinks, snacks and bottled water). There is then an extensive **Duty Free** store, a **Reel Stuff** film memorabilia shop and a new entertainment shop, **Travel Pursuits**, featuring travel games,

Get the Spirit

To really make the most of your American adventure, the Brit's Guide can heartily recommend exploring some other vital destinations direct from Orlando with Florida-based Spirit Airlines, one of the most go-ahead and reliable operators in the US. With low fares – especially if you book well in advance – and a specialist route network that includes New York (La Guardia), Chicago, Atlantic City (the Vegas of the East Coast), Detroit and San Juan (on the Caribbean island of Puerto Rico) non-stop from Orlando, Spirit can extend your holiday in the best possible way. In November 2005 it introduces a direct service to Nassau in the Bahamas, adding still further possibilities.

Spirit is introducing a new fleet of Airbus A-320 family aircraft, it has one of the best reliability records in the US and only alcoholic drinks and snacks cost extra on board. For a low-cost carrier it is rare in offering a business class upgrade at less than business class prices. In fact, it puts many scheduled services to shame and we at the Brit's Guide have enjoyed many hassle-free flights in its company. Book online (www.spiritair.com) for the best bargains, or call 1-800 772 7117 (in the USA) or 954 447 7965 (from the UK). If you are staying on the Gulf Coast, it also flies non-stop to Detroit and New York from Tampa.

electronic toys, soft toys, Lego and K'Nex sets, mood jewellery and novelty sweets, as well as **News World** for books and magazines. **Altitudes Arcade** (neatly located in one corner) is guaranteed to appeal to the kids, while there is also an **Information and Currency Exchange** kiosk. Smoking is restricted inside the Lounge, but there is an extensive outdoor deck for smokers.

The big extra here, though, is the **Guest House**, a premium lounge (dramatically enhanced in 2005) available to all passengers for a modest fee. It is in a separate annexe from the main lounge and is an oasis of comfort and quiet, more reminiscent of an upscale hotel. Split into 2 distinct halves, it boasts a pleasant café bar, where you can enjoy unlimited tea, coffee, soft drinks and snacks (plus 2 glasses of beer or wine per over-21), or opt for something from its exclusive lunch menu. It also provides 2 home theatre lounges, with widescreen TV and surround-sound, for

recently released films; 2 quiet reading rooms; computer terminals for internet access and e-mail; a youth entertainment centre, with more than a dozen Sony PlayStation 2 consoles; and a separate toddlers' playroom with soft toys and games. The Guest House is billed as an airport lounge with the comforts of home and, to my mind, it is well worth the $20 each extra ($15 for children) to while away the last few hours here. Most tour operators offer it in advance at a discount, or you can book on arrival or with your tour reps in resort. With its increased capacity in 2005 and extra facilities, this is a highly satisfying way to conclude a holiday. See the Guest House (and airport facilities) on www.OrlandoSanfordAirport.com.

Whether you are using Orlando International or Orlando Sanford, you can expect the return flight to be about an hour shorter than the journey out thanks to the Atlantic jetstreams that provide tail-winds to high-level flights. Nevertheless, you will land back at Gatwick,

Fly Transmeridian Airlines

For a *Brit's Guide* recommendation from Orlando Sanford airport, look no further than TransMeridian Airlines (and Vacation Express). This archetypal low-cost carrier is one of Sanford's busiest operators, taking in Washington (Dulles airport), Atlanta, Syracuse (New York State), Toledo (for Ohio and Michigan), Rockford (for Chicago), Harrisburg and Allentown (in Pennsylvania), Louisville (in scenic Kentucky) Cincinnati, Belleville (for sizzling St Louis) and San Juan (seasonally for Puerto Rico and the Caribbean). TMA also operates Vacation Express flights to the Dominican Republic, Costa Rica, Aruba and the big Mexican resorts of Cancun and Cozumel. It uses smaller regional airports, hence getting in and out is much easier. If you've flown EasyJet or Ryanair, you will know the TMA style and ease of use, and its simplicity of flight procedures makes for hassle-free travelling. The in-flight service is also above average (with the option to buy a full meal). No Saturday overnights are required, there are no advance purchase requirements, advance seat selection is available and all seats are pre-assigned. For more info and to make reservations, visit www.IFLY TMA.com (or www.vacationexpress.com) or call toll-free on 1-866 435 9862.

Manchester, Glasgow, etc, rather more jet-lagged than on the trip out because the time difference is more noticeable on eastward flights, and it may take a day or two to get your body clock back on local time. It is even more important not to indulge in alcohol on the flight if you are driving when you get home.

And, much as it may seem like a good idea, the best way to beat Florida jet-lag is NOT to go straight to the travel agent's and book another holiday to Orlando! But, believe me, the lure of this theme park wonderland is almost impossible to resist once sampled – you WILL return!

Your chance to give something back

After hopefully having the holiday of a lifetime, you might like to know about 2 charities helping children with serious illnesses to have a memorable time here, too. **Give Kids The World Village** is an amazing organisation in Kissimmee, providing a week's holiday for children with life-threatening illnesses who wish to visit Central Florida. GKTW works with over 250 wish-granting foundations worldwide to provide an unforgettable Wish Vacation for children – and their families. It is set up as a resort and includes meals, accommodation, transportation, whimsical venues, donated theme park tickets and many other thoughtful touches in a magical setting. It is a charity I am happy to support myself, and I hope you will, too. You can make a donation through the website – www.gktw.org – or send to: Give Kids The World, 210 South Bass Road, Kissimmee, Florida 34746, USA. Equally, **Dreamflight** is a registered UK charity taking seriously ill children (aged 8-14) to Florida annually (since 1987), often with the help of British Airways. It costs around £1,400 per child and, while many people generously donate their time to help, cash donations are essential. You can contribute by writing to: Dreamflight, 3 Saxeway, Chartridge, Bucks HP5 2SH (01494 792 991) or by e-mail to office@dreamflight.org. Look up more on www.dreamflight.org. Thanks for any contributions to these 2 wholly worthwhile organisations.

12

13 Your Holiday Planner

Example: with 5-day Park Hopper Plus Ticket

(Disney's 5-Day Premium Ticket gives 5 Days at the main theme parks, pus 5 visits to Blizzard Beach, Typhoon Lagoon, Pleasure Island, DisneyQuest and/or Disney's Wide World Of Sports™; there may be a separate charge for big events at Wide World Of Sports).

Day	Our Example	Your Planner
ONE (Sun)	Arrive 2.40am local time, Orlando Sanford airport; transfer to resort – check out local shops and restaurants	
TWO (Mon)	Attend tour operator Welcome Meeting; rest of day at UNIVERSAL STUDIOS	
THREE (Tue)	Chill-out day at Disney's Blizzard Beach water park	
FOUR (Wed)	All day at DISNEY-MGM STUDIOS (Fantasmic! Show at 9pm)	
FIVE (Thurs)	All day at MAGIC KINGDOM Park (Wishes fireworks at 10pm)	
SIX (Fri)	All day at EPCOT Park (IllumiNations at 9pm)	
SEVEN (Sat)	Have a lie-in! Try some shopping at Orlando Premium Outlets and Lake Buena Vista Factory Shops	
EIGHT (Sun)	DISNEY'S ANIMAL KINGDOM Park – Eve: Medieval Times Dinner Show (8pm)	
NINE (Mon)	ISLANDS OF ADVENTURE – Eve: CityWalk and dinner at Hard Rock	
TEN (Tue)	Kennedy Space Center – Eve: International Drive	
ELEVEN (Wed)	All day at SEAWORLD ADVENTURE PARK (Mistify at 10pm)	

Day	Our Example	Your Planner
TWELVE (Thur)	Have a chill-out day; head for Disney's Typhoon Lagoon water park	
THIRTEEN (Fri)	UNIVERSAL STUDIOS Eve: Medieval Times Dinner Show	
FOURTEEN (Sat)	Have a lie-in, then head for MAGIC KINGDOM Park (Wishes at 9pm)	
FIFTEEN (Sun)	Gatorland/Back to airport; return flight at 5.30pm	

Busy Day Guide

Day	Busiest	Average	Lightest
Mon	Disney's Animal Kingdom Magic Kingdom	Epcot	Disney-MGM Studios Universal Studios Islands of Adventure Busch Gardens Kennedy Space Center SeaWorld Water Parks
Tues	Epcot Disney-MGM Studios Universal Studios	Islands of Adventure Magic Kingdom	Disney's Animal Kingdom Busch Gardens Kennedy Space Center SeaWorld Water Parks
Wed	Epcot Islands of Adventure	Disney's Animal Kingdom SeaWorld Water Parks	Magic Kingdom Disney-MGM Studios Busch Gardens Kennedy Space Center Universal Studios
Thurs	Magic Kingdom Universal Studios	Busch Gardens Disney-MGM Studios SeaWorld Water Parks	Epcot Disney's Animal Kingdom Islands of Adventure Kennedy Space Center
Fri	Disney's Animal Kingdom Epcot SeaWorld Water Parks	Disney-MGM-Studios Islands of Adventure Busch Gardens Kennedy Space Center	Magic Kingdom Universal Studios
Sat	Disney-MGM Studios Busch Gardens Islands of Adventure Kennedy Space Center SeaWorld Universal Studios Water Parks	Epcot Magic Kingdom	Disney's Animal Kingdom
Sun	Magic Kingdom Islands of Adventure Kennedy Space Center SeaWorld Water Parks	Disney's Animal Kingdom Busch Gardens Universal Studios	Disney-MGM Studios Epcot

13

Index

Page numbers in *italics* refer to maps or tables, those in **bold** are major references.
(A) = Animal attraction, (D) = Dinner show, (R) = Restaurant, (T) = Travel company, (W) = Water park.

accommodation 20–22
  American-style 60–61
  bed and breakfast 90
  Budget hotels 70–71
  buying a holiday home 90–92
  camping 68
  Deluxe hotels 78–85
  Disney Hotel Plaza 69–70
  golfing resorts 82–85, 86–7
  holiday homes 85, 87–90
  holiday resorts 85–87
  hotels 60–85
  International Drive *84*
  Kissimmee *81*
  Lake Buena Vista *76*
  looking for on arrival 61
  rental accommodation *89*
  Standard hotels 71–73
  Superior hotels 73–77
  timeshare 68–69, 85–87, 93, 94
  Universal Orlando 79–82
  Walt Disney World Resort 61–70, *76*
adults, entertainment in Orlando 39–40
Adventure Island (W) 193
air conditioning 60
Air Scandic 28
aircraft/aviation attractions 18, 206–207, 229, 225–226, 228–229
airboat rides 224–225, 232–233
airports *see* Orlando International Airport; Orlando Sanford Airport
Airtours (T) 24
Alamo (car hire) 49, 50, 53, 54
Altamonte Mall 302
ambulance emergency number 43
American banknotes 47
American clothes and footwear sizes 41
American football 247, 248
American measurements 41
American words and meanings *38*
Arabian Nights (D) 45, 194, 252, **261**
Arthur's 27 (R) 290, 291
arts
  arts museums 222–223
  Cultural Corridor, Downtown Orlando 215
  Morse Museum of American Art 34, 41, 194, 222
  Sidewalk Arts Festival 18
Astronaut Hall of Fame *12*, 194, 198–199
Atlantic coast 21, 25
ATMs 45
attractions 6–7, 9–10, *12*, 29–30 *see also individual attractions*
  closed 203
  evening 30, 67, 251–269
  free 34
  further afield 33, 310, 311
  new for 2006 17
  repeat visitors 40–41
  theme park attendances (2004) 36
  tickets 10–11, 13–14

B–Line Diner (R) 284
baby facilities 32, 37
Bahama Breeze (R) 283

Bahamas 26, 33, 226–227
balloon trips 225–226
banks 45
bars 30, 268–269
baseball 247
basketball 247
beach escapes 235–238
BeautiVacation project (highway 192) roadworks 21
Belz Festival Bay mall 17, 32, 296–297
Benihana (R) 70
Best Western Lake Buena Vista 69
birthdays 42–43, 182
Black Hammock Fish Camp and Restaurant 225, 232–233
Blue Spring Manatee Festival 18
Blue Spring State Park 18
bluezoo (R) 40, 66, 290–291
boating 22, 245–246 *see also* airboat rides; fishing
Boggy Creek Airboat Rides 29, 41, **224–225**
Botanical Gardens 199, 204 *see also* gardens
Brit's Guide website 5 *see specific sections for all other websites*
British Airways Holidays (T) 25
British Consulate 43
Busch Gardens (A) 10, *12*, 29, 30, 36, 37, **183–193**
  Adventure Island combination 193
  African theme 185
  at a glance 183
  Bird Gardens 191
  Congo River Rapids 186, 189, 190
  dinner programmes 192–193
  Edge of Africa 10, 187
  getting there 185
  guest services 186
  guided tours 192–193
  Gwazi coaster 186, 191
  Kumba coaster 186, 189–190
  Land of the Dragons 191
  map *184*
  Montu coaster 186, 192
  Myombe Reserve 10, 187, 188
  places to eat 186, 187, 188, 189, 190, 191
  Python coaster 186, 190
  Rhino Rally 10, 186, 188
  RL Stine's Haunted Lighthouse 10, 186, 189
  Scorpion coaster 188–189
  Serengeti Safari 192
  SheiKra coaster 10, 17, 186, 190
  shopping 186, 188, 190
  shows 186–187, 188
  Stanley Falls Log Flume 186, 190
  Tanganyika Tidal Wave 186, 190
  tickets 13
  Tours Centre (bookings) 186
Busch Shuttle Express 51
Busy Day Guide 313

Cadillac Diner (R) 16
Café Tu Tango (R) 284
California Grill (R) 64
canoeing 22, 233, 234, 245–246
car hire *see also* driving
  accidents and breakdowns 58
  car hire companies 49, 50, 54
  car sizes 53, 54
  driving licence 54
  insurance 54
  need for credit cards 45
  Orlando International airport 48–49
  Orlando Sanford airport 50

provision of a map and directions 55
  rates and other costs 53–54
  returning the car 305
car safety 45–47
Caribbean 26, 33
Carnival Cruise Lines 231
cash machines 45
casino cruises 231
Cast Members (Disney) 7, 42, 95
Celebration town (Disney), shopping 303–304
Central Florida Zoological Park (A) 232
Chalet Suzanne (R) 202
Chamber of Magic Show & Dinner (D) 265
character meals 37, 96, 171–172
charities, holidays for sick children 311
Cheesecake Factory (R) 284
chemists (drug stores) 35
children
  age to take to Orlando 35–36
  dining out 36–37
  character meals 37, 96, 171–172
  effects of the heat 36, 37
  hire or buy pushchairs 39
  reactions to loud fireworks 37
  shorter queueing for rides 36
  sun protection 36
  travelling to Florida 35–36
children's holiday charities 311
Christmas time 19, 109, 134, 145
churches and places of worship 42
Cirque du Soleil® 9, 254, 268
Citricos (R) 65
CityWalk 6, 30, 33, 39, 146
  evening entertainment 251, 256–258
Clearwater Beach 28, 237, 238
climate in Florida 14
clothes, American sizes 41
clothing and comfort 32–33
Cocoa Beach 22, 235
Cosmos (T) 27
couples, entertainment in Orlando 39–40
credit cards 45
crime prevention 43
cruise-and-stay options 22
cruising 22, 23, 24, 26, 91, **230–232**
  Carnival Cruise Lines 231
  Disney birthday cruise 42
  Disney Cruise Line 45, 230–231
  Epcot 123–124
  rivers and waterways 199, 231–232, 233, 236
Customs and Excise advice 292
Cypress Gardens Adventure Park (A) 10, *12*, 17, 29,194, **199–200**

Daytona, motor sports 18, 249, 250
Daytona Beach 236–237
dentist 35
dining out
  'all you can eat' buffets 270
  American diners 278–279
  BBQ diners 280
  British-style pubs 277–278
  chain restaurants 274–275
  character meals 37, 96, 171–172
  Chinese 284–285
  Continental 286–287
  cost of park meals 30, 31
  cowboy-style diners 279–280
  Cuban 286
  dining out with children 36–37
  Disney character meals 37, 96

Downtown Disney 253, 254
drinking 273–274
eating 24/7 273
family restaurants 275–277
for adults 39
Indian 285–286
International Drive 21
Irish pubs 278
Italian 281, 288
Japanese 285
'kids eat free' deals 270
Lake Buena Vista 20–21
novel dining 283
ordering 271–272
seafood restaurants 281–2, 287–9
special diets 272–273
steakhouse diners 282
Thai and Vietnamese 286
tipping and service 271
top 10 burgers 274
top 10 diners 283
top 10 romantic restaurants 40
top restaurants 64–67, 287–291
Universal's CityWalk 256–258
variety 270, 271
vegetarian options 270, 272–273
Winter Park area 223
dinner cruises 199, 231–232
dinner shows 6, 30, 171, 194,
259–266
disabled travellers 38–39
drivers 38–39, 58
passengers 23
Discovery Cove (A) 12, 179–182
Aviary 181
birthday packages 182
Coral Reef 180
disabled visitors 180
Dolphin Lover's Sleepover 179
Dolphin Swim 181–182
entrance fees and other costs
179, 182
getting there 179
places to eat 179
Ray Lagoon 180
shopping 179
Trainer For A Day programme 179
Twilight Discovery dinner
programme 182
wedding packages 182
Disney Cruise Line 45, 230–231
Disney Hotel Plaza 69–70
Disney-MGM Studios 9, 12, 29, 30,
36, 39, 40, 125–134
at a glance 126
attractions for different age
groups 134
Christmas 134
Disney Stars and Motor Cars
parade 132–133
Fantasmic! 29, 132
getting there 125
Guest information 125–126
Indiana Jones™ Epic Stunt
Spectacular 9, 127
Jim Henson's Muppet*Vision
3-D 129
Lights, Motors, Action!™
Extreme Stunt Show 9, 127,
129–130
main attractions 126–132
map 128
Muppets 9
places to eat 132, 133
Rock 'n Roller Coaster Starring
Aerosmith 9, 127, 131, 132
shopping 133–134
Skywalker and Co. 134
Star Tours 127, 129
Star Wars™ 9
Twilight Zone™ Tower of Terror
9, 126–127, 131, 133

Voyage of the Little Mermaid
127, 131
Who Wants to be a Millionaire –
Play it! 127, 130
Disney resort restaurant
reservations 64
Disney special occasions 42–43
Disney tickets 10, 11, 13, 93
Disney's All-Star Resorts 20, 20, 62
Disney's Animal Kingdom Lodge
20, 40, 67–68
Disney's Animal Kingdom Theme
Park (A) 9, 12, 29, 30, 36, 39, 40,
135–145
Africa 141–143
Asia 143–144
at a glance 135
attractions for different age
groups 145
behind the scenes tours 144
best times to see the animals 137–8
Camp Minnie-Mickey 139
Christmas 145
DinoLand USA 139–141
DINOSAUR! 140
Discovery Island 138
Expedition Everest 17, 143–144
Festival of The Lion King 139
getting there 137
It's Tough To Be A Bug! 138–139
Kali River Rapids 143
Kilimanjaro Safaris 128, 142
Maharajah Jungle Trek 143
map 136
Mickey's Jammin' Jungle
Parade 144
nature and conservation
emphasis 135, 137
Pangani Forest Exploration
Trail 142
places to eat 137, 139, 141, 144
Rainforest Café 137, 144
shopping 139, 141, 144
The Oasis Tropical Garden 138
The Tree of Life 138, 141
Disney's Blizzard Beach Water Park
(W) 9, 12, 30, 216, 218–219
Disney's Boardwalk Resort 34, 62,
67, 68
evening entertainment 39, 67,
251, 255–256
Disney's Caribbean Beach Resort
62, 63, 69
Disney's Contemporary Resort 40,
64
Disney's Coronado Springs Resort
63–64
Disney's Extra Magic Hours 20, 30,
62
Disney's Fantasia Gardens
Miniature Golf Courses 243
Disney's Fort Wilderness Resort &
Campground 40, 61, 62, 68
Disney's Grand Floridian Resort &
Spa 42, 61–62, 65
Disney's Home Away From Home
resorts 62, 68–69
Disney's Magical Express (luggage
transfer) 25
Disney's Old Key West Resort 62, 68
Disney's Polynesian Resort 20,
64–65, 72
Disney's Pop Century Resort 20,
61, 62–63
Disney's Port Orleans Resort 34,
40, 61, 63
Disney's Saratoga Springs Resort &
Spa 62, 68–69
Disney's Typhoon Lagoon Water
Park (W) 9, 12, 13, 30, 56,
216–218

Disney's Wide World of Sports
Complex™ 247–248
Disney's Wilderness Lodge and
Villas 62, 66–67
Disney's Wilderness Preserve (A)
41, 235
Disney's Yacht and Beach Club
Resorts 39–40, 42–43, 65–66
Disneyland Resort in California 95
DisneyQuest arcade 9, 30, 43, 255,
260
Dolly Parton's Dixie Stampede (D)
264–265
dolphins 179, 181–182, 227–228,
236, 239
Downtown Disney 6, 9, 12, 39,
252–255
Cirque du Soleil® 9, 254, 268
DisneyQuest arcade 9, 30, 43,
255, 260
evening entertainment 252–255
Marketplace 9
Pleasure Island 9, 251, 252–253
shopping 294–295
Virgin Megastore 9
West Side 9, 253–254
Dreamflight 311
Dreams Unlimited Travel service 28
drinking
alcoholic drinks 273–274
and driving 58
fluid intake 32–33
water 31
driving in the US 48, 55–59
see also car hire
AA members' savings 58
accidents and breakdowns 58
and alcohol 58
car controls 55
car safety 45–47
disabled drivers 38–39, 58
from the airports 49–50
key routes through Orlando
58–59
maps and directions 55–56, 59
petrol and petrol stations 59
radio traffic news 50
restrictions 57–58
return to the airports 305–306,
308
roadworks (highway 192) 21
rules of the road 56–58
signs and road names 55–56
speed limits 57
tolls 56–57
traffic lights 57
drug stores (chemists) 35
Duty Free allowances 292
Duty Free shopping 307, 308, 309

Easter 19
Ebookers (T) 28
Eclipse Direct (T) 25
eco-tourism 234–235
electrical voltage 72
Electrical Water Pageant 260–261
emergencies
medical aid 33, 35, 43
phone number (police, fire,
ambulance) 43
Epcot 9, 12, 29, 30, 36, 39, 40,
111–124
at a glance 111
attractions for different age
groups 123
banks 45
fireworks (IllumiNations) 34,
119, 123–124
Food and Wine Festival 124
Future World 9, 113, 114–118
getting there 113.

Guest Relations (information and bookings) 113
guided tours 122–123, 124
Honey I Shrunk The Audience 116
IllumiNations: Reflections of Earth 34, 119, 123–124
Innoventions West and East 118
International Flower and Garden Festival 124
map *112*
Mission: Space 9, 113, **114–115**
places to eat 113, 117, 118, 119, 120, 121, 122
planning your visit 123
shopping 118, 119, 120, 121, 122
Soarin' 9, 113, 116–117
Spaceship Earth 118
speciality cruises 123–124
Test Track 9, 113, 114, 115
The Living Seas 117–118
Universe of Energy 113, 114
World Showcase 9, 113, **118–123**
evening entertainment 30, 67, 251–269
Everglades 21, 226–228, 238
Excel Airways 28
excursions 52, 226–228
Extra Magic Hours 20, 30, 62

Fantasy of Flight 10, *12*, 30, 194, **206–207**, 208
Fiascos (D) 265–266
fire department emergency number 43
First Choice (T) 24–25
fishing 22, 233, 244–245, 304
fitness centres 248
flea markets 303
flight-only 28, 33 *see also* travel companies
Florida *8*
Central Florida festivals 18
weather 14, 19, *20*, 37
Florida Eco-Safaris (A) 194, 234–235
Florida Everglades 21, 226–228, 238
Florida Keys 21, 25, 26
Florida Mall 53, 300–301
Florida Sales Tax 45, 294
Florida State Fair 18
Florida's Beach (St Pete/Clearwater) 237, 238, 239
fly-drive packages 22, 23, 24, 25, 26, 27
flying 229, 225–226 *see also* aircraft/aviation attractions
Flying Tigers Warbird Air Museum 228–229
food *see* dining out
footwear 32–33
American sizes 41
Fort Christmas Historical Park 34
Fort Myers 237
Fun 'n Sun (aviation festival) 18
Fun Spot Action Park 30, 194, **209–210**, 211
Funway Holidays (T) 26

gardens 34, 223 *see also* Botanical Gardens; Historic Bok Sanctuary
Gatorland (A) *12*, 29, 194, **205–206**
gay clubs and bars 268
Gaylord Palms Resort 32, 40, 78–9
George Washington's birthday 19
Give Kids the World Village 311
Go Orlando Card 194
golf 21–22, 24, 82, **238–243**, 304
Grand Bohemian Hotel 40, 41
Great Outdoor Festival 18
Green Meadows Petting Farm (A) 229–230

Grosvenor Resort 69
Gulf Coast 21, 25, 26, 27, **237–238**
gyms 248

Halloween 109, 167
Hard Rock Café 257, 284
Hard Rock hotel 146
heatstroke, avoiding 32–33
hiking 232, 233, 234–235
Hilton hotel 70
Historic Bok Sanctuary *12*, 20, 41, 194, **200–202**
Historic District of Kissimmee, shopping 303
Holiday Inn in the Walt Disney World Resort 69
Hoop-Dee-Doo Musical Revue (D) 260, 269
horse riding 35, 232, 234, 235, **246**
hospitals 33, 35
Hotel Royal Plaza 69–70
hotels 60–85
airport 48–49
American-style 60–61
beyond Disney 70–85
Budget 70–71
deals across the US 33
Deluxe 78–85
Disney Hotel Plaza 69–70
hairdryers 72
security 43–44
Standard 71–73
suite hotels 60
Superior 73–77
Universal Orlando 79–82
Walt Disney World Resort 61–70, 76
hurricanes and storms 37
Hyatt Regency hotel (airport) 48–49, 75

I-Ride Trolley 51, 53, 207–208
ID, need for 45
IllumiNations cruises 42
Independence Day (July 4) 18
insect repellents 35
insurance 35
International Divers 52, 227–228, 246
International Drive (I-Drive) 49, 57, 58–59
accommodation 21
attractions 30, 207–212
I-Ride Trolley 51, 53, 207–208
shopping 32, 295–297
Internet sites *see within specific sections*
Interstate 4 (I-4) 58
Islands of Adventure 9, 29, 30, 36, 146, **158–167**
at a glance 158
attractions for different age groups 167
Dr Doom's Fearfall 161, 162
Dudley Do-Right's Ripsaw Falls 161, 163, 165
Duelling Dragons 164–165
getting there 159
Halloween Horror Nights 167
Jurassic Park River Adventure 33, 161, 163, 164
map *160*
places to eat 159, 162, 163, 164, 166, 167
Popeye and Bluto's Bilge-Rat Barges 161, 162–163, 164
Seuss Landing 161, 166
shopping 159, 162, 163, 164, 166, 167
The Amazing Adventures of Spider-Man 161, 162

The Flying Unicorn 165
The Incredible Hulk Coaster 161
tickets 146
Toon Lagoon 21, 162–163
Universal Express 146
Itinerary Planning Service 5

Jamaica 26
jazz evenings 41
jet-lag 55, 310–311
jet-skiing 245–246
Jetsave (T) 27
Jiko (R) 67, 289, 291

Kennedy Space Center 6, 10, *12*, 22, 29, 30, **194–195**, **197–198**
kids deals 23, 24, 25, 26
Kissimmee 7, 49, 59
accommodation 21
Old Town 32, 34, 40, 297–298
shopping 297–298
Kuoni (T) 27

Labor Day 19
Lake Buena Vista 76
accommodation 20–21
shopping 299–300
Lake Buena Vista Factory Stores 44, 52–53, 299–300
Lake Buena Vista Resort Village and Spa 17
Lake Eola 34, 214
Lake Wales 41, 200–202
Lakeridge Winery and Vineyards 34
Leu Gardens 34
limousines and town cars 52
Lynx public bus system 48, 50–51

Magic Kingdom Park 7, *12*, 29, 30, 36, 39, 40, **97–110**
Adventureland 101–102
Africa 7
at a glance 98
attractions for different age groups 110
attractions for young children 101, 104–107, 110
banks 45
Big Thunder Mountain Railroad 103
Buzz Lightyear's Space Ranger Spin 105, 107
Christmas 109
Cinderellabration 105
City Hall (information, bookings) 99, 101
Fantasyland 104–106
Frontierland 102–103
getting there 97–99
guided tours 109–110
Halloween 109
It's a Small World 104
Jungle Cruise 93, 102
Liberty Square 103
Main Street USA 99, 101, 108
map *100*
Mickey's PhilharMagic 7, 105
Mickey's Toontown Fair 106
parades 107–108
Pirates of the Caribbean 102
places to eat 99, 102, 103, 106, 107, 109
shopping 95, 102, 103, 106, 107
Space Mountain 7, 106
Splash Mountain 102–103
Stitch's Great Escape! 107
The Haunted Mansion 103
Tomorrowland 106–108
Wild West 7
Wishes firework show 108
Magical Midway 30, 210, 211

Mall at Millenia 301
malls 227, 300–303
manatee encounters 228, 234
  Blue Spring Manatee Festival 18
Marco Island 237–238
Marine Science Center, Daytona
  Beach (A) 236
Mears shuttles 51–52
medical aid 33, 35
medical insurance 35
medicines, alternative names in the
  US 35
Medieval Times (D) 262–263
Memorial Day 19
Miami 21, 25, 26
Mickey's Backyard Barbecue (D) 260
mini-golf 30, 194, 212, **243–244**
mobile phones 37, 50
money and travellers' cheques 45, 47
Morse Museum of American Art
  34, 41, 194, 222
mosquito repellents 35
motor sport 249–250
multi-centre holidays 21–22, 25, 26,
  50
museums and arts *see* arts
music, live 30, 34, 266–267 *see also*
  evening entertainment

Naples 237–238
Narcoossee's (R) 65
nightclubs and bars 30, 266–269 *see
  also* evening entertainment

'Ohana (R) 64, 65
Old Town, Kissimmee 32, 34, 40
  shopping 297–298
older people *see* seniors
Omni Champions Gate Resort 16,
  73, 82
Orange County 7
Orange County Regional History
  Center 12, 213–214
Orlando 7, *8*, *15*, 17
  attractions and routes 12, 196,
    212–216
  'no-go' areas 47
  recommended maps of Orlando
    area 59
Orlando FlexTicket 146
Orlando International airport
  48–50
  arrivals 48
  check-in and departure 305–308,
    309
  detailed guide 305–308, *309*
  driving from and back to 49–50,
    305–306
  Duty Free shopping 307, 308
  Hyatt Regency hotel 48–49, 75
  the return journey 310–311
Orlando Premium Outlets 32, 53,
  299
Orlando Sanford airport 7, 50
  arrivals 50
  car hire 50
  check-in and departure 308–310,
    309
  detailed guide 308–310, *309*
  driving from and back to 50, 308
  Duty Free shopping 308, 309
  Guest House departure
    lounge *309*, 310
  the return journey 310–311
Orlando Science Center 194, 212–3
Osceola County 7
Osceola County Pioneer Museum
  230
out-patients departments 33, 35
Oviedo Marketplace 302–303

Palio (R) 66
parasailing 245
passports, visa requirements 14, 15
personal liability insurance 35
Personalised Itinerary Planner 46
petrol stations 59
phone calls 37, 60–61
phonecards 43, 61
Pirate's Dinner Adventure (D) 194,
  253, 262
Planet Hollywood® (R) 253, 284
planning your visit 6, 18
  avoiding heatstroke 32–33
  avoiding theme parks' busiest
    times 30–31
  Busy Day Guide 313
  busy times of year 19, *20*
  clothing and comfort 19, 32–33
  cruise-and-stay options 22
  exploring further afield 33, 310,
    311
  fluid intake 32–33
  fly-drive packages 22, 23, 24, 25,
    26, 27
  footwear 32–33
  Itinerary Planning Service 5
  returning home 305–311
  split holidays 21–22
  strategies for getting around the
    parks 31
  sun protection 32
  time required for different
    attractions 29
  top 10 things to do for free 34
  travel companies 22–28
  when to go 19, *20*
  where to stay 20–22 *see also*
    accommodation
  Your Holiday Planner 312–313
Plant City Strawberry Festival 18
Pleasure Island 9, 39
  evening entertainment 251,
    252–253
police service 43–47
  emergency number 43
  information numbers 47
Portofino Bay hotel 146
pregnancy, theme park rides to
  avoid 37–38
Premier Holidays (T) 27–28
prescriptions drugs, alternative
  names in the US 35
President's Day 19
Prime Outlets 17, 205
public transport 50–51
pushchairs or strollers, to hire or
  buy 32, 39

Race Rock (R) 284
Rainbow Wheels 39
Rainforest Café (R) 284
Real Florida Excursions 52, 227
Renaissance Orlando Resort 40
Reptile World Serpentarium (A) 230
Resort Tax 45
restaurants *see* dining out
return trip
  baggage allowance 292
  Duty Free allowances 292
Reunion Resort 17
Ripley's Believe It or Not 12, 21,
  29–30, 194, **208**
river cruises 231–232, 233 *see also*
  cruising
Rivership Romance (D) 231–232
rodeo 41, 248–249
roller-blade park 297
Ron Jon's Surf Park 17, 297
Royal Caribbean International
  (cruise line) 231
Royal Pacific Resort hotel 146

safety and security 43–47
sailing *see* airboat rides; boating;
  cruising
Sales Tax 45, 294
Sanford city 233
Sanford Museum 34
SeaWorld Adventure Park (A) 10,
  12, 29, 30, 36, **168–178**
  at a glance 170
  attractions for different age
    groups 178
  behind-the-scenes tours 168,
    170–171
  Blue Horizons 10, 17, 173, 177
  character meals 171–172
  educational and environmental
    message 168, 170–171
  fireworks 177–178
  getting there 171
  Journey to Atlantis 10, 176–177
  Kraken 10, 177
  main attractions 172–178
  map *169*
  Mystify finale 177–178
  Odyssea 174, 176
  places to eat 171–172, 173–174,
    175–176, 178
  Sealion and Otter Stadium 172–3
  Shamu the Killer Whale 172
  Shark Encounter 175
  shopping 173–174, 176, 177, 178
  Sunset Celebration 177
  tickets 13, 168, 170–171
  Waterfront district 10
  Wild Arctic 172
security and safety 43–47
Seminole County 7, 232–234
Seminole Towne Center 302
seniors
  discounts and special deals 40
  entertainment in Orlando 39–40
Shingle Creek Resort 17
shopping 6, 21, 31–32, 40, 44
  Belz Festival Bay 17, 296–297
  CityWalk 256
  Disney's town of Celebration
    303–304
  Downtown Disney 253, 254,
    294–295
  Duty Free allowances 292
  electrical goods 294
  flea markets 303
  Florida sales tax 45, 294
  golf shops 304
  Historic District of Kissimmee
    303
  International Drive 21, 295–297
  jeans 304
  Lake Buena Vista 20–21, 299–300
  malls 227, 300–303
  Marketplace (Downtown
    Disney) 294
  Old Town, Kissimmee 297–298
  Orlando's shopping centres 292,
    293, 294
  Pleasure Island 294
  return trip baggage allowance 292
  specialist shops 304
  sports 304
  supermarkets 43, 304
  The Loop, Kissimmee 298
  The Pointe Orlando 295–296
  West Side (Downtown Disney)
    294–295
  Winter Park area 222–223
  Winter Park Village 303
Shula's Steak House 66
shuttle services 51–52, 52–53
Sidewalk Arts Festival 18
Silver Springs (A) 10, *12*, 29, 30, 37,
  194, **202–205**

Silver Spurs Rodeo 18
single-parent discounts 23
singles, entertainment in Orlando 39–40
skateboarding 297
Skull Kingdom 21, 30, 194, **209**
SkyCoaster 298
SkyVenture 41, 194, 208, **211–212**
Skyy Limousines 52
Sleuth's Mystery Dinner Shows (D) 263, 264
smoking 95
Spirit Airlines 33, 310
split holidays 21–22, 25, 26, 50
sports 35, 238–250, 304 *see also specific activities*
sports bars 269
St Petersburg Beach 237, 238
State Parks 233, 234
storms and hurricanes 37
strollers or pushchairs for hire in the parks 32, 39
Style Holidays (T) 26–27
sun protection 32, 216
Sunstart (T) 25
supermarkets 43, 304
surfing 297
Swamp Buggy Adventure 41, 225

Tampa 25
taxes
 Florida Sales Tax 45, 294
 Resort Tax 45
taxis 53
Tchoup Chop (R) 80, 291
tennis 22
Thanksgiving 19
The Holy Land Experience *12*, 213, 215–216
The Loop, shopping 298
The Mercado 295
The Pointe Orlando 17, 30, 32, 39
 evening entertainment 251, 258–259
 shopping 295–296
Thomas Cook (T) 25–26
Thomson (T) 23–24
tickets for attractions 10–11, 13–14 *see also individual attractions*
 advance purchase discount 10
 Busch Gardens 13
 direct-sell ticket brokers 13–14
 Disney 10, *11*, 13
 Go Orlando Card 194
 Orlando FlexTicket 146
 SeaWorld 13
 Universal 13
timeshares 68–69, 85–87, 93, 94
tipping 14, 73
Titanic – The Exhibition *12*, 208–209
tour operators *see* travel companies
tourist information 47
tourists,
 numbers from Britain 7
 safety precautions 43–47
tours *see* excursions
town cars and limousines 52, 53
Trailfinders (T) 27
TransMeridian Airlines 33, 311
Transolar Holidays (T) 27
transportation *see also* car hire; driving
 Orlando without a car 50–53
 public transport 50–51

shuttle services 51–52, 52–53
taxis 53
town cars and limousines 52, 53
Travel City Direct (T) 22–23
travel companies 22–28
travel insurance 35
Travelbag (T) 27
travellers' cheques and money 45
Twilight Discovery programme 182
two-way radios 44

Universal Orlando 9, *12*, 30, 146–167
 CityWalk 6, 30, 33, 39, 146, 251, **256–258**
 Islands of Adventure 9, 30, 36, 146, 158–167
 Orlando FlexTicket 146
 resort hotels 146
 tickets 13, 146
 Universal Express 146
 Universal Express Plus 146
 Universal Studios Florida® 9, 29, 30, 36, 40, 146, **147–157**
 Wet 'n Wild (W) 9, *12*
Universal Studios Florida® 9, 29, 30, 36, 40, 146, **147–157**
 at a glance 147
 attractions for different age groups 157
 Back To The Future… The Ride 149, 153
 Earthquake – The Big One 149, 151–152
 Fear Factor Live 17, 152–153
 fireworks 157
 getting there 149
 Guest Services 149
 Jaws 149, 152
 map *148*
 Men In Black – Alien Attack 149, 153–154
 places to eat 150, 151, 153, 154, 155
 Revenge of the Mummy 17, 149, 150–151
 seasonal entertainment 156–157
 shopping 150, 151, 153, 154, 155–156
 Shrek 4-D 149, 150, 152
 Terminator 2: 3D Battle Across Time 149, 155
 tickets 146
 Universal Express 146
 Woody Woodpecker's Kidzone 154–155, 156
Universal's Royal Pacific Resort 40
USAirtours (T) 27

Vacation Express 311
Venice 237
Victoria and Albert's (R) 65
Virgin Holidays (T) 23, 24
visa requirements 14, 15
Visitor Center, Orlando 47

wakeboarding 246
Walt Disney World Resort in Florida 7, *8*, 9, *12*
 accommodation 20, 61–70, 76
 autograph collecting 94–95, 121
 Cast Members 95
 character dining 37, 96
 'char swap' 95
 Christmas time 19, 109, 134, 145
 dinner shows 260–261

discounts and free tickets 93–94
Disney-MGM Studios 9, *12*, 29, 30, 36, 39, 40, **125–134**
Disney's Animal Kingdom (A) 9, *12*, **135–145**
Disney's Blizzard Beach Water Park (W) 9, *12*, 30, 216, **218–219**
Disney's FASTPASS Service 94, 95
Disney's Typhoon Lagoon Water Park (W) 9, *12*, 13, 30, 56, **216–218**
Downtown Disney 9, *12*, 39, **252–255**
Epcot 9, *12*, 29, 30, 36, 39, 40, **111–124**
golf 241
Happiest Celebration on Earth 95
Magic Kingdom 9, *12*, 29, 30, 36, 39, 40, **97–110**
motor sports 249–250
Official Visitor Center 93
Pal Mickey 95
pushchair rental 94
ratings and restrictions for rides 94
smoking 95
Swan and Dolphin Hotels 40, 66
tickets 93
timeshares (Disney Vacation Club) 93, 94
water sports 245–246
Wedding Pavilion 9, 36, 41
Warbird Adventures 229
water, drinking 31
Water Mania (W) *12*, 30, 194, **221**
water parks 204–205, 216–221
water sports 245–246
weather 14, 19, *20*, 37
website for *Brit's Guide* 5 *see specific sections for all other websites*
weddings in Florida 23, 24, 26, 27, 32, **41–42**, 202, 228
 Discovery Cove 182
 Walt Disney World's Wedding Pavilion 9, 36, 41
West Side, evening entertainment 253–254
Wet 'n Wild (W) 9, *12*, 21, 30, 216, **219–221**
what's new 17
wheelchair accessibility 38–39
Wild Waters (W) 203, 204–205
wilderness trails, 233, 234, 234–235
windsurfing 245–246
Winter Park 34, 40, 41, **222–224**
Winter Park Scenic Boat Tour 194
Winter Park Village, shopping 303
Winter-Summerland Miniature Golf 43, 243
Wishes cruises 42
Wolfgang Puck's (R) 254, 290
WonderWorks 21, 30, 194, 208, **210–211**
 The Outta Control Magic Show (D) 263–264
Wyndham Palace Resort & Spa 40, 70

Yachtsman Steakhouse (R) 65
Your Holiday Planner 312–313

Zellwood Corn Festival 18

The author and publisher gratefully acknowledge the provision of the following photographs.

320 ——————— ACKNOWLEDGEMENTS ———————

The authors wish to acknowledge the help of the following in the production of this book: The Orlando Tourism Bureau in London, the Orlando/Orange County Convention & Visitors' Bureau, Visit Florida, The Kissimmee/St Cloud Convention & Visitors' Bureau, Walt Disney Attractions Inc., Universal Orlando, The British-American Chamber of Commerce, The Greater Orlando Aviation Authority, Orlando-Sanford International airport, The Busch Entertainment Corporation, Seminole County Convention & Visitors' Bureau, Central Florida Visitors' and Convention Bureau, St Petersburg/Clearwater Area Convention & Visitors' Bureau, Daytona Beach Area Convention & Visitors' Bureau, Alamo Rent A Car, The Kessler Collection Hotels Group.

In person, Margaret Henrikson (Orlando Tourism Bureau) and Zoe Ward (Icas PR), Nicole Walsh, Louisa French, Jason Lasecki, Geoff Pointon (Walt Disney), Danielle Courtenay, Rick Gregory (Orlando CVB), Larry White, Abby Montpelier and Oonagh McCullagh (Kissimmee CVB), Wit Tuttell (St Petersburg/Clearwater CVB), Susan McLain (Daytona Beach CVB), Kelly Rote (Central Florida CVB), Kate Burgess, Tanya Hillman (Visit Florida), Carol Williams, Andy Wade (Travel City Direct), Michael McLane, Susan Storey, Chris Bielecki (Universal), Sally Hinds (Alamo Rent A Car), Carolyn Fennell (Orlando Aviation Authority), Lynne Koreman (Spirit Airlines), Ron Menke (TransMeridian), Lorraine Ellis (Get Married In Florida), Andy James (International Divers), Susan Flower (Discovery Cove), Oliver Brendon, Sarah Rathbone (Attraction Tickets Direct), Becca Bides and Jacquelyn Wilson (SeaWorld), Aimee Jeansonne-Becka (Busch Gardens), Anthea Yabsley (Synergy PR), Suzan Bunn (Seminole County CVB), Alyson Gernert (Cypress Gardens Adventure Park), Laura Richeson (Bennett & Company), Mary Kenny (The Kessler Collection), Michael Caires, Greg Dull (Orlando Sanford International Airport), Allan Oakley (Alexander & Associates), Nigel Worrall (Florida Leisure), Bob Mandell (Greater Homes), Christen Svendsen and Bill Cowie (BACC), Wrenda Goodwyn (International Drive/I-Ride), Lori Babb (Renaissance Orlando Resort), Trevor Thompson (SkyVenture), Jeff Stanford (Orlando Science Center), Kristin Rutkowski (Wet 'n Wild), Michelle Harris (Gatorland), Terry Lynn Morris (Lake Buena Vista Factory Stores), John Stine (Dixie Stampede), Donna Turner (Medieval Times), Ouafa Elkasmi (The Holy Land Experience), Jean Briggs (Arabian Nights), Donna Connelly, Lance Lancaster (Sleuths), Jonathan Robinson (Orange Blossom Balloons), Susan Phelan (Keith Prowse Attraction Tickets), Marcus Lund (Reunion Resort), Stormy Washington (Disney's Wide World of Sports), Phillip Jaffe (Pro Golf Guides of Orlando), Sally March (Mall at Millenia), Leigh Jones (Orlando Premium Outlets), Siobhan Corcoran (The Pointe Orlando), Margie Long, Michele Peters (Boggy Creek Airboats), Rod Wiltshire (Alpha Retail Services), Naomi Lewis, Emma Pridmore (Virgin Holidays), Serena Andrews (British Airways Holidays), Claire Headicar (First Choice), plus Michele Plant, Michael McRaney, Gerard Mitchell and travel writer Karen Marchbank.

Big thanks to Pete Werner and all at the DIS – you know who you are!

Got a red-hot Brit Tip to pass on? The latest info on how to beat the queues or the best new restaurant in town? We want to hear from YOU to keep improving the guide each year. Drop us a line at: Brit's Guide (Orlando), W. Foulsham & Co Ltd., The Publishing House, Bennetts Close, Cippenham, Slough, Berkshire SL1 5AP. Or e-mail simonveness@yahoo.co.uk.

Reader tips from: Sally Harley, Zoe Brown, Fiona Newby, Richard & Donna Worssam, Gill Dancyger, Mike, Roy and Maurice from London, Tracey Cooper, Cedric & Anita Hill, Helen Potter, Lawler family, Chris & Paula Darvell, Barbara Hargreaves, Simon Hillyard, Steve Kenney, Mark Champken, John & Fiona Low, Claire Hunt, Kevin Salter, Louise Sutherland, Mark Henderson, John Green, Carolyn Dorey, Les & Denise Owen, Mike Elston, Paul Gannon, Bassett family, Janey & Paul Ginman, and Jonathan & Sarah Lee.